Boogie Down Predictions

BOOGIE DOWN PREDICTIONS
HIP-HOP, TIME AND AFROFUTURISM

EDITED BY

ROY CHRISTOPHER

Boogie Down Predictions
Hip-Hop, Time, and Afrofuturism

Edited by Roy Christopher

ISBN: 9781913689285

Introduction Copyright © Ytasha L. Womack
First Published by Strange Attractor Press 2022
This print on demand edition 2023
Texts Copyright © 2022 The Authors

Cover image by Savage Pencil

Layout by Dominic Rafferty
www.dgrafferty.com

A CIP catalogue record for this book is available from the British Library.

Strange Attractor Press
BM SAP, London, WC1N 3XX, UK
www.strangeattractor.co.uk

Distributed by The MIT Press, Cambridge, Massachusetts.
And London, England.

Contents

Part 2: Technology

Part 3: The Future

Dedicated to the memories of

Karl Gold, Shelton Lee, Daniel Dumile,
Earl Simmons, Gregory Jacobs,
Robert E. Davis, Malcolm McCormick
Ermias Asghedom, Jahseh Onfroy
Jarad Higgins, Shar Jackson
Marcel Hall and Greg Tate

My first memory was hearing my first sound.
— Maria Chavez[1]

I have to extend time.
— Grandmaster Flash[2]

Preface
Roy Christopher

> It's harder to imagine the past that went away than it is to imagine
> the future.
> — William Gibson[3]

> What can you do? You can't turn back the clock. That's why you keep on
> moving, and you don't stop.
> — Babbletron, "The Clock Song"[4]

"The past is a foreign country; they do things differently there." So begins the prologue
to L.P. Hartley's 1953 novel *The Go-Between*.[5] Time is as inescapable as it is impossible
to conceive. Technology tries to tame it, chopping it into discrete bits and arranging
them in manageable lines: the alphabet, the printing press, the clock, the Internet.
Marshall McLuhan once wrote, "Just as *work* began with the division of labor,
duration begins with the division of time, and especially with those subdivisions
by which mechanical clocks impose uniform succession on the time sense."[6] From
Frederick Taylor's studies of time and scientific management to the division of labor
of Taylor and Henry Ford, the inventors of modern industrialization, *division* and
duration are operative terms for the technologies of time.

If you were asked to name the salient elements that define hip-hop music,
sampling would be among the first things to come to mind. If you're reading this,
you know it started manually with fingers finessing black vinyl, chopping and
stretching tones on two turntables. The manual mixing of recorded sounds by
DJs allows them to, as Naut Humon puts it, "Manipulate time with your hands!"[7]
Reconfigured and recontextualized notes lift hip-hop out of the linear, tying it
equally to both forgotten pasts and lost futures. Because of sampling, hip-hop's
manipulation of sound is also its manipulation of time. More so than any other
musical genre, hip-hop toys with temporality.

Further stretching this frame, the aesthetic of hip-hop's early days feels like
possible futures. Way before Tupac and Dr. Dre danced in the desert and Chuck D was
doorman to the Terrordome, things were always already going down in the Boogie
Down Bronx. The post-apocalyptic scene there in the early 1970s, the repurposing

of left-behind technology, the hand-styled hieroglyphics on every building wall, and the gyrating dance moves: an entire culture assembled from the freshest of what was available at hand.[8]

Whereas the dominant (read: "European, white, male") culture of the 20th century regularly pictured the next century through stories and inventions, that hasn't been the case as much among those same folks so far in the 21st.[9] Even as far back as Edward Bellamy's *Looking Backward*, which viewed its 1887 present from a fictional year-2000 wherein the United States had evolved into a technologically enabled, Marxist utopia. Twenty-first century tales that venture to look that far ahead rarely find such positive results, especially where technology is concerned.

With that said, it would be remiss to talk about hip-hop and its tumultuous relationship with time without mentioning Afrofuturism. "Afrofuturism is me, us [...] is black people seeing ourselves in the future," says Janelle Monáe, whose futuristic R&B concept records *The ArchAndroid*, *The Electric Lady*, and *Dirty Computer* imagine android allegories in alternative futures.[10] Afrofuturism addresses the neglect of the Black diaspora not only historically but also in science-fiction visions of the future. Through its relationship with time and its technological manipulation thereof, hip-hop also invites us to view different vantages of the future. Just as it recycles and revises the past, hip-hop also invites us to re-imagine the future. As we will see, these re-imaginings are far from apolitical. William Gibson is fond of saying that the future is already here, it's just not evenly distributed yet.[11] Any reader of history knows that the past isn't evenly distributed either. Drawing different conclusions from the past and picturing a future that is different from the present are the very essence of resistance.[12]

"Hip-hop is imprisoned within digital tools like the rest of us," writes the technologist and musician Jaron Lanier. "But at least it bangs fiercely against the walls of its confinement."[13] That banging is the rhythm. That banging is the beat. That banging is the celebration of days past and the longing for better ones to come. As Kodwo Eshun writes in his 2003 essay, "Further Considerations on Afrofuturism," reprinted herein,

> Afrofuturism approaches contemporary music as an intertext of recurring literary quotations that may be cited and used as statements capable of imaginatively reordering chronology and fantasizing history. Social reality and science fiction create feedback between each other within the same phrase.[14]

Though this dialog between social reality and its fictional futures has occurred since we started telling stories, mechanical and digital reproduction has made the exchange easier and much wider spread. The division of sampling and duration of remixing keeps the feedback flowing in time. As Jacques Attali puts it, "Our music foretells our future. Let us lend it an ear."[15]

Acknowledge the Knowledge

All of these issues are explored through the pieces in this collection. I attempted to assemble a variety of voices, from poets to scholars, emcees to journalists. I tried to bring together a looser view than you're used to. I tried to put together what Brian Cross would call *a literary mixtape*. Like any good cassette or DJ set, the playlist includes the freshness of original pieces interspersed with recent classics. There was no call for papers for this book. Rather, I called three friends and they called three friends and so on and so on and so on.

To that end, I have to thank all of the contributors and co-conspirators, without whom none of this, as well as the ones who led me to others, and ones who wished us well, including Mankwei Ndosi, Tiffany Barber, Tananarive Due, Veronica Fitzpatrick, Nisi Shawl, Krista Franklin, Saul Williams, Vijay Iyer, Su'ad Abdul Khabeer, Charlena M. Wynn, Melvin Williams, Alondra Nelson, Ingrid LaFleur, Scott Heath, D. Scot Miller, Kahley Emerson, Dave Allen, Hannah Liley, Courtney Berger, Steve Jones, Mark Dery, William Hutson, Jonathan Snipes, Peter Relic, Priya Nelson, Greg Tate, Harry Allen, Adam Bradley, Chuck D, Charles Mudede, Josh Feit, Hanif Abdurraqib, Jeff Chang, Dan Charnas, Brian Cross, Brian Coleman, S. H. Fernando Jr., Andrew Rausch, Paul Edwards, M. Nicole Horsley, Kevin P. Eubanks, Sha'Dawn Battle, CalvinJohn Smiley, H. Samy Alim, Gino Sorcinelli, Curly Castro, Timothy Baker, Matt Freidson, Zilla Rocca, Geng PTP, Scorcese Lorde Jones, Call Out Culture, M. Sayyid, H. Prizm, Beans, John Morrison, Mike Ladd, Will Brooks, Mike Manteca, Alap Momin, Erik Larson, everyone at AfroFuturist Affair and Metropolarity. Thanks to Doug Armato, Jason Weidemann, and Dani Kasprzak at the University of Minnesota Press and Gianna Mosser and Trevor Perri at Northwestern University Press. Extra special thanks to Travis Terrell Harris.

Many thanks to Jamie Sutcliffe and Mark Pilkington at Strange Attractor for their guidance and enthusiasm, Dom Rafferty for the layout and design, and to Edwin Pouncey for the dopest book cover. And as always to my partner Lily Brewer. I cannot even tell you.

Credits

"Molemen" by Kevin Coval was previously in *A People's History of Chicago* (Haymarket Books, 2017), and "Bop Shop" was in *Everything Must Go* (Haymarket Books, 2019).

"Further Considerations on Afrofuturism" by Kodwo Eshun previously appeared in *CR: The New Centennial Review* 3/2, 2003, 287–302.

"Constructing a Theory and Practice of Black Quantum Futurism" by Rasheedah Phillips was previously published in *Black Quantum Futurism: Theory & Practice, Vol. 1* (Afrofuturist Affair, 2015).

Notes

1. Chavez, Maria, *Of Technique: Chance Procedures on Turntable,* Brooklyn, NY: self-published, 2012, 14.

2. Flash, Grandmaster, *The Adventures of Grandmaster Flash: My Life, My Beats,* New York: Broadway, 2008, 74.

3. Quoted in Wallace-Wells, David, 2011, "Summer, William Gibson, The Art of Fiction, No. 211", *The Paris Review,* https://www.theparisreview.org/interviews/6089/william-gibson-the-art-of-fiction-no-211-william-gibson.

4. Babbletron, "The Clock Song." On *Mechanical Royalty* [LP], New York: Embedded Music, 2003.

5. Hartley, L.P. *The Go-Between,* London: Hamish Hamilton, 1953, 17.

6. McLuhan, Marshall, *Understanding Media: The Extensions of Man,* New York: Mcgraw-Hill, 1964, 157-158.

7. Quoted in *SCRATCH* (2002), directed by Doug Pray.

8. For a much longer exploration of this idea, see Christopher, Roy, *Dead Precedents: How Hip-Hop Defines the Future,* London, UK: Repeater Books, 2019, pp. 29-349.

9. See Bruce Sterling & Benjamin Bratton in Conversation, SCI-Arc Channel, 2018: https://www.youtube.com/watch?v=Zo__x5SG8WY.

10. Quoted in Barrett, Gena-mour (2018, May 7) "Afrofuturism: Why Black Science Fiction 'Can't Be Ignored'", BBC News. Retrieved March 17, 2019 from http://www.bbc.com/news/newsbeat-43991078. As the cultural critic and writer Mark Dery, who coined the term in 1993, writes, revisiting the idea in 2016, "Afrofuturism speaks to our moment because it alone... offers a mythology of the future present, an explanatory narrative that recovers the lost data of historical memory, confronts the dystopian reality of black life in America, demands a place for people of color among the monorails and the Hugh Ferris monoliths of our tomorrows, insists that our Visions of Things to Come live up to our pieties about racial equality and social justice." See Mark Dery, 2016, February 1. "Black to the Future: Afrofuturism (3.0)", *Die Fabrikzeitung.* Retrieved March 17, 2019 from http://www.fabrikzeitung.ch/black-to-the-future-afrofuturism-3-0/.

11. See Scott Rosenberg, 1992 April 19, *San Francisco Examiner,* Section: Style, "Virtual Reality Check Digital Daydreams, Cyberspace Nightmares," Page C1, San Francisco, California.

12. Paul Gilroy calls these two processes the "politics of transformation" and "politics of fulfilment." See *The Black Atlantic: Modernity and Double Consciousness,* Cambridge, MA: Harvard University Press, 1993, passim.

13. Lanier, Jaron, *You Are Not a Gadget: A Manifesto,* New York: Knopf, 2010, 135.

14. Eshun, Kodwo, "Further Considerations on Afrofuturism", this volume, 260.

15. Attali, Jacques, *Noise: The Political Economy of Music,* Minneapolis, MN: University of Minnesota Press, 1977, 11.

Introduction
Ytasha L. Womack

The future is my home, it all came from here.
— Saul Williams, *The Noise Came From Here*

How does hip-hop intersect with science fiction? How does it not.

From Afrika Bambaataa's "Planet Rock" in the 80s to OutKast's *ATLiens* at the turn of the century; Ras G's space bass in the 2010s, to Moor Mother's *Analog Fluids of Sonic Black Holes* at the dawn of 2020 – hip-hop articulates alienness, otherworldliness, aspiration, community, and the metaphysics of nonlinear time.

The hip-hop production alone and the tonal mastery of looped samples and digital drumming is clearly channeled from the future.

Visual artist Alisha Wormsley is known for her billboard proclaiming that black people are in the future. Perhaps black people are from the future, too. It would certainly explain things, as jazz icon Sun Ra discovered. He claims Saturn. What swirling rock around the sun do you spring from?

"We came to Africa on a spaceship," chants Shabazz Palaces in "Afrikan Spaceship". "Do you know where we're coming from?"

That answer is no. Much of society doesn't know the social, time travelled Sankorarration process the poet descended from, the fragments of memory remixed in time, the racial traumas reconciled with nor the urgency in reconciliation of a fragmented human whole. No, much of the world may not understand why a Black American born poet would find surreptitious joy in rolling Bugatti style to the African motherland in a craft designed for astral travel — that he's not just saying it because it sounds cool or questionably absurd but because it reclaims his space in the universe.

Is he talking about going to Africa from the States? Is he talking about arriving in Africa from afar? Is he talking about both, the ultimate time paradox à la Dr. Manhattan in the 2019 *Watchmen* series where actress Regina King's character discovers she is both the cause and the result, the chicken and the egg in her current debacle?

Whether it's comic book inspirations in the likes of rapper David Banner, adopting the Incredible Hulk's alter ego or DMC of Run-DMC aka Darryl McDaniels whose flipped his iconic King of Rock mantra into comic books, hip-hop is all about the hero's journey.

That epic trek is a murky story, often spaceborne, inherently Afrofuturist, nearly always Afrosurrealist, thoroughly surreal and wields sci fi tropes with the acumen of a deejay digging in crates. Call it a lens on the altered reality. Hip-hop lyricism is not a binary story with saints and sinners but rather the duality of high stakes winners who defy the odds. Who is the victor? The poet. He tells the story, a testament to winning the war. What war? The war of who gets to tell the story and how the story is told.

Part of hip-hop's appeal is that everyone yearns to tell their story, as the data collectors behind our social media have discovered.

Everyone needs a hero.

Hip-hop projects a human centric future/now in what some call the temporal post-apocalypse.

Welcome to the Post-Apocalypse. You've Been Here for Some Time.

Many people in this world have been reconciling with cyborg and alien identities for a minute... aka awhile. Hip-hop creatives are not shy in exploring, embodying, and sometimes exploiting the human as conflicted cyborg in a very meta now space.

> Your freedom's in your mind. Your freedom's in a bind
> — Janelle Monáe, aka Cindi Mayweather, aka Django Jane.

Although Janelle Monáe is most popular for her android dualities, all of hip-hop poetics is in a philosophical tug and pull with otherness projected and identities presented.

Fear of a Black Planet, the title of Public Enemy's iconic album, in colloquial phrasing is "a thing." The alien metaphors in the Western sci fi canon are thinly veiled allegories for fears of otherism in all forms. The creation of race through force, law, and violence being example number one of putting humanity in the balance. For some the ultimate apocalypse was centuries ago, for others it's a war still waging.

The uninitiated will understand hip-hop's logic best when they think of it as music born of the post apocalypse. The 21st century dueling relationship between chorus and verse, stitched in time with space tropes and memories of lives not lived; the superhuman posturing of the antihero; the cognitive dissonance spawned by samples; aggression as hyperbole; loops; vulnerability, as sonic fragment; juxtaposition of pop locking, footwork, breaking as time deconstruction all take on new meaning in the liminal space.

Hip-hop's fighter spirit doubles as optimism threaded through temporal states. There's irony, there's humor, there's absurdity, there's lore, there's love, there's desire. "You have to laugh at the zombie in your front yard," says Janelle Monáe in "Dance Apocalyptic". It's this ironic humor amid chaos where magic meets poetic technology meets subversion.

Unlike hip-hop's cyberpunk literary brethren, who paint pictures of moving towards the ultimate calamity, hip-hop often juxtaposes an Afrofuturist narrative where it's moving out of one. In the hip-hop nation, technology is not here to kill us. We are the technology. We are the cyborg in the alien world called home. We are the capital, the capitalist, the rebel rolled in one. The hero, the antihero, the believer and the nonbeliever. "What's a god to a nonbeliever who doesn't believe in anything" sings Frank Ocean in "No Church in the Wild" a song helmed by Jay-Z and Kanye West who have Judeo Christian aliases, Hova and Yeezus respectively. Irony undisputed. Call it the vortex, the Matrix, the portal, the Spider Trap, the trap, or the wav, the truth, and the light, hip-hop is cozily wedged after the big bang and before the birth of the universe.

The post-apocalypse is not the end of the world. It's the end of "a" world but not "the" world for there are many rocks circling the sun. The post apocalypse is not utopia. The post apocalypse is not inherently anarchist as some of our sci fi narratives would lead us to believe. But it is layered, messy, hopeful, emotional, and charged. Hip-hop knows this territory all too well.

Sun Ra's rhetorical chant "it's after the end of the world" is a reminder of the impacts of enslavement and colonialism as apocalyptic moments. Public Enemy's *Fear of a Black Planet* are reminders of progress made and yet to be gained while Childish Gambino's "This is America" speaks to the surreal art of navigating epic chaos in classic trickster tradition.

> Grandma told me 'Get your money' black man.
> — Childish Gambino, "This is America"

In the video a tense and cool Gambino dances shirtless in the midst of sporadic violence and dancing children, fully adjusted to the madness at hand. He is the orisha Elegba, the gateway to life on one plane and the next. He is shapeshifting before our eyes. He is walking the thin line of realities of space/time. Is it the future, is it the past, or is it the ever present now?

> World getting warmer we're going the other way
> — billy woods says in *Marlow*, a metaphor for climate change and chaos.

Moor Mother's work is nearly exclusively about time, often exploring cultural trauma as trapped in time loops. Industrial, melodic, and bold, she samples spirituals and sound fragments, using heavy distortion as she bridges the horrors of enslaved Africans with the prison industrial complex, and police brutality.

In the post apocalypse, survivors are superheroes.

"Trying to save my black life by fantasizing my dead life," she says in "Deadbeat Protest." "You can see my dead body at the protest."

> Black Girl Magic, y'all can't stand it
> They been trying hard just to make us all vanish
> I suggest they put a flag on a whole 'nother planet
> — Janelle Monáe, *Django Jane*

Hip-hop is inherently about winning, survival, and triumph.

We are not Tupac riding with Dr. Dre in the video "California" à la *Mad Max Beyond Thunderdome* nor are we Lil Wayne falling from one dimension to the next in his *Inception* inspired video for "6 foot 7 foot." We are none of these things but at times we feel like it — somewhere between Princess Nokia's supernatural resistance in "Brujas" and Shabazz Palaces' dreamy trek through *Quazarz: Born on a Gangster Star*. Are we King Britt/Fhloston Paradigm's "The Phoenix" hurling through space like cyborgs on a mission? Can we just nestle in Ras G's *Stargate Music* soundtrack for, say, a millennium?

Afrofuturism claims a trajectory of resilience, a power tool to navigate the madness. This delicate ebb and flow of change and tension to navigate new worlds requires a mastery of rhythm.

Hip-hop is all rhythm. I personally like my rhythm with bass. Nevertheless, hip-hop technicians have swallowed the proverbial drum. How you ask, did they swallow the drum?

A Hip-Hop Trinity Reconfigured

Hip-hop technician embodies an altered trinity: the superhero, the curious hacker, the dreamy unborn child. They are what John Akomfrah depicted in his Afrofuturist documentary *The Last Angel of History* as the Data Thief, a time traveler, seeking to know black culture through musical artifacts.

Hip-hop is as now as it is later, remixing life's conundrums, with a faith that the artist's ability to speak truth to power or emotion to capital is modern day alchemy. If they do it right, they will be immortal, soaring above the drudgery of the pixilated post apocalypse. If they have skill, they will create something akin to Sun Ra's Alter Destiny, living a timeline parallel to the world's they hailed from, and shapeshifting into something epic that transmutes trauma and elevates dreams. They will be forces to reckon with. They will be visible in a world bewitched by dehumanizing color paradoxes. They will be superheroes.

Rapper alias and tagger names are superhero armor. They are Superman's glasses or T'Challa's vibranium suit, god head identities chiseled to be of rare form. They are what old school Baptist born African American Christians called "a covering," an inspired supernatural protection. Such names and identities are the verbal variation of the African mask reconfigured in a technology with naming power for a reborn soul, a twin soul, an altered self, an empowered self.

Digable Planets, Del the Funky Homosapien, Black Star, André 3000, Flying Lotus, King Britt, Gang Starr, Fhloston Paradigm, Black Thought, Future are aliases plucked from star-bound inspirations. Some names are godly (Queen Latifah) and others are the ultimate in overcoming archetypes (Cardi B, Nipsey Hussle, Chance the Rapper, Big K.R.I.T.). Others ditch the moniker and transmute anyway (Vic Mensa, billy woods).

> Hacker. I'm a hacker, I'm a hacker in your hard drive.
> Hundred thousand dollar Tesla ripping through your hard drive
> — Saul Williams, "Burundi"

Hip-hop technicians are Neo in their own Matrix, questioning, yearning, and claiming the superhero within because their higher visions of themselves, as dancers, MCs, deejays, producers, and writers, require that they channel higher frequencies. They are fine tuned. They are antennas, catching noise, data, fragments, and transmitting an emotion, a story, a forward charge.

They are the unborn child in *Daughters of the Dust*. In Julie Dash's masterpiece of a film, a family on the Gullah Islands of South Carolina at the onset of the 20th Century are torn. Do they leave their community, one which preserved African traditions during and after the transatlantic slave trade, and head North for opportunity? A yet to be born little girl narrates. The question? How does one keep the culture in the face of change and new technology? What does one do if they are moving away from being technology, the labored body that is both the product and the maker?

Clock Parts on the Lawn

A professor of mine at Clark Atlanta University talked to his students at length about the swallowing of the drum. A visiting artist who was once mentored by luminary Renaissance man Paul Robeson, he reminded us that the drum, a communication technology, was snatched from enslaved Africans in the United States. Africans in

Antebellum America were prohibited from using the drum. As a result, a heavy dose of drum patterns was evident in our vocals. Why? Because African Americans had to swallow the drum. Think scatting in jazz, think the vocal runs up and down the scale in R&B and gospel. Think of them as drum patterns, sonic hums. Now think of lyricism in hip-hop.

Lyricism, as rhythm, is an act of agency and reclamation. Hip-hop reminds us that language is technology. Poets speak to the prophetic and profane. Deejays are archivists, producers are time travelers, and those in the culture adopt the superhero near god personas as armor.

Rhythm is identified as a core artistic aesthetic in African Diasporic artforms by Negritude philosopher Leopold Senghor. The aesthetic is used to contextualize contours in African masks but could also speak to the internalized drum, a cyborg tool for communicating to the future now. Hip-hop reminds us that language is technology. That slang, dialect, language itself has a philosophy and worldview of its own.

> My cranium is vibranium, my brain is of uranium and titanium.
> — Black Thought, "Streets."

Hip-hop's foundation is fundamentally Afrofuturist. The construction of the aesthetic from the arrangements of lyrics to sounds as quilted word time machines is Afrofuturist. But all subject matter in hip-hop songs isn't Afrofuturist even when science fiction is the clear playground.

Hip-hop as a practice claims both time and space, creating an altered today with logic defying sample mash ups from disparate eras that screw with all manner of linear thought. Whereas, Afrofuturism is a way of looking at the world or alternate realities through a black cultural lens. Afrofuturism intersects black culture, the imagination, liberation, technology, and mysticism while engaging the divine feminine and nonlinear time.

Hip-hop has its own time travel device framework. This logic centers around what comic and hip-hop arts scholar John Jennings calls Sankofarration. The term references the Sankofa bird and symbolizes a Twi ideology that's evolved into an African Diasporic technology. Sankofarration is the process of pulling the best of the past and repurposing it for the future now.

A paradigm of inversions, at hip-hop's core, it questions all matters of reality, a philosophical modality inherited from their funk, jazz, and poetic predecessors. George Clinton, Sun Ra were king among those space tinged inspirations. Clinton and Sun Ra's lyricism and hyperbole, not to mention, the celestial costumes are obvious musical ancestors.

However, the line of poets and time defying rhythms is an African Diasporic/ Continental cultural aesthetic, the poetry of Nikki Giovanni among them. The time inversions are as evident in the clave count in Cuban rhumba as they are in the mbalax drumming of Senegal or the Malian strings or the soul clap in Chicago House. The polyrhythms that denote many African traditional music forms are evident in thinking of lyrics as drum patterns layered over digitized beats.

Nile-Born Memories

I've been reading about Ancient Egyptian art lately. I was reminded in my readings that Ancient craftsmen created grand public works to ensure immortality for those depicted. I can't help but think of hip-hop's grandiosity and self-affirmation as related — an ancient practice reclaimed to remix the status quo — a statement of existence that transcends all dimensions.

This book, edited by Roy Christopher, is a moment. It is the deconstructed sample, the researched lyrical metaphors, the aha moment on the way to hip-hop enlightenment. Hip-hop permeates our world and yet it is continually misunderstood. Hip-hop's intersections with Afrofuturism and science fiction provide fascinating touchpoints that enable us to see our todays and tomorrows. This book can be, for the curious, a window into a hip-hop infused Alter Destiny — a journey whose spaceship you embarked on some time ago. Are you engaging this work from the gaze of the future? Are you the data thief sailing into the past to u turn to the now? Or are you the unborn child prepping to build the next universe? No, you're the superhero. Enjoy the journey.

Moor Mother by Bob Sweeny

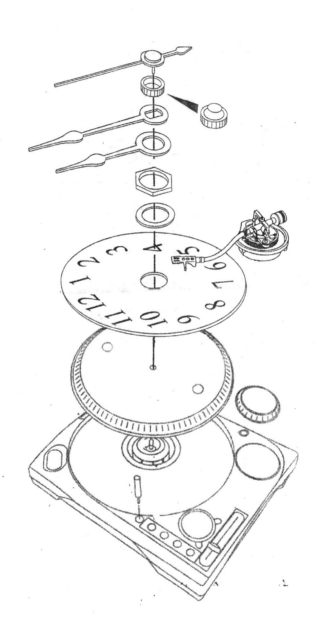

I. Time

Take Me Back: Ghostface's Ghosts
Steven Shaviro

Ghostface Killah's track "Can Can" was originally supposed to be on his 2006 album *Fishscale*. Advance copies were all over the Internet, but the track was withdrawn at the last moment, I presume because of copyright clearance issues. The track has never been officially released, but you can hear it on one on Ghostface Killah's semi-illicit mixtapes (*Hidden Darts Volume Four*, released 2008).

Ghostface Killah himself produced the track. It is built around a sample taken from the Pointer Sisters' 1973 hit "Yes We Can Can," itself a cover of a song originally written by Allen Toussaint, and performed by Lee Dorsey in 1970. The backbone of Ghostface Killah's track is the opening rhythm track from the Pointer Sisters' version of the song: first we hear the bass line, and then the drums and the funky rhythm guitar kick in. This is looped over and over again during the rap. In the Pointer Sisters' recording, we first hear the rhythm track by itself, making for a long introduction; finally, after about thirty seconds, this leads into Anita Pointer's opening verse: "Now's the time for all good men/To get together with one another..." In Ghostface Killah's track, this opening verse comes in twice to interrupt the rapping: first in the middle of the track, and then again at the very end. But the sample (and the track as a whole) ends in a weird suspension, with the words "we got to..." In the Pointer Sisters' version, these words lead to the triumphant chorus ("we got to make this land a better land/Than the world in which we live/And we got to help each man be a better man/ With the kindness that we give," etc.). But Ghostface withholds this chorus from us, so that his track ends on an unresolved note.

I don't know what the story is about Ghostface Killah's failure to get copyright clearance for "Yes We Can Can." Not only has the song itself been covered by numerous artists, it has also been sampled in hip-hop something like forty-three times, by artists ranging from NWA to De La Soul, and from Big Daddy Kane to MC Lyte. I haven't listened to most of these other samplings, but I doubt that "Yes We Can Can" has ever been used quite in the way it is used here, as the backdrop to a knockdown argument between Ghostface Killah's persona and that of an irate girlfriend. It's a drawn-out lip battle. Ghostface Killah alternates between outrageous threats of violence — "shut up 'fore I break your jaw," and "your girlfriend, I had to have her smacked up, she had it coming" — and expressions of contrition; she curses him out as a "stupid ass punk faggot mark trick," and complains that "all I do is cook, clean, and watch all the children." There's a lot of back-and-forth here, and a tentative movement towards reconciliation; but the narrative, like the vocal sample, ends without any firm resolution.

It's significant, I think, that, although Ghostface Killah is in charge of the story, and although the overall import of the song is one of self-justifying masculinity, we do nonetheless get at least some sense of the woman's perspective. She may be greedy and materialistic, with her "bullshit perms" and her "alligator Gucci bag" and "Donatella Versace sweatsuit"; but rhetorically, at least, she gives as good as she gets — and in hip-hop, there is no belittling that. In any case, Ghostface Killah moves in the course of the track from telling her off to begging her forgiveness and asking her to marry him. He seems to be taking to heart the original song's exhortation: "And do respect the women of the world/Remember you all have mothers." Ghostface Killah comes out managing to have it both ways. He shows that he is able to apologize, and be something of a sensitive man; but he still maintains his patriarchal privilege. It's all well and good for him to recognize that "a real man would never disrespect or hurt his family"; but nobody will mistake this phrase, with its emphasis on what makes a "real man," for a formula of egalitarianism and feminist empowerment.

I am not going to go over the words of the song in any greater detail; suffice it to say that nearly every line is packed with incident and with significance. Past relationships are recalled, somebody comes to visit, and so on — all in the course of a track that is less than three minutes long. In any case, others have written, better than I could, about Ghostface Killah's brilliance as a storyteller, his amazing way with words, how aptly he moves between finely rendered naturalistic details, on the one hand, and bizarre non sequiturs and invented slang, on the other. He's like a great noir novelist one moment, a whacked-out surrealist the next, a postmodern metafictionalist the verse after that. But for all the games he plays with words, I think that Ghostface Killah is ultimately more an expressionist than a formalist, more concerned with projecting emotions than with foregrounding, and calling attention to, his (considerable) skills. As Greg Tate nicely put it,

> you scratch your head every fourth line, but you get the ones about roaches in the cornflakes, the wifey back home boning your boy while you're on tour, and the Shaolin crime narratives where fists and bullets are foreverever flying — all like he's Burroughs, Ellroy, and Bukowski rolled into one garrulous gregarious grungy gruesome ghettofied writer.

By calling Ghostface Killah an expressionist, I am trying to get away from all those tired old debates about authenticity and "realness" in hip-hop. If talking about roaches in the cornflakes, or for that matter brand-name bags and sweatsuits, is "real," then talking about epic gunfights, and adopting aliases from kung-fu movies and

Marvel comics very clearly is not. Ghostface Killah's lyrics, as the RZA says in *The Wu-Tang Manual*, "are colorful and abstract, their sound and shape as important as their meaning." What I am calling expressionism includes all of this, cutting across the opposition between reality and fantasy. The opposite of expressionism is rather formalism, by which I mean that stage in every genre when the practitioners become more interested in reflecting on the genre itself, and on making minor refinements and innovations therein, than on projecting an emotional content. The Wu-Tang Clan has its formalist moments, but I don't think that this is the center of what Ghostface Killah is doing in his solo work.

Why does this matter? Well, one common response to charges of misogyny and violence in rap lyrics is to say that the artists are just telling it like it is, describing the world that poor black people are forced to live in. While this is true enough in its way, it doesn't get at the full measure of what somebody like Ghostface Killah is actually doing with his rhymes. He is dramatizing, or projecting, a way of life; but his *manner of speaking* — his incessant fabulation, his invention of a language — is itself a crucial part of this way of life. I won't attempt to work through the whole history of rapping in African American culture, from the dozens and the signifyin' monkey to the ways in which success in "the rap game" in the twenty-first century reflects the importance of "gettin' paid." But Ghostface Killah's masculine posturing, his complex position in the gender wars, must itself be seen in the light of this complex process of fabulation and invention.

Let me try to put this in another way, one that acknowledges race and class as well as gender. There is certainly what can be called a "realist" side to Ghostface Killah's raps. You can see it in all his tales of ghetto life. These are songs and stories about contemporary African American experience. More precisely, they are situated within the northern, urban, working-class (or unemployed, sub-working-class) male heterosexual African American experience in the 1980s and 1990s, and they convey this experience with an intense, and carefully crafted, verisimilitude. Beyond this, there is the way that Ghostface Killah evokes a general attitude, or a form of life: what Greg Tate, again, called "that je ne sais quoi we know as unrepentant, unreconstructed, around-the-way negritude."

I am strategically quoting Tate here, because this is something that is problematic for me, or any other white person, to talk about. It's all too easy for white folks (and for some black folks as well) to romanticize crack dealing, or pimping, or what have you, as the "essence'" of the African American condition. This is a tendency that already existed full-blown in Norman Mailer's notorious "white Negro" essay from 1957; of course, its roots go back a lot further than that. I said "romanticize," but I could just as easily have said "vilify" or "pathologize" — as these are just two

sides of the same coin. Norman Mailer in the 1950s, and Daniel Patrick Moynihan in the 1960s, were pretty much saying the same thing about black people. And their attitudes still persist today, in what we would like to think of as our more enlightened, "post-Civil-Rights" era. (This is something, incidentally, that Spike Lee has a lot to say about, in his 2000 film *Bamboozled*). Now, I am not accusing Ghostface Killah of a commercially calculated pandering to this sort of mentality: which could be called blackface minstrelsy, even if a black person is doing it. Most likely, Ghostface Killah just doesn't give a fuck. But I think that we do need to take the reality of white people's vicarious enjoyment of what they see as black culture into account: when we consider, for instance, how Ghostface Killah moved from the broader emotional range of his underrated *Pretty Toney Album* (2004), which didn't sell very well, to the narrower focus, two years later, on that old standby, crack dealing, that marked his universally acclaimed *Fishscale*.

This brings me back to Tate's comments on "negritude." Ghostface Killah's expression of "blackness" is more a matter of style and attitude than it is one of content. It is something that comes from the singer, not the song. It has more to do with the specificities of *how* Ghostface Killah expresses himself, than it does with the actual — often violent — content of the stories he tells, or the particular — often weird and crazy and hyperbolic — things he says. It's not just a question, therefore, of Ghostface Killah's words, but also, and perhaps even more importantly, of just *how* these words are presented to us. This means that we need to consider, on the one hand, his speaking and singing voice, and on the other hand, his use of samples. These can be thought of as, respectively, the inner and outer dimensions of a rapper's mode of expression. The voice, with its tones and inflections, expresses the inside, or the underlying character, of the person speaking — or more accurately, of the persona (since it may well be a consciously crafted fiction). The sample, on the other hand, is the outside. It is something like the voice's context, the otherness that it must confront, the field of forces in which it must be located, and the memory traces that it reactivates, and to which it responds.

Ghostface Killah's rapping voice is unique. It doesn't sound like anyone else's in hip-hop — or in any other musical genre, for that matter. Many masculine voices in hip-hop are tough-guy voices: they can be characterized by their sheer bravado; or they have an air of authority that comes, at least in part, from a certain undercurrent of menace. A tough-guy voice may be boasting, but it can just as well be quietly matter-of-fact. Other rap voices are more open and relaxed, even ebullient: think of Lil Wayne, for instance. Still others are colloquial to the point of mumbling; though this itself is a carefully crafted effect, as in the case of Young Thug (arguably the most innovative rapper of the 2010s). Then there are the sexy, even seductive voices — though in this case, we are already starting to cross over from speaking to singing, or from rapping voices to male R&B loverman voices. And beyond that, there are those rap voices that are delirious or crazy, that seem to be out of control (think of Ghostface Killah's Wu-Tang bandmate, the late Ol' Dirty Bastard). And this typology could be extended, to encompass styles like those of alternative rap (MadLib), white working-class rap (the unique vocal stylings of Eminem), and so on. But Ghostface Killah's voice doesn't really fit into any of these categories. It's wary and tough, rather than relaxed or open; but it also has a certain twang, or a slight shaking — or perhaps I should even say a whine. You have to take it seriously, and give it a certain authority; it never crosses over into Ol' Dirty Bastard-style buffoonery. But at the same time, it always seems to be derailing itself slightly. You can hear this, for instance, if you compare Ghostface Killah's voice to Raekwon's, on the albums in which they appear together: like the latter's *Only Built 4 Cuban Linx* (1995), or Ghostface Killah's earlier solo efforts (e.g., *Ironman*, 1996).

You can't help sensing a true degree of charm in Ghostface Killah's voice — and thereby, a certain distance, a certain sense of this-is-not-quite-to-be-taken-seriously — even when he is threatening to break his girlfriend's jaw. The twang is what allows him to get away with it. It makes him sound a little more self-conscious and reflective. Yet at the same time, it gives his voice an added dimension of emotionality, which allows it to slide from self-assertion into romantic pleading — as when he begs his woman to come back to him, and give him another chance. This twang or whine even fuels the metamorphosis into what Ghostface Killah calls his "crying voice": the tonality of remembered woe, which he drifts into when he is recalling roaches in the cornflakes, or "babies with flies on the cheeks" (in "I Can't Go To Sleep," from the Wu-Tang Clan's *W*, 2000) or being whipped by his Mama when he was a child (in "Whip You With A Strap," from *Fishscale*). In short, Ghostface's voice is unique in the way it is able to continually *modulate* its affective tone: from tough-guy fatalism to wacky humor to begging to almost-crying, and back again.

This flexibility can be disconcerting. Even Robert Christgau — who rates most of Ghostface Killah's solo albums quite highly in his "Consumer Guide" — dismissed *The Pretty Toney Album* (2004) with the rather snarky one-liner: "Don't worry, Ghost — no matter how much you cry we'll never call you 'faggot.'" The truth behind Christgau's comment is that there is indeed only a thin line between mastery and victimization; or between masculine assertiveness and control, and the kind of enforced submission that is coded as 'feminization' in our patriarchal (misogynistic and homophobic) culture. Let there be no mistake: I'm referring here to United States/American culture *in toto*, and not specifically to working class American culture, or African American culture, or prison culture, or hip-hop culture. If we are to find a particular "negritude" in Ghostface Killah's voice, it has to do, not with this globally oppressive situation, but with the culturally specific resources that he uses to negotiate it. It's as if Ghostface Killah were always teetering on the edge between self-congratulatory sneering and maudlin self-pity, or between asserting that he's a top, and confessing that he's a bottom — but without ever quite falling into either side.

And this is where I would like to turn from Ghostface Killah's own voice to that other dimension of his sound, the one that comes from without rather than within: the way that he uses soul music samples. Ghostface Killah's willingness to compromise his hardcore gangsta stance with unabashed appeals to sentiment — his genre switch, you might say, from nihilistic crime narrative to melodrama or even romantic comedy — goes together with his taste for soul music from the late 1960s and early 1970s. Ghostface Killah was born in 1970; he never tires of saying that soul of that era is the music that he likes the best, because it is the music his parents would listen to when they were fucking. It's the music to which he was conceived. Such a return to his own sonic origins, if I may call it that, is sufficiently weird and outrageous that it *has* to be taken seriously.

Ghostface Killah's use of soul samples is certainly indebted to the RZA's deployment of them on the Wu-Tang Clan's first album, *Enter the Wu-Tang (36 Chambers)*, back in 1993. Nate Patrin has argued that this move revolutionized hip-hop. And retro soul samples became well-nigh ubiquitous in both hip-hop and R&B in the early 2000s, thanks to Kanye West — as well as to other producers such as Rich Harrison. But I want to suggest that Ghostface Killah's use of these samples is unique, precisely because of the way that they call up his scene of origins. Of course, nobody can really go back to the moment of their own conception. My scene of origins is necessarily beyond my grasp. It's an experience, or a life-world, that absolutely, materially concerns me — but also one that I can never grasp directly. It is lost; and it can only be imagined, retrospectively, as already having been lost. Ghostface Killah's sampling practice is a sort of time travel: but it is one that can only access the past in a distant, wavering, spectral form.

I don't mean this only in personal, autobiographical terms — after all, I know nothing about the life of Dennis Coles (to call him by the name his parents gave him), aside from what he has chosen to reveal (or perhaps remix and fabulate) in his lyrics. What I am calling Ghostface Killah's scene of origins has a crucial social and historical dimension. For the time of his birth, or of his parents' generation, is a unique moment in African American history. It's the moment of Black Pride, after the victories of the 1960s Civil Rights Movement — and before the economic crisis of the 1970s, and then the crack epidemic of the 1980s, utterly ravaged urban African American communities like the one in which Ghostface Killah grew up. Indeed, it's the time of blaxploitation cinema, one of the sources of hip-hop's gangsta mythology. But even those were exhilarating, in a way that their echo in hip-hop of the 1990s and later is not. The soul era was a time of hope rather than despair. And, though it wasn't exactly a utopia of gender equality, it was also a time that was still largely free of what Greg Tate called "the self-inflected misogyny of the modern [hip-hop] era."

In short, the soul music that Ghostface loves belongs to a moment that — excuse the hyperbole — might almost be thought of as a second Emancipation. You can hear it directly in the music: just listen to a compilation like *Black Power: Music Of A Revolution*, released by Shout! Factory in 2004. There's an amazing degree of political engagement and radical passion there, even in the most mainstream soul and R&B acts. You can hear that passion in the positivity of a song like "Yes We Can Can": a positivity that is scarcely imaginable today. Of course, we now know how limited that moment of Black Pride and Soul Power was: how partial its victories were, how quickly its gains were eroded away. This was already evident in 2006, when Ghostface Killah recorded "Can Can". It is even more desperately the case today, in the age of Black Lives Matter and overt racism in the White House.

For now, I just want to emphasize how shocking and disjunctive and crazy the irruption of "Yes We Can Can" into Ghostface Killah's domestic dispute really is. There's just too much of a gap between the personal, private register of the track's slice of life narrative, and the public call-out to "all good men" of the original song. There's too much of a distance between the rap's litany of complaints and curses, and the anthemic exuberance of the Pointer Sisters. When Ghostface Killah calls upon soul sounds in this way, he is not acting out of anything so simple as nostalgia: since he is evoking a past that he cannot recover or even remember, but only experience in the form of a trace, a mark of absence, a haunting.

At the same time, Ghostface Killah is not just using the soul sounds in order to get an emotional reaction, or to give his own track an authority that it would otherwise lack. Rather, his call to the past works to register difference and distance, to create and express disjunction. His rapping both echoes and opposes the music to which it is set. His voice adapts itself to the rhythm and flow of the samples, while at the same time his tone — sometimes desperate, more often dry and deadpan, at times comedically mock-hysterical — cuts against it. Ghostface Killah reverts to the moment of his conception in order to tear a hole in the heart of the moment at which he is rapping, and of the ghetto world that he describes with such economy and precision. In other words, Ghostface Killah is working with the fact that soul music *signifies* or connotes emotionality. It stands for passion: for longing, desperation, and blocked desire, on the one hand, and warmth, fulfillment, drawn-out erotic bliss on the other. In this way it stands at an opposite pole from the ethos of the Shaolin warrior (the big theme in Wu-Tang mythology), or from the pimp/thug/gangsta/Iceberg Slim/ Donald Goines lineage of so much rap. Soul is about emotional outpouring, while hardcore rap is about maintaining a reserve of cool, never letting yourself go. These opposing trends can be seen as the two sides of black music, and can further be seen (stereotypically) as "feminine" and "masculine'" modes. Soul includes men singing to women as well as women singing for women; hardcore rap is usually addressed by men to other men, and is filled with masculine bravado. Ghostface Killah negotiates the boundaries of this dichotomy, and to some extent steps beyond it.

I will conclude by briefly citing another Ghostface Killah track, one that resonates strongly with "Can Can." "Tooken Back" from *The Pretty Toney Album* is another plea to a woman (here, Jacki-O) for forgiveness. Throughout the song, a soul sample pleading "take me back" — from a 1972 song of that name by The Emotions — loops in the background, and swells up to the foreground during the chorus. The intonations of both rappers pass through a number of affective states, from derision to desperation to love. The soul sample makes the emotion seem over the top and larger than life, while the voices' nuances introduce subtlety and qualification. Both speakers are calculating in everything they say, yet the soul sample drags them into a warmth, and an erotic pull, that are beyond calculation. The sample loops and loops with the stirrings of desire, while the raps rationalize and then give way, giving a narrative shape to that underlying pulse. The song manages to be heartfelt rather than ironic, even as it shows a fully ironic, self-conscious awareness of what's going on. And that's what Ghostface Killah has always been about.

Two Dope Boyz (In a Visual World)
Tiffany E. Barber

From lyrics to production to sonic and visual themes, OutKast shifts conventional understandings of contemporary black life and love in the post-civil rights era. Post-civil rights black cultural production — work by artists of African descent born after the civil rights era, also referred to as post-black and post-soul — responds to the political gains of the Civil Rights Movement. Before the civil rights era, African Americans were excluded from the electoral and policymaking arenas of U.S. institutionalized politics. But as a result of the Civil Rights Movement, "The major foundations of the Jim Crow order had been toppled, and for the first time since Reconstruction it seemed possible that a progressive and racially inclusive coalition might prevail in American politics," political theorist Richard Iton explains.[1] Formal political equality, or movement towards it, was seen as a viable remedy to centuries of black degradation and a way to establish a multiracial, national community. Black cultural production was part and parcel of this political transformation. Black music specifically, from the blues to avant-garde jazz to soul to funk, offered empowered visions of blackness. Black music during this time carried a message of liberation and was seen as a way to bring people together through sound and dance. This is particularly true in the case of the American South, the epicenter of the Civil Rights Movement and "a space that has alternately been a place of origin, exile and return in the African-American imaginary," as curator Thomas J. Lax puts it.[2]

OutKast's otherworldly musical stylings extend this tradition. The group's debut album *Southernplayalisticadillacmuzik*, written and produced when its members Big Boi and André "3000" Benjamin were just teenagers, went platinum in 1995. That same year, the duo won the Source Award for Best New Artist Group of the Year. This recognition effectively changed the face and sound of hip-hop and popular black music more broadly. OutKast's award recast the boundaries of the rap genre's east coast-west coast turf wars and brought critical attention to the emerging sounds of American Southern hip-hop, an intervention that was met with disapproval. During the acceptance speech for the award amid a sea of tastemakers and music executives, Benjamin proclaimed, "The South's got something to say," and OutKast was unceremoniously booed. In this moment, detractors dismissed the post-civil rights American South as a legitimate hip-hop cypher. But more than Benjamin's elevation of the region and of a sub-genre of hip-hop apart from the musical form's east-west predominance caused a stir; the duo's sonic and visual aesthetic was equally disruptive.

From dandies to aliens, OutKast has shaped black visual culture to complicate well-worn assumptions about both the American South and the sociopolitical realities of our post-civil rights present. But their visual language has garnered little attention in the scholarly and popular record; critics typically focus on their place in hip-hop history and their innovative sound. This essay addresses this dearth. Adding to the literature that focuses on OutKast's sound, this chapter focuses on the group's music videos to explicate the postmodern visions of blackness they construct.

Contemporary black cultural production — from post-black to post-soul — continues to play a significant role in the negotiation of history, place, memory, and identity in the decades after the Civil Rights Movement. Post-black "artists [are] adamant about not being labeled as 'black' artists," curator Thelma Golden cheekily proclaims, "though their work was [or is] steeped, in fact deeply interested, in redefining complex notions of blackness."[3] Introduced on the occasion of Golden's 2001 blockbuster exhibition *Freestyle*, post-blackness is part of an exhibition history that begins in the mid-1980s amidst varying ideas about identity politics in American art and has since become a highly contested term. "Racism is real, and many artists who have endured its effects feel the museum [world] is promoting a kind of art — trendy, postmodern, blandly international — that has turned the institution into a 'boutique' or 'country club,'" artist David Hammons quips.[4] Golden herself admits that post-black is "both a hollow social construction and a reality with an indispensable history."[5] In other words, to be post-black is to be rooted in but not restricted by blackness, to avoid identity labels and the social expectations that come with them. For all its controversy, post-blackness represents a sea change in how we conceive of aesthetic categories and values in racial terms.

Post-soul follows a similar impulse as post-black. According to Bertram D. Ashe, post-soul artists address "the peculiar pains, pleasures, and problems of race in the post-Civil Rights movement United States; the use of nontraditionally black cultural influences in their work; and the resultant exploration of the boundaries of blackness."[6] But more importantly, black cultural producers in the post-civil rights era repudiate a "proper" relation between their racial identities and their art.[7] On this front, OutKast troubles monolithic, essentialist understandings of blackness, and the imagination of a unified (often male and heteronormative) black body often associated with the Civil Rights Movement, or hip-hop for that matter. Whereas racial respectability and uplift formed the foundation of the civil rights agenda, black intellectuals and artists of the post-civil rights era prefer new, less didactic forms of expression not constrained by racial responsibility.

No song in OutKast's oeuvre exemplifies this phenomenon better than "Rosa Parks." Named after the civil rights icon who brought national attention to the problem of segregation in Montgomery, Alabama's public transportation system by refusing to move to the back of the bus, the song is the third track on the album *Aquemini* and was the first video to be released for the project. The first two sentences of the song's hook, "Ah ha, hush that fuss/Everybody move to the back of the bus," recall the early years of the Civil Rights Movement. The back of the bus is equivalent to inferior status, and this line signifies on the condition of black riders forced to sit in colored-only sections of public transport prior to desegregation.

Though there is no explicit mention of Rosa Parks, the song's evocative chorus attracted the attention of the civil rights icon and her lawyers. She sued the duo and their record label for the unauthorized use of her name in a song she deemed profane and vulgar.[8] Parks' lawsuit and reaction to the song detail a rift — generationally and politically — between civil rights memory and the distance that accumulates the farther away from the era we move. Put differently, "the generation(s) of black youth born after the early successes of the traditional civil rights movement are in fact," popular music scholar Mark Anthony Neal avers, "divorced from the nostalgia associated with those successes and thus positioned to critically engage the movement's legacy from a state of objectivity that the traditional civil rights leadership is both unwilling and incapable of doing."[9] For these reasons, Parks regarded OutKast's song as disrespectful.

Bearing in mind the many references to black musical forms old and new, the visual codes, and the landscape depicted in "Rosa Parks," the post-civil rights American South that OutKast constructs for us is one in which blackness is more than historical memory; it is at once sonic, visual, and geographical. The video animates the afterlife of civil rights struggle with sonic and visual references that expand outmoded conceptions of blackness and its history, from the marching band and choreography akin to formations and movements seen in black Greek step shows to a rousing harmonica breakdown accompanied by a collective soul clap. The presence of the marching band and step choreography recall the significance of these traditions as sites of community building within African American expressive culture as well as formal organizations such as Historically Black Colleges and Universities and the National Pan-Hellenic Council, an organization of nine historically black and international Greek lettered fraternities and sororities headquartered in Decatur, Georgia. Furthermore, the landscape depicted in the video is undeniably black and Southern. The video was filmed on Auburn Avenue in downtown Atlanta, just blocks away from where Martin Luther King, Jr. was born. The legendary club, Royal Peacock, is in the background as is a huge, blinking neon sign that reads, "TRAP." Aside from calling attention to the building to which it is affixed, TRAP in this context also marks the often inescapable grit of urban life, which the folks in the street attempt to mitigate with improvised dance and sound along with the subgenre of Southern hip-hop that life in the "trap" inspired in the late 1990s.[10]

Bridging civil rights history and contemporary popular culture, this milieu casts the song's chorus anew, complicating the generational anxieties of Southern black folks that Parks herself raises. The back of the bus in this schema is where the cool kids congregate to plot, to be mischievous, and to be rowdy, creating an enclave in the back seats away from the watchful eye of the bus driver. From this angle, the main purpose of the song is to valorize OutKast's position in the rap game and the sonic revolution they initiated at the time; the creative community the duo coalesces in calling together and moving everybody to the back of the bus boasts the duo's lyrical prowess and hip-hop excellence. After all, unlike their peers, "[they] the type of people make the club get *crunk*" (emphasis mine).

Extending the metaphor of the back of the bus as a space of coolness and ruckus, OutKast's creative — *crunk* — labor also engenders the ways the pair disrupts long-held assumptions about the boundaries of hip-hop and black respectability more broadly. Crunk here unfolds in two directions. It at once refers to another blossoming subgenre of hip-hop, crunk music, characterized by the repetition of shouted catchphrases and electronic bass beats.[11] Crunk also signals alternative affective possibilities for black Southerners. Spanning joy and excitement, having a good time, and uninhibited liveliness that spills over into disorderly conduct and downright rowdiness, these forms of disruption extend past the upright, uniformed, and disciplined behavior performed and expected of African Americans during the civil rights era.

Consequently, OutKast brings new meaning to Rosa Parks' principled stand against segregation. OutKast's vision of the South according to 3000 entails a futuristic orientation that plays a more menacing role than the unauthorized use of Parks' name. Less concerned with staying true to Parks' legacy, Benjamin pushes for "some space futuristic type things" because, as he declares in the video's opening dialogue, "they scared of that." With this prompt, Benjamin envelops listeners and viewers in an exercise of defiance, turning away from previously held assumptions about the political value of black cultural production in the past and present. "Black creative life has too often been determined by this impulse to 'keep it real,'" explains sociologist Alondra Nelson in her writings on Afrofuturism's early permutations.[12] "In order to be taken seriously, we have fostered and encouraged a long tradition of social realism in our cultural production. And we feared that to stop keeping things real was to lose the ability to recognize and protest the very real inequities in the social world."[13] As a result, Nelson continues, "we created a cultural environment often hostile to speculation, experimentation, and abstraction."[14] "Rosa Parks," by contrast, embraces speculation and experimentation. It traffics in the futuristic ethos OutKast initiated with their sophomore album *ATLiens*, one that recognizes a black historical past but is oriented toward "the beyond" marked by nebulous, psychedelic, digital backdrops and manipulated shots.[15] Rather than post-soul pastiche, then, the visual culture of OutKast extends the speculative, Afrofuturist impulses of Sun Ra, the Bar-Kays, and George Clinton and the Parliament Funkadelic, bands that all have roots in the South (Birmingham, AL; Memphis, TN; and Kannapolis, NC respectively). "Rosa Parks" serves

Overleaf: Big Boi by Timothy Saccenti

as a launching pad for the world OutKast envisioned beyond constraining historical paradigms. Ultimately, the lyrics and video for "Rosa Parks" reflect OutKast's efforts to redefine contemporary American popular music and the South.

André 3000's song, "Prototype," visualizes what the ATLiens were up to in the wake of four jointly recorded studio albums and critical acclaim. "Prototype" is the seventh song on Dré's contribution to *Speakerboxxx/The Love Below*, the pair's fifth project. In "Prototype," the possibilities of sound and text expose the limitations of the visual, thereby spurring alternative ways of "seeing" black intimacies, the world, the present, and the future. In so doing, "Prototype" highlights how science and speculative fiction elements — namely the presence of aliens and human-nonhuman relations that result in unconventional forms of reproduction and filial intimacy — supply metaphors for blackness and queerness.

In the opening sequence of the video, a multiracial band of seven blond aliens — "a family of *extra* extraterrestrials," in the narrator's description — lands on earth. The sun shines brightly as the motley crew exits their polyhedron spaceship.[16] Glowing, they step into a field of green grass, taking in the strange scenery. Dré, the tallest and darkest of the lot, senses they are being watched as a woman snaps photographs of them from behind a tree, fascinated by the scene before her. André 3000 and his fellow extraterrestrials freeze and make eye contact with the woman as she fixes their image.

After basking in the sun, the aliens magically appear behind the woman. The crew examines her as they tilt their heads and sing, "Today must be my lucky day/Baby, you are the prototype." Finally Benjamin extends his hand. She stands, their eyes meet, and they proceed to show each other pieces of their respective worlds. For Benjamin, this is the way he and his alien kin walk and perform supernatural feats like healing impaired eyesight or playing rousing guitar solos without ever having touched the instrument before. For her, it is a fetish for the role of technology in everyday life, from cars, plastic drinking glasses, vinyl records, and news magazines to vintage cameras.

In the video's final frames, 3000 departs from his alien "family," relinquishing his supernatural attributes for human ones to start a family of his own with the woman. Most notably, the couple's offspring originates from a simple kiss rather than copulation. This thematic queering of filial and sexual relations — alien kin and procreation that results from nonsexual contact — is reinforced by formal elements. There is no realistic continuity to the video, from narrative to shot composition to editing. From the outset, we are in strange territory. Aliens magically move from one place to another, still black-and-white images interject color frames that depict motion, and time jumps forward and backward. But the human and non-human relations are the strangest of all in that they celebrate racial harmony and black intimacy while embracing the risk of failure and loss.

But this scenario runs counter to both the lyrics of the song and the speculative imaginings that constitute OutKast's aesthetic ethos. The title of the song epitomizes this investment. A prototype is an archetypal example, a preliminary model from which other forms are developed or perfected. In the context of the video, it is a framework for how to engage the world. When Benjamin's alien self sings of luck upon encountering his soon-to-be mate, it is tempered by speculation. He hopes that she's "the one;" "if not, [she is] the prototype," setting the foundation for possible future relationships. As the song progresses, he thinks he's in love, but he's not altogether sure. To this end, he anticipates failure while at the same time holding out hope for self-transformation: "if we happen to part … we can't be mad … we met today for a reason/I think I'm on the right track now." For Benjamin, the *practice* of love, rather than the *attainment* of perfection or mastery, is enough for now, and he remains cautiously optimistic until the song's final lines. In these lines, Benjamin combines a common phrase for expressing gratitude — "thank you very much" — with "smell you later," a black vernacular saying for goodbye popularized in the 1990s.[17] Thus, the prototype is useful insofar as it is a guide to an improved sense of self, one that incorporates hope and risk but does not require relational bliss. He could very well end up alone.

OutKast restages this relationship in the video for "The Whole World (featuring Killer Mike)," this time in more obvious, albeit darker terms. The setting for the video is a circus, the most freakish of places. There are crying clowns, exotic dancers, little people, sword swallowers, illusionists, and magicians, most of whom are phenotypically black, all of whom are racialized others. These "freaks" gesticulate in front of a mass of mostly white male spectators dressed in corporate garb. At one point in unison, the spectators throw their heads back to laugh with mouths wide open. This dynamic between black circus freaks and white spectators is a historical one activated in the first moments of the video.

Words in vaudevillian font, "Big Boi and Dre Present 'The Whole World,'" introduce the video and a red curtain parts to reveal a darkly lit film screen. As the sepia-and-white (digital) tape rolls, it appears to flicker, recalling early cinema technologies. After the image changes to color and the Big Top is fully illuminated, we are completely immersed in an arena that approximates what Tom Gunning calls the cinema of attraction, an early filmmaking strategy that showcased the capabilities of the technological apparatuses of film itself rather than that of narrative continuity. The cinema of attraction takes the spectator outside of the realm of "illusory imitativeness," or that of "exhibitionist confrontation rather than diegetic absorption."[18] In other words, the camera takes the place of the theater and fairground entertainer by performing tricks for the eye.

For early avant-garde filmmakers, in contrast to the static viewing experience of traditional theater, the cinema of attraction was revolutionary in its emphasis on direct engagement with the spectator. Notably, this form of early cinema holds "a vital relation to [both] vaudeville, its primary place of exhibition until around 1905" and an emerging mass entertainment industry.[19] This industry coincides with the practice of exhibiting exoticized bodies at state and world's fairs, amusement parks, and human

zoos in the nineteenth and twentieth centuries. The visual cues in "The Whole World" foreground this link. By juxtaposing shots of the American flag with the world of the circus and its historical significance, OutKast shows just how constitutional black struggle and suffering are to the U.S. national project. Additionally, lyrics such as, "And the whole, world, loves it when you're in the news/... loves it when you sing the blues," demonstrate how indispensable both black abasement and black music traditions are to American politics and popular culture.[20] Circuses, then, are analogous to blackness; they are sites of difference — of otherness — par excellence.

OutKast's forays into film and video as well as their far-out fashion — a form of black dandyism that includes outfits worn inside out, blonde wigs, and unconventional pattern play — pushed the boundaries of blackness at a time when experimentation in rap was largely unexplored. With "Rosa Parks," "Prototype," and "The Whole World," we are no longer simply in the South. These videos in the latter years of OutKast's artistic output display an engagement with national and global issues at the turn-of-the-twenty-first century to which human and non-human relations, precarious intimacies, and black spectacle are pivotal. Together, the three music videos bring into view myriad ways of seeing and being black in the world that are weird, nonteleological, and alien. They elucidate a postmodern vision of blackness that short circuits Eurocentric conceptions of identity, time, and space by veering away from the redemptive, heteronormative ethos to which black cultural production has long been tethered. To this end, OutKast's visual worlds consistently posit possible black futures but not necessarily ones oriented toward progress or self-mastery, a departure from both the annals of civil rights discourse and liberal humanism. As a result, the music videos provide unique insight into the sociopolitical realities of our post-civil rights present.

Significantly, hip-hop and the South are the spaces in which these transformations take place. "At once a homeland and place of exile," Thomas Lax opines, "the South is a cipher for a culture understood as obstinately regional and global, determinedly historic and contemporary."[21] The same could be said about hip-hop. In both contexts, ideas about blackness, reclamation, and the potential for racial and economic uplift circulate. But OutKast and their output exceed these parameters. The group's innovative sonic content along with their visual deployment of science fiction elements has propelled the duo to extraterrestrial heights. Furthermore, the duo's skillful adaptations of the pop music video form offer alternative visions of black life populated by ATLiens, postmodern dandies, and prototypical scenarios that give new, sometimes counterintuitive meaning to the possibilities of love and racial belonging. In so doing, they invite us to question hegemonic ways of seeing and being black by constructing new images and ultimately new worlds.

OutKast by Nettrice Gaskins

Notes

1. Iton, Richard. *In Search of the Black Fantastic: Politics and Popular Culture in the Post-Civil Rights Era* (New York, NY: Oxford University Press, 2008), 5.

2. Lax, Thomas J. "In Search of Black Space," *When the Stars Begin to Fall: Imagination and the American South* (New York, NY: The Studio Museum of Harlem, 2014), 10.

3. Golden, Thelma. "Post ...," *Freestyle*, Exh. Cat. (New York, NY: The Studio Museum of Harlem, 2001), 14. *Freestyle* was presented at The Studio Museum in Harlem in 2001 and featured work by 28 contemporary black artists. The first in an ongoing series of survey exhibitions of contemporary black art at The Studio Museum under Golden's direction, *Freestyle* has since been followed by *Frequency* (2005), *Flow* (2008), and *Fore* (2012). It is important to note that there is at least one instance in which the term post-black enters art historical and scholarly discourse prior to Golden's proclamation. In "Afro Modernism," a September 1991 *Artforum* review of *Africa Explores: 20th Century African Art*, Robert Farris Thompson writes, "A retelling of Modernism to show how it predicts the triumph of the current sequences would reveal that 'the Other' is your neighbor — that black and Modernist cultures were inseparable long ago. Why use the word 'post-Modern' when it may also mean 'postblack'? (91). While Thompson's review appears to be the first published use of the now pervasive term, Thompson's use of post-black differs from current iterations of the term.

4. David Hammons quoted in Solomon, Deborah. "The Downtowning of Uptown," *The New York Times Magazine* (19 August 2001), http://www.nytimes.com/2001/08/19/magazine/the-downtowning-of-uptown.html?pagewanted=1.

5. Thelma Golden quoted in Valdez, Sarah. "Freestyling — Studio Museum in Harlem," *Art in America* (September 2001), 138.

6. Ashe, Bertram D.. "Theorizing the Post-Soul Aesthetic: An Introduction," *African American Review* 41, 4 (Winter, 2007), 611.

7. For accounts of this proper relation and its rupture, see Thaggert, Miriam. *Images of Black Modernism: Verbal and Visual Strategies of the Harlem Renaissance* (Amherst, MA: University of Massachusetts Press, 2010) and English, Darby. *How to See a Work of Art in Total Darkness* (Cambridge, MA: MIT Press, 2007).

8. Neal, Mark Anthony. *Soul Babies: Black Popular Culture and the Post-Soul Aesthetic* (New York, NY: Routledge, 2002), 21.

9. Neal, 103.

10. The origins of trap music are debatable. But Atlanta, along with Houston, TX and Memphis, TN, are all cities that lay claim to trap's origins during the 1990s.

11. Fellow Atlanta rapper Lil Jon popularized crunk music.

12. Nelson, Alondra. "Afrofuturism: Past-Future Visions," *Color Lines* (Spring 2000), 37.

13. Ibid.

14. Ibid.

15. These effects appear again and again in later videos, including "B.O.B." and "So Fresh, So Clean."

16. Though I do not take them up in this essay, it is important to note the references to numerology (seven aliens) and sacred geometry (polyhedron spaceship) that OutKast deploys. Numerology and sacred geometry are two cosmological components of Afrofuturism. Supernatural weather events, rainstorms and flooding in both "Idlewild Blue" and "Ms. Jackson," also bear some relation to Afrofuturism, rootworking, conjuring, and other black speculative spiritual practices.

17. "Smell ya later" was featured in the theme song for the 1990s TV show, *The Fresh Prince of Bel-Air.*

18. Gunning, Tom. "The Cinema of Attraction: Early Film, Its Spectator and the Avant-Garde," *Wide Angle* 8, 3-4 (Fall 1986), 66.

19. Ibid.

20. See Hartman, Saidiya. *Scenes of Subjection: Terror, Slavery, and Self-Making in Nineteenth-Century America* (New York, NY: Oxford University Press, 1997).

21. Lax, 13.

Close to the Edge: "This Is America" and the Extended Take in Hip-Hop Music Video
Jeff M. Heinzl

When Childish Gambino's music video for "This Is America" appeared on YouTube in May 2018, it provoked a wide range of responses on social media and web publications. Just over four minutes in length, the clip shows Gambino (aka Donald Glover) dancing shirtlessly in an enormous warehouse, sometimes with a group of black children following and dancing along. Occasionally, he pauses from dancing to shoot and murder a number of black people around him, including a guitarist and a robed choir. Chaos builds in the background as the routine continues: we see people running, cop lights flashing, fires raging. At one point, after the chaos has died down, Gambino hops onto the roof of a car to show off some impressive footwork and wild moves. The video then ends with an image of him running for his life, a pack of others following close behind.

Released in the immediate wake of Gambino's appearance on *Saturday Night Live* (where Gambino first performed "This Is America"), the music video went on to garner over 500 million views on **YouTube** and win the 2019 Grammy Award for Best Music Video. Many viewers reacted positively and indicated their appreciation for its all-too-accurate portrayal of black American realities. Tre Johnson (2018), writing for *Rolling Stone*, called the video "an upsettingly vivid illustration of the Faustian bargain that black America makes on a regular basis, trading our bodies for our expression and freedom." Music history professor Guthrie Ramsey, in dialogue with *Time*'s Mahita Gajanan (2018), noted, about the video's ending, "Gambino's sprint goes back to a long tradition of black Americans having to run to save their lives."

But not everyone was here for the video's accolades and enormous viewership. Israel Daramola (2018) described the video, in a piece for *SPIN*, as "infuriatingly cheap," "pandering," and "callous and inconsequential." A number of viewers took issue with the scene that portrays the gunning down of the choir, since it seemed to directly recall white supremacist Dylann Roof's 2015 shooting at the Emanuel African Methodist Episcopal Church in Charleston, South Carolina. Writer and researcher Huda Hassan (2018) tweeted, "when you are murdering black people in your music video, with no warning, to prove a political point, i really can't help but wonder who your art is for. Surely it isn't black folks." Artist and activist Zalika

Umuntu Ibaorimi (2018) wrote, "It . . . has become extremely normalized to depict Black trauma or death. In an effort . . . to turn some heads and be controversial, the video wasn't controversial at all." And Aida Amoako (2018), while noting the video's ability to jerk viewers out of passivity, highlighted that the video's effect on black viewers is especially traumatizing. She asked, "If the scene is meant to evoke an atrocity committed by a white terrorist with a specifically anti-black agenda, what does it mean to see a black man re-create it?"

Implied in both praise and criticism of the video was a consideration of the video's aesthetics. It consists of only six steadicam shots (disguised, at certain points, to look like separate parts of a single shot), each of which moves fluidly, even calmly, through space. Thus, when writers like Amoako (2018) described the video as jarring, she was, in part, referring to its extended-take aesthetic. She notes,

> An internal struggle begins in the viewer's body, which is pulled between joy and horror. Just as the video questions how we can dance when there is pandemonium all around, the audience struggles with whether to continue moving, too, after witnessing such brutality, especially after Glover shoots an entire choir of gospel singers, supposedly in reference to the 2015 murder of nine churchgoers by Dylann Roof in Charleston, South Carolina.

Amoako doesn't describe extended takes directly, but her reference to "moving" seems directly connected to the camera's graceful, unaffected motion. This ties to Gambino's continued dancing and contrasts with audience repulsion: we feel the need to recoil, to turn away, but the video's camera work, in combination with its refusal to cut and desire to follow Gambino's movements, gives us no opportunity to do so. Daramola's (2018) takedown in *SPIN* similarly, implicitly, critiques the video's aesthetics, which he argues only work to anesthetize viewers further. He describes the video as "capitalizing on the culture's growing *numbness* to seeing black people being murdered while claiming to be making a point" (emphasis mine). The numbness seems embedded in the video's camera work and editing style, which do not seem to directly react to the video's violence.

Both positive and negative reactions to the video draw attention to the complicated, somewhat muddled history of the hip-hop music video. I argue that, if we begin with the concept of the sample and hip-hop's most important early video clips, we can see that extended takes (i.e., shots that go on for several sublime moments before editing removes them from our line of sight) are central to hip-hop music video aesthetics. Moreover, these extended takes — defiant to their core — move us both backwards and forwards in time, along a feedback loop of black media that includes blaxploitation and hood films from their respective eras. I also argue that hip-hop video's extended take aesthetic becomes more pronounced in the wake of DJ Screw, who further emphasized the affective, material qualities of expansion and slowness. While "This Is America" exists within this defiant, extended-take tradition, the video also reveals the receptive and transformative limits of that tradition, which allow exploitation and trauma to relentlessly coexist.

It's worth pointing out, first of all, that hip-hop music video is itself a nebulous form with a fraught history, and both critics and scholars have had difficulty attempting to define and assess it. Early music television monographs, such as Andrew Goodwin's (1992) *Dancing in the Distraction Factory*, tended to position rap as one popular genre among many others, even if they did see the genre as significant in drawing attention to key political issues related to racism (such as police brutality and urban poverty); others make little mention of rap or hip-hop at all, perhaps partially because of MTV's discriminatory relationship with the genre. Carol Vernallis' (2004) seminal *Experiencing Music Video* highlights the important relationship between hip-hop and the music video ("Given that hip-hop represents a departure from pop songwriting practices . . . it is safe to say that the audience needed to 'see' the song in order to understand the genre's concerns and issues" [288]) and excels at describing the importance of setting to hip-hop music video but hesitates to describe it as entirely distinct, in terms of editing and cinematography, from other kinds of music video. The most recent work on music video, by writers like Vernallis (2013), Steven Shaviro (2017), and Mathias Bonde Korsgaard (2017), has tended to de-emphasize music genre and music video genre in order to highlight the importance of hybridity and impurity.

Yet a specifically hip-hop music video has always been embedded in the genre, from hip-hop's very beginnings, and it remains important to examine as a unique form, distinct from other kinds of music video. Jeff Chang (2005) recounts the origins of hip-hop music in the Bronx when he describes how DJ Kool Herc and Coke La Rock, who had immigrated to New York from Jamaica, "set off their dances by giving shout-outs and dropping little rhymes" (78). Like any worthwhile DJs, Herc and La Rock wanted to find ways to encourage more dancing with the way they selected and played their records (78). So when Herc realized that dancers most enjoyed the section on disco and funk records called the break (what Chang calls the "song's short instrumental break, when the band would drop out and the rhythm section would get elemental" and "the fundamental vibrating loop at the heart of the record"), he found ways to isolate and extend the break from a few seconds to several minutes (79). This was the genesis of the hip-hop beat.

Chang's (2005) description suggests that at the heart of hip-hop is the expansion of time: a few seconds become a few minutes; a few minutes of time are, in the end, only a few seconds. Even as sampling itself has massively transformed over the years since Herc and La Rock — it had become a predominantly digital process by the late 1980s, and, as Michail Exarchos (2019) has recently noted, now many artists pull from commercial sample libraries instead of copyrighted fragments from pre-existing songs — hip-hop remains rooted in the manipulation of time. Exarchos goes on to describe, for example, new sampling and composition processes that involve interpolating elements that *sound* sampled or retro, even though they are actually not (443). Such processes lend a level of sonic authenticity to hip-hop beats without truly relying upon pre-existing sound recordings. In other words, a new beat can sound more authentic due to its sonics, even though that new beat might be sampling something that's brand new, created purely for the sake of the new record, or not sampling anything at all. In this a further, thicker manipulation takes place: the vibrating loop at the heart of the record, if it's convincingly hip-hop, exists forever without ever having really existing at all.

Andrew Bartlett (1994) connects sampling to a long history of reading, archiving, and production in African-American musical traditions, including spirituals and various forms of jazz. It allows, he argues, multiple temporalities and perspectives to exist simultaneously. In his view, this is not a function of postmodernism but rather of black history, aesthetics, and sonic innovation This co-existence taps into the bodies of black listeners, who respond almost automatically to sounds that echo into previous eras of black community and resistance. In the context of new sampling techniques, this means locating sounds that connect with black audiences through a particular instrument, rhythm, or timbre. Sampling, still fundamental to hip-hop as a genre, moves listeners — and calls the bodies of listeners to move — through time, even as it loops them back to the present track and the future songs that will pull from its elements in the future.

Early hip-hop music video also revealed itself to be invested in this matter of time manipulation, particularly through a kind of expansion similar to the process that extended a portion of an already existing song in time. Two key music videos mark the foundations of the hip-hop music video form: Afrika Bambaataa & Soulsonic Force's "Planet Rock" and Grandmaster Flash and the Furious Five's "The Message," both of which initially came out in 1982. These tracks have traditionally been understood as landmarks in hip-hop music: George Lipsitz (1994) remarks that "Planet Rock" "hailed the utopian potential of Black music to transform the entire world into a land of 'master jam'" (26), while Greg de Cuir Jr. (2017) states that "Hip-hop first gained a conscience in 1982 with the release of the song 'The Message' by Grandmaster Flash and the Furious Five" (54). Catherine Appert (2018), too, positions these two tracks as marking hip-hop's initial movement away from partying to political action (3). Both also play a major role in Jeff Chang's (2005) momentous history of hip-hop music, *Can't Stop Won't Stop*, since "Planet Rock" allows us to see hip-hop's diasporic, utopian ambitions, while "The Message" testifies to hip-hop's emergence in unjustly derelict urban environments.

However, very little has been written about their accompanying videos, which likely would have been broadcast on local television; other, non-MTV cable channels; and DJ service RockAmerica (due to MTV's racist, rock-centric programming

approach, which I'll discuss further below). The visual dynamism of these and other early hip-hop videos existed in close relation to the new fashions, dance styles, DJ techniques, and graffiti they portrayed. "Planet Rock," for example, features a breakdancer spinning on his head while his legs swirl around in the air, intercut both with footage of Afrika Bambaataa and his crew performing the song while dressed in long, vibrantly colored robes, capes, and headdresses against a background of flashing lights and with various kinds of space and satellite imagery. The song foregrounds a diverse array of samples (including Kraftwerk's "Trans Europe Express," Yellow Magic Orchestra's "Rap Phenomena," and Ennio Morricone's soundtrack from *For a Few Dollars More* [1965]) and synthesizes them with sonics emerging from recent technological developments, specifically the Roland TR-808 drum machine. With these musical elements moving across, under, and through, the video's imagery suggests that the pixelated, funky-as-hell future has already arrived. "You gotta rock it, pop it, 'cause it's the century/There is such a place that creates such a melody/Our world is but a land of a master jam, get up and dance/It's time to chase your dreams," the song insists, and the video strengthens these sentiments with its colorful, psychedelic images of dancing crowd members, performers, and Atari-style cosmic representations.

"The Message," on the other hand, is not about dance styles and partying but rather situates rap in a heterogeneous, busy, crowded, and dangerous urban context with a pestering and blatantly racist police presence. This connects closely with the song's lyrical content, which describes impoverished circumstances and the city-centric fallout from drug business and addiction (*"Junkies in the alley with a baseball bat"*) and various sorts of sexual exploitation (*"She had to get a pimp, she couldn't make it on her own"*). The images from the video display a number of New York City scenes, including traffic jams, puppet shows, pedestrians, displaced individuals, and empty alleys. These often directly connect to the song's lyrics. For example, as a line about a person getting *"pushed...in front of the train"* plays on the audio track, the video shows us an image of an approaching train. The song's sound, too, gestures towards urban chaos: while it doesn't sample any iconic songs like "Planet Rock," it combines genres like funk, disco, dub, and electro into a thick, propulsive piece of music (Cairns 2008). The video suggests that these are the sounds of the city, in all their everyday disarray.

Although it has proved fruitful for critics to see "Planet Rock" and "The Message" as opposed to one another, both find hip-hop music video working less as an advertisement for purchasable songs (a barb initially used to ridicule and diminish the music video form in general) and more as a necessary tool for the spread of hip-hop's pre-existing visual language alongside its music. These early hip-hop music videos did not isolate the song they featured; instead, they saw the song as part of a broad set of practices that necessarily coexisted. The artists who produced these videos figured that, as rap gained wider circulation, it was necessary for new listeners to see that this music was part of a larger New York urban hip-hop context with a strong visual element.

At the same time, these videos began developing a strong visual language of their own, not merely in terms of their hip-hop-inspired mise-en-scène but also in terms of their cinematography and editing. One crucial component of the videos' language is an element of slowness — that is, their cameras linger on a scene for longer than we might expect. This isn't to say that these videos necessarily have what we would call long takes in the context of Hollywood or art cinema, but they certainly contain takes that go against the grain of the music's driving tempo by continuing past expected edits. The opening shot of the "Planet Rock" video is an extended take (about fourteen seconds long), and five other shots in the video last longer than ten seconds. Many of these shots feature multiple screens and/or computer animation and so have a different effect from purely photographic shots, but they have a durational quality to them nonetheless. The first shot of "The Message" is also an extended take (it lasts around 19 seconds), and the video as a whole continues this extended-take aesthetic: it features nine shots that last longer than nine seconds and reaches a sort of pinnacle in its last two shots, one of which lasts thirty-eight seconds, the other of which lasts forty-seven seconds. These shots feature, for the most part, the MCs themselves, who rap while a crew of their friends nods and postures around them.

The extended takes of "The Message" function according to a different kind of revelation: the video reveals the poisonous racism within — and poignant dereliction of — black urban environments. We look beyond the individual here, too, in order to see unjust urban decay. The video's final take makes this injustice especially clear, as Melle Mel (a member of the Furious Five) stands on the street corner and talks with his crew about girls. It's a long shot, so we don't see any of the speakers too clearly — what's more important is that they're black and on an urban street corner. For when the camera zooms out (around seventeen seconds in), it reveals a police cruiser that enters from the right side of the frame and out of which two policemen emerge to forcibly push the men into the vehicle for no specific reason (other than the fact that they're black and on an urban street corner). The message is clear: any sense of freedom or justice for black individuals is fleeting, since the current authorities in place trample it violently and ignore the ways in which they could actually work to improve, say, the neglected state of the apartment building and abandoned lot that provide the setting for this final shot. The extended takes near the end of the video emphasize this by showing events play out in slow, real time: the implication is that these black individuals are, thanks to a corrupt policing presence, especially unsafe in an already unsafe place.

Both videos offer up a distinct mode of defiance: Afrika Bambaataa & Soulsonic Force dare viewers to suggest that hip-hop is not the future, while Grandmaster

Flash and the Furious Five take a stand against a blatantly racist system of legality and policing. More generally, the extended take in these videos highlights the importance of duration to hip-hop as a distinctive musical form. Their extended takes highlight one of hip-hop's key formal elements: the sample-driven loop. Yet even while the term *loop* may seem to suggest stasis or cyclical repetition, the two videos locate a kind of looping that shifts overarching systems and refuses satisfaction with the present moment. "Planet Rock" drops a new sort of future-past into an imperfect present, while "The Message" offers a radical pessimism that seeks to overturn the present moment by presenting it as is. "Keep tickin' and tockin', work it all around the clock," Afrika Bambaataa commands — the clock moves forward and back, the video finds its groove. "It's like a jungle sometimes/ It makes me wonder how I keep from goin' under," Grandmaster Flash observes — the video reveals many possible ways to be swallowed up, and the edge of the frame reveals destruction yet desires otherwise.

Additionally, the two videos represented a position that stood in opposition to MTV as the primary mode music television broadcasting. S. Craig Watkins (1998) describes how the creators of MTV "were driven by one main goal: to develop a programming concept designed specifically for a youth aggregate" (179). In order to do so, MTV sought to synthesize two media, television and radio, "to create, in essence, a visual radio station with youth appeal" (180). Yet when MTV launched in 1981, hip-hop video had no presence on the station. This was true not because MTV took issue with hip-hop specifically but rather because MTV disallowed black music generally, a move Watkins ascribes to "a combination of market calculation and racism" (180). MTV believed, in its early days, that any music styles other than (white-fronted) rock would "alienate its predominantly white constituency" (180). It was only in 1986, when they realized that the opposite was the case and that its competition could take advantage of MTV's refusal to play black videos, that MTV began to play non-rock, non-white music videos in wider circulation (the station had agreed to show a few Michael Jackson videos, prior to 1986, including "Billie Jean," "Beat It," and "Thriller") (Christian 2006, 18). "Planet Rock" and "The Message" stand in oppositional testament to this point in music video history by showing that a thriving hip-hop visual culture existed outside of racist corporate strategizing.

Thus, the two videos together represent one convincing origin story for the hip-hop music video form. Neither of them needed MTV to circulate their visions, and both thrived upon their resistance towards present injustices. Yet they also represent one moment in a broader black aesthetic history whose key points of intersectional influence begin with 1970s action-crime cinema and push forward towards the present moment. Just as Bartlett ties hip-hop music to older forms of black music and expression, we can tie hip-hop music video's extended takes to a still-existing tradition of expanded black temporality. Paula Massood (2003) discusses such temporality as deeply related to a black cinematic tradition focusing mainly on urban spaces as sites of both conflict and possibility. Using Mikhail Bakhtin's concept of the *chronotope*, Massood emphasizes black cinema's tendency to interweave multiple locations and histories in its depictions of the city. She writes, "[T]he play between visual and aural signifiers contributes meaning to a film, anchors the narrative in an historical moment, and acknowledges the existence of complementary or contradictory spaces and times in a single text" (5). This is clearly present in early hip-hop music video as well, where the extended take displays, for example, both a relaxed, convivial atmosphere among black men and the destruction of the atmosphere at the hands of police. To be clear, extended takes make up only one small part of the cinematic tradition to which Massood refers, but a careful look at key examples from 1970s black cinema and hood films from the 1990s — both of which are key parts of Massood's study — finds extended takes functioning to reveal, through duration, "complementary or contradictory spaces and times in a single text."

Many of the extended takes referenced above provide a powerful counterpoint to the rhythmic structure of the music played alongside them. Vernallis (2004) points out that video directors "rarely choose to use material that replicates our cultural and biological understanding of the song"; they instead create videos that "teas[e] . . . our perceived conceptions of the music's uses" (203). Although blaxploitation cinema predates the arrival of the music video in full force, the dominant role of music — often composed and performed by well-known black funk and soul artists (from whom hip-hop draws a significant amount of its vocal and rhythmic samples) — in many blaxploitation films allows us to find a fascinating analogue and trace out a certain artistic lineage between the two forms. Blaxploitation cinema, like early hip-hop music video, includes the deployment of images to purposely contrast (or "tease," as Vernallis puts it) the music at hand. The use of the extended take over an accelerated groove creates an audiovisual contrast that piques our attention, helping us hear a cool, relaxed quality in the music, even as we understand the sometimes frenetic content of the image in productive tension with it.

The so-called hood film, another influential trend in black cinema, shows the influence of previous blaxploitation flicks, as well as early hip-hop music video; it would also have a major influence on the hip-hop videos and hip-hop-inspired cinema that would come out in its wake. Massood (2003) states, "Like blaxploitation, hood films are shot with specific cinematic techniques that connote both temporal immediacy and documentary verisimilitude" and goes on to say that hood films "focus, through quotation, allusion, and homage, on the plethora of images associated with African American urban youth culture in film, television, and music video" (145). In other words, we can see certain aesthetic trends through time and across media that lend hip-hop its particular audiovisual style and that these trends do relate very directly to precedents in African-American cinema. Scenes in *Set It Off* (1996) and *Menace II Society* (1993), for example, explicitly reference this by including extended takes at party scenes where commonly sampled songs from the 1970s and early 1980s (Parliament's "Flash Light" and "Atomic Dog," respectively) play a prominent role. These shots embed the characters in present and past at once, and confirm this multiplicity by using their narratives to motion towards the past (thriving factories for the mass employment of black workers in *Set It Off*, Los Angeles' Watts riots in *Menace II Society*). Another hood film, *Juice* (1992), allows its characters to carve out their own time, to their own music, in the space of the city. It is in these scenes that we are reminded of Paula Massood's observation that "[c]ity spaces . . . were often meccas that, in their promise of decreased racial discrimination, offered social, economic, and political mobility" (8). There is a sense of mobility in these extended takes, as characters move steadily and happily through a space in which they feel comfortable. In these moments, the present seems more like an everlasting utopian future, although this disintegrates entirely by the film's end.

Around the same time as the appearance of hood films, another black tradition of slowness emerged through the artistry of DJ Screw (aka Robert Earl Davis, Jr.), an influential Houston DJ who, in the 1990s, mixed and manipulated a slew of hip-hop sounds (both original and pre-existing) to create a series of mixtapes commonly known as screwtapes.[1] A key element of these tapes — and the element most prevalent in their influence on contemporary hip-hop — is their slowed-down tempo. Matthew Kent Carter (2019) writes, "The slow tempo of a screwtape . . . is its most recognisable and omnipresent characteristic. Through decreasing a track's original speed by roughly 30%, a screwed track's length is extended and its pitches are much lower, creating timbres that are increasingly muddy and distorted" (162). Screw's process also highlighted the sonic chaos uncapped by the process of sampling. Instead of merely isolating an instrumental portion of a track for the purpose of looping, Screw would allow long portions of tracks to play over one another, thus accentuating hip-hop's multilayered, multitemporal nature. On top of this, Langston Collin Wilkins (2016) describes how DJ Screw's tapes would often feature the sounds of laid-back parties in the background: "Along with freestyles and Screw's turntable virtuosity, a screwtape consists of drinks being poured, and other elements that mark a party atmosphere" (74). Wilkins quotes local rapper E.S.G., in regards to the setting where these recording sessions would take place: "You come in the big room, you know what I'm sayin'. You chillin' with your partners . . . . Everybody sittin' around talkin' and chillin', listenin' to Screw make a tape" (74). E.S.G.'s comments highlight the relaxed nature of these gatherings, which provide their own kind of slowness to the layering that already occurs on a screwtape.

DJ Screw and Houston hip-hop culture more generally connect the slowed-down Screw sound to a particular substance: syrup, described by Wilkins (2016) as a "codeine-based drug concoction" that "complements the hazy, slow-tempo soundscape of the screwtapes" (77). Although Screw distanced his music from the drug, many locals found syrup and screwtapes the perfect match. The link has continued well beyond the local Houston communities where it originated. Wilkins writes, "Houston's rise to the mainstream, while brief, left one lasting mark of identity on mainstream hip-hop: syrup" (107). Popular rappers that consume the substance advertise their consumption through both lyrical content (to lean, syrup, double-Styrofoam cups, and the color purple) and a slowed-down sound marked especially by slow-motion, deeply resonant vocals. Sheldon Pearce (2017), writing for *The Guardian*, chronicles the spread of the Screw sound, noting, "Screw culture has come to represent more than just chopping and screwing records in recent years: it's an aesthetic now, one that's come to represent a laid-back sense of cool, a transporting, almost disorienting atmosphere, and . . . codeine and opiate abuse." Pearce credits both Drake's popular 2009 mixtape, *So Far Gone*, and A$AP Rocky's "Purple Swag" (2011) with expanding the reach of the Screw sound and lifestyle to other rappers, hip-hop producers, and artists from a range of genres, including Miley Cyrus (pop) and Grizzly Bear (indie rock).

This DJ Screw aesthetic of slowness does not replace the tradition of black aesthetics that preceded it; in fact, the earlier tradition influenced its sample-heavy, multitemporal origins. (Screw described, for instance, how he initially wanted to become a DJ after watching *Breakin'* [1984], an early and influential film about hip-hop culture [Wilkins 2016, 71].) But DJ Screw's artistry further emphasized the temporal expansion at the heart of hip-hop, and screwed-ness has effectively merged with other strands in hip-hop visuality to place further emphasis on the extended take as a central element in the hip-hop video. We see this in videos ranging from several works by A$AP Rocky and A$AP Mob ("Purple Swag" [2011], "L$D" [2015], "Yamborghini High" [2016]) to Kendrick Lamar's "God Is Gangsta" [2016], The Weeknd's "The Hills" [2016], Young Chop's "Around My Way" [2016], ScHoolboy Q's "By Any Means" [2016], Jaden Smith's "Fallen" [2016], and multiple others. (The presence and mentions of other drugs in these videos and their accompanying songs also gesture towards the possibility that Screw's slowed-down sound has expanded to include other substances, such as weed, cocaine, alcohol, and various kinds of pills.) Many of these videos also include flashes of bright color and digital graphics, but their feeling of expansion and slowness remains key to comprehending their links to both hip-hop's sample-driven core and the DJ Screw aesthetic that effectively magnified this core.

This brings us back to Childish Gambino's "This Is America," a video fully engrained in hip-hop's extended take traditions. If "Planet Rock" and "The Message" deploy extended takes to represent two sides of the same coin ("Planet Rock" a futuristic video that acknowledges the tragic present only by implication, "The Message" a realist video that acknowledges a better future only by implication), we see that the extended takes in "This Is America" emphasize that the present moment is both futuristically dystopian and joyfully realist. It is a video that defiantly calls attention to contradictions: terrible, shocking violence on the one hand and inspired, communal dancing on the other. Such contradictions also play out across Gambino's body, which hovers in a zone between spasm and grace, facial contortion and sinuous machismo. The transitions in the song between melodic prettiness and trap ruggedness emphasize such contradictions further by drawing attention to an ugly, jolting kind of coexistence — the movement from one sound to another occurs without warning.

Two key components of the song and video help connect its extended takes to DJ Screw's brand of slowness. First, there are the ad-libs from rappers Young Thug, Blocboy JB, 21 Savage, Slim Jxmmi (of Rae Sremmurd), and Quavo (of Migos). These artists, as well as the video's replication of Blocboy JB's "shoot" dance, represent the lean-and-other-drug-induced sound of lived-in, semi-conscious bliss (a sound that tends to be associated with trap music, which also draws from DJ Screw's pitched-down sound), even while Gambino himself tends to be distant from it. Frank Guan (2019) notes the following in a piece for *Vulture*:

> The incongruousness of Glover, raised middle-class and a NYU graduate, bragging about his Mexican drug supplier and threatening to have you gunned down, is intentional: it's a tribute to the cultural dominance of trap music and a reflection on the ludicrous social logic that made the environment from which trap emerges, the logic where money makes the man, and every black man is criminal.

Guan's statement taps into the contradictions that "This Is America" exploits, whereby blackness comes to connote both infectious, artistic wealth (monetary and emotional) and criminality.

Second, there's the crucial pause, about three minutes into the video, where Gambino — in medium shot — goes from making a gun gesture with his arms and hands to pulling a joint from his pocket, which he summarily lights before moving out of the frame. The action occurs right after the line about his Mexican drug supplier ("I got the plug in Oaxaca [woh]/They gonna find you like blokka [blaow]"), during a moment of almost total silence — all we can hear are the sounds of scattering feet and (eventually) the sound of Gambino's lighter. The moment acknowledges Gambino's own position between two societal expectations related to blackness: the "positive role model" that reflects white desire for black cultural transformation (Gambino puts down the gun) and the drug user that reflects continued white criminalization of black individuals for their use of substances that are, in many places, no longer illegal (Gambino pulls out, and begins to smoke, the joint). It also highlights the privileged place of self-medication to help cope with the traumas of black American life, a strategy also present in a trap music lifestyle that, at the same time, continuously acknowledges the presence of — and sometimes threatens — terrible violence. As viewers, we are invited to reflect on this moment of silence in the extended take, which continues for a beat after Gambino's exit.

At the same time, the video also acknowledges that the video's "us" sits in the same ugly, jolting kind of coexistence that the song represents. Its empty factory setting and extended-take aesthetic directly recall an earlier Gambino video for his 2011 song, "Freaks and Geeks." The song which shares a producer (Ludwig Göransson) with "This Is America," features the kinds of lines with which many "This Is America" viewers took issue, such as "Alright, I'm down with the black girls of every single culture/Filipino, Armenian girls on my sofa" and "Love is a trip, but fuckin' is a sport/Are there Asian girls here? Minority report." Daramola (2018) opens his critical piece about "This Is America" by describing Gambino's uncomfortable status in the minds of black viewers familiar with his "Asian girl fetishizing" and his claims about dating "the black girls of every race." He goes on to note, "Glover has long had a fixation on how black people come off to the white gaze. It's an understandable anxiety, but he's less concerned with how this fixation distances himself from the actual black people for whom he claims to be making art."

By emphasizing visual similarities between "Freaks and Geeks" and "This Is America," Gambino ties its contradictions to his own polarizing presence, whereby he has traditionally represented a figure palatable to white audiences and (at the very least) frustrating to black audiences. "This Is America" accentuates this palatability — and, by extension, the general palatability of hip-hop music to white, suburban audiences — in order to show its disturbing qualities, qualities that allow white audiences to separate widely admired black celebrities from everyday instances of racialized violence and police brutality against black individuals and communities. In other words, white audiences seem to shrug off this contradiction, separating out "good" black celebrity figures from "criminal" black people and considering their spectatorial position as the only possible position. The video for "This Is America" embraces the extended take to force such viewers to sit in this contradiction and acknowledge Gambino's own position at its center as someone whose career has exacerbated it, since he has actively distanced himself and his art from black audiences. "This Is America" by no means amends this contradiction; instead, it defiantly gestures back towards it. It's a gesture that necessarily, urgently, calls to mind the extended takes of blaxploitation, early hip-hop music video, hood films, and screwtapes. These, too, were full of contradictions that white audiences and artists were all too ready to exploit in order to associate blackness with (coolly glorified) violence, drug use, and poverty for their own entertainment and financial gain. This is the ugly power of the extended take, so central to hip-hop aesthetics: it powerfully forces viewers to recognize the contradictory temporalities and valences of the present, even as this recognition is traumatic for some and still, somehow, enjoyable for others. (Google "this is america memes," and you'll see what I mean.) The vibrating expansion at the heart of hip-hop — the sample, the loop, the extended take — clearly and irreverently pushes for something better and simultaneously derails attempts to find a way out by asserting the terror of continuation.

Note

1. The sound may not, however, have actually originated with DJ Screw. Wilkins (2016) points out that two earlier DJs, Darryl Scott and Michael Price, claim to have experimented with slowing music as early as the late 1970s and 1980s.

Bibliography

"Afrika Bambaataa & Soul Sonic Force — Planet Rock [Rockamerica] (1982)." Video file, 06:33. YouTube. Posted by Erick Monasterio, November 5, 2014. Accessed August 27, 2019. https://www.youtube.com/watch?v=8KhK8kvzlL4.

Amoako, Aida. "Why the Dancing Makes 'This Is America' So Uncomfortable to Watch." *The Atlantic*. Last modified May 8, 2018. Accessed August 27, 2019. https://www.theatlantic.com/entertainment/archive/2018/05/this-is-america-childish-gambino-donald-glover-kinesthetic-empathy-dance/559928/.

Appert, Catherine. *In Hip-Hop Time: Music, Memory, and Social Change in Urban Senegal*. New York: Oxford University Press, 2018.

"A$AP Mob — Yamborghini High (Official Music Video) ft. Juicy J." Video file. 05:12. YouTube. Posted by asapmobVEVO, May 11, 2016. Accessed August 27, 2019. youtube.com/watch?v=tt7gP_1W-1w.

"A$AP Rocky 'Purple Swag.'" Video file. 02:27. YouTube. Posted by ASAPROCKYUPTOWN, July 5, 2011. Accessed August 27, 2019. https://www.youtube.com/watch?v=KuZ2QZKYj7c.

"A$AP Rocky — L$D (LOVE x $EX x DREAMS)." Video file. 05:27. YouTube. Posted by ASAPROCKYUPTOWN, May 19, 2015. Accessed August 27, 2019 https://www.youtube.com/watch?v=yEG2VTHS9yg.

Bartlett, Andrew. "Airshafts, Loudspeakers, and the Hip-Hop Sample: Contexts and African American Musical Aesthetics." *African American Review* 28, no. 4 (Winter 1994): 639-52.

Cairns, Dan. "Song of the Year: 1982 Grandmaster Flash 'The Message.'" *The Sunday Times* (London), September 28, 2008.

Carter, Matthew Kent. "All Day in the Trey: DJ Screw, Screwtapes, and the Sonic Representation of Houston in Hip-Hop Culture." In *Pop Culture Matters: Proceedings of the 39th Conference of the Northeast Popular Culture Association*, edited by Martin F. Norden and Robert E. Weir, 161-71. Newcastle upon Tyne, UK: Cambridge Scholars, 2019.

Chang, Jeff. *Can't Stop Won't Stop: A History of the Hip-Hop Generation*. New York: Picador, 2005.

"Childish Gambino — Freaks and Geeks (HD Music Video)." Video file. 03:46. YouTube. Posted by PumpkinSmasherz, March 2, 2011. Accessed August 27, 2019. https://www.youtube.com/watch?v=27d138zhyZQ.

"Childish Gambino — This Is America (Official Video)." Video file. 04:04. YouTube. Posted by Donald Glover, May 6, 2018. Accessed August 27, 2019. https://www.youtube.com/watch?v=VYOjWnS4cMY.

Christian, Margena A. "Why It Took MTV So Long to Play Black Music Videos." *Jet*, October 9, 2006, 16.

Daramola, Israel. "The Cynicism of Childish Gambino's 'This Is America.'" *SPIN*. Last modified May 8, 2018. Accessed August 27, 2019. https://www.spin.com/2018/05/donald-glover-this-is-america-review/.

de Cuir, Jr., Greg. "'The Message' Is the Medium: Aesthetics, Ideology, and the Hip-Hop Music Video." In *Music/Video: Histories, Aesthetics, Media*, edited by Gina Arnold, et. al., 53-65. New York: Bloomsbury Publishing, 2017.

Diawara, Manthia, ed. *Black American Cinema.* AFI Film Readers. New York: Routledge, 1993.

Exarchos, Michail. "(Re)Engineering the Cultural Object: Sonic Pasts in Hip-Hop's Future." In *Innovation in Music: Performance, Production, Technology, and Business*, edited by Russ Hepworth-Sawyer, 437-54. London: Routledge, 2019.

Foxy Brown. Directed by Jack Hill. 1974. Santa Monica: MGM Home Entertainment, 2001.

Gajanan, Mahita. "An Expert's Take on the Symbolism in Childish Gambino's Viral 'This Is America' Video." *Time*. Last modified May 7, 2018. Accessed August 27, 2019. https://time.com/5267890/childish-gambino-this-is-america-meaning/.

Ganja & Hess. Directed by Bill Gunn. 1973. Alexandria, VA: All Day Entertainment, 1998.

Goodwin, Andrew. *Dancing in the Distraction Factory: Music Television and Popular Culture*. Minneapolis: University of Minnesota Press, 1992.

"Grandmaster Flash & The Furious Five — The Message (Official Video)." Video file. 05:59. YouTube. Posted by Sugarhill Records, August 24, 2015. Accessed August 27, 2019. https://www.youtube.com/watch?v=PobrSpMwKk4.

Guan, Frank. "What It Means When Childish Gambino Says 'This Is America.'" *Vulture*. Last modified May 7, 2018. Accessed August 27, 2019. https://www.vulture.com/2018/05/what-it-means-when-childish-gambino-says-this-is-america.html.

Hassan, Huda A. "when you are murdering black people in your music video, with no warning, to prove a political point, i really can't help but wonder who your art is for. surely it isn't black folks." Twitter. May 6, 2018, 8:45 a.m. https://twitter.com/_hudahassan/status/993154868465586176.

Ibaorimi, Zalika U. "In reference to the Childish Gambino video, yes I understood it; however, I found it sensationalistic. It is has become extremely normalized to depict Black trauma or death. In an effort, to turn some heads and be controversial, the video wasn't controversial at all. Here's why." Twitter. May 6, 2018, 5:53 a.m. https://twitter.com/zaluibaorimi/status/993111554185924608.

"Jaden Smith — Fallen (Official Music Video)." Video file. 04:39. YouTube. Posted by Nostalgic Jams, December 4, 2016. Accessed August 27, 2019. https://www.youtube.com/watch?v=Fof9lHaApXc.

Johnson, Tre. "Donald Glover's 'This Is America' Is a Nightmare We Can't Afford to Look Away From." *Rolling Stone*. Last modified May 8, 2018. Accessed August 27, 2019. https://www.rollingstone.com/music/music-news/donald-glovers-this-is-america-is-a-nightmare-we-cant-afford-to-look-away-from-630177/.

Juice. Directed by Ernest R. Dickerson. 1992. Hollywood: Paramount, 2001. DVD.

"Kendrick Lamar — God Is Gangsta." Video file. 07:20. YouTube. Posted by KendrickLamarVEVO, January 13, 2016. Accessed August 27, 2019. https://www.youtube.com/watch?v=4wZytWFm7xo.

Korsgaard, Mathias Bonde. *Music Video after MTV: Audiovisual Studies, New Media, and Popular Music*. London: Routledge, 2017.

Lipsitz, George. *Dangerous Crossroads: Popular Music, Postmodernism and the Poetics of Place*. London: Verso Books, 1994.

Massood, Paula. *Black City Cinema: African American Urban Experiences in Film, Culture and the Moving Image*. Philadelphia: Temple University Press, 2003.

Menace II Society. Directed by Albert Hughes and Allen Hughes. 1993. New York: New Line Home Video, 2009.

Pearce, Sheldon. "From DJ Screw to Moonlight: The Unlikely Comeback of Chopped and Screwed." *The Guardian*. Last modified January 24, 2017. Accessed August 27, 2019. https://www.theguardian.com/music/2017/jan/24/chopped-screwed-hip-hop-dj-screw-moonlight.

"ScHoolboy Q — By Any Means." Video file. 08:57. YouTube. Posted by ScHoolboy Q, June 24, 2016. Accessed August 27, 2019. https://www.youtube.com/watch?v=DDmSvVOogFc.

Set It Off. Directed by F. Gary Gray. 1996. N.p.: New Line Home Video, 1999.

Shaviro, Steven. *Digital Music Videos*. Quick Takes: Movies and Popular Culture. New Brunswick, NJ: Rutgers University Press, 2017.

Super Fly. Directed by Gordon Parks, Jr. 1972. Burbank, CA: Warner Home Video, 2004.

Sweet Sweetback's Baadasssss Song. Directed by Melvin Van Peebles. 1971. Santa Monica: Xenon Pictures, 2002.

"The Weeknd — The Hills." Video file. 03:54. YouTube. Posted by The Weeknd, May 27, 2016. Accessed August 27, 2019. https://www.youtube.com/watch?v=yzTuBuRdAyA.

Vernallis, Carol. *Experiencing Music Video: Aesthetics and Cultural Context*. New York: Columbia University Press, 2004.

Vernallis, Carol. *Unruly Media: YouTube, Music Video, and the New Digital Cinema*. Oxford: Oxford University Press, 2013.

Watkins, S. Craig. *Representing: Hip-Hop Culture and the Production of Black Cinema*. Chicago: University of Chicago Press, 1998.

Wilkins, Langston Collin. "Screwston, TX: The Impact of Space, Place, and Cultural Identity on Music Making in Houston's Hip-Hop Scene." PhD diss., Indiana University, 2016.

"Young Chop 'Around My Way' Feat. Vic Mensa & King 100 James (WSHH Exclusive — Official Music Video)." Video file. 04:48. YouTube. Posted by WORLDSTARHIPHOP, June 10, 2016. Accessed August 27, 2019. https://www.youtube.com/watch?v=bXfmTv2oj6Y.

MF DOOM mask collage by Roy Christopher

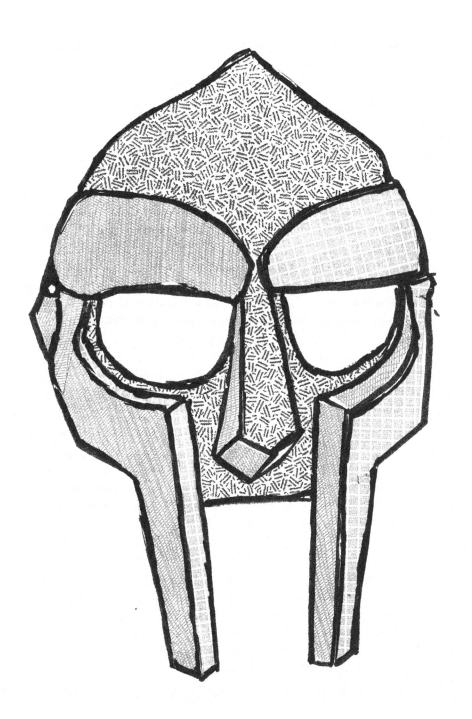

Glitched: Spacetime, Repetition & The Cut
Nettrice R. Gaskins

Introduction

In black culture, the thing (the ritual, the dance, the beat) is 'there for
you to pick it up when you come back to get it.' If there is a goal in such a
culture, it is always deferred; it continually 'cuts' back to the start, in the
musical meaning of 'cut' as an abrupt, seemingly unmotivated break (an
accidental da capo) with a series already in progress and a willed return
to a prior series.[1]

Much like Einstein working with his thought experiments, so jazz
improvisers construct mental patterns and shapes when they solo.[2]

In "Repetition as a Figure of Black Culture" (1984) James A. Snead describes
improvisation — the spontaneous and inventive use of things — as foundational and at
the heart of black cultural and creative production. Improvisation is the tool that acts
upon a thing (i.e., a sequence), or changes it. Repetition and cutting are the methods.
Without these organizing principles, improvisation would not be possible. The 'cutting'
of cycles of repetition is aesthetic and political, signaling a level of resistance.[3] According
to Snead, black culture in 'the cut' builds accidents into its coverage, as a way to control
the unpredictability. The cut is like a glitch in *The Matrix*, or when Neo sees the same
black cat walk past a door twice. Neo assumed it was déjà vu and mentioned it to the
rest of the crew, which let them know that the Agents had made a change and knew
they were there. We hear James Brown's 'cut' in the song "Cold Sweat," when, after the
band has played for a certain time, Brown and other performers interject with sonic
cues to direct the music to another level. This essay examines such strategies in artistic
and cultural improvisation, from James Brown to Public Enemy, specifically how these
performances engage repetition and technological disruption, which generate visual
and sonic patterns and use algorithms to remix and disrupt time.
    In R&B/funk, jazz, rap and other related musical forms, most of the harmonic
progression is cyclical. Musicians and producers improvise over a composition that

typically loops or repeats certain elements of a song, and a phenomenal amount of change and development can occur in the accompaniment. Improvisation around a theme such as in Afrofuturism is a fundamental principle in music, patternmaking, and computation, as a deliberately cultivated, creative method. Music is the tip of the iceberg; leading scholars to find broader strategies of circulation and 'cutting' that regenerate what has come before in the present and imagine future scenarios. Snead references John Coltrane who made rhythmic and melodic statements by cutting away from the initial musical sequences.[4] A similar phenomenon is found in physics when using music to manipulate waveforms on a computer. Music visualizations and charts represent the physics of vibration through sound. Coltrane learned this when he composed "Giant Steps" and created a circular diagram that illustrates the harmonic progression in the song.[5] Besides using a cycle as the basis of this song, Coltrane applied substitute patterns over the chord changes of other songs to which he composed new melodies. Later, hip-hop music producers such as Grandmaster Flash, Marley Marl and Hank Shocklee would build on this method through the use of sound systems, computers and software.

"Cold Sweat", often called the first true funk song, contains patterns or *grooves* that, when interrupted, produce changes in rhythm, timbre and tone. Hip-hop music producers have extensively sampled "Cold Sweat" and reproduced its structure by using machines such as the Roland TR-808 and E-mu SP-100. Black music can generate computer-based visualizations that mimic the visual patterns in traditional African textiles and African American quilts.[6,7] The visual and algorithmic nature of the music has seldom been addressed in academic discourse. "Cold Sweat" consists of sequences or statements, which are similar to instructions that might be used to tell computers to complete certain tasks, also referred to as algorithms. For the purposes of this essay, "Cold Sweat" is in a jumping off position for the study of works that exist where code meets cultural art. In continental African traditions, a thing often has a variety of applications. If you see someone wearing a beautiful piece of cloth, the cloth can not only protect the body, but also rely on the fabric to record history and culture. The same visual polyrhythms in the cloth can be found (sonically) in black music. Afrofuturism, as a speculative practice, helps to tie these concepts and works together.

The Black Ghost in the Machine

Travelers who have been in *The Matrix* long enough are able to see glitches before the changes occur. In the film, Neo gains the newfound power to perceive and control the Matrix and, as Thomas Anderson, he is known to be a hacker and coder. By understanding how computation (i.e., the algorithm) in "Cold Sweat" works, we can begin to see ways in which real-life performers use computational thinking — expressing problems and solutions in ways that a computer can execute — to disrupt mainstream technologies. Replace hacking with cutting and this method becomes performative or embodied in different art forms. James Brown was known to do this once his band had established the groove of a song, then instantly change different parts of it based on what he heard.

> He put the lyrics on it. The band set up in a semicircle in the studio with one microphone. It was recorded live in the studio. One take. It was like a performance.[8]

Repetition and the practice of cutting (to replace hacking) was mastered by James Brown and passed along to hip-hop producers and performers who made an art out of sampling from his songs decades later. The dynamic rhythms of "Cold Sweat" and other songs from that era inspired breakbeats, or the sampling of drum loop beats found in soul or funk tracks and their subsequent use as the rhythmic basis for rap music. Perhaps not coincidentally a short break in rap music is known as a "cut" and cutting in funk and hip-hop requires repetition and "abruptly skipping it back to another beginning" that was previously played. Hip-hop music producers use cutting and scratching with equipment such as turntables and a DJ mixer, which is a small mixer with a crossfader (slider) that is used to cut in and out of the main track. Sampling, scratching, or cutting touches on an aesthetic impulse that is linked to the discourse of repetition and the cut. These methods inspired software developers from the Massachusetts Institute of Technology to create Scratch visual (computer) programming language that relates the ease of mixing sounds to the ease of mixing projects, thus allowing users to improvise with code.

Improvisation leads to embodied interaction in different art forms, which includes the body's direct, iterative engagement with materials, tools, machines and objects.[9] The performativity of embodied improvisation, especially through cutting, can be thought of as a language which functions as a form of social action and has the effect of change.[10] This scholarship provides a theoretical and conceptual framing for black creativity and the idea that humans (performers) and machines (sound systems) can work together such as in call-and-response participation in which one performer offers a verse (call) and the next performer answers. The "call and recall" aspects of black creativity and culture are essential to understanding creative practices and inventions that engage repetition, cutting and variation.[11] The "call and response" aspect of jazz was essential to visual artist Romare Bearden's practice in that his spontaneous approach required each move in his making of a work to determine subsequent actions. Producer Hank Shocklee equates his creative process to Bearden's collages, once again indirectly referencing the cut.[12]

The connections between sonic, visual, computational and performance-based creativity are strengthened and supported by embodied improvisation, or the "black ghost in the machine". Human-machine interactions are often sensory: the machine or system receives and responds to inputs by live human performers. Performers enable this interaction, which calls forth images of cyborgs with enhanced abilities due to the integration of some artificial component or technology that relies on some sort of feedback.[13] We can see how this works in music production and in Afrofuturism. Initially, music producers opted for analogue rather than digital sounds such as when the Roland TR-808 first became popular with Afrika Bambaataa & Soulsonic Force's "Planet Rock." As computers and software became more ubiquitous, producers assembled multiple devices and the music became more layered and complex. The use of sound to generate images adds another dimension to this domain.

Chaos Theory, Performance & Sonic Space

> [T]he Bomb Squad actually cut songs into pieces surgically and put them in the precise places they wanted for maximum impact, sometimes even changing the original in the process...[14]

The Bomb Squad, a music production team known for their work with the rap group Public Enemy, made use of early funk production through sampling and noise generation. Funk pioneer George Clinton wrote that Public Enemy's music helped him to understand the way that sound could either organize upward into music or dissolve into chaos.[15] This production sits at the "edge of chaos" that, in physics, is the transition space between order and disorder that engenders a constant dynamic interplay between order and disorder.[16], [17] Public Enemy, specifically The Bomb Squad music production team, attached improvisation (and time) to this space. They used chaos in the form of noise to create sonic space. A sample from James Brown's "Cold Sweat" appears in Public Enemy's "Welcome to the Terrordome," specifically at the 0:09 and 4:12 minute marks. You can hear Brown's vocal cut that follows the groove and supports the emphasis of "the one," which is the first beat in a measure.

> [T]he one is not so much a musicological place as it is a spiritual place, as the navigation of that beat is invested with age-old rhythms and nuances that end up propelling the rest of everything else — the tune, the band, the audience and Brown himself — into a strutting, rump-shaking beatitude.[18]

Funk musicians are "on the one" when several rhythmic lines are performed simultaneously, or in the moment where the players "lock" and the rhythmic output sounds as if it's one voice. The rhythmic lock is a specific performance technique closely related to groove and feel.[19] Loose correlations can be made between Neo as the "One" in *The Matrix* and performers responding to rhythm. Both embody improvisation, bringing order, or control to chaos through their performances. The idea of using computation to simulate this interaction was something Sun Ra, the grandfather of Afrofuturism, was exploring when he collaborated with Bill Sebastian of Visual Music Systems to create the OVC or Outerspace Visual Communicator. The original OVC was a complex hybrid visual music machine with various control interfaces. The recent version is called the OVC-3D and it features a 360-degree alternate-reality experience using Oculus Rift headsets.[20] Afrofuturist Onyx Ashanti created the "Beatjazz controller," a hybrid sound system that allows him to produce and improvise with sounds using the movement of his own body. The sound system of decades past is now becoming a part of the human body.

Emerging technology combines visuals, sound and artificial intelligence (AI). AI can be used to create new ideas by producing novel combinations of familiar ideas, exploring the potential of conceptual spaces, and by making transformations that enable the generation of previously impossible ideas.[21] Google's NSynth is based on an algorithm, which uses a deep neural network technique to generate sounds. Rather than generating music notes, NSynth replicates the sound of an instrument. What makes the algorithm unique is that it continuously learns the core qualities of what makes up an individual sound and is able to combine various sounds to generate something completely new. It is the generative, algorithmic nature of improvisation that makes it possible to expand repetition and the cut to new forms of AI such as neural networks that use sequential information. In order to create music, AI machines need to learn the patterns and behaviors of existing songs so that these machines can reproduce something that sounds like actual music.

Conclusion

In *Matrix: Reloaded*, Neo meets a program called the Architect, who explains that Neo is an intentional part of the Matrix, which is now in its sixth iteration. For James Brown and other artists, the "one" is the Architect; it contains the secret code of black creative and cultural production. Hank Shocklee is often referred to as an architect of sound and, like a hacker, gets under the hood of the code during production. The response is the glitch in which performers can change or modify the code, or make the music do anything they want it to do. The Bomb Squad's use of the cut encouraged social action. James Brown's cut is the driver in "Welcome to the Terrordome." The repetition of this brief sequence provides the foundation for the entire song. "Terrordome" is what post-colonial scholar and theorist Homi Bhabha would refer to as a *third space of enunciation* in which cultural systems are constructed, including the construction of culture and the invention of tradition.[22]

This theory extends the notion of the real and the virtual by suggesting a hybrid space that allows participants to engage in social relations with one another or with music-making devices of all types.

The third space theory explains the uniqueness of performers, or contexts as hybrids. Sonic hybridity blurs the real and the virtual, and this is expanded in the third space through distributed presence and distributed physical spaces, essentially, referring to a shared electronic performance space. Emerging technologies act as hybrid sound systems and multi-track music machines, building on sonic innovations such as the cut in "Cold Sweat" or the sample (of the cut) in "Welcome to the Terrordome." This development enables performers to collaborate with machines in new ways to compose polyrhythmic sounds that incorporate the style and methodology of funk, rap, etc. Space and time carry a cacophony of vibrations with textures and timbres as rich and varied as the din of sounds in a recording studio or even an AI music-making machine. Through this noise emerges the rhythm and culture of a diaspora, captured and manipulated with zeroes and ones, and atomized so that past, present and future genres can be studied and shared in ways or forms perhaps not yet invented.

Notes

1. Snead, James A. "Repetition as a figure of black culture", in *Black Literature and Literary Theory*, ed. Henry Louis Gates, Jr. New York, NY: Methuen & Co, Ltd., 1984.

2. Ibid.

3. Mathes, Carter. *Imagine the Sound: Experimental African American Literature after Civil Rights.* Minneapolis; London: University of Minnesota Press, 2015.

4. Snead, 68.

5. Alexander, Stephon. *The Jazz of Physics: The Secret Link Between Music and the Structure of the Universe,* New York, NY: Basic Books, 2017, 5.

6. Rajagopalan, Ramgopal, Eric Hortop, Dania El-Khechen, Cheryl Kolak Dudek, Lydia Sharman, F László Szabó, Thomas Fevens, & Sudhir P. Mudur. "Inference and Design in Kuba and Zillij Art with Shape Grammars." Concordia University, 2006.

7. Wahlman, Maude S. *Signs and Symbols: African Images in African-American Quilts.* New York: The Museum of American Folk Art, 2001.

8. "James Brown's Musicians Reflect On His Legacy." *Down Beat,* 2007.

9. El-Zanfaly, Dina. "[I3] Imitation, Iteration and Improvisation: Embodied interaction in making and learning." *Design Studies,* Vol. 41, Part A, 2015, 79-109.

10. Cavanaugh, Jillian R. "Performativity." *Anthropology,* March 10, 2015.

11. Andreae, Christopher. "Bearden Created the Visual Equivalent of Jazz." *The Christian Science Monitor.* October 4, 2004. https://www.csmonitor.com/2004/1004/p18s02-hfes.html.

12. Muhammad, Ali Shaheed, and Frannie Kelley. "Hank Shocklee: 'We Had Something to Prove'." NPR. April 16, 2015. Accessed August 10, 2019. https://www.npr.org/sections/microphonecheck/2015/04/16/399817846/hank-shocklee-we-had-something-to-prove.

13. Carvalko, Joseph. *The Techno-human Shell: A Jump in the Evolutionary Gap.* Sunbury Press, 2012.

14. Clinton, George. *Brothas Be, Yo Like George, Ain't That Funkin' Kinda Hard on You?* New York, NY: Atria Books, 2017, 307.

15. Ibid.

16. Wotherspoon, Tim and Alfred Hübler. "Adaptation to the edge of chaos with random-wavelet feedback," *The Journal of Physical Chemistry,* 2008.

17. Waldrop, M. Mitchell. *Complexity: The Emerging Science at the Edge of Order and Chaos.* New York, NY: Simon & Schuster, 1992.

18. Reynolds, Mark. "That Thing That Makes Funk Funky: 'The One: The Life and Music of James Brown'." PopMatters. February 24, 2018. Accessed August 7, 2019. https://www.popmatters.com/157147-that-which-makes-funk-funky-the-one-the-life-and-music-of-james-brow-2495863634.html.

19. Davis, Robert. *Who Got Da Funk? An Etymophony of Funk music from the 1950s to 1979,* University of Montreal, 2006, 158.

20. Gaskins, Nettrice. "Cosmogramic Design: A Cultural Model of the Aesthetic Response," in *Aesthetics Equals Politics.* Cambridge, MA: The MIT Press, 2019.

21. Boden, Margaret A. "Creativity and Artificial Intelligence," in *Artificial Intelligence* Volume 103, Issues 1—2, August 1998, 347-356.

22. Bhabha, Homi K. *The Location of Culture.* Abingdon: Routledge, 2004, 55.

Bibliography

Alexander, Stephon. *The Jazz of Physics: The Secret Link between Music and the Structure of the Universe.* New York: Basic Books, 2017.

Andreae, Christopher. "Bearden Created the Visual Equivalent of Jazz." *The Christian Science Monitor.* October 4, 2004. https://www.csmonitor.com/2004/1004/p18s02-hfes.html.

Bhabha, Homi K. *The Location of Culture.* Abingdon: Routledge, 2004.

Boden, Margaret A. "Creativity and Artificial Intelligence," in *Artificial Intelligence* Volume 103, Issues 1—2, August 1998, 347-356.

Carvalko, Joseph. *The Techno-Human Shell: A Jump in the Evolutionary Gap.* Sunbury Press, 2012.

Cavanaugh, Jillian R. "Performativity." *Anthropology,* March 10, 2015.

Clinton, George. *Brothas Be, Yo Like George, Ain't That Funkin' Kinda Hard on You?* New York, NY: Atria Books, 2017.

El-Zanfaly, Dina. "[I3] Imitation, Iteration and Improvisation: Embodied interaction in making and learning." *Design Studies,* Vol. 41, Part A, 2015, 79-109.

Gaskins, Nettrice. "Cosmogramic Design: A Cultural Model of the Aesthetic Response," in *Aesthetics Equals Politics.* Cambridge, MA: The MIT Press, 2019.

Kimmel, M., Hristova, D., & Kussmaul, K. Sources of Embodied Creativity: Interactivity and Ideation in Contact Improvisation. *Behavioral Sciences* (Basel, Switzerland) 2018, 8(6), 52.

Mathes, Carter. *Imagine the Sound: Experimental African American Literature after Civil Rights.* Minneapolis; London: University of Minnesota Press, 2015.

Muhammad, Ali Shaheed, and Frannie Kelley. "Hank Shocklee: 'We Had Something to Prove'." NPR. April 16, 2015. Accessed August 10, 2019. https://www.npr.org/sections/microphonecheck/2015/04/16/399817846/hank-shocklee-we-had-something-to-prove.

Reynolds, Mark. "That Thing That Makes Funk Funky: 'The One: The Life and Music of James Brown'." PopMatters. February 24, 2018. Accessed August 7, 2019. https://www.popmatters.com/157147-that-which-makes-funk-funky-the-one-the-life-and-music-of-james-brow-2495863634.html.

Snead, James A. Repetition as a figure of black culture, in *Black Literature and Literary Theory,* ed. Henry Louis Gates, Jr. New York, NY: Methuen & Co, Ltd., 1984.

Wahlman, Maude S. *Signs and Symbols: African Images in African-American Quilts.* New York: The Museum of American Folk Art, 2001.

Waldrop, M. Mitchell. Complexity: *The Emerging Science at the Edge of Order and Chaos.* New York, NY: Simon & Schuster, 1992.

Wotherspoon, Tim and Alfred Hübler. "Adaptation to the edge of chaos with random-wavelet feedback," *The Journal of Physical Chemistry,* 2008.

"The Theology of Timing"
Black Consciousness and the Origin of Hip-Hop Culture
Omar Akbar

The title of this essay is a "remix" of the title of a lecture series by the Honorable Elijah Muhammad from the early 1970s, titled "The Theology of Time."[1] In the original lecture series, the Honorable Elijah Muhammad summarized that the "Theology of Time", as "knowing the time and what must be done." When put into context, Elijah Muhammad's conceptualization of time provides a multi-layered framework for the analysis of the origins of hip-hop culture, African Semiotics and Black Consciousness. In context to hip-hop culture, "knowing the time and what must be done" could be interpreted as a manifesto of rhythm, as it relates to music and dance. Deeper analysis of the concept can be extended to the work of graph artists that purposefully choose subject matter for murals, in specific locations to make a poignant, if not provocative message regarding an issue relevant to a particular community. In essence these interpretations are valid and very relevant to the practices of hip-hop culture; however, at best these interpretations only offer a surface analysis of how and why hip-hop culture came into existence, and what hip-hop culture truly is. This essay will analyze the ways in which youth of the South Bronx recognized "the time and what must be done" as the necessity to redirect the energy of a genocidal gang war into a state of moderate peace, that would become a cultural paradigm that would change the world.

The origins of hip-hop culture are an extension of African Semiotics, Black Consciousness, urban youth clubs (also known as outlaw gangs), and the conceptualization of time. Hip-hop culture is an African paradigm formed by the descendants of formerly enslaved African people in the United States of America during the 20th century and has become a global phenomenon in the 21st century. In African cultural paradigms, the concept of time is non-linear and often refers to events and cycles in both the natural and super natural realms. African epistemology, ontology, axiology categorize time as "what is and what was", with various levels of access to these temporal planes available to human, animal, geological and supernatural actors. In the Bantu language of Swahili, the word Sasa, is translated as "the present", while the word Zamani means "the past", while there is no specific word for the future. The absence of a linguistic term for the concept of the "future" in an African language is not due to the lack of an understanding, for what is considered the future is an aspect of the past and present, rather than a separate concept in itself. African conceptualizations of time are circular; thus, events are repeated, which would make the future an aspect of the past and present interchangeably. Another manifestation of the African principle of time is demonstrated in rites of passage, by which the event of fulfilled ritual activity marks the stages of the temporal plane, with conception, birth, puberty, parenthood and death as temporal markers that were not fixed to a particular age or date, but instead to the events that correspond with each stage. From antiquities to the age of globalization, the construct of time holds multiple meanings, and functions in African cultures, and hip-hop culture is no exception to this principle. African cosmology, Black Consciousness and hip-hop culture are ultimately bound in origin, theory and practice.

Black Consciousness is a fundamental element in the process by which hip-hop culture became a reality. The context of a lecture series by The Honorable Elijah Muhammad to provide an analysis of the origins of hip-hop culture is deep and essential towards a proper understanding of why and how hip-hop culture came into existence. The works of the Honorable Elijah Muhammad are rooted in Black Consciousness and Black Collectivism, and he must be acknowledged as one of the most profound and prolific purveyors of Black Consciousness in the 20th century. Black Consciousness functions as a cognitive framework, purposefully implemented by people of African descent to deconstruct and reject white supremacy, while acknowledging and becoming accountable to the larger history, traditions, and collective of African people, materialized by the intergenerational preservation and development of African people and their descendants. The term "Black Consciousness" was popularized by Caribbean psychiatrist Frantz Fanon in his 1952 work titled *Black Skin: White Masks*, in which Fanon states:

> The dialectic that introduces necessity as a support for my freedom expels me from myself. It shatters my impulsive position. Still regarding consciousness, black consciousness is immanent in itself. I am not a potentiality of something; I am fully what I am. I do not have to look for the universal. There's no room for probability inside me. My black consciousness does not claim to be a loss. It is. It merges with itself.[2]

Though Fanon can be credited for the term "Black Consciousness", the formation of the uncompromised Black identity and psychological perspective that Fanon describes was a collective effort formed by African people during chattel slavery, and was first articulated in a literary manifesto in the 19th century by David Walker in his work *The Appeal*.[3] The cognitive framework of Black Consciousness was further developed by other great minds of Africa and its diaspora during the 19th and 20th centuries. Various forms of African based concepts such as African Humanism, Negritude, and Afrocentrism can be combined with the paradigm of Black Consciousness towards forming models of Pan-Africanism and Black Collectivism. Black Consciousness is the cognitive framework by which culture and community are codified through principled behavior.

Many of the issues of racism, violence, poverty, and drugs in the community were compounded by the assassination of Malcolm X in 1965; and Martin Luther King in 1968 after which the popularization of Black Consciousness became a stronger force in Black communities. The urban rebellions that were prevalent in the United States during the 1960s, also manifest in Harlem, New York in 1964. These urban rebellions were connected to a state of Black Consciousness that sought an aggressive manifestation of Black action in the face of wholesale racial oppression and white supremacy. Although the urban rebellions of the 1960s were not necessarily rooted in a calculated ideology, philosophy or organization, the mass mobilization of resistance during this time period further facilitated the state of Black Consciousness that would become a staple in the popular aesthetic of Black youth, music, art and culture during the late 1960s and early 1970s. J. Herman Blake further elaborates on the nature of the youth movements during the 1960s:

> Furthermore, a new generation of black people is coming to maturity, young people who were born and raised in the urban black communities. They do not use a previous Southern pattern of living as the framework through which they assess their current situation, but use an urban, mainstream-America framework, usually learned from the mass media rather than experienced. These youth comprise a very large proportion of the urban residents and are less enchanted by the view that, although things are bad, they are better than they used to be. As such, they are very critical of attitudes of those blacks who see the situation of the black man as improving.[4]

Blake goes on to elaborate on Black youth and the trend towards Black Consciousness and cultural nationalism during the late 1960s:

> The heightened interaction of black youth as a result of urban living, the coming-of-age of a generation of post-World War II youth, and the rejection of some white middle-class values in the attempt to articulate values which grow out of the black experience are some of the internal dynamics of black communities in the 1960's which are producing a new upsurge in nationalism.[5]

In New York City during the 1960s, the paradigm of Black Consciousness and the movement of Black cultural nationalism were spearheaded by the Nation of Islam through Muhammad Temple #7 in Harlem, Muhammad Temple #7C in Brooklyn and Muhammad Temple #7D in the Bronx. Blake also elaborates on the impact of the Nation of Islam as follows:

> The Nation of Islam places great emphasis upon black consciousness and racial pride, claiming that a man cannot know another man until he knows himself. This search for black identity is conducted through the study of the religious teachings of Islam, as interpreted by Elijah Muhammad, and through the study of Afro-American and African history.[6]

Blake also elaborates on the widespread influence of the Nation of Islam in the ideologies of Black Consciousness that were prevalent in the late 1960s:

> The Nation of Islam had a profound effect upon the development of contemporary trends in black nationalism. There are very few ardent black nationalists today who have not had some contact with the Nation of Islam either through membership or through having come under the influence of one of its eloquent ministers.[7]

The form of Black Consciousness offered by the Nation of Islam did not promote revolutionary or criminal activity, but rather the emphasis of the Nation of Islam's ideology was based on the psychological and spiritual reform of the descendants of enslaved African people in the United States. The Nation of Islam also identified the nature of all human beings as a part of the Human family, with indigenous peoples from Meso-America and Asia as being "Original" peoples that were simply another tone of "Black" peoples.[8] This broader context of "Original" Human Beings represented by Meso American and Asian peoples, would also be a critical element in the formation of hip-hop culture in Afro and Meso American communities. The Nation of Islam is the catalyst for the Black Consciousness ideologies represented by the Nation of Gods and Earths in Harlem and the Black Arts Movement with Amiri Baraka.

Though hip-hop culture is most popularly known for the artistic elements of DJing, B-Boying, graph art and MCing, the ideological ethos of the culture resides in the "Knowledge" element, which is deeply and specifically rooted in the Black Consciousness paradigm and the movements it spawned in New York City during the 1960s and early 1970s. The ideology of Black consciousness became a staple of popular Black art and youth culture during the 1960s, and its aesthetical principles played a role in the formation of the symbolism and ethos of hip-hop culture.

The Bronx: Birth of a Ghetto

The historical context by which hip-hop culture was formed is essential in developing a proper understanding of the "Theology of Timing", thus it is crucial to develop a proper historiography of the pre-hip-hop culture period in New York City. New York City has been the home of many cultural, and social movements such as the Harlem Renaissance and the Black Arts Movement. This section seeks to properly analyze the historical backdrop of the Bronx Borough of New York City in the period from 1945 to 1975, with emphasis on the economic and social conditions that would contribute to the genesis of hip-hop culture.

The southern region of the Bronx Borough of New York City is the birthplace and home of hip-hop culture. Prior to the 1960s and 1970s, the Bronx Borough had been a predominantly blue collar and working class area, with a predominantly white population.[9] The Bronx became more ethnically diverse after World War Two, due to the mass migration of African Americans from the South, Puerto Rican expatriates, and war veterans seeking to build a new life after the war. This massive influx of new residents contributed to a gradual change in the ethnic demographic of the Bronx during the late 1940s, and early 1950s.[10] The influx of minority groups seeking a new life in New York City after World War Two, combined with White flight to the newly formed suburban areas north of the Bronx, caused drastic change in the ethnic make-up of the Bronx from 1950 to 1970.[11] Another major factor that contributed to the shift in the demographics of Bronx residents was the undertaking of major public works projects such as the building of the Cross Bronx Expressway, which displaced large numbers of longtime Bronx residents and businesses.[12] The surge of new residents who had come from Puerto Rico, and African American residents from the south, sought better housing than what was offered in the Manhattan tenements. The new population of minority citizens who were mostly unskilled laborers and domestics, combined with the departure of the traditional white middle class residents to the newly formed suburbs, caused a severe loss of the tax base of the Bronx, causing a downward shift in the economic status of the borough.[13]

With the large number of Puerto Rican immigrants coming to the Bronx Borough, many of the large immigrant families crammed into small apartments with minimum upkeep and exploitative landlords, creating what was considered slum conditions in the community.[14] The slum conditions and the influx of new residents increased over the decades after World War Two, and by 1960, New York City Public Housing began to replace the older slum tenements with public housing projects, designed to accommodate the high concentration of residents in the borough.[15] These public housing projects in the Bronx would become catacombs of human interaction between diverse ethnic groups that had various positive and negative outcomes.

During the 1950s, the Bronx Borough of New York City would become home of a youth gang culture that became a primary foundation of hip-hop culture in the late

1960s and early 1970s. The Bronx suffered many of the struggles that impoverished urban American communities faced during the 1960s and 1970s, and the youth of these impoverished communities coped with these experiences in many different ways. The economically impoverished segments of society often suffer from a lower quality of educational institutions, higher crime rates, and psychological attacks from those who deem the lower class and minority groups as innately inferior. One of the coping mechanisms for many of the youth who lived in impoverished and newly integrated urban communities was the formation of youth clubs; or "gangs" as they became more popularly known by the larger society. Although, many gangs were not formed based on simply poverty and urban decay, but as a means to form a community within a larger community.

By the 1960s, somewhat of an urban plague had become commonplace in New York City, and that plague was heroin. Between 1950 and 1961, only 1,586 deaths were reported due to heroin use; from 1964-1967 the reported amount of heroin users in New York City was 64,890, with a median age of 27 years old; and that number increased to 145,577 between the years 1971-1974, with a median age of 22 years old.[16] The crime rate in the Bronx during this time also increased and would continue to increase drastically from 1960 to 1970.[17] Another phenomenon that played a critical role in the downward turn of the community of the Bronx was arson; as many landlords determined it was more profitable to burn down the tenements and collect insurance, rather than trying to collect rent from impoverished tenants.[18] The loss of a strong tax base, the new majority population of impoverished peoples, the influx of heroin, higher crime rates, arson, and urban decay had a tremendous impact on the Bronx Borough socially, economically and culturally in every stratum of the community. By the 1960s, the formerly 2/3 White population of the Bronx had shifted to a 2/3 Black and Latino majority in the Bronx and the youth gangs represented by this new majority became the force du jour of the Bronx neighborhoods. These various elements that were indicative of life in the Bronx would contribute to the climate and environment that gave birth to the culture of hip-hop.

Clubs, Outlaws and Hip-Hop

The earliest youth gangs in the Bronx were predominantly European American groups that had existed in New York City since the 19th century.[19] After the influx of African American and Puerto Rican populations following the Great Migration and World War Two respectively, White youth often felt resentment toward the new Black and Puerto Rican residents. The early phenomenon of gangs in the Bronx was described by Jill Jonnes as:

> The steady of influx of Blacks and Puerto Ricans was transforming the old neighborhoods. The young expressed the hostility most forcefully.

Gangs of teenagers gathered to challenge the "spics", not just in the Bronx but all over the City. (A heavily romanticized version of gang warfare, *West Side Story*, would later captivate the world and send even the most middle-class of boys into imitations of Sharks and Jets.)[20]

The aggression of White youth gangs to non-White youth gangs effectively served as a catalyst for the formation of Black and Puerto Rican youth gangs, and the conflict between White and non-White gangs would persist into the 1970s.[21] The Black and Latino youth gangs that would emerge during the 1950s and 1960s, formed in part as a response to urban decay, as well as the desire to create in-groups for minority youth who were considered pariah to the former majority "white" community.

The gang entities functioned as communities within larger communities and this aspect of the gang culture would also function as a critical framework in the formation of hip-hop culture. Sociologist R.L. Warren describes the gang conceptualization of community as follows:

> The term "community" implies something both psychological and geographical. Psychologically, it implies shared interests, characteristics, or association, as in the expression "community of interests". . . Geographically, it denotes a specific area where people are clustered. Its reality exists only in constituting a social entity, only in the behaviors and attitudes which its members share, only in the patterns of their interaction.[22]

The gang structure is a highly codified rite of passage, and the youth based outlaw gangs of the South Bronx were no exception. Sociologists of the "Chicago School" of gang research have developed a model using five criteria to define the gang experience:

1. Social organization: associated with experiences of migration to a new area and control over territory.
2. Competition: competition with other gangs reinforces loyalty to the group, external competition reinforced internal loyalty and identity.
3. Hierarchy: the gang structure is characterized by hierarchy, with a clearly defined set of roles within the gang.
4. Identity: the gang produces identity, with a significant ritual dimension, from rites of initiation to rites of exclusion.
5. Counter culture: the gang emerges in social and spatial contexts characterized by the weakening of traditional forms of community authority (linked to the loss of parents, particularly the father, as a result of immigration experience), and finally in context involving

barriers to fully participate in the new society — these could be the school system, racism, or other forms of stigmatization.[23]

The Chicago School model of gangs offers elements consistent with authentic hip-hop culture, as social organization (crews), competition (battles), hierarchy (pioneers, champions), and identity (formation of alter ego for various artistic disciplines) are staples of the culture.

Although gang culture alone is not synonymous with hip-hop culture, there are undeniable overlapping principles. The codified practices of youth clubs reflect the origins of hip-hop culture as a collective action, where the individual's behavior is accountable to a larger community. The notion of honor is essentially an assertion of ethical principles, within the context of the gang and are related to status, self-esteem, courage, loyalty, and machismo.[24] The value of respect is held in the highest regard and is often the element that conflict between gangs is most connected to. The hierarchy of youth gangs is implicitly based on a rite of passage and age rank for the members.[25] The youth gangs were deeply embedded in concepts of 1. protection of territory, and 2. "notions of honor."[26] These fundamental elements of the gang ethos when used for the purpose of peace are critical aspects of the later influence of gang culture on the ethos of hip-hop culture.

The Gangs That Would Become Hip-Hop Culture

Some of the most prevalent gangs in the Bronx during the period of the mid 1960s and early 1970s were: the Seven Immortals, the Ghetto Brothers, the Bronx Aliens, the Saints, the Javelins, the Royal Charmers, the Seven Crowns, the Uptown Organization, Inter Crime, and White youth gangs such as Bronx Aliens, White Angels, and the Golden Guineas; and the most powerful gangs in the Bronx with chapters throughout NYC: the Savage Nomads/the Savage Skulls, and the Black Spades.[27] Gangs such as the Black Spades and the Savage Skulls were derivative of early Bronx gangs from the 1950s that had a resurgence during the late 1960s. The gangs were often agents of criminal activity, while engaging in conflict with each other through gang warfare. The Black and Puerto Rican "outlaw gangs" of the Bronx that came into prominence during the period of the mid 1960s, though often violent, would also be the organizations that provided the cultural framework for hip-hop culture. Arthur Armstrong, an early hip-hop event promoter, and owner of Bronx venues Galaxy 2000 and Ecstasy Garage; describes the origins of hip-hop culture in gang culture:

Rap was territorial. It came from the gang wars; I don't know if a lot of people know that many of the rappers came from the gang wars of the

70s. Some became DJs, MCs; some became security. So, it melted over into rap music, protecting their territory. So that's basically how it started.[28]

Alien Ness, an early hip-hop pioneer and member of breakdance pioneers the New York City Breakers, Rock Steady Crew and Bronx hip-hop crew Boogie Down Productions, describes the origin of B-Boying or breakdancing as also being a staple of the pre-hip-hop gang culture:

> The B-Boying didn't start at the Herc parties. You could take the B-Boys back to the outlaw gangs of the late 60s and 70s. They were the original B-Boys, and it was part of their war dances. That's why the competitive level is always going to be there with the B-Boy. It's not just entertainment and flash; there is a competitive level, and that comes from its true essence and roots, from the competitive levels of the outlaws.[29]

Pop Master Fabel, hip-hop dance pioneer, also elaborated on the origin of the B-Boy dance style being directly derived from the "outlaw gangs of the late 60s and early 70s":

> The first groups I ever saw dance were actually outlaw gangs. Back in those days we had the Black Spades, the Savage Nomads in the Bronx, the Ching-a-Lings. In my neighborhood, you had the Savage Samurais on 123rd to 117th. Back then those gang members wore leather vests, similar to Hell's Angels, with the name on the back. They had younger brothers called the Young Samurais, and then they had even younger guys who were the Baby Samurais. The first B-Boys I ever saw were the Baby Kings — the youngest members of the Spanish Kings — and they were about my age. I was eleven or twelve, and I was seeing some of the most incredible dancing. The style of dance was different from B-Boying, where one guy went out and then you had to go out and burn him with better moves. With the outlaw dance they would do it at the same time; they would sort of dis the guy they were battling with a series of moves, and then they'd flash their colors.[30]

The hip-hop element of graffiti art also had its origins in the gang culture and was often used to mark the territory of a certain gang. BOM5 describes early Bronx member of the Savage Nomads and pioneer of graffiti, Smiley 149:

> The famous Smiley 149 (RIP), he was my cousin's friend. Smiley was an original Savage Nomad. I always call him my grandfather in graffiti; he's a forefather. A lot of people talk about writing in the 60s, but I only know

of one person who was writing in the 60s. Smiley was his gang name, so he was already in there with the Savage Nomads, who were a brother/sister gang to Savage Skulls. My cousin was always coming to pick me up — he was 5 years older than me. He told me, "Yo, if you want to survive in this neighborhood you got to stick with me." He told me everything that I know about fighting, and since I was really good with art, they told me, "Hey, you're going to be the one putting up the name" — a quick skull and crossbones and SS with lightning lines. I used to do it all over. I never used spray paint. I used a can of paint and a brush, and I'd dip it in and write 174 Spider (Savage Skulls) all over the place, and to this day I got a tag left in the Bronx.[31]

From War to Peace

Though the youth gangs of the Bronx had various forms of recreation and art, the mainstay of activity remained violence and crime. Throughout the 1960s the gang activity and the crime rate in the Bronx began to reach epic proportions. Intense urban decay, poverty, high crime rates, heroin epidemic, institutional racism, racially motivated gang wars and youth gang wars were a focal point for both community activists, and government officials in New York City. Activists and local government officials sought to address and remedy the community issues collectively, with a diverse group of citizens and organizations. During the mayoral administration of John Lindsay, a liberal Republican, several initiatives were formed to reduce gang violence in New York City in 1967.[32] Mayor Lindsay also implemented initiatives to create programs for urban youth, such as the "street academy" programs in conjunction with the Urban League and the Nation of Gods and Earths in Harlem.[33] The Nation of Gods and Earths was founded by man called "Allah", formerly known as Clarence 13x, former captain of the Temple #7, Fruit of Islam military force of the Nation of Islam in Harlem. Although Allah had left the Nation of Islam to teach youth in the Harlem community, his teachings were mostly based on those taught by the Nation of Islam, with the exception that Wallace Fard was not considered the Supreme Being, and all Black or "Original" people were Allah or God. This form of Black Consciousness was also centered on the reform of delinquent behavior and a respect for authority and law, as it relates to the local, state and federal government. The Nation of Gods and Earths would have a direct impact on the culture of hip-hop in its genesis, as well as in the long term. Hip-hop musical pioneer and original hip-hop DJ Kool Herc describes how the Nation of Gods and Earths acted as security at his early parties in the West Bronx:

> So even the gang members loved us, because they didn't want to mess with what was happening. You know? They come in, keep to themselves.

Not only that, a lot of Five-Percenters used to come to my party...you might call them "peace guards", and they used to hold me down: "Yo Herc, don't worry about it." So, we was just having a good time.[34]

The language of the Nation of Gods and Earths remains as a cultural artifact in the vernacular of hip-hop culture with terms such as "word", "word is bond", or "word up", which are directly extracted from the "120" Lessons used by Allah from the inception of the Nation of Gods and Earths, as well as in Fruit of Islam Training in the Nation of Islam. The original context of the term "word' and "word is bond" is drawn from Lost Found Muslim Lesson #1 as follows:

> 11. (Question): Have you not heard that your word is your bond regardless to whom or what? (Answer): Yes, my word is bond and bond is life and I will give my life before my word shall fail.[35]

There are several other ideological and aesthetical aspects of the Nation of Gods and Earths that are found in the early formation of the culture of hip-hop, such as the traditional "B-Boy stance". The "B-Boy stance" is typically associated with the crossing of the arms and standing straight up at 90 degrees, which is directly borrowed from the "standing on the square" stance used by the Nation of Gods and Earths. The act of "standing on the square" has a more ancient origin, as "the square" refers to the Nile Valley deity Maat, who represents truth and justice. The foundation of buildings and other structures were based on the square foundation of Maat, which represented truth and justice. The influence of the Nation of Gods and Earths further demonstrates the impact of Black Consciousness in the community of youth that originated hip-hop culture. After a slight decline in gang activity during the beginning of the Lindsay administration, gang wars began to crescendo between 1969 and 1973 after the death of Allah in 1969. By 1971, the vacuum left by the passing of Allah was slowly beginning to fill with youth that had been exposed to his teachings, and the Ghetto Brothers youth club began to work toward efforts for a truce between the gangs of the South Bronx.

In December of 1971, Ghetto Brothers leader vice-president Cornell Benjamin, also known as "Benji", was killed in the process of trying to facilitate a truce between the Black Spades and the Seven Immortals gangs prior to a pending rumble between the warring factions.[36] The murder of a gang member seeking to create a peace treaty between the gangs gave cause for the remaining Ghetto Brothers to work harder to make a truce reality. The efforts to honor the memory of Benji were a critical factor in ending the all-out war between the gangs in the South Bronx, as the death of Benji was the signaling of a time of peace rather than a time to escalate the violence in retaliation.[37] However, the violence between gangs would not immediately subside despite the efforts of the Ghetto Brothers, several gang members from warring factions, city government and community organizations. The violence would continue to escalate before a truce was finally a consensus amongst the non-White gangs.[38] A notable phenomenon that occurred with the gangs of the South Bronx during this period of resurgence, was the gang activity to remove drug dealers from the communities that were claimed by the gangs. Acts of vigilantism by the gangs against the dope dealers in the Bronx became a new agenda of the gangs, as efforts to diminish inter gang warfare increased.[39] By 1973, the gang warfare was still a major factor, but a shift towards efforts of peace became more commonplace; even in the midst of persistent violence.[40] 1973 would prove to be the year of transition from the "outlaw gang" culture, to a new culture called hip-hop.

Despite the fact that the slow process of implementing a gang truce had not quelled the violence in the Bronx, the seeds for the decline in gang warfare had been planted in the tragic death of Benji and the burgeoning efforts of various segments of the community to diminish the violence. In 1972, New York City police said many of the new gang wars were between "Negro-Spanish gangs and the whites", as new gangs began to form in White communities in the North Bronx.[41] Although the new resurgence of gang war included a racial element between White and non-White groups, the warfare between the Black and Latino gangs was still prevalent at the beginning of the 1970s. However, the truce would produce a cultural renaissance that would become hip-hop culture and eventually would become a global phenomenon of personal and collective expression, reconciliation, protest and education.

When the concept of "knowing the time and what must be done" is contextualized within the cognitive framework of Black Consciousness, the most profound example of "knowing the time and what must be done" is materialized by a population of disenfranchised youth, who were the descendants of formerly enslaved people, that would defy the economic, social and cultural agendas of hegemony, in a time of hyper capitalism, toxic consumerism, mass media, and disposable art, to give birth to one of the most impactful global cultural movements of the late 20th and early 21st centuries in hip-hop culture. Elijah Muhammad's creed of "knowing the time and what must be done" represents the ethos of hip-hop culture as a Black cultural paradigm, with origins triggered by the desire for peace amongst warring factions of youth organizations, catalyzed by the death of Soul Brother Benji in 1973. The Theology of Time in this regard speaks to the ability of impoverished youth to seek to end a cycle of destruction, while providing the DNA for what would become the most dominant cultural phenomenon of the late 20th and early 21st centuries. Despite the 21st century marginalization of authentic hip-hop culture, and the culture industry's commodification of pseudo-hip-hop culture in the form of so called "rap music," the "Theology of Timing" is still present. Despite the mass marketing of ignorance and anti-culture, hip-hop culture was and remains the function of the sacred and metaphysical action of human beings who "knew the time and what must be done."

Notes

1. Muhammad, Elijah. *The Theology of Time: The Secret of the Time*, Atlanta, GA: Secretarius M.E.M.P.S, 1997.

2. Fanon, Frantz. *Black Skin, White Masks*, New York, NY: Grove Press, 2008, 114.

3. Walker, David. *David Walker's Appeal, in Four Articles: Together with a Preamble, to the Coloured Citizens of the World, but in Particular, and Very Expressly, to Those of the United States of America : Third and Last Edition, Revised and Published by David Walker, 1830*, Boston, MA: David Walker, 1830.

4. Blake, J. Herman. "Black Nationalism," *Annals of the American Academy of Political and Social Science*, 382, 1969: 21, http://www.jstor.org/stable/1037110.

5. Ibid.

6. Ibid., 19.

7. Ibid., 20.

8. Muhammad, Elijah. . "Lost and Found Muslim Lesson #2," in *The 120*, by Master Fard, Detroit: Nation of Islam, 1934.

9. Roby, Megan. "The Push and Pull Dynamics of White Flight: A Study of the Bronx Between 1950 and 1980," *The Bronx County Historical Society Journal* XLV, no. 1&2 (Fall 2008): 35, accessed March 2, 2014, http://www.bronxhistoricalsociety.org/M.Roby.pdf.

10. Jonnes, Jill. *South Bronx Rising: The Rise, Fall, and Resurrection of an American City*, New York: Fordham University Press, 2002, 102.

11. Roby, Megan "The Push and Pull Dynamics of White Flight: A Study of the Bronx Between 1950 and 1980," *The Bronx County Historical Society Journal* XLV, no. 1&2 (Fall 2008): 35, accessed March 2, 2014, http://www.bronxhistoricalsociety.org/M.Roby.pdf.

12. Jonnes, Jill. *South Bronx Rising : The Rise, Fall, and Resurrection of an American City*, New York: Fordham University Press, 2002, 123.

13. United States, State of New York Comptroller, Office of the State Deputy Comptroller for the City of New York, *The Bronx: An Economic Review*, by McCall, H. Carl. Report 1-2003, New York: Office of the State Comptroller, 2002, 4, accessed March 2, 2014, http://www.osc.state.ny.us/osdc/rpt103/rpt103.pdf.

14. Jonnes, Jill. *South Bronx Rising: The Rise, Fall, and Resurrection of an American City*, New York: Fordham University Press, 2002, 112.

15. Ibid., 118.

16. Frank, Blanche. "An Overview of Heroin Trends in New York City: Past, Present and Future," *The Mount Sinai Journal of Medicine* 67, no. 5&6 (October/November 2000): 342, accessed March 2, 2014, http://www.drugpolicy.org/docUploads/meth340.pdf.

17. Jonnes, Jill. *South Bronx Rising : The Rise, Fall, and Resurrection of an American City*, New York: Fordham University Press, 2002, 227.

18. Ibid., 7.

19. United States, U.S. Department of Justice-Bureau of Justice Assistance, Office of Juvenile Justice and Delinquency Prevention, *History of Street Gangs in the United States*, by Howell, James C. and Moore, John P. vol. 4 (Washington, D.C.: U.S. Dept. of Justice, Bureau of Justice Assistance, Office of Juvenile Justice and Delinquency Prevention, 2010), 2, accessed March 3, 2014, http://www.nationalgangcenter. gov/content/documents/history-of-street-gangs.pdf.

20. Jonnes, Jill. *South Bronx Rising: The Rise, Fall, and Resurrection of an American City*, New York: Fordham University Press, 2002, 109.

21. Markham, James M. "Stabbing of Washington High School Student Points Up a Resurgence of Youth-Gang Violence in City," *New York Times*, April 19, 1972, ProQuest Historical Newspapers.

22. Goldstein, Arnold P. *Delinquent Gangs: A Psychological Perspective*, Champaign, Ill.: Research Press, 1991, 114.

23. Kontos, Louis, Brotherton, David and Barrios, Luis. *Gangs and Society: Alternative Perspectives*, New York: Columbia University Press, 2003, 66.

24. Goldstein, 37.

25. Kontos et al., 66.

26. Goldstein, 34.

27. Fricke, Jim, Ahearn, Charlie and Experience Music Project., *Yes Yes Y'all: The Experience Music Project Oral History of Hip-hop's First Decade*, Cambridge, MA: Da Capo Press, 2002, 6.

28. Ibid., 3.

29. Ibid., 9.

30. Ibid.

31. Ibid., 8.

32. "City Acting To Bar Summer Violence," *New York Times*, April 3, 1967, ProQuest Historical Newspapers.

33. Bennett, Charles G. "City Panel of 55 to Help Prevent Summer Trouble," *New York Times*, April 29, 1967.

34. Fricke, et al., 26.

35. Muhammad, Elijah. "Lost and Found Muslim Lesson #1," in *The 120*, by Master Fard, Detroit: Nation of Islam, 1934.

36. "Bronx Gang Leader Is Slain Trying to Arrange Peace," *New York Times*, December 3, 1971, Murders and Attempted Murders sec., ProQuest Historical Newspapers.

37. Francis, X. Clines. "South Bronx Gang Seeks Peace Role," *New York Times,* December 4, 1971, ProQuest Historical Newspapers.

38. Cook, Lee. "Groups Seeking Halt in Gang Violence," *New York Amsterdam News,* May 13, 1972, ProQuest Historical Newspapers.

39. Markham, James M. "Stabbing of Washington High School Student Points Up a Resurgence of Youth-Gang Violence in City," *New York Times,* April 19, 1972, ProQuest Historical Newspapers.

40. Breasted, Mary. "Youth Gangs and Their Crimes Are on the Rise," *New York Times,* July 2, 1973, ProQuest Historical Newspapers.

41. Darnton, John. "New Problems Encountered By Resurgent Street Gangs," *New York Times,* New York, February 21, 1972.

Bibliography

"9 Hurt in Raid on Gang's Dance; Rival Bronx Group Is Suspected." *New York Times*, July 17, 1972.

Alim, H Samy. *Roc the Mic Right : the Language of Hip-Hop Culture*. New York; London: Routledge, 2006.

Allah, Beloved. "The Bomb: Greatest Story Never Told." *The Word*, o.s., One, no. 1, 3, 4, 5 (1987). http://lafivepercent.wordpress.com/the-bomb-the-greatest-story-never-told/.

Barrett, Richard A. *Culture and Conduct: an Excursion in Anthropology*. Belmont, Calif.: Wadsworth Pub. Co., 1984.

Bennett, Charles G. "City Panel of 55 to Help Prevent Summer Trouble." *New York Times*, April 29, 1967.

"Biaggi Meets With Leaders of Bronx Street Gangs." *New York Times*, April 22, 1972.

Blake, J Herman. "Black Nationalism." *Annals of the American Academy of Political and Social Science* 382 (1969): 15—25. http://www.jstor.org/stable/1037110.

Breasted, Mary. "Youth Gangs and Their Crimes Are on the Rise." *New York Times*, July 2, 1973.

"Bronx Gang Leader Is Slain Trying to Arrange Peace." *New York Times*, December 3, 1971, sec. Murders and Attempted Murders.

Callahan, John P. "Mayor, After a Walking Tour, Goes Aloft With 86 Harlem Youngsters." *New York Times*, August 6, 1967.

Chang, Jeff. *Can't Stop, Won't Stop: a History of the Hip-Hop Generation*. New York: St. Martin's Press, 2005.

"City Acting To Bar Summer Violence." *New York Times*, April 3, 1967.

"City Youth Board Chairman to Resign." *New York Times*, December 9, 1973, sec. GN.

Clines, Francis X. "South Bronx Gang Seeks Peace Role." *New York Times*, December 4, 1971.

COLLINS, H.C., and New York City Police Dept 1 Police Plaza New York NY 10038. *STREET GANGS — PROFILES FOR POLICE*. United States, 1979.

Cook, Lee. "Groups Seeking Halt in Gang Violence." *New York Amsterdam News*, May 13, 1972.

Darnton, John. "New Problems Encountered By Resurgent Street Gangs." *New York Times*. February 21, 1972.

Doggett, Peter. *There's a Riot Going on: Revolutionaries, Rock Stars and the Rise and Fall of '60s Counter-Culture*. Edinburgh: Canongate, 2007.

Domestic Intelligence Division. Freedom of Information Act: Five Percenters, 1 Freedom of Information Act: Five Percenters §. BUFILE: 157-6-34 (1964). http://vault.fbi.gov/5percent.

Dwyer, Jim. "LINDSAY GREASE BOUGHT PEACE." NY Daily News, December 24, 2000. http://www.nydailynews.com/archives/news/lindsay-grease-bought-peace-article-1.895399.

Elijah, Muhammad. *Message to the Blackman in America*. Chicago: Muhammad's Temple #2, 1965.

Fanon, Frantz. *Black Skin, White Masks*. New York, NY: Grove Press, 2008.

Fard, Master, and Elijah Muhammad. "Lost and Found Muslim Lesson #1." In *The 120*. Detroit: The Nation of Islam, 1934.

Farrell, William E. "Harlem Militants Offer Peace Vow: They Say They Will Stay In School Despite Slaying." *New York Times*, June 15, 1969.

Fasi, M. El, ed. *General History of Africa: Africa from the Seventh to Eleventh Century*. Vol. III. London: Heinemann, 1988.

"The Fivepercenters: Youth Gang or Social Workers?" *New York Amsterdam News*, September 18, 1976.

Frank, Blanche. "An Overview of Heroin Trends in New York City: Past, Present and Future." *The Mount Sinai Journal of Medicine* 67, no. 5 & 6 (2000): 339—46. http://www.drugpolicy.org/docUploads/meth340.pdf.

Fraser, Gerald C. "Unarmed Citizen Patrol to Get 5-Day Harlem Test." *New York Times*, March 15, 1968.

Fricke, Jim, Charlie Ahearn, and Experience Music Project. *Yes Yes Y'all : the Experience Music Project Oral History of Hip-Hop's First Decade*. Cambridge, MA: Da Capo Press, 2002.

Gardell, Mattias. *In the Name of Elijah Muhammad : Louis Farrakhan and the Nation of Islam*. Durham, N.C.: Duke University Press, 1996.

Gennep, Arnold van. *The Rites of Passage*. Chicago: University of Chicago Press, 1960.

Goldstein, Arnold P. *Delinquent Gangs: a Psychological Perspective*. Champaign, Ill.: Research Press, 1991.

Hoenig, Gary. "Execution In The Bronx." *New York Times*, June 17, 1973, sec. IV.

Honigmann, John Joseph. *The Development of Anthropological Ideas*. Homewood, Ill.: Dorsey Press, 1976.

Hugh, Barry. "Racial Peace Keeper." *New York Times*, November 1, 1967.

Johnson, Thomas A. "City Ghettos Get Plans For Summer." *New York Times*, June 11, 1967.

Jonnes, Jill. *South Bronx Rising: the Rise, Fall, and Resurrection of an American City*. New York: Fordham University Press, 2002.

Kett, Joseph F. *Rites of Passage: Adolescence in America, 1790 to the Present*. New York: Basic Books, 1977.

"Lindsay Aides at Funeral For Slain Black Militant." *New York Times*, June 17, 1969.

Maeroff, Gene I. "Anxiety Growing at Stevenson High Over Gangs and Violence at School." *New York Times*, March 31, 1972.

Markham, James M. "Hunts Point Youths Draw Gang Battle Lines." *New York Times*, September 2, 1971, sec. Crime and Criminals.

"Mayor's Aide Helped Keep 'Cool'." *New York Times*, December 16, 1967.

Monti, Daniel J, and Scott Cummings. *Gangs: the Origins and Impact of Contemporary Youth Gangs in the United States*. Albany, N.Y.: State University of New York Press, 1993.

Obenga, Theophile. *A Companion to African Philosophy*. Edited by Kwasi Wiredu, W. E. Abraham, Abiola Irele, and Ifeanyi Menkiti. Malden, MA: Blackwell Pub., 2004

Office of Juvenile Justice and Delinquency Prevention, James C. Howell, and John P. Moore. History of street gangs in the United States, 4 History of street gangs in the United States § (2010). http://www. nationalgangcenter.gov/content/documents/history-of-street-gangs.pdf.

Office of the State Deputy Comptroller for the City of New York, and H. Carl McCall. The Bronx: An Economic Review, The Bronx: An Economic Review §. Report 1-2003 (2002). http://www.osc.state.ny.us/osdc/rpt103/rpt103.pdf.

Plog, Fred, and Daniel G., Bates. *Cultural Anthropology*. New York: Knopf, 1976.

Robson, David. *The Black Arts Movement*. Detroit, MI: Lucent Books, 2008.

Roby, Megan. "The Push and Pull Dynamics of White Flight: A Study of the Bronx Between 1950 and 1980." *The Bronx County Historical Society Journal* XLV, no. 1 & 2 (2008): 34—55.

Short, James F. *Gang Delinquency and Delinquent Subcultures*. New York: Harper & Row, 1968.

Tolchin, Martin. "Gangs Spread Terror in the South Bronx." *New York Times,* January 16, 1973.

"Two Shot Dead in Bronx Duel." *New York Times,* January 11, 1975.

United States Census Bureau. 1960, 1970, 1980, and 1990 Censuses of Population and Housing Income Statistics Branch/HHES Division, 1960, 1970, 1980, and 1990 Censuses of Population and Housing Income Statistics Branch/HHES Division § (n.d.). http://www.census.gov/hhes/www/income/data/historical/county/county3.html.

Warren, Roland Leslie. *The Community in America*. Chicago: Rand McNally, 1971.

Breakbeat Poems
Kevin Coval

Flashdance ending on a theme from The Jimmy Castor Bunch
(after Nick Makoha & Pat Rosal)

we had a VCR, bootleg tapes stacked
around a tiny black & white television.
a secondhand library some boyfriend copped
from a flea market & gifted my moms, haphazardly.
this was her story: a working woman with aspirations
greater than her lot. no conservatory art school.
no Jennifer Beals. but the desire to stop being
on the other end of a man's punch
clock. she was knocked out after
a long day of selling or snorting
or some mix therein.

i was 8, the year my parents split
& began to memorize *The Message*;
broken glass everywhere.

i was a bad sleeper, wide awake
tape rolling, when down an alley
a little kid, maybe my age, ticking
to a boombox, is joined by Mr. Freeze
i'd later learn; white gloved & moon
walking, an umbrella gliding under acid
rain. magic on the cobble stone;
one minute & thirteen seconds worth
of Crazy Legs dazzling footwork
a Ken Swift windmill, steel mill
to make a working woman smile

& call a community together
to soul clap, to witness
young people inventing
on the spot, something
unseen prior. in that moment
Frosty Freeze flips a suicide
& resurrects, for the time being
legs popping like oil in a hot pan.
G-d damned! i'd back spin, the tape
a thousand times, more
on cardboard, wanting to make
a working woman smile, my mother
stop. *watch me now*
cuz i *don't know what*
we're running from
but i'll come to know
it's just begun

brothers

Phife: *you on point Tip* / Q-Tip: *all the time Phife*
Check the Rhime, A Tribe Called Quest

Phife & Tip seemed like brothers.
gave brothers a routine, a way

to latch key in front of Yo!
i was the Abstract, the distant.

you were the 5-footer, not even
tho. Phife, the always little brother

bother. back & forth on the blvd.
of Linden or Shermer. trading rhymes

jabs, teaching ourselves to be men
boys. east coast stomping around

the planet rock, the far away galaxy
of the suburbs. low end appeared

in the record city bin: a '91 jazz
-simmered schoolyard shit talk
bar-mitzvah manual from Queens.
the first time we'd stop fighting

& treat one another like brothers
Kings. a phantom microphone

in our balled fists, an imaginary
ave filled with heads, brothers

bouncing to our speech, back
& forth on the rooftop, forever

or at least 'til moms got home
or 'til some higher power called us

                there   Rest in Power Phife
                                                         3/12/16

ode to the clown prince

for Biz Markie

boogers & vapors.
the odd long islander
from new jerusalem.
big brother of the native
tongues. who let hip-hop
be weird & hilarious
who let/lead a youth culture
of hard knocks keep a schoolyard crush
& expand the possibility of what
a generation could feel. he couldn't
sing but sang from the gut
a blues with such great longing
we cried from laughing & sung
too & surprised ourselves
of what we might become. we grew
with each note, each record. party
-rockin clown prince of the people
in a powdered wig & gold rope.
an alchemist mixing the improbable
improv-able, in-the-moment entertainer.
improving the sound of the reagan ridden
80s when the faces of a generation crack rocked
& mean mugged. he cracked us up.
nobody beats the Biz, even the Biz
-ness said sampling is taking
& that is only acceptable
in the empire. now the record
companies are failing
& scrambling & sampling's considered
high art, post-modern pastiche.
dissertated at all the museums.
later for Gilbert O'Sullivan
i need a haircut, too. a master
of the technique & techniques
& ceremonies. controller of the needle
& the 45. jack-of-all-trades, beloved
court jester telling the king(s)
where they could sit & spin

knowledge is king / Queen

moms threw a surprise party
for me at my pop's restaurant
a few months before he closed
the doors forever. they were
split for years, but she said
i should always be cool
with him. i knew a surprise
was coming. no one could keep
a secret. it all spilled in the kitchen
at some point.
my homies held menus to hide
their faces like horrible PIs. all guys
i hooped with. moms the only
female. two sons & all the men
at her; dudes trying to holler, bill
collectors trying to holler, police
& pops hollering. she held a quiet
space in her head somewhere
must've practiced a meditative
art not to go mad.

(& isn't that what all women do
to deal with the idiocy of male-dumb)

Matt Wenska got me a CD,
the first i ever had. Kool Moe Dee's third
record, *Knowledge is King.* i already
got the tape of course, a bootleg
off Maxell St. i'd play the shit out it
before basketball practice, especially
i go to work. i was literal like that
& not great at anything unless
i worked. moms taught me that
just like a doctor but paid dumb less.

CD's came wrapped in cardboard
the size of a forearm. it stayed propped
in my room, a make-due mini-poster
i was too poor to play. Kool Moe Dee

stared at me in all Black leather.
the universe hovering behind
his shaded eyes like everything
might open if i kept my fist
balled around an idea or pen
if i wouldn't give up.

               i knew that
we were in some kind of war

& i knew which side we were on:
the side of longing & desire
of want & the necessity
of invention, of knowing
more than the other side.

moms & Kool Moe Dee taught me
that, stylin in '89. droppin gems
i wasn't able to open yet.

molemen beat tapes

were copped from Gramophone.
cassettes jammed into a factory-
issued stereo deck of the hoopty
i rolled around in. a bucket. bass
and drum looped with some string
sample, fixed. a sliver of perfect
adjusted. the scrapes of something
reconstituted. there was so much
space to fill. an invitation to utter.
Iqra- Allah said to the prophet
Muhammad (peace be upon Him).
a- to b-side and around again. a circle
a cipher. i'd drive down and back
in my mom's Dodge for the latest
volumes of sound. i'd stutter
and stop and begin again. lonesome
and on fire. none. no one i knew
rapped. i'd recite alone on Clark St.
free, styling, shaping, my voice
a sapling, hatchling, rapping
my life, emerging in the dark
of an empty car.

there was a time when hip-hop felt like a secret
society of wizards and wordsmiths. magicians
meant to find you or that you were meant to find
like rappers i listened to and memorized in history
class talked specifically to me, for me.

& sometimes
you'd see a kid whisper to himself
in the corner of a bus seat & you
asked if he rhymed & traded a poem
a verse like a fur pelt/trapping.
some gold or food. this sustenance.
you didn't have to ride solo anymore.

Jonathan was the first kid i met who rapped. he was Black
from a prep school, wore ski goggles on top his head & listened
to Wu-Tang which meant he was always rhyming about science
and chess. his pops made him read Sun Tzu. his mans was Omega
a fat Puerto Rican who wrote graffiti and smoked bidis.

& they'd have friends
& the backseat would swell
& the word got passed/scooped like a ball
on the playground. you'd juggle however long
your mind could double Dutch. sometimes you'd take
what you were given/lift off like a trampoline
rocket launch. sometimes you'd trip & scrape
your knees. tongue-tied, not quick. words stuck
on loop, like like words, stuck, like that. but break
thru, mind, knife sharp, mind darts
polished & gleaming we'd ride
for the sake of rhyming. take the long way
home or wherever the fuck we were going
cruise down Lake Shore & back, blasting
blazing. polishing these gems.
trying to get our mind right.

Overleaf: Bop Shop by Langston Allston

The Bop Shop

i was there when liquid kitty used to be The Bop Shop — J.U.I.C.E.

jazz embraced its son.
old heads in Kangols
recognize the snot-nosed
foul-mouthed motherfuckers
in over-sized denim. a Tuesday
work night to put in work.
when a freestyle was off the dome
in the tradition of they city's
great improvisers; Phil Cochran & Viola Spolin.

glasses sweat like the crowd
gathered in layers before the band
stand; hoodied monks, strong heads
nod in approval, a ritual to keep
the crowd moving. young bucks might
fuck up which meant heads would stop
& you could get stomped but homeboy
could return next week after practice.
rap's gymnastics, kids flipping in empty lots
on a mattress, an art & kung-fu dance.
when emcees were swordsmen
who carried words in a velvet case
& polished brass when they'd get to the bar.
all day long, a generation mumbling
to themselves over the rumble of L trains.
mad men superheroes who hold down day
jobs & emerge in the night with bombastic
nome-de-plumes: *Shadow Master, Eyespy
Longshot, J.U.I.C.E, Ang 13, Prime, Capital D.*

Tuesday's a proving ground, wordshop
work shop, masterclass, shogun swap meet
spot to see new poets from sides of the city
the city didn't want you to see.

we were out there, on Division
catching wreck & getting open.

the cactus album as a mirror / the cactus album as crystal ball

high-top fade and graphix.
big nose dancing hip-house
praise   the percolator
                    percolating.
the first time i see a version of me. corny
but present. stepping thru the am
stepping thru a step line.
white as exception. acceptation:
a baron on fertile land, a history
i couldn't know cuz
all the white lies buried
but
                         Search
was Nice, Pete & i didn't know
the difference between them
& me or other white folk.
i didn't know other white folk
who wanted to be in the mix
who wanted to be something
other than white so bad.

this was
a way to be an ally or something
something other
                   than   every white person
i ever heard of.
i hadn't heard of KMD:
Subroc & Zev Love X.
the Bomb Squad co-sign
meant everything. something
other than a history
of white take over
before Jay-Z. the Beastie
Boys felt schtick-y Gilbert G-dfrey, i was
no joke. i was dead
serious & stupid
& stupid fresh.

i never heard of jump blues;
Robert Johnson, Muddy Waters.
i didn't know Vanilla.
i didn't know the concerts
would swell with white mouths
comfortable with the *n-word*.
i didn't know the neighborhood
would swell with white families
cool with deleting. i was white   out
unaware of the forces i announced
unaware of the forces /faces   yet to come

The Free Space/Time Style of Black Wholes
Juice Aleem

Black Whole Freestyles

A black hole, in science, is described as being a section of Space/Time that contains so much gravity that nothing, not even light, can escape it. Everything that passes close enough by is drawn into the black hole by its gravitational pull.

Freestyle, as far as Rap goes, can be described as an impromptu rhyme made up on the spot from the mind of the MC to either an a cappella or previously unused beat.

Science also tells us the black "hole" is anything but, the amount of density within a black hole leads me to call them the same as the title of a compilation from the Big Dada Records label by the name of *Black Whole Styles*.

Over the years, Freestyle has been defined and redefined: From many of the east-coast tri-state originators of hip-hop describing a freestyle as a written rhyme that hasn't been heard before or that verse being spat on a new beat. To the previous meanings of the word 'Freestyle,' in pretty much every human endeavor has seen it being a mostly or totally made up on the spot execution of that particular genre or skill. From Freestyle skiing to freestyle fighting. There is a known form and an unknown form, the freestyle allows the two to blend with up to the time malleability.

A Black Whole is said to contain all the information of everything that has previously been drawn into its gravity well. This means every single atom of mass that has passed into the Black Whole is still inside. Every particle, every burst of radiation, is still there in the form of data. The inside of a Black Whole is filled with the most dense body of information. The density of this information, increases the gravitational pull and size of the Black Whole.

Black (W)holes are observed to be born of old stars collapsing in on themselves.

Over the years, the body, likeness, culture and expressions of African peoples have not always been in their own control. In the diaspora this has been represented through chattel slavery, European colonialism, medical apartheid, state legalized brutality, the legal and prison system, rape, torture, anti-African laws and education. So, for a diasporic African to gain control of themselves and their culture, in the worlds of Mentos, The Blues, Soca, Ska, Rocksteady, Reggae, Dancehall, hip-hop, Reggaetton, Baile Funk, Drill or Grime is socially a big thing. And any control of Intellectual Property, economics and the body itself makes a person not simply black but Black. For those who have lost the direct knowledge of their family histories, ethnicities and names, the terminology known as "Black" is a response, an answer to the question of "where do you come from?" To be lacking the original cultural heritage but to know inside that there is more information through feeling, intent and DNA Memory, is to be aware of one's own gravity but not fully in control of what the self draws in. For black to be Black it must have a reason to have a capital letter the same way Asian, European, Parisian, Japanese, English, Kenyan and African have a capital letter. The reason for "Black" being the name, descriptor, history, resistance and verb is that it was chosen by the Black mass themselves. The vast majority of the world have a recognized ethnicity or culture to claim, so they do not need to be defined by the depth of color in their skin. Black is not simply a colour, it is a collective and individual response. Black is a politik. Black is a culture. Black is not a monolith. Noble Drew Ali explained that black was death, Sun Ra told us Blackness could beat death.

Socially, Black is a big thing. For black to be Black, it must be Whole. The technology of Black is survival. Black is me!

Most modern scientists would contend that the concepts of black holes were put forth in the 18ᵗʰ Century. The real work of them starting to be understood happened in the 20ᵗʰ Century with an abundance of papers on the phenomena occurring during the 1950s and 60s. Black holes are observed to be born of old stars collapsing in on themselves.

An Astro Black overstanding of the universe has us pondering Indigenous creation myths and if the Dogon had already seen/heard of Black Wholes as the Egg of Amma or if Kemet had already put forth the concept through the tales of Amun/Atum/Atom/Adam. Since many naturally occurring circumstances have been observed and noted by the ancients as part of their folk and spiritual lore it can be difficult to know where and when the hard science comes in. A host of cultures worldwide have designed their folk-lore around the making of calendars, times and the movements of stellar objects — or vice-versa.

Those who freestyle to a high level have been known to be "In the Zone" or even to "Black Out". This is when the skillful find those special pockets of space/time, rhythm, tone, meaning and intensity where they have navigated a new path through the Universe. Word, Sound & Power coalesce from the mind of the MC to take all listeners/feelers to new places. The great MC makes a new calendar by initiating a new creation-myth.

The secret to freestyling is working on the creation of thought and it being expressed from your cerebral cortex, to the air in your lungs, to your larynx, pharynx, to your tongue to form a word via whatever consonants and

vowels you're working with as well as having a sense of style, cadence, and rhythm.
— Myka Nine

So where is the thought before it enters or exists in the brain, and though it is an old debate: how close/far are mind and brain from one another?

Modern, Western scientists tend to remove the possibility of us controlling black holes and being able to shift objects to other parts of the Universe through them. The navigation of a black hole would take an immense amount of statistics in the fields of physics, engineering and quantum physics in particular. Not only that but in a craft it would take piloting of the highest levels at the speed of light and near light-speeds.

In Speculative Science-Fiction though, we find numerous examples of what are known as wormholes taking people through time and space. In this thinking, humans can go through black holes and exit them as wormholes or simply go through wormholes from one end of the universe to another by folding the Space/Time matrix. Science-Fiction often becomes Science-Fact. One of the people that helped popularize the idea of wormholes was a little known scientist by the name of Albert Einstein, with what was called the Einstein-Rosen Bridge.

Dark Energy and Dark Matter are posited to make up around 90% of the known (and unknown) Universe. Dark Energy balances gravity, and both sides cannot be 'seen' without observing other outside phenomena. Dark Matter does not react to stimulus in ways that modern orthodox science can measure.

> The Neutron Star
> Too heavy for you to spar
> Equations to every sum is within the Black Sun
> Light can't escape its fate
> So here we come
> — New Flesh For Old, "Adoration of Kings"

The MC, through either control of Mind/Energy and riding of Mass and Gravity is that Great Information Super-Highway. The Freestyle MC is a scientist who knows the Einstein-Rosen Bridge can carry them sumwhere over the rainbow. Using The Mind as an antenna to tune in and grab universal information. The MC who blacks out becomes a living manifestation of Black Whole styles. Moving from the idea/ energy that draws everything into a super-dense mass and enabling themselves to travel. A folding of the Time/Space map with it being re-opened in new positions. This travel can be a solitary thing but the greats manage to bring in the audience and make them co-pilots to destinations unknown.

Myka Nine by B+

Envision the density of information contained within an MC: the storyteller, folk-hero, wordsmith, duelist, lover, comedian, social scientist, activist, historian, porno star, musician, magician, artist, philosopher, lyrical genealogist, criminologist, hustler, rebel and entertainer in one body.

Think on the MC who can tap into this on command and in the moment, in The Zone.

Dark Matter/Energy, are so-called due their unknown qualities. Science knows it is out there but not exactly the How or Why of it.

The true Freestyler is in touch with the known and unknown of Space/Time and is sumhow able to defeat their own Gravity to bring the light through themselves, magnified, back into the physical reality as vibrational waves called R.A.P. On the spot Dark Energy/Matter manipulation. Rhythmic wordholes bringing us from one unsafe black body to another Black Whole reality.

Light is provided by sparks of energy
By the mind that travels in rhyme form
Giving sight to the blind

The dumb are mostly intrigued by the drum
— Masta Killa, from Wu-Tang Clan's "Triumph"

As time is measured by the motion of bodies such as The Sun, Moons and Stars, black holes are to a greater degree outside the realm of normal Time. Inside a black hole the flow of time works differently depending on how far into the hole a body has gone.

There are moments that forever remain outside of time due to the need for a person to have physically been there to understand how things went down. Any recording is a copy, and clones are weaker than the original. These are those moments of pure freestyle magic where an MC takes themselves and listeners to new worlds, weaving centuries into seconds, changing timelines from black holes to Black Wholes.

Do you realize that if you fall into a black hole, you will see the entire future of the Universe unfold in front of you in a matter of moments, and you will emerge into another space-time created by the singularity of the black hole you just fell into?
— Neil deGrasse Tyson

The MC in whatever genre who makes these possibilities a reality is to be applauded. There's a lot more going on than what on the surface might seem like a few nursery rhymes. This is an important addition to human history in the form of live interactive documentation. These special moments where empty spaces are made into liquid light shows of super-dense information. The known and unknown colliding and refracting faster than the speed of light. The speed of darkness can only be fathomed by the mind that was already there before the light approached. It's this type of mind that makes all kinds of things happen. A Sun or sum other body that implodes on itself but brings in all around it bending space-time to its will. Holding on to past realities of dark bodies while becoming Whole new bodies of shining Blackness. Both external and internal melanin hold a few of these keys to creation. Through this process, the freestyling MC makes the socially inert Dark Matter, mentally active in their audience. This would be outside of your normal Time.

MCs are of course a particular bunch. With a world of humans out there who now claim to be MCs it might be that many can lock into this form of design/ making. Not only artists whose brains already work in different patterns but all humans who look at words in different ways.

A cadre of free-flowing free-associating free minds using and utilizing their Black Whole Free Styles.

I made an Einstein-Rosen bridge out of a smoken spliff And unrequited love notes, that I wrote when I was a hopeless kid My road wasn't paved with golden bricks It was paved by the decaying bones of slaves in rows who didn't know to quit
— Tabs, "The Center of A Black Hole"

Chopping Neoliberalism, Screwing the Industry: DJ Screw, the Dirty South, and the Temporal Politics of Resistance
Aram Sinnreich and Samantha Dols

Introduction

DJ Screw, born Robert Earl Davis, died too young to see the music that he invented (and to which he gave his name) become the globally celebrated musical genre it is today. Chopped and screwed music, which began as a local Houston hip-hop subculture, distributed physically via mixtapes at parties and local brick-and-mortar retail establishments, has now become a widely recognized genre embraced and emulated by pop stars and promoted by major record labels. While DJ Screw and his creative partners in Houston's Screwed Up Click are now far more widely known than they were before his death at the turn of the century, their legacy has a monodimensional and even pejorative aspect to it — one in which the music has become a sonic marker of drug abuse, and a symbol of the degradation and decadence of the "Dirty South." In this article, we aim to broaden Screw's legacy, and to valorize the politically resistant aspects of chopped and screwed music, by illuminating the articulation between hip-hop as a political art form and the rise of the "slow media" as a global counterhegemonic movement.

Hip-Hop as Resistance

From the earliest years of its emergence out of the Bronx and onto the world stage, the one thing that hip-hop's most ardent supporters and most vitriolic detractors have typically agreed upon is that it is fundamentally political. Especially during its first two decades or so, before it became the lingua franca of global commercial youth culture, hip-hop was widely understood as an organic and authentic expression of African American resistance to white hegemony.

This audible resistance took on very different valences depending on the vantage point of the listener. White audiences and critics frequently focused on the music's palpable anger, interpreting it as an expression of reflexive and retributive rage against a society built on racist exploitation. In an infamous 1990 cover story for

Newsweek, for instance, editor Jerry Adler described hip-hop as "primarily a working-class and underclass phenomenon" that lacked the capacity to inspire a "sensible discussion" about politics, because it never rose above the level of "homeboys talking trash."[1] The opposite polarity was staked out in 1989 by Public Enemy frontman Chuck D, who credited hip-hop as nothing less than an alternative news media platform, the "invisible TV station that black America never had", a perspective that by 1997 he had crystalized into the now-canonical "I call Rap the Black CNN."[2]

Over the following decade, scholarly treatments of hip-hop emerged across a range of fields, many of them bolstering and expanding on Chuck D's claims for the art form by documenting and celebrating its resistant potential. Not only was hip-hop a vector for black-centered news and perspective, they argued, it was a platform for coordinated political resistance and deliberation;[3] a model for seizing the means of production through conspicuous mastery and *détournement* of media technology;[4] and a redistributive act of appropriation that modeled black entrepreneurship and celebrated economic independence.[5]

Claims for hip-hop's resistant potential, both in the U.S. and around the world, are still central to the scholarly discussion of the art form.[6] Yet this narrative continues to have its detractors, and just as arguments in favor have become more nuanced and convoluted through the years, so have the arguments against. In his pan of Thomas Chatterton Williams' book *Losing My Cool*, for instance, Richard Beck inveighs against the premise that "hip-hop is fundamentally a mindset . . . that just happened to get into the world as a set of sonic practices."[7] Instead, he argues, we must understand that "hip-hop is a music before it is a sociological lens, an urban newscast . . . or anything else." It's not that Beck rejects the premise that hip-hop is a powerful cultural and political force; it's just that he considers the power to be rooted in aesthetics, rather than vice versa. And even among those scholars and critics who do see hip-hop as politically causative, many reject blanket claims for its emancipatory potential, arguing, for instance, that it may serve to further hegemonic ideologies including patriarchy,[8] heteronormativity,[9] and American empire.[10]

While the debate over hip-hop's resistant capacity, writ large, continues to churn, it is important to remember that DJ Screw wasn't merely a hip-hop artist. He was, first and foremost, a mixtape producer, and that unique subgenre of hip-hop carries its own political implications. Although mixtapes have been a widely practiced folk art form, across a broad range of subcultures and musical styles, since cheap and accessible microcassette recording technology first emerged in the 1970s, they have also been a canonical aspect of hip-hop culture since it first emerged, at roughly the same time.

Initially, mixtapes were integral to hip-hop because there were no commercial distribution platforms for rap music recordings. This was due in part to the ambiguous legality of sampling at the time, but also attributable to racist and Eurocentric attitudes within the music industry, which devalued music perceived to be a localized, ghettoized, Afrocentric phenomenon — what Adler would later call "homeboys talking trash."[11] Once the commercial potential of the genre became clear in the late 1980s and 1990s, the role of mixtapes shifted. They became an alternate distribution network — one where the relative lack of copyright policing meant that greater artistic liberties could lead to greater aesthetic innovation than work circulated within the highly consolidated commercial recording, distribution, and broadcasting sectors,[12] and where free, discounted, and even industry-subsidized mixes could be used as a shadow promotional vehicle, providing both a test market and a patina of street authenticity for soon-to-be commercial tracks and acts.[13]

Not only were the mixtape networks that emerged in the 1990s structural alternatives to commercial distribution and marketing platforms, they were also *ethical* alternatives. While major record labels, retail chains, and radio and television networks were national or international in scope, and therefore focused on music with the broadest possible audience, mixtape networks were rooted in local social and cultural institutions, distributed in barber shops, strip clubs, and grocery stores strung together in ad hoc regional networks, and therefore committed to local, primarily Southern, and emphatically African American styles and aesthetics.

Collectively, these networks and regions are often referred to as the "Dirty South" or, more politely, the "Third Coast."[14] Yet even these regionalized designations bely the highly localized nature of mixtape hip-hop in this era. DJ Screw wasn't merely Southern, he was from Houston, which gained the local sobriquet "Screwston" in the mid-2000s, based entirely on the popularity and cultural relevance of the subgenre he invented and gave his name to.[15] In other words, chopped and screwed music isn't some idiosyncratic local delicacy, too weird to make it in the mainstream music industry; as Wilkins argues, it is *"the central component* of Houston's hip-hop identity"[16] (emphasis added), and therefore a "source of empowerment"[17] in which "space becomes a way that subjugated peoples can resist vulnerability."[18]

In short, even aside from the aesthetic particularities of the genre he helped to invent, DJ Screw was an avatar of resistance to commercialism, to global cultural homogenization, and to white hegemony. By distributing aesthetically localized recordings of dubious legality via regional networks built by black entrepreneurs, his mixtape series (titled "The Screwtapes") exemplified some of the core principles of African American autonomy, codified in Kwanzaa tenets such as *Ujima* (collective work and responsibility), *Ujamaa* (cooperative economics), and *Kuumba* (creativity).

DJ Screw and Purple Drank

Perhaps unsurprisingly, much of the academic scholarship on DJ Screw focuses on the relationship between the chopped and screwed genre and drug use, specifically "purple drank," a fusion of cold medication (containing promethazine and codeine) and sweet soda. To be fair, this association is valid for several reasons. DJ Screw himself spoke candidly of his experimentation with purple drank, infusing advocacy for, and tales about, the drug into his mixtapes. For example, his song "Sipping Codeine" with Big Moe includes the lines: "I sip codeine/It makes a southside playa lean... And I'm playa made/Keeps a tight ball fade, sippin' syrup in the shade." And "Barre Baby," another Big Moe collaboration, includes the lyrics "now I'm the codeine fiend" and "now I got the whole world sipping drank with me." These lyrics perpetuated a certain brand — a creative ethos that allied "sizzurp" with the Screwed Up Click; "lean" with the idiosyncratic quality of the music's sonic deceleration. And sadly but also unsurprisingly, the lyrics anticipated the demise of DJ Screw himself, who overdosed on codeine in November 2000 and died at the age of 29.

Fans and scholars alike have long argued that screw music is manipulated to emulate, induce, and/or promote the psychobiological state of purple drank intoxication[19] — one characterized as slow, mellow, and easy. Agnich et al.,[20] credit DJ Screw for popularizing purple drank but expose patterns of its use beyond the hip-hop scene in Houston, arguing that the drug is a potential problem for urban male youth of all racial backgrounds and all regions, as well as individuals who identify as part of the LGBT community. Hart et al.,[21] examine the empirical correlation between musical preferences and experimentation with purple drank, showing that those who prefer rap/hip-hop music and rock/alternative have the highest risk for use. And while acknowledging the "ingenious and unparalleled art form" conceived by DJ Screw, Peters et al., posit that codeine addiction has spread with the diffusion of the chopped and screwed genre, and conclude that the "modeled messages of reckless CPHCS use found in screw music...outweigh its contributions to society."[22]

While these publications raise legitimate concerns about drug abuse, they also serve the ideological function of reducing chopped and screwed music — and DJ Screw's oeuvre in particular — to the status of pro-drug propaganda, overlooking and diminishing the value of his aesthetic and subcultural contributions.

At a fundamental level, the academic discussion of drug use tends to be inherently pejorative and limited. In most cases, the etic perspective assumed about drug culture by social researchers leaves a considerable distance between the observer and subject. This is problematic in several ways. Firstly, it can be difficult to study drug use either phenomenologically or semiotically; the mind-altering effects elicited by purple drank, for example, will not be felt by an onlooker, nor will its cultural significance be fully appreciated as long as drug use is treated as a social ill or personal failing *a priori*.

More importantly, perhaps, this pathologizing frame, applied to chopped and screwed music and the broader subculture it signifies, perpetuates a historical cycle of outsiders (who are typically white) delegitimizing artistry and achievement within marginalized communities and undermining the recognition of the art form as a mechanism of social autonomy. Thus, we view this chapter in part as a scholarly intervention, aiming not only to shed additional light on the aesthetic and cultural legacy of an influential musician, but also in order to recuperate the resistant aspects of his music and to articulate it with broader media movements taking place within other subcultures around the globe.

The Rise of Slow Media

In recent years, even as the chopped and screwed music genre has grown beyond its Houston origins, another, seemingly unrelated cultural trope has gained currency across a range of platforms and locales: the concept of "slow media." Although it is relatively new, it has already been analyzed and discussed in a diversity of ways: as a social movement,[23] a subculture,[24] and a luxury commodity that both requires and signifies wealth and social power.[25] Evolving from the slow food movement, which began as an act of resistance against fast food institutions and their role as "symptoms of incipient globalization,"[26] the slow media movement serves as parallel form of resistance against consumerist hegemony. It aims to promote alternative methods for engaging with media, in order to contribute to a more satisfying and sustainable global ecosystem.[27] As another tactic of defense "against the universal folly of 'the fast life',"[28] slow media can be understood as a deliberate subversion of the industrially regulated pace of media production and reception.[29] Slow media writ large includes specific subgenres including slow TV, slow storytelling, slow web, slow news, slow music, slow journalism, and more; the movement is still evolving and innovating. Though perhaps as innocuous on the surface as "detox" health fads, the slow media movement is a vector for powerful critique against not only concentrated media industries but the broader apparatus of industrial capitalism that they serve, inviting audiences to resist what Horkheimer and Adorno called "the consolidation of temporal consciousness,"[30] and what Honore refers to as our contemporary "roadrunner culture."[31]

Slow media operate as a mechanism of critique and resistance in several ways. First, at its most rudimentary level, the slow media movement challenges the widely perceived trend toward sensory and information overload. People are increasingly exposed to a daily deluge of data, accessed through computers, phones, television, and any number of other channels, and the increasing social centrality of these data makes it increasingly difficult to slow down or "unplug," to trust that something will be gained, not lost, by quieting the noise.[32] By defining criteria for "good" media[33] and establishing parameters for consumption, the slow movement promotes "knowledge not information"[34] and encourages people to reconsider the quantity and pace, as well as the quality, of the content they consume.

Second, the slow movement builds on precepts of intentionality and deliberation. Within the media landscape, pursuing slowness allows individuals to engage in practices of "reflection and consciousness" and promotes a "thoughtful process"[35] of deliberation regarding what and what not to consume. The priority is having timely and present engagement, rather than reacting to every real-time update or request and perpetuating a false sense of urgency. Echoing Benjamin's idea that in a society of oppression, "the 'state of emergency' in which we live is not the exception but the rule,"[36] the aim with slowness is for audiences to break free from the hegemonic tempo of programming and communications, and to engage with the media on their own terms.

Third, the slow movement emphasizes leisure, community, and the practice of monotasking,[37] or doing one thing at a time rather than many. In an age when distractedness and fragmentation are normative, advocates argue that "slow ideals restore a sense of community and conviviality...which sustain political resistance."[38] The movement seeks to intervene at both the psychological and social scales, empowering individuals and communities through practices like "mindful emailing" and "contemplative computing."[39] Through the process of slowing down, the movement holds, people can more holistically incorporate playfulness and joy into their lives. By reprioritizing relaxation, and opting to do nothing, "living" transforms from a race wherein time is linear and finite into something real, raw, and breathing.

Finally, the slow movement highlights and challenges the ways in which the pace of media consumption serves as an instrument of hegemony. Individuality, competitiveness, achievement, wealth — all of these values are central to the overarching image of success in western culture. Yet, these values serve primarily to generate profit for the corporate sector and to normalize the neoliberal ideologies that run much of the developed world. Fast-paced media consumption is presented in advertisements and dominant cultural narratives as a competitive edge, and therefore as a mandate to succeed: to keep up and stay up-to-date, we must follow the temporal standard or risk "falling behind" and becoming valueless. But, for voices in the slow movement, another option exists. People can defy the pervasive expectations or standards of time and decide to *slow down*; doing so is a political, ethical choice that emphasizes autonomy and community over competition and conformity. Slowness, in other words, embodies values that are inherently resistant to, and critical of, neoliberalism — it is communal,[40] collaborative,[41] and "about allowing room for others and otherness."[42]

In light of this growing global subculture, we believe that the work and legacy of DJ Screw must be reinvestigated and argue that he should be understood as not only an example of resistance through hip-hop, but also as an early and influential avatar of the slow media movement.

DJ Screw: Slow Media Avatar

Because it originated in the Dirty South and not in Europe, or within online hipster culture, chopped and screwed music isn't typically seen as a part of the slow media movement. Yet if we examine DJ Screw's oeuvre in its entirety — including his musical choices, business practices, lyrical contributions, and political stance — it clearly reflects the core values of the movement and can even be seen as an early and influential exemplar of its principles.

First, resisting sensory and information overload. On the face of it, the most obvious connection between DJ Screw and the slow media movement lies in the music itself.

Overleaf: Screwed Up Records & Tapes by Peter Beste

In contrast to the songs that characterized mainstream "urban" musical culture at the end of the 20th Century, which tended to hover in the range of 100 beats per minute (BPM), Screw's tempos were manipulated to 60-70 BPM.[43] He also incorporated other sonic features that challenged listeners' sense of regulated temporality, such as repeating vocal phrases, glitches and disruptions to the flow of the music, and phasing (layering two versions of a single source, slightly out of synch), creating an almost cosmic aural experience — vast, hypnotic, and echoey. Screw used slowness as a mechanism to contest the aesthetic standards and temporal dictates of the music industry. Rather than conforming to the formulaic expectations of hip-hop, e.g., protocol regarding tempo, vocal pitch, tonality, song form and length, Screw carved out a space and time of his own. Using the materials distributed by the global recording industry, in the service of what de Certeau would call bricolage, or "making do,"[44] he created an environment that *he* controlled, tailored to the local, subcultural needs and values of Screwston.

Second, intentionality and deliberation. DJ Screw practiced intentionality in several dimensions of his music making. As discussed above, he was intentional with his artistic method and creative output. Yet, he was also intentional in his professional and cultural relationships, prioritizing localism, communalism, and the upkeep of his Screwed Up Click over traditional competitive and egoistic models of success in the music industry. In the words of SUC member Big Hawk, "[Screw would] give you the shirt off his back ... as our careers were blossoming, he never wanted any credit." Screw also provided support and mentorship to his local community in other ways. As his mother remembered, "he had guys calling him from prison...he would send them money...he'd say 'Mom, they just want to talk.'" And when aspiring rappers approached him on the street, Screw always listened, even going so far as to give out his personal phone number, offering the possibility of professional assistance.[45] He began his mixtape series by making "personals," or specialized tapes for his closest friends, complete with requested songs and shoutouts. Finally, Screw was intentional in his localism, rooting both his aesthetic and his ethic in his neighborhood. His music deliberately reflected and constructed a sense of place, creating a sonic identity that persists today, two decades after his death. Just as the initial slow food movement revolved around the culture of local communities, on reveling in the "conviviality of sharing locally produced seasonal food and wine,"[46] chopped and screwed both emerged from *and* defined Houston — its weather, its *terroir*, its pace of life.

Third, valorizing leisure and community. Communal play was central to DJ Screw's ethic. These values are reflected in the structure of his Screwed Up Click, a collective comprised of more than a dozen rappers and friends from the neighborhoods of Houston's South side, who also served as a business cooperative for the music.[47] When record labels tried to get Screw to sign as a solo act, he refused; the contract would need to include the entire collective or none of them.[48] Additionally, much of the music from the Click evoked leisure through imagery and sound, with stories about "ballin', hanging out with your buddies in H-town, [and] swangin' and bangin' (slowly driving while listening to music)."[49] These lyrics, and the ethics they embrace, amount to far more than "homeboys talking trash." We argue they can best be understood as a form of "work refusal"[50] — a longstanding tactic of labor to resist the dictates of capital and to carve out a space of agency within hegemonic systems. Work refusal has been interpreted and promoted through subcultural art forms in the past; Grindon, for example, makes similar claims for Dada and Surrealism.[51] Even Screw's use and celebration of purple drank can be understood through this lens; as both anarchists[52] and criminologists[53] have long argued, drug use itself can be understood as a tactic of work refusal.

Fourth, defying societal norms. The principles of labor upheld by DJ Screw and the Screwed Up Click presented a contrast to the industry standards of the time. Though subtle, Screw offered a counterbalance to the mainstream, celebrity-focused, automated music machine of the "culture industry", in which "the mechanically differentiated products prove to be all alike in the end."[54] Screw modeled something different, something new, both in process and in product; he created a slow counterculture by investing expressively in people, place, and sound.

For the Screwed Up Click and its followers, "choosing to get lost in slow music felt like a way of dissociating from having so much stimulus, with music and the Internet, so much input to manage."[55] Even before the popularization of the Internet, Screw's slowness could be seen as a form of retreat, a way to resist the potential that information or demands might grow overwhelming, and instead curate an artistic process that worked for him and his community. In this way, he was a pioneer of the "slow music" philosophy, a subset of the broader slow media movement, which "advocates a cultural shift towards slowing down life's pace & connecting more meaningfully with others, our surroundings and ourselves."[56]

Conclusion

As we have argued in this chapter, DJ Screw, the Screwed Up Click, and the chopped and screwed music they helped to popularize should be understood and remembered as fundamentally resistant, combining the black self-empowerment of hip-hop and localism of mixtape culture with the counterhegemonic capacity of the slow media movement to produce a locally-rooted but globally-recognizable sound of rebellion against neoliberal ideology.

However, we do acknowledge several potential limitations to these claims. Firstly, although we have identified the celebration of purple drank as a symbol of work refusal and therefore of community empowerment, we also acknowledge that opioid abuse is economically and culturally devastating on a global level, and that it exacerbates existing challenges and vulnerabilities for low-income communities of color such as Screwston.[57] Of course, the fact that Screw himself died from opioid abuse adds an extra dimension of tragic irony to these claims. Yet we cannot allow the pathologization of drug use to dominate the discussion of his legacy to the exclusion of other, more celebratory and emancipatory readings.

Second, we acknowledge that our claims for chopped and screwed music become more complex when considering its recent commercial resurgence. Established hip-hop artists are now producing screw music, and deejays are emulating the techniques and sonic attributes in tracks reminiscent of the Screwed Up Crew. While some of these are explicit in their homage to the roots of the genre, such as Drake's "November 18th", we speculate that they do not *necessarily* embody or promote the foundational values and counterhegemonic practices of DJ Screw.

Rather, the screw music revival — and the slow media movement writ large — must be understood through the lens of what Sharma[58] calls "power-chronography." She views time as multiple and relational, rather than fixed and static, and argues that the negotiation of time is a social and political process, influenced by labor relations and other vectors of power and status.

While acknowledging the potentially empowering dimensions of slowness, Sharma posits that not everyone has the economic power to benefit from it — for instance, comparing the divergent temporalities of frequent business travelers (for whom slowness is relaxation) and taxi drivers (for whom slowness is precarity). This perspective helps to shed light on the newer politics of new chopped and screwed music. An artist like Drake, whose status in the hip-hop firmament is cemented, has the luxury of producing screw music from his position of wealth and power; he has the freedom to repurpose the musical tropes, and to adopt the associated revolutionary stance, without substantial financial or reputational risk. But an emerging artist, say from a poor neighborhood in Texas, might not have the same luxury to slow down just yet — first, if he desires to emulate Drake's success, he needs to hustle, establish credibility, make money and touch fame. Then, once his reputation holds, might he be able to afford a slowdown. Thus, chopped and screwed music, when appropriated into commercial codes and practices, becomes an engine of neoliberalism, exacerbating the divide between haves and have-nots by creating diametrically opposite financial incentives to people who occupy different positional roles within the industry.

In this way, the evolution of chopped and screwed reveals an all-too-common path for grassroots innovation, especially within black culture. What began as a political act of resistance within a marginalized community is later seized and appropriated by the mainstream, subverting and depoliticizing its cultural origins. This is why it's so important to deemphasize the relationship between screw music and drug abuse, and instead to refocus on its articulations with the slow media movement. The former reinforces interpretive paradigms that naturalize and essentialize the subjugation of local, low income African American communities, while the latter clarifies DJ Screw's historical role as an organic intellectual, and an avatar of global resistance to neoliberalism. Ultimately, the sound of screw music may lose its resistant capacity altogether, but the act of chopping and screwing, and the valorization of localized temporalities, will continue to serve Screw's own aims, and to burnish his legacy.

DJ Screw's nephew at his headstone by Peter Beste

Notes

1. Adler, Foote, and Sawhill, "The Rap Attitude."

2. D, *Fight the Power: Rap, Race, and Reality.*

3. Martinez, "Popular Culture as Oppositional Culture: Rap as Resistance"; Stapleton, "From the Margins to Mainstream: The Political Power of Hip-Hop."

4. Rose, *Black Noise: Rap Music and Black Culture in Contemporary America.*

5. Smith, "Method in the Madness: Exploring the Boundaries of Identity in Hip-Hop Performativity."

6. Christopher, *Dead Precedents: How Hip-Hop Defines the Future*; Clark, *Hip-Hop in Africa: Prophets of the City and Dustyfoot Philosophers.*

7. Beck, "Express Yourself."

8. Rebollo-Gil and Moras, "Black Women and Black Men in Hip-Hop Music: Misogyny, Violence and the Negotiation of (White-Owned) Space."

9. Penney, "'We Don't Wear Tight Clothes': Gay Panic and Queer Style in Contemporary Hip-Hop."

10. Aidi, "The Grand (Hip-Hop) Chessboard: Race, Rap and Raison d'état."

11. Adler, Foote, and Sawhill, "The Rap Attitude."

12. Sinnreich, "Music, Copyright, and Technology: A Dialectic in Five Moments."

13. Sinnreich, *Mashed up: Music, Technology, and the Rise of Configurable Culture.*

14. Sarig, *Third Coast: OutKast, Timbaland, and How Hip-Hop Became a Southern Thing.*

15. Wilkins, "Screwston, TX: The Impact of Space, Place, and Cultural Identity on Music Making in Houston's Hip-Hop Scene."

16. Ibid., 188.

17. Ibid., 192.

18. Ibid., 193.

19. Peters Jr. et al., "Codeine Cough Syrup Use Among African-American Crack Cocaine Users"; Peters et al., "Codeine Cough Syrup Use among Sexually Active, African-American High School Youths: Why Southern Males Are Down to Have Sex."

20. Agnich et al., "Purple Drank Prevalence and Characteristics of Misusers of Codeine Cough Syrup Mixtures."

21. Hart et al., "'Me and My Drank:' Exploring the Relationship Between Musical Preferences and Purple Drank Experimentation."

22. Peters Jr. et al., "Codeine Cough Syrup Use Among African-American Crack Cocaine Users," 101.

23. Honore, *In Praise of Slowness: Challenging the Cult of Speed.*

24. Rauch, *Slow Media: Why Slow Is Satisfying, Sustainable, and Smart.*

25. Sharma, *In the Meantime: Temporality and Cultural Politics.*

26. Petrini, *Slow Food: The Case for Taste,* 8.

27. Rauch, *Slow Media: Why Slow Is Satisfying, Sustainable, and Smart.*

28. "The Slow Food Manifesto."

29. Parkins and Craig, *Slow Living.*

30. Horkheimer and Adorno, *Dialectic of Enlightenment,* 21.

31. Honore, *In Praise of Slowness: Challenging the Cult of Speed.*

32. Persson, "Attention Manipulation and Information Overload"; Thomas, Azmitia, and Whittaker, "Unplugged: Exploring the Costs and Benefits of Constant Connection."

33. David, "The Slow Media Manifesto and Its Impact on Different Countries, Cultures, and Disciplines."

34. Cheng, "The Slow Web."

35. David, "The Slow Media Manifesto and Its Impact on Different Countries, Cultures, and Disciplines," 111.

36. Benjamin, *Theses on the Philosophy of History.*

37. David, "The Slow Media Manifesto and Its Impact on Different Countries, Cultures, and Disciplines."

38. Berg and Seeber, *The Slow Professor: Challenging the Culture of Speed in the Academy.*

39. Rauch, *Slow Media: Why Slow Is Satisfying, Sustainable, and Smart.*

40. David, "The Slow Media Manifesto and Its Impact on Different Countries, Cultures, and Disciplines"; Rauch, *Slow Media: Why Slow Is Satisfying, Sustainable, and Smart.*

41. Petrini, *Slow Food: The Case for Taste; Honore, In Praise of Slowness: Challenging the Cult of Speed.*

42. Berg and Seeber, *The Slow Professor: Challenging the Culture of Speed in the Academy.*

43. Petrusich, "JAM NOTHIN' BUT THAT SCREW."

44. de Certeau, *The Practice of Everyday Life,* Volume 1, 29.

45. Hall, "The Slow Life and Fast Death of DJ Screw."

46. Le Masurier, "What Is Slow Journalism?"

47. "DJ Screw Photographs and Memorabilia."

48. Walker, "DJ Screw: A Fast Life In Slow Motion."

49. Hall, "The Slow Life and Fast Death of DJ Screw."

50. Cleaver, "Work Refusal and Self-Organisation."

51. Grindon, "Surrealism, Dada, and the Refusal of Work: Autonomy, Activism, and Social Participation in the Radical Avant-Garde."

52. Zerzan, "Anti-Work and the Struggle for Control."

53. Burrows, "Glue Sniffing: The Psychosocial Context."

54. Adorno and Horkheimer, "The Culture Industry: Enlightenment as Mass Deception."

55. Caramanica, "Seeping Out of Houston, Slowly."

56. "What Is Slow Music?"

57. James and Jordan, "The Opioid Crisis in Black Communities."

58. Sharma, "Temporality and Difference from the Agora to the Airport: Towards a Theory of Power-Chronography"; Sharma, "Critical Time"; Sharma, *In the Meantime: Temporality and Cultural Politics*.

Bibliography

Adler, Jerry, Jennifer Foote, and Ray Sawhill. "The Rap Attitude." *Newsweek* 115, no. 12 (March 19, 1990): 56—61.

Adorno, Theodor, and Max Horkheimer. "The Culture Industry: Enlightenment as Mass Deception," 1944.

Agnich, Laura, John M. Stogner, Bryan Lee Miller, and Catherine D. Marcum. "Purple Drank Prevalence and Characteristics of Misusers of Codeine Cough Syrup Mixtures." *Addictive Behaviors* 38 (2013): 2445—49.

Aidi, Hishaam. "The Grand (Hip-Hop) Chessboard: Race, Rap and Raison d'état." *Middle East Report* 41, no. 3 (260) (October 2011): 25—39.

Beck, Richard. "Express Yourself." n+1, September 9, 2010. https://nplusonemag.com/online-only/book-review/express-yourself/.

Benjamin, Walter. *Theses on the Philosophy of History*, 1942.

Berg, Maggie, and Barbara K. Seeber. *The Slow Professor: Challenging the Culture of Speed in the Academy*. University of Toronto Press, Scholarly Publishing Division, 2016.

Burrows, Gerard. "Glue Sniffing: The Psychosocial Context." *Australian & New Zealand Journal of Criminology* 16, no. 3 (1983): 163—71. https://doi.org/10.1177/000486588301600304.

Caramanica, Jon. "Seeping Out of Houston, Slowly." *The New York Times*, November 4, 2010, sec. Music. https://www.nytimes.com/2010/11/07/arts/music/07witch.html.

Certeau, Michel de. *The Practice of Everyday Life*, Volume 1. Berkeley, CA: University of California Press., 1984.

Cheng, Jack. "The Slow Web," 2012. https://jackcheng.com/the-slow-web.

Christopher, Roy. *Dead Precedents: How Hip-Hop Defines the Future*. Watkins Media, 2019.

Clark, Msia Kibona. *Hip-Hop in Africa: Prophets of the City and Dustyfoot Philosophers*. Ohio University Press, 2018.

Cleaver, Harry. "Work Refusal and Self-Organisation." In *Life without Money: Building Fair and Sustainable Economies*, 48—68. Pluto Press, 2011.

D, Chuck. *Fight the Power: Rap, Race, and Reality*. Delacorte Press, 1997.

David, Sabria. "The Slow Media Manifesto and Its Impact on Different Countries, Cultures, and Disciplines." *Acta Univ. Sapientiae, Social Analysis, Slow Media Institute* 5, no. 1 (2015): 107—12.

"DJ Screw Photographs and Memorabilia." *University of Houston Digital Library* (blog), n.d. https://digital.lib.uh.edu/collection/djscrew.

Grindon, Gavin. "Surrealism, Dada, and the Refusal of Work: Autonomy, Activism, and Social Participation in the Radical Avant-Garde." *Oxford Art Journal* 34, no. 1 (2011): 79—96.

Hall, Michael. "The Slow Life and Fast Death of DJ Screw." *Texas Monthly*, no. April 2001 (2001). https://www.texasmonthly.com/articles/the-slow-life-and-fast-death-of-dj-screw/.

Hart, Melanie, Laura Agnich, John Stogner, and Bryan Lee Miller. "'Me and My Drank:' Exploring the Relationship Between Musical Preferences and Purple Drank Experimentation." *Southern Criminal Justice Association*, 2013.

Honore, Carl. *In Praise of Slowness: Challenging the Cult of Speed.* HarperOne, 2004.

Horkheimer, Max, and Theodor W. Adorno. *Dialectic of Enlightenment.* Edited by Gunselin Schmid Noerr. Translated by Edmund Jephcott. Stanford University Press, 2002.

James, Keturah, and Ayana Jordan. "The Opioid Crisis in Black Communities." *The Journal of Law, Medicine & Ethics* 46, no. 2 (2018): 404—21. https://doi.org/10.1177/1073110518782949.

Le Masurier, Megan. "What Is Slow Journalism?" *Journalism Practice*, May 9, 2014, 1—15.

Martinez, Theresa A. "Popular Culture as Oppositional Culture: Rap as Resistance." *Sociological Perspectives* 40, no. 2 (1997): 265—286.

Parkins, Wendy, and Geoffrey Craig. *Slow Living.* Berg Publishers, 2006.

Penney, Joel. "'We Don't Wear Tight Clothes': Gay Panic and Queer Style in Contemporary Hip-Hop." *Popular Music and Society* 35, no. 3 (2012): 321—32.

Persson, Petra. "Attention Manipulation and Information Overload." *Behavioural Public Policy* 2, no. 1 (2018): 78—106.

Peters Jr., Ronald J., Mark Williams, Michael W. Ross, John Atkinson, and George S. Yacoubian Jr. "Codeine Cough Syrup Use Among African-American Crack Cocaine Users." *Journal of Psychoactive Drugs* 39, no. 1 (March 2007): 97—102.

Peters, Ronald J., Charles Amos Jr., Angela Meshack, Charles Savage, Michael M. Sinclair, Lena T. Williams, and Christine Markham. "Codeine Cough Syrup Use among Sexually Active, African-American High School Youths: Why Southern Males Are Down to Have Sex." *The American Journal of Addictions* 16, no. 2 (April 2017): 144—45.

Petrini, Carlo. *Slow Food: The Case for Taste.* Columbia University Press, 2004.

Petrusich, Amanda. "JAM NOTHIN' BUT THAT SCREW." *Oxford American* Winter 2014, no. 87 (December 1, 2014). https://www.oxfordamerican.org/item/509-jam-nothin-but-that-screw.

Rauch, Jennifer. *Slow Media: Why Slow Is Satisfying, Sustainable, and Smart.* Oxford University Press, 2018.

Rebollo-Gil, Guillermo, and Amanda Moras. "Black Women and Black Men in Hip-Hop Music: Misogyny, Violence and the Negotiation of (White-Owned) Space." *The Journal of Popular Culture* 45, no. 1 (2012): 118—32.

Rose, Tricia. *Black Noise: Rap Music and Black Culture in Contemporary America.* Middletown, CT: Wesleyan University Press, 1994.

Sarig, Roni. *Third Coast: OutKast, Timbaland, and How Hip-Hop Became a Southern Thing.* Cambridge, MA: Da Capo Press, 2007.

Sharma, Sarah. "Critical Time." *Communication and Critical/Cultural Studies* 10, no. 2—3 (2013): 312—18.

Sharma, Sarah. "Temporality and Difference from the Agora to the Airport: Towards a Theory of Power-Chronography." York University, September 2006.

Sinnreich, Aram. *Mashed up: Music, Technology, and the Rise of Configurable Culture.* Amherst, MA: University of Massachusetts Press, 2010.

Sinnreich, Aram. "Music, Copyright, and Technology: A Dialectic in Five Moments." *International Journal of Communication* 13 (2019): 422—39.

Smith, Christopher Holmes. "Method in the Madness: Exploring the Boundaries of Identity in Hip-Hop Performativity." *Social Identities* 3, no. 3 (1997): 345—74.

Stapleton, Katina R. "From the Margins to Mainstream: The Political Power of Hip-Hop." *Media, Culture & Society* 20, no. 2 (1998): 219—34.

"The Slow Food Manifesto," 1989. https://www.slowfoodusa.org/manifesto.

Thomas, Virginia, Margarita Azmitia, and Steve Whittaker. "Unplugged: Exploring the Costs and Benefits of Constant Connection." *Computers in Human Behavior* 63 (2016): 540—48.

Walker, Lance Scott. "DJ Screw: A Fast Life In Slow Motion." *Red Bull Music Academy* (blog), May 20, 2015. https://daily.redbullmusicacademy.com/2015/05/dj-screw-feature.

"What Is Slow Music?" *The Slow Music Movement* (blog), July 1, 2018. https://www.theslowmusicmovement. org/blog/what-is-slow-music.

Wilkins, Langston Collin. "Screwston, TX: The Impact of Space, Place, and Cultural Identity on Music Making in Houston's Hip-Hop Scene." Doctoral dissertation, Indiana University, n.d.

Zerzan, John. "Anti-Work and the Struggle for Control." *Telos* 50 (1981): 187—93. https://doi. org/10.3817/1281050187.

II. Technology

Scratch Cyborgs: The Hip-Hop DJ as Technology
André Sirois

Introduction

In 2009, I began research for my dissertation and eventual book,[1] in which I chronicled the role of hip-hop DJs in the evolution of products that catered to their culture. I spoke with some of the key players in the DJ product industry and in DJ culture itself, and asked them something simple: "What do you think is the most important technical innovation in the history of DJing?" As you might imagine, most people suggested products like the Technics 1200, digital vinyl systems, and sharp, contactless crossfaders like the one invented by DJ Focus in the late 90s.

These answers make perfect sense; these products disrupted the industry and advanced the culture by allowing DJs' ideas to come to life in new ways. But, by foregrounding advancements in machine technology, these answers only tell a part of the story. Consider, for example, the answer that Bay Area scratch legend DJ Quest gave to my question.[2] When I asked him his opinion about the most significant technical innovation in the history of DJing, he suggested, "The thing that has advanced the most ... has been the hand."[3]

Quest's answer is central to this chapter and to technocultural synergism as I present it. A common misconception, I argue, is that technical innovation leads to innovations in technique. With respect to hip-hop DJing, I have found that it's the other way around: technical innovation follows innovations in DJ technique, or as Quest puts it, "the hand." Whether finding new ways to use existing machines, or designing, inventing, and engineering their own equipment, DJs have participated in an ongoing feedback loop that shapes new technologies. Technical innovation is in a sense a product of the culture not something external to it. Seen this way, hip-hop DJ culture provides a rich site for exploring innovation as a cycle, a dialectic, and a network.

Technique and technical innovation are grounded in memory as well. For technique, it's muscle memory and sonic memory, and applying these memories via practice. For technical innovation, these memories codified through DJ technique are encoded to products, and through use these mixers are given meaning and develop a unique cultural/historical importance.

In this chapter, I present a number of case studies that illustrate the synergy between hip-hop performance techniques and product development, specifically that of DJ mixers. Although most writing about technological advancements considers the ways that technical innovations affect people, I want to flip the script and show how the development of new DJ mixers were influenced by DJ techniques themselves.

While house, club, and DJs from other electronic genres have had a huge impact on DJ culture and the DJ product industry, it is the hip-hop/scratch/turntablist DJs that have advanced DJ practice far beyond mixing and beat matching techniques foregrounded in other DJ genres. Therefore, as we will see by reviewing some landmark moments in innovation from 1970-2000, hip-hop DJ culture has had the most visible impact on the DJ product industry and the ways in which mixers have been engineered and designed.

The 1970s: Pioneering Technique

Most literature out there suggests that hip-hop culture began as a reaction to disco,[4, 5] with impoverished black/brown teenagers rejecting the adult, mostly white, mostly middle-class culture of mid-to-late 1970s Manhattan clubs. While that is true in many ways, before disco was a genre it was a diverse subculture in New York City, that, like hip-hop, was commodified and sanitized by the music industry.

The documentary *Founding Fathers*,[6] which focuses on the early Brooklyn mobile disco scene, showcases some of the ways that disco influenced hip-hop culture. For me, what stands out is the centrality of the DJ to both hip-hop and disco. Furthermore, some of the basic techniques pioneered by disco DJs, such as slip-cueing using slipmats and beatmatching, predated and thus influenced hip-hop DJ culture (even if indirectly). Therefore, disco is fundamental to understanding how DJ techniques were first encoded into DJ products.[7]

The DJ most commonly cited as a pioneer of mixing two records together was Francis Grasso,[8] who worked at downtown disco clubs, such as The Sanctuary and The Haven.[9] In the late 1960s, Grasso was using a Rek-O-Kut mixer, a product designed for mixing audio for radio and television broadcast, to seamlessly blend two songs together. As his popularity grew, so did his need for a mixer that could accommodate his style of mixing. Most broadcast mixers used both upfaders and rotary knobs to mix signals, but it was rare for them to have a headphone cue. The headphone cue turned out to be a major technical innovation that followed from DJ technique.

In the early days of NYC's disco subculture, there were no mobile DJ products, which meant that the earliest mixers were designed as installation pieces for specific nightclub venues. In 1971, Alex Rosner designed a simple stereo mixer named "Rosie" (after its red colored faceplate) for Grasso to use at the Haven Club. The prototype was simple: two phono inputs, a tape input, a mic input, and a headphone cue system. It was designed with Grasso's style of mixing in mind and a reflection of his art and technique.[10] Rosie enabled Grasso to cue mix on headphones, previewing his blends of different recordings before playing them over the club's speakers.

Rosie was also the bi-product of collaboration and modification; Rosner was able to use a mono mixer made by Louis Bozak for radio broadcasting and adapt it for Grasso's style of club mixing, and of course Grasso gave feedback on what he needed. This collaboration would be vital to the history of DJ mixers, as it was Rosner along with another iconic sound engineer, Richard Long, who convinced Bozak that there was a market for a club DJ mixer, and in 1971 the Bozak CMA-10-2DL was released and installed in clubs around New York.

While the CMA-10-2DL was the first mass-produced mixer, it was really only accessible to established DJs playing in disco clubs. That limitation meant that the mobile DJs of Brooklyn and hip-hop DJs in the South Bronx would need to develop alternative solutions and techniques that would have a major impact on future products.

Founding Fathers[11] specifically looks at how some of these DJs modified products on the market to suit their mixing needs. In the film DJ Vernon recalls the technical ingenuity of Ricky Grant. Vernon explains how Grant took a Sony MX 14 mixer made for microphone mixing in live sound applications and "y-jacked" the channels, allowing him to mix with independent control of the volume levels coming from the turntables (now a standard "gain" or "trim" feature on modern DJ mixers). Vernon continues: "And from that, slick ass engineers at GLi saw the idea, copied it, and came out with the first 3800. They stole ideas from Ricky Grant."[12] This story of DJ innovations being copied and encoded into commercial DJ products is common in the history and development of DJ mixers.

The 3800, which came out in 1974-1975, around the same time that GLi, Inc. was founded in Brooklyn, was one of the first commercially available mobile DJ mixers and one of the first mixers that Kool Herc supposedly used.[13] Despite what anybody has said, this is likely the first DJ mixer with a horizontal crossfader, an integral component in the history of hip-hop DJ technique because it's the most natural tool for heavy duty sound manipulation using the hand. Almost all companies designing and manufacturing mixers in this era were from NYC or elsewhere in the tri-state area because of the proximity to DJ culture. But, the parks and rec centers were also the first research and development labs for these companies. With so much technical and technique innovation happening in the parks, engineers at these companies saw what DJs were doing and the potential market for these types of products, and the GLi 3800 was likely the bi-product of "borrowed" park jam innovation.

There are many accounts of the early hip-hop culture and DJ Kool Herc bringing out the breakbeats with his "Merry-Go-Round," Grandmaster Flash's "Quick Mix Theory," and how Theodore serendipitously stumbled across scratching.[14] So, while BK's mobile disco scene was popping, teenage DJs in the South Bronx had developed

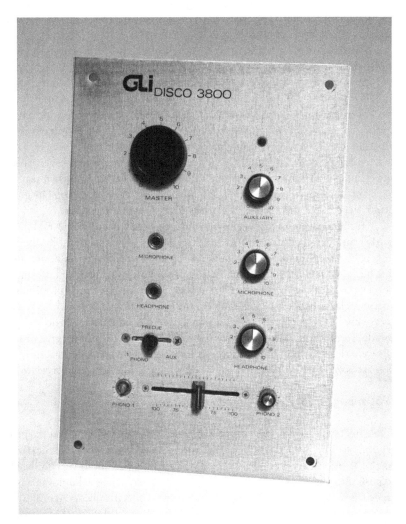

GLi 3800
Photo: André Sirois

their own style of mixing, largely centered on isolating, repeating, and manipulating the drum break sections of their records.

Massively important here was that these DJs were making groundbreaking innovations in technique, developing new dexterous skills with the hand, as early as 1973. With the only DJ mixers available being club installs, young, poor, black and brown kids from the South Bronx, just like Ricky Grant, had to make technical modifications to products to allow for their style of mixing to advance. In the early days of hip-hop culture, DJs would modify and use microphone mixers. They would also find ingenious ways of using multiple stereo receivers to cut between breakbeats. One notable innovation was to use a stereo receiver and plug one turntable into the left channel and the other turntable into the right channel and then use the stereo pan control to cut between records. Plain and simple, these hip-hop DJs in the South Bronx lacked access to the few DJ mixers that were on the market.

Throughout most the 1970s, DJ mixers were aimed at the mobile disco DJ market and designed to perform long transitions between songs. By the late 1970s, mixers like the GLi 3800, CM Labs CM 607 or Meteor Light & Sound's Clubman line (i.e., the One-One, Two, and Two-Two) grew in popularity and use amongst hip-hop DJs. Again, these products were not designed for their style of mixing, cutting, and scratching, as most of these mixers were large (often 19" in width), and relied on rotary knobs or upfaders to control signals; but hip-hop DJs made do and continued to adopt and adapt into the 1980s. Manufacturers were paying attention to what DJs were doing in NYC, but largely ignoring the style and innovations in the city's poorest borough. However, they could only ignore this innovative style for so long.

1980s: Legendary Style

While the 1970s gave birth to the foundational practices of DJing and the products to try and accommodate club DJs, the 1980s was a decade of serious technical innovation. As the breakbeat style of DJing spread outside of NYC, notably to Philly, DJs began to push the possibilities of the human hand while technological innovations followed. These DJs took from the pioneering hip-hop DJs — specifically, scratching and cutting breakbeats on time — and brought that to the next level. Scratching became faster and more precise, while cutting two copies of the record went from just being on time to funky re-arrangements of songs (also known as beat juggling). The human hand was developing at a speed much faster than DJ mixers.

The mixer that defined much of the early 1980s style and served as a great segue from the decade before was the GLi PMX 9000. Despite being a 19" wide mixer geared towards club use, the PMX 9000 had a horizontal crossfader, a semi-rarity when this came out in 1979/1980, and thus became a favorite mixer of DJs like Jam Master Jay, UTFO's Mixmaster Ice, Whodini's Grandmaster Dee, and DJ Cheese. In fact, DJ Cheese used this mixer when he won the DMC World DJ Championships in

1986, effectively introducing scratching to the annual competition. Because of the size of the mixer, Cheese (and others) would set up their turntables on one side of the mixer in order to be a bit faster with both hands, a style known as "Axe Style." While more mixers of the time used rotary dials, the 9000 was all faders. Despite its popularity amongst hip-hop DJs, it did not reflect their style of DJing. Thus, the true innovation was in the hand and how this mixer was used.

Seeing a need for DJ mixers that were more compact, essentially more "mobile," two iconic brands emerged to prominence in the 1980s: Numark and Gemini. The brands' popularity was relegated to hip-hop DJs on each coast in the U.S,, although both were based in New York, with Gemini taking over in Philly and NYC and the Numark rising to fame amongst DJs in Los Angeles and in the Bay area. At the time rap music and hip-hop in general was still considered to be a youth fad that would fall from popularity, and thus none of the DJ mixers reflected the style and needs of the hip-hop DJ.

If you were coming up in Philly, then the Gemini MX-1100 was the mixer of choice during the early-to-mid 80s. It was the mixer that DJs like Cash Money, Jazzy Jeff, Tat Money and other DJs in the 215 likely developed two fundamental DJ techniques on: the transform and chirp. Before he helped make the Gemini MX-2200 an iconic mixer, the 1100 was DJ Cash Money's mixer of choice.[15] It had a super clean and simple layout, a horizontal crossfader, and was small. It marked the movement away from the monolithic 19" mixers towards the 10" battle/hip-hop DJ styled mixers that would rise to prominence in the 90s.

Modern beat juggling as we know it developed because DJs in Philly and NYC started messing with these smaller Gemini mixers, allowing them to put the turntables closer together. With the turntables closer together and flipped horizontally into Philly "battle style," the tonearm was out of the way and DJs were able to move more rapidly and freak their records into new compositions. This arrangement also enabled the advancement of body tricks (manipulating the crossfader and records with body parts other than the hands).

Of course, to perfect scratch techniques like the transform and chirp DJs needed a faster fader. The slope of faders was still engineered to accommodate the slow transitions between songs that were prominent at disco clubs. Philly's hip-hop DJs would modify their mixers by blasting crossfaders with WD-40 or graphite. Although this made their faders move faster, it did nothing to sharpen the slope (the rate at which the signal from one turntable or the other would cut off and on). But in this moment, we can see DJ techniques like scratching and beat juggling pushing ahead against mixer technologies that aren't yet capable of fully supporting these practices.

Although initially well behind NYC, west coast hip-hop DJs became known for taking the Philly innovations of the transform and chirp techniques and making them faster. On the west coast, Numark was the go-to brand mixer (particularly the bulky and cluttered DM-1650 and DM-1800). Gaining popularity with its larger

models in the mobile scenes in the major cities, the Numark DM-500, which came
out in 1981, was a nice, clean little mixer. It was marketed as a budget-priced product
in competition with the Gemini MX-1100. Like most Numark mixers, it had a short-
stemmed crossfader that was awkwardly placed in the lower left hand corner of
the mixer. Inferior in many ways to the Gemini mixers, the Numark's main selling
points were its cost and size. However, there was one feature that Numark had that
unintentionally allowed hip-hop DJs to push their techniques to new heights.

The DM-500 had a phono/line switch, a small switch that allowed a DJ to select
if the channel input would be a phono signal (an unamplified turntable) or a pre-
amplified line signal (i.e., a tape player). However, if you were playing sound from a
turntable and positioned the switch to line it would effectively turn that signal off
to dead silence, and it could be turned back on to a full level turntable signal. At the
time, a crossfader was a gradual on/off switch for musical signal while a phono/line
switch is instant on/off.

West coast DJs figured out that you could use the phono/line switch for
scratching instead of a crossfader. This eliminated the need for a fast fader and
also solved the general problem that the slope of the crossfader was slow, meaning
you'd have to quickly move the fader from its off position to the center position, to
off position, to transform and chirp. On the west coast, DJs like Joe Cooley and
Aladdin used this switch, dubbed the "clicker," to execute super fast and precise
chirps and transforms because the clicker needed to travel a very short distance to
have an instant on/off for the signal.[16]

The mixer that really allowed these DJs to push these techniques in the mid-
1980s was the Numark DM-1150a. Unlike many of its predecessors in the DM line
(DM stands for disco mixer), the 1150a's phono/line switch used longer shaft style
switches instead of small button switches. This gave Aladdin and Cooley something
they could hold onto and move quickly up and down. And like the DM-500, the
crossfader was awkwardly placed in the lower left, encouraging west coast DJs to
favor the clicker. Furthermore, the 1150a was about 10" wide, so it also allowed the
turntables to be placed closely together. If you watch the 1989 USA DMC Finals or
World Championships, it's hard to forget jheri curled DJ Aladdin absolutely crushing
it. Aladdin, who was from Compton, was up there doing east coast style cutting over
west coast style beats, and doing it all super fast on the DM-1150a.[17]

And you can imagine how all the east coast DJs felt when they heard some of
the techniques they pioneered being done by Aladdin with incredible funkiness and
speed. In the competitive world of battling, however, the clicker was considered a bit
of a cheat by NYC and Philly DJs who clung to the authenticity of the crossfader.[18]
While the 1150a was ruling the West in the late 80s, the wood veneer paneled Gemini
MX-2200 was the mixer favored amongst DJs in the East. Although a version of it came
out in 1983 with a clicker switch,[19] this classic mixer became an icon of 1980s hip-hop
DJ culture when DJ Cash Money won the 1988 DMC World Championships using it.

"Gemini wasn't that expensive for those times," says Cash Money. "They came out with the MX 1100 and I loved that mixer. So after that mixer the MX-2200 came out. I was like 'Wow, that mixer looks dope,' so I used it all the time."[20] The mixer was the perfect size to go between two turntables and cut it up. "I loved the size of it. The size, the crossfader... this was all I need," says DJ Jazzy Jeff, who had a rotation of six MX-2200s.[21]

But the 1150a and MX-2200, although used extensively by hip-hop DJs, were not made for their style of DJing. Therefore, DJ technique impressively advanced during the 1980s without technical innovations to support their style. That is, the hand advanced well ahead of the products. As DJ technique developed, it became clear that the proper style of mixer to suit hip-hop DJ style needed a few things: a simple layout and design that was especially clean around the fader area, a width that would allow the turntables to be close together, and a way to turn sound on and off for scratching fast, preferably using a crossfader.

The 1990s: Turntablism

If the first 20 years of hip-hop DJing was defined by the DJ adapting to technologies pioneered for other styles of DJing, it was the 1990s, an era that witnessed the rise of "turntablism" as an underground genre with thousands of aspiring practitioners, when the DJ product industry finally began catering to hip-hop style. What happened during this decade was that manufacturers finally began to encode the ideas and practices of hip-hop DJs into their mixers. The most direct way was that DJs were included in product research and development (R&D), giving manufacturers ideas about design and function. Sometimes DJs would be offered product endorsement deals for signature DJ products that reflected their preferences. Furthermore, manufacturers indirectly incorporated hip-hop DJ intellectual properties into products by including design elements and functions that would accommodate DJ technique advancement outlined in the previous section, such as the ability to increase the slope on crossfaders to an instant on/off setting.

While I will look at the Vestax 05Pro as the blueprint for all hip-hop styled mixers that would follow, there were two products that segued us into the turntablist era: the Melos PMX-2 and Vestax PMC-05 TRIX, both of which were released around 1990.

The Melos brand PMX-2 was the mixer everybody wanted in the early 90s. Co-branded with DMC as the official mixer of its World DJ Championships from 1990-1996, this was quite an advanced piece of gear, light years from the Geminis and Numarks of the previous decades. This model boasted a super clean layout, LED VU meters, a nice fader with faster than average cut-in, and importantly, a phono/line switch for the ultra sharp transform scratches.[22]

Melos was manufactured by Ozaki Denshi Co, Ltd., a Japanese company that also made and designed mixers for other brands (i.e., GLi and Vesta Fire, which would go on to become Vestax). DMC's founder Tony Prince wanted to make a

Molos PMX-2
Photo: Zane Ritt

DMC-branded mixer, and eventually met Isao Ozaki of Melos, who was surprised by the ways in which DJs were using the mixers at the DMC battles.[23] Basically, Prince collected design ideas from world-class DJs and worked with engineers at Melos, such as its master engineer, Mr. Moriya, to make 50 PMX-2s a month. Primary design concepts, however, came from three UK battle DJs: Cutmaster Swift, DJ Pogo, and Mysterious K.

At the time, Swift, who won the 1989 DMC World Championships against Aladdin, was a tech for DMCs, and was going nuts soldering new faders into Gemini mixers (you have to remember that with the MX-2200 or Numark 1150a, the crossfaders were hardwired in). The PMX-2 was designed to be a mixer that they could actually service quickly, and was essentially Swift's wishlist as a service tech.

At the time, TRIX was using the Vestax PMC-05mkII mixer, a product whose features he liked, but he thought that its layout design was all wrong. TRIX thought he had a better design. "I drew a design using the components of the PMC-05mkII but laid the mixer out as I wished, I also included the Vestax logo and my signature," he says.[24] TRIX submitted the design to Vestax and by 1990 Vestax released the PMC-05 TRIX battle mixer, a carbon copy of TRIX's initial concept.

The PMC-05 TRIX was one of the first symmetrical 2-channel mixers geared towards hip-hop/scratch DJs. It was also one of the early mixers that had a replaceable

Gemini MX 2200
Photo: Zane Ritt

crossfader. At the time of the PMC-05 TRIX's release, the only way manufacturers could get a sharper cut-in time for scratching was to use smaller crossfaders, so the standard 45mm fader could be replaced with a 20mm fader, which was a borderline clicker switch.

The mixer is notable because it made TRIX the first DJ to have a signature mixer, which included his signature on the faceplate, and it marked one of the first major instances of a DJ's design concept being executed in a product. TRIX thinks that the mixer represents the turn when hip-hop and DJ culture were taken seriously.[25] This would become the standard practice for Vestax, and eventually the industry: using DJs in research and development and then in marketing and branding. But, Shiino san was a pioneer in this way because he listened to DJs and then used them to brand products, and thus Vestax used catchphrases like "We give DJs what they want" or "For DJs By DJs."

And while the TRIX signature mixer surely blazed a path for Vestax, it was its 05Pro that became the blueprint for the modern hip-hop/battle/turntablist style DJ mixers and the flurry of mixers that dropped to cater to the boom in hip-hop DJs in the 1990s. To be honest, there is a bit of a difference in opinion on where the design ideas came from for the 05Pro, but it's best to look at it as an example of the results of impressive collaboration and networked creativity.

In 1993, DJ Shortkut was winning battles and doing demos for Numark at trade shows. He had been thinking about what he liked and disliked about the then-standard Melos PMX-2, and one day drew a design concept on a napkin and showed it to the Numark rep (Numark was still focusing on 19" mobile disco mixers). "Numark wasn't really feeling me. You know, I was just a little kid," says Shortkut.[26] Later that year he went to NAMM with fellow Beat Junkie, Rhettmatic. There they met with an engineer and later president of Vestax, Toshi Nakama. At the time, Toshi-san, based on his design of the Vestax PMC-05, was already conceiving a mixer that would not be a piece of audio equipment but a musical instrument. At NAMM, Rhettmatic and Shortkut liked Toshi's ideas, and also gave him feedback based on Shortkut's napkin design.

In 1994, Vestax began developing the PMC-05Pro — a game-changing mixer and eventual standard for hip-hop DJs because of its smooth crossfader, control over the crossfader's cut-in curve/contour (i.e., slope), its clean layout, and compact design at 10" wide. Aside from Shortkut and Rhettmatic, Vestax also got feedback from Qbert and Mix Master Mike, as well as Japanese DJs, including Takada and GM Yoshi. But, as specced by Vestax, the retail cost would be significantly higher than anything on the market. However, Shortkut and Rhettmatic were excited about the idea and felt like hip-hop DJs would pay a lot for a mixer with these features. "The retailers in the U.S. shot down my idea, saying, 'Are you crazy? People can buy 10 Gemini mixers with this price... You don't understand the market in America,'" Nakama tells me. "However, I was eager to develop this dream model to meet everyone's needs."[27]

The 05Pro hit market in a super limited quantity of 50 units in the rare grey colorway in 1995. To everybody's surprise it sold out: "At first when we made it they were like 'oh, this mixer is not going to sell,'" says Qbert.[28] And then Vestax released the classic gold on black 05Pro, which went on to sell 300,000-400,000 units.[29] The success was not only because of the quality of the mixer itself, but Vestax used the Invisibl Skratch Piklz to brand the mixer and authenticate it within hip-hop DJ culture.

Other than layout and design, it was the crossfader system on the 05Pro that helped open creative doors in scratch styles. By this time DJs were already developing more complex sounding scratch techniques like the twiddle and crab scratches where the DJ's fingers would tap the fader knob 3-4 times per second. The 05Pro crossfader had a contour adjust (slope adjust) to set it to a quick on/off like the clicker, or a slower transition like all crossfaders that preceded it. Because of this mixer and the fader, it allowed a lot of DJs to execute creative ideas and progress technique advancements they were already testing, and the Vestax 05Pro was the mixer at the forefront of one of the most innovative periods in DJ technique from 1995-2000. While the mixer was advanced for the time, even when it first came out it was already behind the innovations in DJ technique; in fact, new DJ products are, as I've detailed here, always following advancement in technique.

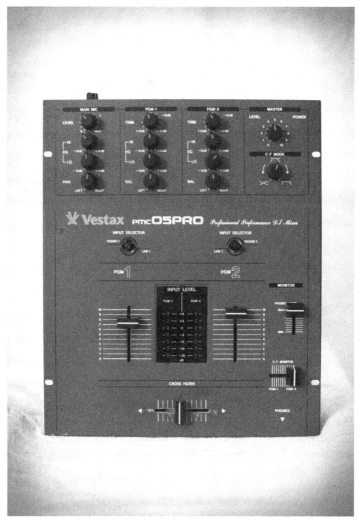

Vestax 05Pro
Photo: Zane Ritt

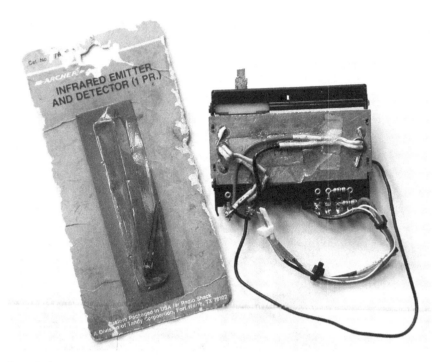

Focus Fader prototype
Photo: André Sirois

It was the fader's system that changed the game, not just the fader itself. The Vestax 05Pro, and later mixers made by Rane, started using voltage controlled amplifier (VCA) circuitry. Instead of passing more/less musical signal like the Melos, Gemini and Numark mixers, VCA systems passed more or less voltage through the fader, which was then expressed in signal loudness. While VCA circuitry was an advancement in itself, it's what one DJ, DJ Focus, did with VCA that changed the future of the industry and culture. "There was such a burden with the old faders that held back how you could practice," Focus explains.[30] Most faders in the late 1990s were made of graphite that used a trace from one end to another that allowed progressive electrical resistance and thus musical signal to pass through the fader. "The grand epiphany was like 'oh shit, I just can hook up an optical sensor and transmitter to it because it's voltage, and that will work,'" Focus recalls.[31]

In 1998, DJ Focus, a bedroom inventor from Mesa, Arizona, invented a disruptive technology that would change the DJ product industry and culture: the first optical contactless crossfader. Prior to this innovation, crossfaders would eventually wear out and bleed, which in the 80s meant you needed a whole new mixer, or in the 90s that you needed to buy a new replacement fader (and, if you were a scratch/battle DJ, you went through many faders). Focus' innovation had no contacts, which meant it could possibly last forever. Focus made 4 original Focus Fader mods using the famous ALPS crossfader used in the 05Pro, and when Focus brought this mod to the company Stanton Magnetics they were impressed.

The Focus Fader first went into the Stanton SK-2F, an imitation of the Vestax 05Pro, but it also worked on the Rane and Vestax mixers that used VCA circuitry. One of the issues for Focus was how Stanton interpreted and produced his faders, and in the production process cut corners, so the products were never like his original concepts. Regardless, the fact that a contactless fader could work and exist, was groundbreaking; eventually other manufacturers and third parties created their own contactless faders. This innovation allowed DJs to practice longer, practice more, and further develop hand technique. But, it came from the culture and it came from innovation by DJs.

Conclusion

This is not the whole story of technical and technique innovation in hip-hop DJ culture as it relates to DJ mixers. I've written elsewhere about many of these products, such as the Rane TTM 54 and magnetic crossfader or many of the other products Vestax put out, as examples of technocultural synergism.[32]

This dialectic between technique and technical innovation in hip-hop DJing demonstrates how DJs are the technology. DJs emerge as the combination of human and machine and I've tried to delineate how the faders, buttons and knobs have always followed technique and represent the encoding of memories on multiple levels. And, without someone behind a mixer making it do amazing things with sound, all you really have are buttons and sliders. It's the DJs' memories, of mind and muscle, that get encoded into these products. But also, it's important to consider how memories get attached to these products through DJs' uses of them (similar to how guitarists attach meaning to a guitar).

Hip-hop DJs show the various ways in which culture and industry can converge and collaborate, as well as how they need each other to move forward. But, I do want us to rethink what "technology" is and what makes it, and hip-hop DJ culture is an interesting site for reconsidering how we conceptualize technology. With that said, it may be worth resisting writing impact narratives about technical innovations, and instead look at our effect on those objects through our use of them.

Following my narrative here, we can see a connection between Ricky Grant and Francis Grasso to Cash Money and Aladdin to Focus and Shortkut. Their ideas and innovations connect on many levels as they envisioned beautiful ways of making what they had access to work for them. But, they didn't stop there; they pushed the gear and they didn't let the limitations of the products burden their creativity. It's easy to suggest that DJ products are designed and made by companies, but I hope we can look beyond that and see how advancements are truly designed from scratch.

Notes

1. Sirois, André. *Hip-Hop DJs and the Evolution of Technology: Cultural Exchange, Innovation, and Democratization*, New York: Peter Lang Publishing, Inc., 2016.

2. The DJ who gave a name to an influential style of scratching, Hamster Style.

3. DJ Quest, telephone interview with author, December 26 2009.

4. Technocultural synergism is a way of looking at how grassroots culture and corporations converge to make new products. Collaboration creates a greater whole and is a cycle of thesis and antithesis that produces new technological systems as its synthesis. Furthermore, this collaboration also creates inequity as much as it creates creative opportunity. At the core of this concept is the idea that Hip-Hop DJs are and create valuable intellectual properties that are capitalized on by industry.

5. For example, see Toop (2004) or George (1998).

6. *Founding Fathers*, April 7, 2014, accessed April 20, 2014, https://www.youtube.com/watch?v=1G13bRoBo-8&sns=fb.

7. In the 1970s, and frankly most of the 1980s, the DJ product industry (just like the recording industry), saw Hip-Hop as a fad and thus failed to cater to the robust Hip-Hop DJ culture/market. Thus, most of the products to hit the market were designed with DJs whose primary techniques were beatmatching and mixing between two or more songs for discos and clubs, and not the heavy duty manipulation and cutting, scratching, and beat juggling prominent amongst Hip-Hop DJs of that era. Hip-Hop DJs had to improvise with and modify what they had access to.

8. Grasso called mixing two records together a "change."

9. See Lawrence, Tim. *Love Saves the Day: A History of American Dance Music Culture, 1970-1979*, Durham, North Carolina: Duke University Press Books, 2004.

10. **See** *The Note Episode 1 | Alex Rosner: Shaping the Sound of New York*, May 17, 2016, accessed August 22, 2019, https://www.youtube.com/watch?time_continue=372&v=Nv8mju2-gHI.

11. *Founding Fathers*, April 7, 2014, accessed April 20, 2014, https://www.youtube.com/watch?v=1G13bRoBo-8&sns=fb While the documentary *Founding Fathers* contests the popular narrative behind Hip-Hop culture, it also looks at the creativity of DJs like Pete "DJ" Jones, the Disco Twins, and DJ Hollywood. The film explores how these largely Brooklyn-based crews impacted DJ technique and products. And the popularity of these mobile DJ parties, where the DJs would engineer and build their own sound systems, would soon catch the attention of those in the pro audio and sound industry.

12. I pulled that clip from *Founding Fathers*. See *GLi 3800 Innovation*, April 11, 2016, accessed August, 20, 2019. https://www.youtube.com/watch?v=bdLRo4MPmEI. The GLi 3800 was one of the first commercially available mobile DJ mixers.

13. It is said that this is the mixer that Grandmaster Flash would watch Herc to the merry-go-round on. Flash noted how sloppy Herc's technique was, and thought that if Herc used the headphone cue function on the mixer instead of needle dropping, that his sound could be much cleaner. This, along with Flash using Pete "DJ" Jones' mixer with a headphone cue, was what inspired Flash to engineer what he called a "peak-a-boo" (a headphone cue) on his Sony MX-8 microphone mixer and allow him to execute his precise, on-time cutting of breaks with his "quick mix theory." While Flash didn't invent the headphone cue, he re-invented how to use it to DJ with.

14. You can read about that in Chang (2004), Katz (2012), and Toop (2000).

15. You can see Cash and Marvelous posing with one on the back of the "Ugly People Be Quiet" 12".

16. Essentially these two techniques rely on sharp on/off of the sound you're scratching.

17. In the 1990s, companies would incorporate a clicker switch as a "kill" switch on mixers; essentially it would perform the same function as the phono/line switch but only turn the signal on/off and give DJs another way to perform scratch techniques.

18. On a historical note, it was the 1150a mixer that Flare developed the Flare scratch on before the "no clicker" rule. This rule, a sort of cultural ethic, pushed Flare to use the fader to attempt a chirp and in the process accidentally developed the scratch technique of his namesake.

19. Note that this original MX-2200 was the one that Grand Mixer DXT supposedly used to perform the scratches on Herbie Hancock's "Rockit."

20. DJ Cash Money, personal communication with author, August 20 2018.

21. The Gemini 2200, March 9, 2018, accessed August 20, 2019, https://www.youtube.com/watch?v=qAGxpaxvaTw.

22. This mixer was hard to get outside of Asia or Europe as Melos didn't have strong distribution in the Americas. DMC champions and heavy battle heads had them here in the U.S., as well as DJs who travelled to Japan.

23. Most manufacturers didn't realize what Hip-Hop DJs were doing with the products for a long time (until the late 1980s with Gemini Flashformer that at least recognized this style) as most were making products for club use and disco-styled DJs. Also, many still believed that Hip-Hop was a passing fad through most of the 1980s.

24. DJ Trix, email interview with author, April 20 2011.

25. Ibid.

26. DJ Shortkut., telephone interview with author, January 11 2010.

27. Toshi Nakama, email interview with author, January 18 2019.

28. DJ Qbert + Yogafrog + MC UB discuss the development of the PMC-05 Pro, August 3 2011, accessed February 3, 2015. https://www.youtube.com/watch?v=ehKkeKOKTxw.

29. Ibid.

30. DJ Focus, telephone interview with author, April 16 2014.

31. Ibid.

32. Sirois, *Hip-Hop DJs and the Evolution of Technology.*

Digital Underground x Sex Pistols mashup by Roy Christopher

NEVER MIND
THE BIG NOSE

HERE'S THE

SeX PaCKeTS

Public Enemy and How Copyright Changed Hip-Hop: An Oral History
Kembrew McLeod

Artists have traditionally borrowed from each other and have been directly inspired by the world that surrounds them. But what happens — ethically, legally, aesthetically — when digital technologies, such as sampling, allow for very literal audio quotes to be inserted into new works? In Public Enemy's 1988 song "Caught, Can We Get a Witness?," from *It Takes a Nation of Millions To Hold Us Back*, Chuck D famously rapped:

> Caught, now in court 'cause I stole a beat
> This is a sampling sport ...
> Mail from the courts and jail
> Claims I stole the beats that I rail
> Look at how I'm livin' like
> And they're gonna check the mike, right? Sike
> Look at how I'm livin' now, lower than low
> What a sucker know
> I found this mineral that I call a beat
> I paid zero

"It's almost like 'Caught, Can We Get a Witness?' was a pre-Napster record," said "Media Assassin" Harry Allen, a member of Public Enemy. "It's really speaking to the way the industry handles technological change." Just as multitudes of panel discussions about digital downloading were mounted at music industry and academic conferences in the early twenty-first century — which achieved little consensus — Allen recalled how sampling was viewed as the new music-industry boogeyman in the late 1980s. "Even more than a prediction or looking forward to the controversies that would bloom around sampling," he said of Chuck D, "it was really more like looking forward to the controversies that would bloom around Napster." As with the sharing of MP3 music files, many artists and record companies believed that the practice of digital sampling was the equivalent of stealing. Others, like Public Enemy's Chuck D, argued that there should be more freedom to recontextualize found sounds.

However, Chuck D and other similar artists lost this particular argument. By 1991, the music industry began strongly enforcing copyright law, and in the process the industry developed a cumbersome and expensive "sample clearance" system in which all samples, even the shortest and most unrecognizable, had to be approved and paid for. Since this period, the cost of licensing samples has continued to increase, as have the costs associated with negotiating those licenses. This made it impossible for certain kinds of music to be legally made — like Public Enemy's early records — because they contained *hundreds* of fragments of sound, just within one record. Today, it would simply be too expensive to clear copyright licenses for albums such as Public Enemy's *Fear of a Black Planet* — a record considered so culturally important that the *New York Times* included it on its list of the "25 Most Significant Albums of the Last Century" and that the Library of Congress included it in its 2004 National Recording Registry, along with the news broadcasts of Edward R. Murrow and the music of John Coltrane.

Harry Allen gave a hypothetical example of how one would have to sell a record such as *Fear of a Black Planet* for over one hundred dollars per CD to pay for all the licenses. There was a time before the early 1990s when not all sound fragments needed to be licensed, and the ones that were licensed did not reach today's astronomical prices (sometimes $100,000 for a single sample). Many artists and critics have argued that this licensing system had a negative impact on the creative potential of this newly emerging African-American art form before it had a chance to flower. The growth of 20th century jazz music would have been similarly stunted if jazz musicians — who regularly "riffed" on others' songs — had been burdened by a similar legal need to license and get permission from music publishers for the use of every sonic fragment they appropriated. The following oral history is based on interviews Kembrew McLeod conducted with Public Enemy members Chuck D, Hank Shocklee, Keith Shocklee, and Harry Allen.

What are the origins of sampling in hip-hop?

Harry Allen: When we talk about hip-hop and the beginning of hip-hop, we are talking about DJ culture and the use of turntables as instrumental devices. And when I say instrumental devices, I mean to bifurcate tones — to fragment tones, to fragment sounds, to do something different with the turntable. I'm talking about manipulating the sound on a turntable, something different than playing a record as it is recorded.

Chuck D: Sampling basically comes from the fact that rap music is not music. It's rap over music. So vocals were used over records in the very beginning stages of hip-hop in the 1970s to the early 1980s.

Hank Shocklee: Sampling came out of the DJ culture. You would have a drumbeat playing on one record and, using the other record, you would scratch a horn or a guitar riff on top of it.

Harry Allen: DJs, they're working with a very small amount of space on a record. The precision necessary — you can't be off by millimeters. We're talking about very tiny distances on a record. With samplers you could take the sound of the DJ and make it instantly retrievable and customizable. With the increasing complexity of samplers — the increase in sampling memory and sampling fidelity — you were able to get sounds that were true to what you recorded, and what this allowed DJs to do, and producers in this case now, was then to construct tracks, layers, audio layers. Sampling was a way of bringing an unusual delicate form of live performance into the recording medium, and this technology allowed one to replicate and make it more unique.

Chuck D: In the early-1980s, rappers were recording over live bands that were basically emulating the sounds off of the records. Eventually, you had synthesizers and samplers, which would take sounds that would then get arranged or looped, so rappers can still do their thing over it.

Those synthesizers and samplers were expensive back then, especially in 1984. How did hip-hop artists get them if they didn't have a lot of money?

Chuck D: Not only were they expensive, but they were limited in what they could do - they could only sample two seconds at a time. But people were able to get a hold of equipment by renting time out in studios.

Hank Shocklee: I think at the time the only thing that could capture a sample or a recording was in a keyboard called the Synclavier, and that was a $300,000 machine. The only way you could get access to one was in professional recording studios. But then more studios could afford them when samplers lowered in price.

Chuck D: You had a mad dash of creativity, as far as musicianship and technological innovation was concerned... Those technology companies didn't necessarily have any kind of allegiance to intellectual property owners.

Hank Shocklee: The machines that came after that were, for example, the Akai. Akai created the S-900 which now gave you more time, more memory. This created more flexibility and opportunities with what you could do with sound. You could mess with the resonance, the decay and other elements of the sound.

Were you aware of the opposition to sampling on the part of the more traditional musicians?

Harry Allen: I think for a lot of people who weren't used to sampling, it was almost rude, actually, to say, "I'm going to take this song and sample the drumbeat because I like it." Knowing how long he took to work on that drumbeat, to get that drumbeat to where it was, and you're just going to go — *bink* — and just take it right off the record? It seemed rude. Some of those first sampling cases, it wasn't that we were trying to be thieves or trying not to get caught. We were just doing what seemed natural, creatively.

Chuck D: Our sampling wasn't based on thievery, but instead using sampling machines as tools and looking at those tools from musician's point of view. We wanted to blend sound. Just as visual artists take yellow and blue and come up with green, we wanted to be able to do that with sound.

Hank Shocklee: I've always been from the school where, you know, from if I'm sampling, who am I to attack somebody else from sampling from me?

Chuck D: With Public Enemy, a quarter of our intention was to disguise the original sound, but 75% of our intention was that we wanted to create a new sound out of an assemblage of sounds. So it was more about creating a new sound, and not running away from the responsibility of stealing somebody's sound.

How did the Bomb Squad use samplers and other recording technologies to put together the tracks on *It Takes a Nation of Millions*?

Hank Shocklee: When we sampled, we'd take a piece from each section of a song. You may get one part of the sound is from the intro, another part of it is from the drum breakdown, another part of it is from the end, the vamp on the end. So, and all those samples are combined to create one sample. That's what the Bomb Squad did.

Harry Allen: The Bomb Squad was the association of Chuck D, Hank Shocklee, Keith Shocklee, and Eric Sadler. Those four individuals together were the Bomb Squad, and they were the ones that put together the sound of Public Enemy's music, especially on their second album [*It Takes a Nation of Millions To Hold Us Back*]... Hank didn't play any instruments of which I know, I don't think his expertise was expressly or particularly technical. Eric oversaw more of the direct technical stuff and Keith did as well. But Hank was really almost like the composer. He was the person who had the idea in his head and executed that idea.

Hank Shocklee: We would all comb through records to find pieces that would fit. And as we started putting together those pieces, the sound got a lot more dense. Sampling was a very intricate thing for us. We didn't just pick up a record and sample that record because it was funky. It was a collage. We were creating a collage.

Chuck D: The Bomb Squad was supervised by Hank Shocklee. He was kind of like the coach of the team, shaping the overall blueprint.

Harry Allen: Hank was the person who dealt with frequencies, if you will. He was the one who dealt with noise. Hectic was a word that he liked to use and one that Chuck liked to use as well. Chuck was the vocalist, he was the one that this whole had to work behind, and the strength of Chuck was that he has one of the most awesome voices in recorded music. It's a voice that when you hear it, you know it; it's not a voice that you could be indifferent to. It's distinct. He also brought a producer's energy to putting these records together. In a way it's almost like Hank and Chuck worked out the composition, and Keith and Eric did more of the machinery, and then together they all kind of finished it. But no one was ever absent from any part of it. It was like the best combos, collaborative and very much so, but there was definitely like a line of responsibility and difference in terms of focuses and abilities or application.

Hank Shocklee: We would use every technique, no different than in film with different lighting effects or film speeds, or whatever. Well, we did the same thing with audio. There was no genre of record that I didn't collect, whether it was classical, speed metal, folk, or speeches. It didn't matter, a record was a record.

What were some of the ways you used samplers as musical instruments?

Hank Shocklee: My vision of this group was to almost have a production assembly line where each person had their own particular specialty. I'm coming from a DJ's perspective. Eric is coming from a musician's perspective. So together, you know, we started working out different ideas.

Chuck D: We thought sampling was just another way of arranging sounds. Just like a musician would take the sounds off of an instrument and arrange them their own particular way. So we thought we was quite crafty with it.

Hank Shocklee: For instance, our song "Don't Believe the Hype" was one of the strangest ways we made a record. We were looking for blends in particular records, so I might be on one turntable, Keith on another and Chuck on another turntable at the same time.

Chuck D: We would get into a recording session and all four of us would just be playing.

Hank Shocklee: If you were to come into our studio, you'd think it's the worst noise.

Chuck D: Hank recorded the session, and 95% was a mess, and 5% of the music was magical.

Hank Shocklee: There would be a time when we have a nice little groove where Keith is going [*sound effects with mouth*] and Chuck is going [*sound effects with mouth*]. We're all together and there's one little moment when it all meshes together in a nice little vibration.

Chuck D: You would listen to this mess and out of that you'd be like, "Whoa, what happened here?"

Hank Shocklee: That little moment is what we snatched and sampled, and that became the music to "Don't Believe the Hype."

Chuck D: That was the closest thing to a jazz band that you could have, just jamming. Maybe not a conventional jazz band. Maybe someone like Sun Ra. [*laughs*]

Harry Allen: I'm thinking of one of my all-time favorite records from Public Enemy's second album *Nation of Millions*, "Show 'em Watchcha Got." The song is composed of the sounds of a lecture by Sister Ava Muhammad of the Nation of Islam over this incredible slowed down drum and bass — this booming track, this mournful horn. By taking this speech by Sister Ava Muhammad and putting it over this music, what you get is something that has even more pathos and a kind of sadness, yet defiance that I think was in her voice. Public Enemy found and accentuated that defiance by re-contextualizing her voice by sampling her voice and putting it in this new context. A lot of the sound of that album is that not of horns and drums and guitars, but this jittery staccato of digital technology of Louis Farrakhan voice that has been digitally sampled and reedited. You have these screams and hollers and grunts and moans all brought together into this orchestra of human passion, you might say. The interesting thing is that PE used something as cold and brittle as computer chips, and samplers, to give this kind of resurrection and life to the voices of pain of black people as uttered in song and voice.

A song like "Fight the Power," which appears on the album *Fear of a Black Planet*, contains a variety of sounds, not just bits and pieces of music, but also speeches and other nonmusical elements.

Fear of a Black Planet
1990

Harry Allen: On *Fear of a Black Planet*, a lot of the content is the sound and voices of either news reports, or radio reports, journalist interviews. There's a whole a kind of attempt to dramatize both the world of PE and a world at large, especially at that time in the early nineties in a very unsure place, what sampling allows the band to do was to really to create its own sonic world.

Hank Shocklee: Public Enemy was not just a group that made hip-hop records that people can just dance to. It was also a source of information. So, when you think about our song "Fight the Power," well, what are you thinking about? You're thinking about going against the system, so the sounds have to go along with that idea.

Chuck D: "Fight the Power" has so many different layers of sound. You have musical loops going around with vocal samples. And you got the musical loops competing with the words, and the loops are going backwards and forwards.

Hank Shocklee: You're thinking about rebellion, you're thinking about persecution, you're thinking about all those things. So, thus, your musical bed is going to echo that sentiment as well.

Chuck D: The song contains a great deal of black music history from a 25-year period. You listen to it, and it's like [*mock announcer's voice*], "This 25-year period black music is brought to you by Public Enemy." From the beginning to the end, it's filled with musical and political history... It was crazy.

Hank Shocklee: We got so far into sampling, we even sampled ourselves, media coverage of ourselves. Our whole reason for doing music in the first place is because we wanted to sample from culture and spit something new out into the world.

Chuck D: *Fear of a Black Planet* was probably the most elaborate smorgasbord of sound that we did. As a matter of fact, I couldn't even produce the backing tracks after *Fear of a Black Planet* because I was burned out by the matrix of the collecting of all kinds of sounds on that record. It's completely an album of found sounds. I couldn't get into the production mode for seven or eight years after that. *Fear of a Black Planet* just fried my brain. I was done. Zzzzzzzz-t.

Did you have to license the samples in *It Takes a Nation of Millions* before it was released?

Hank Shocklee: No, it was cleared afterwards. A lot of stuff was cleared afterwards. Back in the day, things were different. The copyright laws didn't really extend into sampling until the hip-hop artists started getting sued. As a matter of fact, copyright didn't start catching up with us until *Fear of a Black Planet*. That's when the copyrights and everything started becoming stricter because you had a lot of groups doing it and people were taking whole songs. It got so widespread that the record companies started policing the releases before they got out.

Chuck D: It wasn't necessary to clear those albums, *Fear of a Black Planet* and *It Takes a Nation*. The record companies didn't even know what we were doing, so we had no inhibitions.

With its hundreds of samples, is it possible to make a record like *It Takes a Nation of Millions* today? Would it be possible to clear every sample?

Chuck D: By 1994, it was impossible to do any type of record we did in the late 1980s, because every second of sound had been cleared. It kind of curtailed creativity.

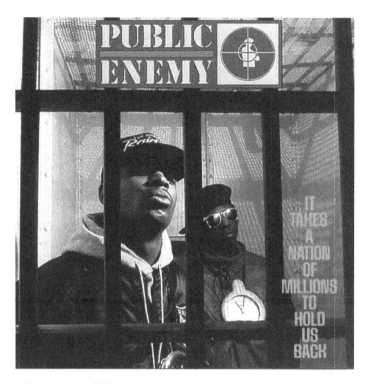

*It Takes a Nation of Millions
to Hold Us Back*
1988

Harry Allen: They were able to even layer sounds and quote other recordings in a way that, just today, because these entities are very familiar with this form of production, would not only charge them an arm and a leg to use, but the amount of publishing income and revenue that would make it simply impossible to release the album. It would amount almost to a form of publishing loan sharking, the amount of — you know, when you use a piece of music that way, the publisher might say this fee plus X percent of publishing income. If they say 50%, and you use six samples, and each person says 50%, that means 300%. That means, in other words, you're paying three times more than you're making even to use it. And so to make an album where really the only thing that's stopping you from adding more layers and more density, or sequentially more samples, is just your imagination — the only thing that's stopping you is just your technique.

Hank Shocklee: It wouldn't be impossible. It would just be very, very costly. The first thing that was starting to happen by the late 1980s was that the people were doing buyouts. You could have a buyout — meaning you could purchase the rights to sample a sound — for around $1,500. Then it started creeping up to $3,000, $3,500, $5,000, $7,500. Then they threw in this thing called rollover rates. If your rollover rate is every 100,000 units, then for every 100,000 units you sell, you have to pay an additional $7,500. A record that sells two million copies would kick that cost up twenty times. Now you're looking at one song costing you more than half of what you would make on your album.

Harry Allen: Those records are kind of artifacts of an earlier time, records that couldn't exist today. They're financially and legally untenable and unworkable records. We can't make those records anymore because you'd have to sell them for, probably, $159 each just to pay all the royalties... What you are hearing on those records is true experimentation unrestrained by suits.

Hank Shocklee: By 1990, all the publishers and their lawyers started making moves. One big one was Bridgeport, the publishing house that owns all the George Clinton stuff. Once all the little guys started realizing you can get paid from rappers if they use your sample, it prompted the record companies to start investigating because now the people that they publish are getting paid.

Chuck D: Corporations found that hip-hop music was viable. It sold albums, which was the bread and butter of corporations. Since the corporations owned all the sounds, their lawyers began to search out people who illegally infringed upon their records. All the rap artists were on the big six record companies, so you might have some lawyers from Sony looking at some lawyers from BMG and some lawyers from BMG saying, "Your artist is doing this," so it was a tit for tat that usually made money for the lawyers, garnering money for the company. Very little went to the original artist or the publishing company.

There's a noticeable difference in Public Enemy's sound between 1988 and the early 1990s. Did this have to do with the lawsuits and enforcement of copyright laws at the turn of the decade?

Chuck D: Public Enemy's music was affected more than anybody's because we were taking thousands of sounds. If you separated the sounds, they wouldn't have been anything — they were unrecognizable. The sounds were all collaged together to make a sonic wall. Public Enemy was affected because it is too expensive to defend against a claim. So we had to change our whole style, the style of *It Takes a Nation* and *Fear of a Black Planet*, by 1991.

Hank Shocklee: We were forced to start using different organic instruments, but you can't really get the right kind of compression that way. A guitar sampled off a record is going to hit differently than a guitar sampled in the studio. The guitar that's sampled off a record is going to have all the compression that they put on the recording, the equalization. It's going to hit the tape harder. It's going to slap at you. Something that's organic is almost going to have a powder effect. It hits more like a pillow than a piece of wood. So those things change your mood, the feeling you can get off of a record. If you notice that by the early 1990s, the sound has gotten a lot softer.

Chuck D: Copyright laws pretty much led people like Dr. Dre to replay the sounds that were on records, then sample musicians imitating those records. That way you could get by the master clearance, but you still had to pay a publishing note.

Hank Shocklee: See, there's two different copyrights: publishing and master recording. The publishing copyright is of the written music, the song structure. And the master recording is the song as it is played on a particular recording. Sampling violates both of these copyrights. Whereas if I record my own version of someone else's song, I only have to pay the publishing copyright. When you violate the master recording, the money just goes to the record company.

Chuck D: Putting a hundred small fragments into a song meant that you had a hundred different people to answer to. Whereas someone like EPMD might have taken an entire loop and stuck with it, which meant that they only had to pay one artist.

So is that one reason why a lot of popular hip-hop songs today just use one hook, one primary sample, instead of a collage of different sounds?

Chuck D: Exactly. There's only one person to answer to. Dr. Dre changed things when he did *The Chronic* and took something like Leon Haywood's "I Want'a Do Something Freaky to You" and revamped it in his own way but basically kept the rhythm and instrumental hook intact. It's easier to sample a groove than it is to create a whole new collage. That entire collage element is out the window.

Harry Allen: When you see artists more interested in playing a piece that they then sample and use in a sample way, as opposed to lifting pieces from records where other great performances which is its own thing, its own kind of technique, and its own kind of timbre — has its own kind of timbre. So I'm mostly talking about that. I'm talking about the failure of music business' imagination to say that this is a — it's almost like the business forced an evolutionary dead end in the case of an album like that. Since 1988, you've not seen or heard really anything like it.

Chuck D: The lawyers didn't seem to differentiate between the craftiness of it and what was blatantly taken.

Hank Shocklee: If I sampled a kick drum from someone, I sampled a snare from someone, and now you're saying that I have to now get clearances for those tiny fragments?

Chuck D: That's when the sound of hip-hop music shifted and people started to only sample one hook, because it was cheaper than paying for 20 or 30 clips in each song — like how we did it.

As you probably know, some music fans are now sampling and mashing together two or more songs and trading the results online. There's one track by Evolution Control Committee that uses a Herb Alpert instrumental as the backing track for your "By the Time I Get to Arizona." It sounds like you're rapping over a Herb Alpert and the Tijuana Brass song. How do you feel about other people remixing your tracks without permission?

Chuck D: I think my feelings are obvious. I think it's great.

Done by the Trickle Trickle: Jbeez With the Ley Liners
Dave Tompkins

I. The Paneling

My uncle was a dowser, attuned to water tables and magnetic vein systems in
Appalachia. Known as Diggy, he listened to calypso on Cuba Radio Marti and welled
up to Ronstadt ballads in Spanish. My mom called him "outdoorsy," which gave him
cover for being out there, or himself. In the late 1950s, he joined a *Barynya* dance
troupe in San Francisco before serving as a codebreaker on the East German border,
eavesdropping on Russian tank commanders. He was shy, knew his rocks, was
nicknamed The Cloud. He was the Bermuda Triangle uncle. The one who gave me
a copy of Ion Hobana's *UFOs Behind the Iron Curtain* when I was 8. That Christmas
I read about a cosmic anti-meteor that "carried on a peculiar form of ballet" before
revising the genetic constitution of the Siberian larch. The blast in Tunguska left no
crater, just eighty million trees flattened in the shape of a butterfly with a 30-mile
wingspan. Shock waves looped the world twice.
        In Christmas 1989, a blue butterfly appeared in a ring of fire in space. Wingspan
was confined to the cassette format, in the upper right corner of the Jungle Brothers'
second release, *Done by the Forces of Nature*. Gently tilt the case and the butterfly,
along with the illustration of the Jungle Brothers (and the World Trade Center at the
foot of a volcano) dissolves into a Zulu Nation emblem. Apparently my uncle gifted
me a hip-hop hologram. Within the folds of the tape's insert was a tiny photo of the
Jungle Brothers, sitting on a sepia chrome beach in Long Island. Afrika Baby Bam,
Mike G, Soundsystem Uncle Sam, and road manager/advisor Baby Chris Lighty. The
Atlantic pulls behind them. Sand fizzes and percolates. They appear to be alone,
watching the overcast skies, as if waiting for Captain Rock's "Dip Ship."[1]
        The Jungle Brothers said they were born to roll like water, the medium through
which humans first hear the world in boom.[2] One could have Jeep-Ass feelings
about air pushed up through limestone passages, a rumble of cave-in-response from
subterranean rivers, the bass we breathe. The Jungle Brothers kept it mineral. Ice
drip was a matter of "trickle trickle," as if on flood watch for rap's expanding future
capital.[3] Sweat beads formed, minds blew. *Done by the Forces of Nature* was layered
with possibility while grounded in truth. J-Ro of the Alkaholiks once called it "an

ode to the regular guy from the ghetto." Baby Bam rapped about clean water, shade, and the pleasures of drinking orange juice buck naked. Called writing *satelliting*, wrote rhymes about writing rhymes in the back of class, splicing in deletions of Black history. Mike G referred to himself as "The Navigator," and at times adopted the alias of a bear park ranger deeply concerned with a world on fire. Though the album title was a carbon credit long overdue, *Done by the Forces of Nature* now carries more ecologic freight and finality, ghostwritten by denial and exploitation. Neither a cosmic deforestation nor Mysterious, less unexplained than just withheld, damage untold and done by the forces of greed.

How the family geomancer happened upon the inventors of Hip House remains unclear, beyond a shared belief that inclusivity is a function of environmental

L-R: Afrika Baby Bam, Navigator Mike G,
Baby Chris Lighty (RIP), Sound System Uncle Sam
Photo by Renee Valerie Cox

Dave Funkenklein and
Afrika Baby Bam circa 1988
Courtesy of Chris LaSalle

awareness and survival. When I look at the photo of the Jungle Brothers on the beach, I half expect to see my uncle wading by, ectoplasmic, pants-rolled, dropping a hydrophone in the breakers for one of his meditation tapes. Once when staying with us, he went out for a walk and left the ocean playing on a boom box in my room all day. I stood outside listening to autoreversed tides crash against the closed door. That sea foam slap.

I asked about the tape two summers ago, when visiting him at the Solace Center, a hospice facility east of Asheville, North Carolina. He remembered UFOs ("I wanted to start you guys early.") and episodes of *In Search Of...* but not the Jungle Brothers. How did he come across them? After performing an exorcism on a fixer upper? Did he hear "I'll Dowse You" in the crawl space clay? Did someone play it for him after a day spent building Cherokee sweat lodges, listening to "Doin Our Own Dang" with its shout out to Loose Ends? Vague from painkillers, he wasn't sure. My uncle did remember the map room in the State Department, the blockade of toy ships off the coast of Cuba. On America's desire to control the Caribbean, he was clear. On Appalachian thunderheads at Max Patch, bark striations, birdsong, the twig integrity of nests lined with invisible mud, a place called Meat Camp — also clear. From his

Richard "Diggy" Crutchfield
in Barcelona, circa early 1960s
Courtesy of John Crutchfield
and Lilian Childress

hospital bed, he took us up the Tanawah Trail in Watauga County, past the Cessna wing claimed by humming ferns, signaling through the spruce and hemlocks, a glint from a fuselage never recovered from a crash in 1978. He rhapsodized about the ley lines on the way up to Calloway Peak, where we once scattered my oldest brother's ashes, jeans powdered by the blowback.

When dowsing, my uncle used a coat hanger with PVC piping. He wasn't just looking for the perfect spring. He dowsed books, relationships, back roads, the health care system. When less mobile, he dowsed with a pendulum on a string, which sat on the nightstand by his bed at the hospice center. That afternoon, I left he and my mom listening to a tape my grandmother made on Christmas Day 1985, when the mic was passed to cousins and sisters from Spartanburg, Savannah and Miami. I went to find a nurse to see if it was okay to take my uncle for a walk. A black bear had been spotted in the mizzle, inspecting a dumpster in the Solace Center parking lot, by the stone maze. I cut through the empty common room and passed a security guard walking by a piano. By the time I reached the doorway, Terry Davis was seated and playing what could've been a lost New Edition slow jam (when Johnny Gill joined and Lutherized the group), as if trying to recall "Can You Stand the Rain" from someone else's memory, alternate versions of why middle school friends outgrew themselves, when accountants got thanked in the liners. The piano drifted down the hallways, the nurses station feeling it, past the harpist playing a few rooms down, shades drawn, past the woodchuck glade print, past the vending machine my mom cussed out for a pack of Cheez-Its, past every time we would replay the afternoon's events in the ride back on I-26 east later that night, so I could listen to my mom listen to Terry's jam on repeat. She leaned forward in the passenger seat, ear to my phone, orange traffic barrels flipping by. On playback, the interlude was a reprise, a fade-in recall at the end of an album that never existed. When memory places Terry Davis in that empty atrium, it takes a few nods for the audio to resolve itself from the brain's default familiar.[4] In this case it was "(No One Knows Me) Like the Piano," by Sampha — the Chopped Not Slopped version.[5] Just before Sampha places the piano in his mother's home, the conflation is sorted and Terry Davis resumes his seat under vaulted ceilings, braids spilling over the back of his gray golf shirt.

My mom likes the Sampha title. She asks me to repeat it and then says it back to herself, slowly, in her own time-stretch drawl to be sure. Barrels fly out of the dark. *What did he call that room in the State Department? The Bureau of Current Indications?*

At the memorial in Asheville, we passed my uncle's walking stick around a Cherokee sidual circle that had been chalked out on the carpet in a common room two floors above his apartment. My cousins suggested that we could contribute an object that reminded us of Diggy. I couldn't find *UFOs Behind the Iron Curtain*, so I brought a copy of the Jungle Brothers tape, purchased from an army veteran who'd moved to Brooklyn from Puerto Rico in the '60s. When I visited his house on Ave M in Canarsie, he answered the door holding a cassette mummified in bubble wrap. It was early May. Dwarf violets nodded in the breeze. He stood in slippers on red flagstones, talking about block parties and dancing to Jimmy Castor, Manu Dibango. We went through our favorites from the Jungle Brothers tape. "Beeds on a String," "JBeez Comin Thru." The Pharoah Sanders joint. "Black Woman": A clavinet from the Four Tops, a few cold morning plucks from the Commodores before the "Assembly Line" cranks up, and Caron Wheeler, in an imaginary session with rust belt loops, the Jamaican-born voice of Soul II Soul. "I love you too," she says. The voice of Gil Scott-Heron hands the planet back over in the breakdown: "We men have messed it up so bad."

"Tribe Vibes" gathered Batman, P-Funk, the Bee Gees, Donald Byrd for a juice cleanse, and still managed to sound skivvied to the bone. Two seconds of this song that the Jungle Brothers called a "level of consciousness" have haunted me since '89 — an instant where two words, "the bongos," get reflected back to Afrika Baby Bam as a question. There's an upfreak drag on his voice, less say-what than where, a call-and-response to self. *The bongos?* In the undertow, on another channel, it happens in reverse at the same time, magnetic tape pulling at the past, an upheave taking it all into the lungs. Hardly a meanwhile, that breath drawn between the drums and their ghost of inquiry. It's a sleight of reverb, technically the echo looking for its source, wide-voiced, bringing interrogations of history, tracing itself. Where did that come from again? (and again). The palms of Perk Jacobs, Donald Byrd's percussionist from Washington, DC, by way of a Pan African sense of gathering that could've taken place in Uncle Red's record crate.[6] It could've happened in Afrika House International in Harlem, when Afrika Baby Bam and Mike G spent time absorbing. The Jungle Brothers knew where to listen.

Rewind a third time, a last time, the tape itself now gathered and then stretching, promising future drag until the past unspools in a regurgitated snarl, spitting us into some outer loop and we're left trying to put it all back together on a porch in Canarsie. I thanked the block party vet for the reverie and replacement. My uncle's gift had been eaten by a Honda Accord back in 1991, at the beginning of "Beads on a String," which had already caught the Undisputed Truth in the breakdown. "(I Know) I'm Losing You." He wished me luck and sent me on my way, popping plastic bubbles.

At my uncle's memorial, *Done by the Forces of Nature* was placed inside the chalk circle left of owl claw. Yona French Hawk, a Cherokee wisdom keeper, had drummed to the southwest as the sun dipped into the Great Smokies along the Tennessee border. My cousin, a playwright and his wife, a Berlin theater actor, rendered a gorgeous Appalachian Traditional by Hazel Dickens, a double bassist from Montcalm, West Virginia. *I feel the shadows now upon me.* My other cousin, a writer and a therapist, recited her dad's favorite passage from Rumi. My mom read a poem she'd written about her brother: ligustrum in restraint, muslin snake sacks, Diggy scaling pines to glimpse a horned owl, lucky to land with his eyes in his head. We cried our faces sore.

During the sidual gathering, I freed the insert from the clear cassette case and shook out eight perforated panels, like a billfold accordion of family photos. Font flea bitten, couldn't see shit in the candlelight. The room of dowsers and healers would have to take my word for it, that *Done by the Forces of Nature* wasn't produced and engineered but "recycled and reincarnated." A family memorial wasn't the best time to hip everyone to the generosity and care the Jungle Brothers imbued in their liner notes, to eulogize an era of rap while making grief about myself. But Diggy always carried a deep reverence of what was before him. I think he would've appreciated "Tribe Vibes," which began with "all are present and accounted for." This could now be heard as an aftermath roll call, making sure everyone's okay and heard, with phones lit up, the check-in tradition of Black radio DJs, connecting community to airwaves.

Giving "Special Dangxz," the acknowledgments in *Done by the Forces...* served as a praise map, a thank you to the hip-hop's parents, aunts and uncles, the family record collections, a gift and a guide, an owl grip-out. The scroll of shouts thickened the print insert, keeping the cassette snug in its case while also transcending its clear dimensions, following ley liners of their own, unfolding and expanding in our heads (and cubbies). Memories keep adding names. Could've sworn George Michael (Red Alert's remix of "J Beez Comin Thru") was in there. A closer inspection of the paneling reveals that Roger Troutman and Zapp are two doors down from Ramsey Lewis, as if you could walk past the Troutman garage in Ohio and hear Roger practicing a Talkbox version

Ladi Luv
'Anything Goes'
(Joey Boy Records, 1989)
Image provided
by Bee Bart

of "Les Fleur," trying catch that Minnie octave with a tube in his mouth. Coltrane next to Earth, Wind & Fire, Scatman Crothers, Chaka Khan. Every name a dang and in every dang, gratitude. There was a paragraph for the sampled past, another for the ever widening present. The Future however is seen, or squinted, in one word: Ultramagnetic. The Future took place in a room in the Bronx wallpapered in Mylar, a polyester film used by NASA for satellite balloons. Best known for its reflectivity, Mylar holds aroma barrier properties and "dimensional stability." That extra wiggle on the air quotes is a molecular disturbance, for anyone who's ever heard Kool Keith repeatedly transmatter himself. He once referred to the SP-1200 as "the panel," sample pads triggered as memory launchers, getting over on borrowed time.[7] Walls ripple. Panels that are actual panels try to keep it all together. The guy in the Elvis helmet is flipping. So sidereal.

I once asked Afrika Baby Bam about Ultramagnetic's solitary landing in the liners, a paragraph in name. "You're reaching back, revering and channeling that while you have another group in your era that's going to outer space, not leaving anything behind. They're (Ultra) taking it all with them." Carry-ons include a crumpled meteor wad of Mylar, spat out of a poster tube.

Within a gatefold, more paneling in comics drawn by Parliament-Funkadelic artist Pedro Bell. George Clinton came up in one of the last conversations I had with my uncle, regarding a slab of concrete in Kannapolis, North Carolina. He wasn't familiar with Uncle Jam, so I attempted a brief rundown: landed UFOs on stage, waterskied on a pair of dolphins in the Bermuda Triangle, Black American folk hero/ revolutionary whose brilliant outdoorsy rhythm guitarist Tawl Ross co-wrote "Music for My Mother" and "Maggot Brain," fled the group under lysergic circumstances that get more attention than what he actually meant to the music (back in our minds), joined the family plumbing business, once spotted on a riding mower in Maxton, North Carolina wearing a canary yellow suit. Tawl Ross is still playing-not-playing to this day.

Diggy was into it. He offered to psychically dowse the slab, site of the outhouse where Julious Clinton gave birth to George in 1941.[8] "There's nothing more ordinary than a dadgum outhouse," my uncle said. "But this one appears to have cosmic repercussions. You're going into the ground in your imagination to the beat of a drum." By the end of our conversation, I realized he might've been dowsing me where I sat, to a reverse bongo under its echo, behind the wall of seep.

II. In the Meantime, All These Reasons

Attrell Cordes, Jr enters a clock shop and passes a gnome made of pecan shells. A giant pair of a black acrylic men's briefs, WWF in XXL, hangs on the wall next to a cuckoo clock. The little wooden door is stuck so the bird marks the hour with a headbutt.

Ye Olde Clock Shoppe was located in Concord, North Carolina, a few miles south of George Clinton's birthplace, across the bridge over Interstate 85. Situated in a former truck stop, the clock repair business also housed 162,000 used records.[9] If one of these records is Spandau Ballet's "True," Attrell Cordes is PM Dawn's Prince Be, who introduced New Romantic pop to "Ashley's Roach Clip." If it's Joni Mitchell and Charles Mingus doing "I's Muggin'," then Attrell is All Those Muthaf*ckin Reasons, a shadow alias he adopted because the name Prince Be had become a professional liability in making hip-hop. For example, one of my favorite songs of 1998: "The Blessin' (Boom Bodya Da)" by Mood Swingaz. The parenthetical boom in the title transcribes one of Mingus' last acts in the studio before he died in Mexico in 1979, the same day, Joni Mitchell would note, that 56 sperm whales had beached themselves. The fine print just credits Reasonz — and there were many — the main one being the time KRS-One bullied Be off stage in 1993. It's also on everyone who bought into the conservatism of what was or wasn't allowed to be hip-hop, myself included. Like I had a claim because I subscribed to *The Source*.

Prince Be had been brought to the Clock Shop by Georges Sulmers, a producer who'd put out the Mood Swingaz on his label Rawshack. I can't speak to anything Be purchased, he showed up there long before me and with an omnivorous ear. (Growing up in a house where Kool and the Gang and Richie Havens had jam sessions in the Cordes living room was helpful too.) By process of elimination (and my dumb luck), I can confirm that Be left without a copy of "Good to the Last Drop." One can be forgiven for bypassing this Miami Bass 12 by a teenager from Camila, Georgia named Ladi Luv. Nor can anyone be expected to notice her logo on the label's pink backdrop — how "Luv" was spelled out in recording tape, a flow of black ribbon that crinkled at the right instants, a distracted cursive. Who drew *that*? I'd like to imagine Ladi Luv's middle school alias, Salenthia Clayton, in math class, blind-scrawling her logo on the corner of her desk, eyes on the board ahead, descrambling a word problem while magnetic tape untangled itself under her pen. Pressure on the nub, ink weight evoking slight twists of ribbon, then a loopy flourish, almost heart-shaped. The effect is name-chain sway, tugged by a South Florida breeze. It was years before I noticed the logo was supposed to be recording tape, freed from the reels. Out of state you might say, this Miami Bass with Georgia plates. Most certainly out of its mind when Ladi Luv's verses get fed through a stroboscopic gate. On the B-side, "Good to the Last Dub," her flow is dispersed as bubbles, words as sounds trying to cohere to their familiars, one of which swore to be *vacuum*. Zoom on the label and see hundreds of actual bubbles, or portals, a porous limestone landscape in a faded pink pastel, just waiting for the water to rise up. The tick-tock breakdowns in the track are just waiting for, if not counting on the next drop, catching "Good to the Last Dub" in an ever state of forward thinking. It's just a matter of time.

TELEPHONE

Dancing On The Edge

FULL RANGE RECORDING
Vocalion
MADE IN U.S.A.   NOT LICENSED FOR RADIO BROADCAST

SHAGGIN' AT THE SHORE
(Nate Leslie)
NATE LESLIE
AND HIS ORCHESTRA
5504

VOLUME 1 No. 1
Sept-Oct 1989

Cynthia Harrell (center with cake) at Charlie's Place by Jack Thompson

Bill Arey, the store owner, was more than happy to oblige these ripples in scheduling. He was known to deadbolt his more committed customers inside the shop overnight. Meanwhile his son Reid continued to hoover up massive collections of Beach Music from the coastal Carolina regions, undeterred by a congenital heart defect or the fact that Beach Music was actually R&B whitewashed by Weejuns.[10] Relabeled so, Beach Music was a designation where its Black creators weren't welcome, yet the only place where white teenagers could hear it.

In 1989, The Clock Shop would run an ad in *Dancing on the Edge*, a Charlotte-based magazine dedicated to Beach Music, with editor Fleur Paysour (now with the Smithsonian's African American Museum of History) preserving the Black origins of Shag, a dance once claimed by the South Carolina legislature as the "State Dance." The first issue features 1930s Shag pioneer Emzie Bubba Caldwell on the cover and an epigraph from *God Emperor of Dune*. "Motives from our darkest past can well up out of an unconscious reservoir and become events with which not only must we live but contend."

With respect to Emzie, Myrtle Beach locals might credit Cynthia Harrell as inventor of the Shag because she taught them. A brilliant dancer, Cynthia was a hostess at Charlie's Place, a Black-owned supper club on Carver Street frequented by white teens sneaking across the marshes from their family vacation rentals. Emboldened by South Carolina's segregationist governor Strom Thurmond, local police/Klan attacked Charlie's Place in august of 1950, leaving owner Charlie Fitzgerald severely beaten. Riddled with bullets, the jukebox from Charlie's would remain in a shed behind the club until it was junked in the early 1980s. "No one thought it had any value," says Frank Beacham, author of *Charlie's Place: How the Ku Klux Klan Tried to Stop the Rise of Rhythm and Blues*. "The records on it were all smashed. None survived." Records like T-Bone Burnett's "Woman Hypin Blues," Stick McGhee's "Drinkin Wine Spo-Dee-O-Dee," Big Jay McNeely's "The Deacon's Hop". The jukebox at Charlie's was in itself an act of defiance. But what was the divider criteria that landed a 45 in the "Beach Music" section at the Clock Shop? Reid and Bill Arey (both now deceased) would be known as one of the central Piedmont sources for R&B singles heard at Charlie's.

While rows of 45s occupied the bins at the Clock Shop, 12 inches and LPs were stashed underneath and largely ignored. How did Organized Konfusion's second album *S.T.R.E.S.S.: The Extinction Agenda* find its way there? Released in 1994, the album was stewarded by Dave "Funkenklein" Klein, a writer and visionary who worked for Organized's label, HollywoodBASIC, in Disneyland, where a day on the job could include taking Boo-Yaa T.r.i.b.e. to Pirates of the Caribbean, or tearing down a bubblewrap-lined hallway in his wheelchair and then writing about it in his Gangsta Limpin column.[11]

In Organized Konfusion's first video from the *S.T.R.E.S.S.* album, they're leaping about snow drifts, shirtless in ski goggles. Pharoahe Monch, who rapped about global warming thirty years ago,[12] introduces himself with a screech of tires on "Thirteen." He's coming like a "redneck trucker," backing over a historical trauma while trying to throw it in reverse at the same time, perhaps catching a lift from "Blowfly's Rapp," when Clarence Reid plowed through the Klan in an 18-wheeler rig, reporting on his CB radio. "That's a 10-4 good buddy!"

For Monch's endless reserve of quotable lines (and advances in neuro-crafting, "shaping your brain like potter-r-r-r-r-r-r-r-y"), the most memorable might be the moment when he burns them all down, dropping everything in mid thought (which in this packed case includes mandatory sentencing, mass incarceration)[13], giving it all up to scoff, "FUCK rapping." Was it written? Did the record label provide health insurance? He says he changed the beat's religion, then does a preacher fire impression of Annie Lennox. "Here Comes the Rain Again" will never sound the same, just as Rev. Eugene McDaniels can be expected every "Black Sunday."[14] The end of "Thirteen" is so hell with it. *What am I some kind of asshole?* For good measure, Prince Po chimes in over his friend's shoulder with "Asshole!" Backing him up, it up, leaving the air jittered with particle tread and tire smoke.

Bill Arey wasn't familiar with Organized Konfusion, much less couldn't locate their album at the Clock Shop. He did however keep a copy of the "I-95 Asshole Song" behind the counter, at the hip. Credited to August and the Spur of the Moment Band, this road-rage country novelty was pressed up in Miami and distributed by truckers through jukeboxes and 24-hour diners along the east coast corridor. Can't help but wonder if a box of "Good to the Last Dubs" hitched a ride, considering Ladi Luv's label Joey Boy shared office space with the A-hole record label Pantera.

One could run themselves off into a drainage ditch on such matters.[15] Like suddenly realizing the Jungle Brothers' infinite wisdom in hearing the dang in thing, doing the damn thing, as they so often did when on the road. There's something in their sound that couldn't wait to get to it, the immediacy of the future. See you at Pottery Brain. Not to get stuck, the thing would heap on to assume the name of a Brooklyn junk shop, so called The Thing, due to its mass assimilation of record collections, souls, and time, yet another version of "The Black Hit of Space," a Human League song about a record that swallows up all the record shops in the universe, a song that was conceived in a Sheffield diner called Nameless. The hours remain the same. Done by the by and by.

III. Like a Plumber Uses a Dang Anti-Meteor

Trees with branches. A seemingly mundane observation in passing, but also a premonition that circles back in days to come, to make sure the trees are still present. The Jungle Brothers were always in consideration of the trunk — it's all about where and how the trees land. In Afrika's verse, that's smack dab between a manmade avalanche and a B-Boy frozen in his favorite stance, arms folded. Then "a prayer to God is a confrontation" followed by a flow chart of environmental extractionism, soil heard as oil, rhyme scheme as geo-acoustic map, ending up sealed in a plastic Ziploc bag. Afrika covers a lot of shifting ground in the title track. Mike G, for his part, walks a mile for a beat, in this case a Pharoah Sanders record that Yann Tomita hooked up to Grandmaster Flash's brainwaves.[16]

Miles turn to decades and Mike G is led to an airbrushed safari rendered in icing. In 2018, the cover of *Straight Out the Jungle* was glazed onto chocolate cake, celebrating the 30-year anniversary of the Jungle Brothers' first album. This means celebrating 30 years of listening to "Black Is Black" finish on the same Prince hard stop that ends "Controversy." (Some nerve right?) The anniversary party took place in Raleigh, North Carolina, 20 minutes southeast of Morrisville, where Mike G has lived with his family for the past 15 years.

I met him once, briefly, at a 4th of July party held at Prince Be's penthouse in Hoboken, watching fireworks shoot across the Hudson, an inverted sky-glass shimmer. New Kingdom's Jason "Nosaj" Furlow made the introduction in Be's arcade room. Could've been by a pinball machine. Could've been Asteroids. Probably high asked him about "Tribe Vibes." Also in the house: Afrika Baby Bam and New Kingdom's Sebastian Christensen, a horologist who currently runs his father Knud's clock shop, Sutton Clocks, in Manhattan. "We make house calls for grandfather clocks," says the outgoing answering machine. Sebastian also repairs vintage barometers, pressure gauges, barometric looking glasses and baro-bezels.

This past summer, I called Mike G in Morrisville to ask him about the liners. We talked cool uncles, Kool Keiths, and memory seepage. "The liners took a life of their own," he said. "The architecture of hip-hop. For me, having Red as an uncle, the DJ was first. That's where you get your education on. That's what the liner notes did. That helped me remember." "The songs (on *Done by the Forces...*) were exchanges of experiences with artists in the liners," added Baby Bam. "It was a community."

The Jungle Brothers also corrected a few errors I'd been propagating over the past three decades. About that reverse bongo reflection in "Tribe Vibes." "The bongos? That's me," said Mike G. "Asking the question."[17] Call-and-response to self becomes Red Alert's nephew chiming in from another channel.

"Between 'Tribe Vibes' and 'Black Woman,' those are my top songs from the album. Caron Wheeler shared her vibe. Wasn't much that needed to be said." Mike G makes another correction: The voice of "I love you" in "Black Woman" was not Caron Wheeler but his girlfriend at the time, Kika of the Safari Sisters, then dancers for Queen Latifah. "Black Woman was a homage to my mom who had passed two years ago, so it was an allotment to her, and my grandmother, who really helped pick me up when my mom passed. It was a heavy time."[18]

On "Feelin' Alright," Mike G gives us the lasting image of his grandmother waving from the stoop as the Jungle Brothers tear off in a Jeep to do another show. The safari bucket flies off his head, gusted by his friend's laughter and a sense of already thereness befitting a group ahead of their time. None rapped better about the thrill and freedom of touring, as well as anticipating its future reflection once back home, giddy and sleepless. "I've got a fine memory of a very fine night." All of this was well underway when the world (or whoever was watching *Yo! MTV Raps*) was introduced to the Jungle Brothers in the video for "I'll House You." We first encounter them cavorting across stages in London, dizzy in spinning lights. What I remembered was a house music all night long (had no idea what that was) and a flash of Baby Bam in a safari vest sitting on a commode. What I missed was a brief glimpse of their tour manager Dave Funkenklein, before he drove to Tijuana to catch Rodney O and Joe Cooley.

We like to have fun by the ton. While reading the lyrics in the liners of *Done by the Forces...,* one may realize (too late), that the panels are cortical folds and that they've disappeared into some over-sparked yet welcoming super-rap brain. You hear the Jungle Brothers goofing around, a release not on tape, but in written unscripted conversations with themselves, and at times, with their records. These too are gatherings. Before the Pharoah Sanders sax cue, Afrika writes in "wipes his mouth," in parentheses. The break between verses is "Recess," back out to the schoolyard (after cutting through the cafeteria, bouncing off lunch tables).

Read along for cues to bridges. There's a "Bridge to Horniness" and a "Bridge to the Rock." There's "James Brown's Getaway Bridge." There are bridges where no bridges exist. Build your own! You can't help but wonder if this was all fiendishly masterminded to make you rewind to make sure Mike G did or didn't say "Stetsasonic" halfway into "Doin' Our Own Dang," right before Monie Love misses her transatlantic flight.[19]

At one point, Afrika attempts to transcribe a sample, some scatting from "Earthquake Shake" by the Undisputed Truth. He finally gives up and tosses the pen to us across the ellipses. *"You Write That Out."* Good luck with that.

This was at a time when printed rap lyrics were decontextualized from Black spaces, weaponized in court (2 Live Crew) and under FBI surveillance (NWA). Reading the transcription for "J Beez Comin Thru," you may notice a serious upgrade in wattage capacity. "5000 boomin watts" gets a boost to "500000000000000."[20] The voice carries well off the page, bringing everything that went into this uncharted *dang* with it, the bass traveling, expanding reach and wavelength, the air from the speakers blowing the map ass-over-expectations down the road. So outta here — the 5000 code for instant egress, or escape, from the studio, the bullshit, America. A version of Harmony Holiday's "acoustics of getting the hell out.[21] It's mobility but also the moment amplified in recall, tacking on more zeros each time the memory unfolds and the Dip Ship loops back home. That's how the story goes. So much joy in "clothes packed neatly."[22] So much looking forward. The endless possibility. The fuck-it-why-not. *We just finished our album and sampled "War Pigs" and our cover is a hologram. Recess.*

When I called Afrika in Daytona Beach, Florida, parts of our conversation were lost to backdrop. The Atlantic rolled and crashed. Turbulence whapped at his phone. I asked about the bongos. "We were recording in reverse with delay and then turned the tape machine back forward. The delay comes before the actual voice. *The bonnngos?*" He sounds just like the record, which is to say, like nothing else. Summoning that backwards-masked wave energy, as if he normally reverse-delayed the tape machine in his mouth in conversation, the machine itself, an Akai now in dust, stored in laryngeal muscle memory and then pitched up by a Daytonian sea wind. No small feat!

According to Afrika, it began when a girl vanishes into a television set after the "Star Spangled Banner" signs off into a blizzard. "I got the idea from *Poltergeist*. The *Mommmmy*. (In 'Tribe Vibes') Your brain registers it spatially, without disturbing the groove. It gives you space."

When Mike G moved to North Carolina, he got space and a journeyman's license in commercial plumbing. Working with drainage systems, his practice becomes increasingly complicated as the eastern part of the state grows more vulnerable to hurricane flooding. "After the Jungle Brothers thing kind of petered out, I learned the trade, literally from the ground up — from the sewer main all the way up to the rooftop vent. Know what I mean? It's kind of a lost art."

Now when I hear Schoolly D saying, "I use a microphone like a plumber use a tool,"[23] I can't help but think of a stray branch from a Siberian conifer, vibrating like a divining rod, still smoking from the blast that tore roofs into the sky. I mention the tape my uncle gave me to Mike G, as well as his found calling in ultramagnetic water sensing and healing. "One of the old guys I used to work under used to do that shit! He'd do it to find water lines. 'Start diggin' over here!' He was in his early '60s. Old farm boy out of Wilson. It (water dowsing) was hard but he showed me some tricks! He was always looking for a main. He popped a couple of 'em! He could pick up a twig and do the little twisty thing. Hold it with two hands, walk it and that thing would just roll. The stick would roll, point down to where the water was. He'd be like, 'That's where it's at.'"

Notes

1. Captain Rock, "Cosmic Blast". NIA, 1985.

2. For extra bass gusto: "Born to Roll (Jeep Ass... Remix)" by Masta Ase INC. Low-end courtesy of "Knowledge Me," Original Concept and Andre "Doctor Dre" Brown and Triple M "Worse Em." Low rider courtesy of Los Angeles' Latinx car culture, which granted "Born To Roll" a new audience and a ground effects kit.

3. "Hurricane Harvey on my wrist, shit flooded out" — 21 Savage and Offset, "Disrespectful" Also: Maxo Kream's "Roaches" which includes a devastating account of the phone call with his mother in Houston during Hurricane Harvey.

4. Every time I hear "Love Is A House" it becomes "Human".

5. Leading piano parents all-timer : "(I Want You) Every Day and Night" by The Springers, released in 1966 on Ves-Thad.

6. Mike G's uncle was DJ Red Alert who had a dedicated following at WBLS. "We was going to a place in Harlem called Africa House, burning incense and reading books, drinking sorrel and not eating meat, and talking with the elders about Bob Marley and Ghana and South Africa and apartheid. And taking all of those experiences back into the studio and making the studio environment almost like our village, our hut — just creating that whole environment." — Afrika Baby Bam talking to Angus Batey, for The Quietus. This would be the same Afrika House International, credited on the back cover as styling the beach photo, full address included. In an extended column right of Past, Present & Future is a parallel scroll, to those "trapped in the concrete jungle," beginning with Lumumba Carson, founder of X-Can.

7. Bedroom studio, homing device, jot landing, Ced Gee.

8. "Can We Get To That." Oxford American, North Carolina Music Issue, 2018. That conversation with my uncle about George Clinton took place late morning, in a coffee shop in Asheville. Afterwards, I walked up towards the center of town and passed a Jeep Cherokee, idling at a significant grade blasting Cybotron's "Clear" next to a quarried wall.

9. Estimation by Clock Shop owner Bill Arey, circa 2003, when I first visited. Chairman Jefferson Mao and Eothen Alapatt first put me up on it. Not surprisingly, Eothen was also one of the customers who requested to be locked in overnight.

10. My introduction to this appellation took place at roughly 3,665 feet above sea level, overhearing someone singing The Embers' 'I Love Beach Music,' while walking away from my grandmother's funeral in Watauga County. Frank Beacham: "I Love Beach Music" is one example of 'bubble gum beach' that got sanitized by the white version. They did a Pat Boone on it. It was called Beach Music because that was the only place whites could hear it." Maurice Williams, who Frank Beacham interviewed for his book, played both Black and white venues to make a living. "He was depressed because his own kids thought Beach Music was white music."

11. Too many to choose from in Funkenklein's Gangsta Limpin columns, which appeared in The Source and The Bomb Magazines.

12. Organized Konfusion "Releasing Hypnotical Gases" (HollywoodBasic) 1991.

13. Ava Duvernay's 13th, nominated for Best Documentary Feature in 2016. Also Pharoahe Monch's new group, 13.

14. "Black Sunday" and "Stray Bullet" also from the *S.T.R.E.S.S.* album. The latter finds its way into one of the Jungle Brothers' more complex tracks, "Sunshine," a block party that ends in tragedy.

15. I fell for it when writing about the Clock Shop for *Wax Poetics* in 2003. The title, "For As Long As That Tick Is Followed by that Boom" was paraphrased from "West Savannah" by way of OutKast, curb detector to trunk. Let panels be mud flaps and let the mud be the clay that soundproofed the Organized Noize basement studio.

16. Pharoah Sanders, "Elevation". Impulse, 1974; Yann Tomita feat. Grandmaster Flash, "Flash To The Bionic Beat And An Analysis Of His Brainwave By Doctor" (For Life Records), 1998.

17. I asked Andrew "Monk One" Mason about the effect. He replied by sending a file of "Tribe Vibes" reverse engineered. He also applied the same effect to a Nate Dogg a capella from a Ludacris song.

18. "I just got the instrumentals." —Mike G. The instrumentals include voice effects and whispers not heard in *Done by the Forces*... most notably in "Black Woman" and "Tribe Vibes." "Soon he lands... clap the same hands...open minds... change in times." It should also be noted that track listing for the tour vinyl begins with "JBs Monorail," which is...*wait what??* In our conversations, both Afrika and Mike both gave it up for engineer Greg Mann for sourcing the Four Tops' source clavinet that would be used for "Black Woman." Memorably identified as Greg "Muthafuckin" Mann in the credits for Brand Nubian's second album *In God We Trust.*

19. He didn't but it's on the page. Go figure! Go Stetsa!

2000000000000000000. I tried counting, went blind, gave up. Those zeros could also be the actions of one under the delirium of deadline and ecstatic to be finished with an album with 5,000 samples uncleared. He also could've just lost track.

21. "What are the acoustics of getting the hell out of here?" Harmony Holiday in conversation with Lynnee Denise, "The Sound of Getting Out," Omniaudience [Side Two], recorded at Coaxial Arts and published in *Triple Canopy*, April 2019.

22. "Travel lytely" — a shout to the fantastic MC Lyte. See "Paper Thin," "10% Dis," "Cappucino."

23. Schoolly D, "Parkside 5-2". Jive, 1987.

Preprogramming the Present
The Musical Time Machines of Gabriel Teodros
Erik Steinskog

Watching the video to Gabriel Teodros' "Greeny Jungle" from the album *Evidence of Things Not Seen* (2014), adds layers to the song. The video opens with demonstrators marching while shouting "We want freedom." From there, a call and response arises. Q: "Whose lives matter?" A: "Black Lives Matter." Then the music comes in, as if the volume is turned up gradually: the sound of steel drums and percussion. When the beat comes in, a voice is heard as if from a distance: "I know how you watch, as you grow older — literally, not a figure of speech, the corpses of your brothers and sisters pile up against you. Not for anything they have done." The images are police spraying demonstrators, holding them to the ground, in combination with images of peaceful demonstrators. Then the MC comes in: "We get hunted in the streets/openly by police/prison is an industry/they don't want us to speak free." I had heard the song on the album before watching the video, but the video added other dimensions to the song. The images of demonstrations, the MC — soon to be accompanied by a guest — are rapping to demonstrators — not simply to a record-listening audience — and engaging in the contemporary political situation. Thus, when the video was released in February 2015, the song got a new and different meaning for me. In hindsight I guess what challenged my preconceptions was that I had heard the song in a context inspired by Afrofuturism, and focused on the lyrics related to fantasy rather than to the here-and-now. The video, on the contrary, insists on the everyday-life struggle in the present, and had me thinking about the relation between Afrofuturism and the contemporary in a different way. This rethinking is, of course, also intimately related to the continuous relevance of Afrofuturism, as well as to the continuous renegotiation of the past, the present, and the future.

Layers of Time

The discourses and practices of Afrofuturism are multifaceted, but a key element is the question about the presence of black people in the future. From Mark Dery's definition back in 1993, about "speculative fiction that treats African-American themes and addresses African-American concerns in the context of twentieth-century technoculture" and "African-American signification that appropriates images of technology and a prosthetically enhanced future"[1] to Ytasha L. Womack's exposition of "an intersection of imagination, technology, the future, and liberation,"[2] the future is an obvious dimension of Afrofuturism. The future, however, is at the same time intertwined with the past and the present. In other words, there is what can be called an alternative philosophy of time and history at stake in Afrofuturism, and when this is brought forward, the notions of the past, the present, and the future are rearranged and reimagined, and other ways of understanding and experiencing time are brought to the fore. Womack's focus upon the imagination is crucial, and is her version of Dery's reference to speculative fiction. In the domain of sound Kodwo Eshun's notion of "sonic fiction" seems to be yet another alternative,[3] underlining how the sonic (sound and music) also takes part in this construction of what Dery in his article calls "other stories" about "culture, technology, and things to come."[4]

This rereading of the understandings of time is, for example, seen in the thinking that the world ended long ago, and that we are, as Sun Ra says, "after the end of the world." If we are after the end of the world, in some post-apocalyptic state, then even parts of our own past become different than they used to be. Sun Ra's statement, heard at the opening of the movie *Space Is the Place*, in June Tyson's voice, seems inclusive: "It's after the end of the world; don't you know that yet?" But not everyone knows this. If this is "the end of the world" as the point in time when West Africans were captured and sent across the Atlantic to the "New World" to become slaves, then the group included in the "we" are the people of African descent in this new world. Such an understanding would be consistent with the alien abduction trope that Dery writes about in the opening pages of his "Black to the Future." Black Americans are the descendants of alien abductees, and they were moved from one world to another, and this other world — this version of the new world — was anything but promising or a place for prosperity. On the contrary, the slaves can much better be conceptualized as sub-humans, functioning as "machines" or "tools," as a kind of proto-robots.[5]

The past future for blacks in America was thus also some kind of science fiction life, and if this is part of the premises for Afrofuturism, then the perspective on the future in Afrofuturism is slightly altered. One begins differently to see how the past, the present, and the future all need to be thought anew, within a slightly different perspective, a perspective based in other stories, in other understandings, in other experiences of what it means to live within "modernity." Such an understanding echoes what Toni Morrison said in conversation with Paul Gilroy: "It's not simply that human life originated in Africa in anthropological terms, but that modern life begins with slavery [...] From a woman's point of view, in terms of confronting the problems of where the world is now, black women had to deal with 'post-modern' problems in the nineteenth century and earlier,"[6] or as Gilroy paraphrases the same argument: "Morrison sees the intensity of the slave experience as something that marks out blacks as the first truly modern people, handling in the nineteenth century dilemmas and difficulties which have become the substance of everyday life in our own time."[7] This is not to claim that Morrison or Gilroy are "Afrofuturists," but rather that there are continuities in thinking the time and history between Afrofuturist discourse and this interview, or elements of Gilroy's thinking in large. A case in point would be to see the spaceship in Sun Ra's understanding or in Eshun's interpretation as the 2.0-version of the slave-ships across The Black Atlantic, but where the earlier version is taking Africans to a New World of slavery and exploitation, the second — Sun Ra's version — could be seen in a more utopian light, as leaving Planet Earth behind to begin a new, black, civilization on a new planet in outer space. This, then, would be one version of thinking blacks in the future.

For my current discussion, however, I am in particularly interested in how these futures and pasts relate to the present. The focus from much Afrofuturist discourse about where black people are in the future thus in a sense is altered, so as to use this futuristic discourse also to say something about the present. Such a focus upon the present, however, is also consistent with elements of Dery's interview-article. As many will remember, and as gives an arguably even more explicit echo today, Dery opens with three epigrams, the first one from George Orwell's *Nineteen Eighty-Four*:

> If all records told the same tale — then the lie passed into history and became truth. 'Who controls the past', ran the Party slogan, 'controls the future: who controls the present controls the past.'[8]

The three modalities used in discussing time — the past, the present, and the future — are all here, but they are at the same time intimately connected with the question of control. Unfolding the connections, the Party seems to be saying that control in the here and now, that is controlling the present, is a prerequisite for controlling the past, and in controlling the past one also and at the same time controls the future. For the Afrofuturist interrogation in Dery's article this also leads to a persistent question, what Dery calls a "troubling antinomy": "Can a community whose past has been deliberately rubbed out, and whose energies have subsequently been consumed by the search for legible traces of its history, imagine possible futures?"[9] Continuing his interrogation, Dery asks: "isn't the unreal estate of the future already owned by the technocrats, futurologists, streamliners, and set designers — white to a man — who have engineered our collective fantasies?"[10] In some kind of contrast to this already owned future — even if it is an unreal estate — he continues to argue that "African American voices have other stories to tell about culture, technology, and things to come."[11] These other stories must, within the present context, also be stories about the past, a past that has been deliberately rubbed out, but that is still possible to unearth, by, for example, Eshun's archaeologists from the future.[12]

When Eshun references these archaeologists, they have returned to our time to find the other stories in our present, but a similar trope could easily be transferred to archaeological work today, also work being done by historians, to find the prehistory of the present. The other stories to be told are thus not solely about the things to come, but are also stories about the other pasts. These other pasts could in one sense be seen as unearthing elements previously untold, the search, as Dery writes, "for legible traces of its (this community's) history," but they are also what Eshun refers to as countermemories. "To establish the historical character of black culture, to bring Africa and its subjects into history denied by Hegel et al., it has been necessary to assemble countermemories that contest the colonial archive, thereby situating the collective trauma of slavery as the founding moment of modernity."[13] Assembling countermemories to contest the colonial archive is clearly the work of historians and the (imagined) team of African archaeologists from the future. Eshun's version of the other stories are also a way to counter "the futures industry,"[14] a term echoing Dery's notion of "the unreal estate of the future already owned by the technocrats, futurologists, streamliners, and set designers." "The futures industry" is, in this particular sense, also about not only who are allowed to imagine the future, but how certain futures have more power than other futures to become what Dery calls "our collective fantasies." Here, then, we also see dimensions of accessibility, of media ecology, of distribution of stories and fantasies. There are also similarities between Eshun's "team of African archaeologists from the future"[15] and "the Data-Thief" from the movie *The Last Angel of History*,[16] a film Eshun participates in, and where his words and the Data Thief's behavior seem to echo each other again and again. In the opening of the film, a black secret technology, the blues, is presented. Robert Johnson learned about it in the Deep South after selling his soul to "the devil." This secret technology is the origin of all black musical forms since, from jazz to hip-hop. The film fast-forwards 200 years introducing the Data Thief, and the scene is set for a moving back-and-forth between music, futurity, and different forms of technology, where the Data Thief becomes a time-traveler throughout history finding glimpses and bits of historical knowledge that he transports backwards and forwards in time.

While Dery speaks about the "unreality" of the future, a similar claim could be made for the present, or at least some dimensions of the present. A version of such a claim is found in the film *Space Is the Place*[17] with Sun Ra, in many ways a core-text for understanding his world-view. While the film is science fiction — with references to blaxploitation as well — it is in one particular sense a very realistic movie, dealing with the "unreality" of black folks in the USA of the early 1970s, something made abundantly clear in the scene where Sun Ra meets a number of young people in a community center in Oakland. As he says in that scene:

> How do you know I'm real? I'm not real; I'm just like you. You don't exist in this society. If you did, your people wouldn't be seeking equal rights. You're not real. If you were you'd have some status about the nations of the world. So we're both myths. I do not come to you as reality. I come to you as the myth because that's what black people are.[18]

On the political level, this unreality is similar to issues at stake for the Civil Rights Movement, as can be seen in Sun Ra's reference to "seeking equal rights." But it is also a statement of an almost ontological or cosmological nature; black or blackness is myth. Is this the incorporation of society's way of ordering race relations? Is it Sun Ra giving up becoming included in the category "human beings"? There is a strand in Afrofuturist discourse arguing in this direction, but where Sun Ra's solution is understood as bypassing the whole category of "the human" and become super- or posthuman.[19] Such a solution can, however, also be seen as a kind of utopian striving, where the utopian dimension necessitates leaving the category of "the human" behind.

Preprogramming the Present

In "Further Considerations of Afrofuturism," Eshun discusses the revisionist histories of Afrofuturism as "a series of powerful competing futures that infiltrate the present at different rates."[20] The multiplicity of futures does not mean that they are unreal, but their reality seems to exist on another plane, which the revisionism brings forward. They are not, however, "merely predictions into the far future," and Eshun quotes Samuel R. Delany in claiming that these futures should be understood as offering "a significant distortion of the present."[21] "To be more precise," Eshun writes, "science fiction is neither forward-looking nor utopian," and he quotes William Gibson claiming, "science fiction is a means through which to preprogram the present."[22] The different rates of the futures disturb linear time, inserting an anachronistic dimension to thought. What Eshun calls "chronopolitics," the politics of time, is thus at the same time what could be termed an "anachronopolitics," highlighting both the revisionisms and disturbances at stake in his project. What these different futures do as well, however, is to "adjust the temporal logics that condemned black subjects to prehistory,"[23] not simply by transposing black subjects into "history," but with the disturbance of linear time, and thus simultaneously the understanding of history following from such a philosophy of time. From this science fiction becomes a genre that "was never concerned with the future, but rather with engineering feedback between its preferred future and its becoming present,"[24] he writes, and thus thinking the future is always already also about changing the present point where this thinking takes place. The present is, in a particular sense, open. Thus, in this particular sense, science fiction is equally much about "the now" or "the present." But this present is floating, it is in the process of being-programmed, the reprogramming is taking place in real time so to speak.

Things Not Seen

With this interrelation between the future and the present as lens, it is time to return to the music video to "Greeny Jungle." In the booklet with the CD *Evidence of Things*

Not Seen, the lyrics to the songs are printed, along with some comments by Teodros. This particular song is important to my argument, not least because he writes at the top of the page "(inspired by Nnedi Okorafor)." Readers of Okorafor will probably immediately associate with her young adult novel *Zahrah the Windseeker*,[25] but I will have to admit that I heard Teodros' song before reading Okorafor's novel. What happened, however, was that in reading the novel some very important dimensions of the song came to the fore differently, and as such this song for me now exists in an intersection between different works of art, in different media. In that I read Okorafor's novel as very much from a female point of view, even the sound of Teodros' voice becomes different when existing in this intersection. In *Zahrah the Windseeker*, "the Forbidden Greeny Jungle" is an important location. Found just outside of the village where Zahrah lives, this jungle is perceived as dangerous, and when Zahrah and her friend Dari try to approach it, they are warned and told they will disappear or die. This danger however is put aside when Dari falls into a coma, and the only thing that can help him is the elgort egg, that Zahrah must fetch from deep in the jungle. Much of the novel thus takes place in this forbidden territory, where slight distortions of myths and folklore seem to meet a fantasy space that is easy enough to follow. In a sense the slight distortions seem to make it easier for a reader (at least for me as a reader) to follow the story, as I enter into the book, into Zahrah's telling of the story, and can follow the story without as much pre-knowledge about the source material as I would expect to have.

Teodros' lyrics reference Okorafor's story, but at the same time alter it. This is not least the case with his subject-position, and lyrics where the "i" is important (he writes everything in lowercase), claiming "i'm from a jungle/that's getting clear cut fast," "from a horn in the east/i grew up with some beasts." This is clearly not the Seattle where he lives, but a reference to the Horn of Africa, and as such bridges the west coast USA and northeast Africa. The video to "Greeny Jungle," however, is, as I pointed out in my introduction, set in the here and now. There are no fantasy elements. On the contrary, the contemporary and current political situation is at stake. As Teodros told *Okay Africa*, the video captures "a moment with the #BlackLivesMatter movement in Seattle when an estimated 10,000 people marched [...] for #ReclaimMLKDay."[26] The video thus intersects even more dimensions than in the album version of the song, and these intersections bring out a multilayered work. There are obviously many layers already in the song; the most explicit is heard in the very opening, when, as if through a megaphone, we hear a voice. It is the voice of James Baldwin, from the 1968 documentary *Baldwin's Nigger*. Directed by Horace Ové, the film documents a conversation between James Baldwin and Dick Gregory discussing the Civil Rights Movement and the black experience in the U.S., as well as in the Caribbean and in Great Britain. The lines from Baldwin are sampled into the music, but with the slight voice-distortion on the album, they sound more like shouts from the past. And arguably this is also how they work in the song. Ending with Baldwin

saying that "when you stand up and look the world in the face like you had a right to
be here you have attacked the entire power structure of the Western world," this is a
call to political action.[27] The historical distance between this call and the present day
makes the call even more persistent, and establishes a historical continuity between
the 1960s and today. The quote from Baldwin also functions, when heard in the music
video, in showing how Black Lives Matter and the Civil Rights Movement belong on
the same political continuum; shows, in other words, how the Civil Rights Movement
arguably never won, but that the fight is still persistently important.

The title of the album is also a reference to James Baldwin, more specifically to
his 1985 book *The Evidence of Things Not Seen*, a nonfiction book about the Atlanta
child murders of 1979-1981.[28] This reference is much less explicit than Baldwin's voice
on the track, but in interviews Teodros has told about the importance of Baldwin
both for his writing and for his life, and says that he was "the biggest inspiration
on [the] album." Unfolding what the inspiration and not least the title mean to him,
Teodros says:

> James Baldwin has been a huge inspiration on my writing and life in
> general these last few years, and he definitely was the biggest inspiration
> on this album in particular. The title Evidence Of Things Not Seen
> has several intended meanings, in the same way I believe it did for
> Baldwin when he authored a book with the same title in 1985. It's about
> the feeling of not being seen in different ways; it's about seeing things
> before they actually happen; it's about how much faith it takes to be an
> uncompromising independent musician in this day & age; and more.[29]

There are a number of elements that could be discussed from this quote; in
addition to Baldwin's importance, the most important seems to be the reference
to the feeling of "not being seen," that at least to me echoes Ralph Ellison's *Invisible
Man*.[30] This invisibility could then subsequently be understood in relation to Sun
Ra's statement of the "unreality" of blacks. But I am equally interested in how a
possible reference to Ellison brings even more historical layers in play. Lisa Yaszek
has described the narrator of Ellison's novel as "a proto-Afrofuturist," in that he
rethinks the relations of "his past and present" and maps "the networks of power
that would propel him into various futures not of his own making," and this
network is made material when he steals electricity to his hiding place to listen
to multiple recordings of Louis Armstrong's "(What Did I Do To Be So) Black and
Blue" simultaneously. Listening to music in the state of invisibility gives, according
to the narrator, another sense of time, the sonic establishes a different temporality
or sense of time. As the narrator writes:

Invisibility, let me explain, gives one a slightly different sense of time, you're never quite on the beat. Sometimes you're ahead and sometimes behind. Instead of the swift and imperceptible flowing of time, you are aware of its nodes, those points where time stands still or from which it leaps ahead. And you slip into the breaks and look around. That's what you hear vaguely in Louis' music.[31]

It may be a stretch to argue that "invisibility" is a reference to Ellison, but the possible echo says something about relating to time, also in the video to "Greeny Jungle." That Baldwin is the more explicit reference is obvious, but from there Teodros' understandings of "the evidence of things not seen" folds out into a broader scheme. As another mode, perhaps, of invisibility is how he claims the time points to "seeing things before they actually happen." Here, rather than relating to the past, there is an almost prophetic dimension, as if one contemplates time travel in the opposite direction, that is to say, into the future, but a mental time travelling, something one can see from the here and now. A possibility of a more prophetic, or at least forward-looking, dimension is found as well when Teodros tells that the title also is about "how much faith it takes to be an uncompromising independent musician in this day & age." The reference to faith may bring us to one of the inspirations for Baldwin's book-title, Hebrews 11:1, where it is written: "Now faith is the substance of things hoped for, the evidence of things not seen." The biblical dimension thus introduces temporal logics of its own, as faith and hope could be seen as spiritual technologies for preprogramming the present.

In an interview from 2012, with references to his album *Colored People's Time Machine*, Teodros speaks about time, race, and music:

One of the original ideas behind *Colored People's Time Machine* came from an Ethiopian man who was of my parents' generation, who told a group of us in Washington, DC that it wasn't until he came to the United States that time became a commodity, something we can lose and something we always chase. He said, 'Here time moves, back home I move through time' and that statement made a lot of sense to me. Also the term 'Colored People's Time' has always had a negative stigma attached to it — it implies people of colour are always late. I wanted to challenge that notion. All music is based on different time signatures; as well as it being something that can capture a moment, it can take you far away to the future, and it can channel voices from the past you didn't even know were there. So our time machine is music, and all of the musical movements in the United States originally came from an experience and expression that was/is specific to people of colour. The ways these ideas are expressed on the album are explicit on the title track, and subtle through the rest of the project. It's a very personal, at times extremely vulnerable piece of music where I touch on subjects that were even hard to talk about before writing these songs. So it deals a lot with the past. The next album we've got coming out starts in the year 2089. The Time Machine on the cover of this album is in the shape of a sankofa bird, an Adinkra symbol that literally means 'go back and get it' and it implies you can't move to the future without first knowing where you're from.[32]

The coming album he references is Copperwire's *Earthbound* (2012), which he did together with Meklit Hadero and Burntface, and where Nnedi Okorafor participated in the world-building. It is a story about a hijacked spaceship on its way to Addis Ababa, and in this sense a more obvious reference to Afrofuturism than any track on *Evidence of Things Not Seen*. But taking a clue from *Colored People's Time Machine*, these different albums may not be that different when it comes to interrogating the different modalities of time. They all partake in capturing the moment, as well as being taken away to distant pasts and futures. His statement above at the same time points to music more generally as a time machine, and how music can take both the musician and the listener into the future, but also "channel voices from the past." It is as one such voice from the past I hear Baldwin's voice in the opening to "Greeny Jungle," but as a layer of time together with other times.

What is happening with the video to "Greeny Jungle" is that yet another context is added to the discourse, not only Okorafor's novel and Teodros' song, but also a contemporary political situation. In a sense, then, there are different layers of time at stake. When he adds the voice of Baldwin and the reference to the Bible, a historical archive not dissimilar to what Eshun called "the colonial archive" is not only brought forward, but is remixed. It is an exploration resembling the Data Thief's, but in a different register. "Seeing things before they actually happens" becomes another way to preprogram the present, two different ways to formulate the same. The last formulation references a kind of premonition, which at the same time indicates that the future is, in a certain sense, present in the present.

Notes

1. Dery, Mark, "Black to the Future: Interviews with Samuel R. Delany, Greg Tate, and Tricia Rose," *Flame Wars: The Discourse on Cyberculture,* ed. Mark Dery, Durham: Duke University Press, 1994, 180.

2. Womack, Ytasha L., *Afrofuturism: The World of Black Sci-Fi and Fantasy Culture,* Chicago: Lawrence Hill Books, 2013, 9.

3. Eshun, Kodwo, *More Brilliant Than The Sun: Adventures in Sonic Fiction,* London: Quartet Books, 1998.

4. Dery, "Black to the Future," 182.

5. Cf. Chude-Sokei, Louis, *The Sound of Culture: Diaspora and Black Technopoetics,* Middletown: Wesleyan University Press, 2016.

6. Gilroy, Paul, *Small Acts: Thoughts on the Politics of Black Culture,* London: Serpent's Tail, 1993, 178.

7. Ibid.

8. Orwell, George, *Nineteen Eighty-Four,* London: Penguin, 2003, 40. Dery, "Black to the Future," 179.

9. Dery, "Black to the Future," 180.

10. Ibid.

11. Ibid., 182.

12. Eshun, Kodwo, "Further Considerations on Afrofuturism," *Boogie Down Predictions: Hip-Hop, Time, and Afrofuturism,* ed. Roy Christopher, London, Strange Attractor Press, 2022, 252-64.

13. Ibid., 252.

14. Ibid., 254.

15. Ibid., 252.

16. From 1996, directed by John Akomfrah.

17. From 1972, directed by John Coney.

18. https://www.youtube.com/watch?v=okEFloBF9MM Quoted in Nabeel Zuberti, "The Transmolecularisation of Black Folk: *Space is the Place,* Sun Ra and Afrofuturism," in *Off the Planet: Music, Sound and Science Fiction Cinema,* ed. Philip Hayward (Eastlight: John Libbey Publishing, 2004), 88.

19. Eshun, *More Brilliant,* 155.

20. Eshun, "Further Considerations," 260.

21. Delany, Samuel R., in *Last Angel of History* (1996).

22. Eshun, "Further Considerations," 254. Eshun, *More Brilliant,* 105.

23. Eshun, "Further Considerations," 260.

24. Ibid., 254.

25. Okorafor-Mbachu, Nnedi, *Zahrah the Windseeker*, Boston: Graphia, 2005.

26. Killakam, "Gabriel Teodros & SoulChef Premiere Their Protest Video For 'Greeny Jungle'," 2015.

27. https://www.youtube.com/watch?v=DeFpzp1pBjc

28. Baldwin, James, *The Evidence of Things Not Seen*, New York: Henry Holt, 1995 (1985).

29. Weg, Z, "Stream Gabriel Teodros' James Baldwin-Inspired 'Evidence Of Things Not Seen LP'" 2014.

30. Ellison, Ralph, *Invisible Man*, London: Penguin, 2001 (1952)

31. Yaszek, Lisa, "Afrofuturism, Science Fiction, and the History of the Future," *Socialism and Democracy* 20/3, 2006, 50.

32. Ellison, *Invisible Man*, 8.

Bibliography

Baldwin, James. *The Evidence of Things Not Seen*. New York: Henry Holt, 1995 (1985).

Brandes, Blake. "Because we can win, and change is inevitable," *Wasafiri* 27/4 (2012), 65-66.

Chude-Sokei, Louis. *The Sound of Culture: Diaspora and Black Technopoetics*. Middletown: Wesleyan University Press, 2016.

Dery, Mark. "Black to the Future: Interviews with Samuel R. Delany, Greg Tate, and Tricia Rose," in Mark Dery (ed.), *Flame Wars: The Discourse on Cyberculture*. Durham: Duke University Press, 1994, 179-222.

Ellison, Ralph. *Invisible Man*. London: Penguin, 2001 (1952).

Eshun, Kodwo. *More Brilliant Than The Sun: Adventures in Sonic Fiction*. London: Quartet Books, 1998.

Eshun, Kodwo. "Further Considerations of Afrofuturism," *Boogie Down Predictions: Hip-Hop, Time, and Afrofuturism*, ed. Roy Christopher, London, Strange Attractor Press, 2022, 252-264.

Gilroy, Paul. *The Black Atlantic: Modernity and Double Consciousness*. London: Verso, 1993.

Gilroy, Paul. *Small Acts: Thoughts on the Politics of Black Culture*. London: Serpent's Tail, 1993.

Killakam. "Gabriel Teodros & SoulChef Premiere Their Protest Video For 'Greeny Jungle'," http://www.okayafrica.com/news/gabriel-teodros-soulchef-greeny-jungle-protest-video-shakiah/ 2015.

Okorafor-Mbachu, Nnedi. *Zahrah the Windseeker*. Boston: Graphia, 2005.

Orwell, George. *Nineteen Eighty-Four*. London: Penguin, 2003.

Womack, Ytasha L. *Afrofuturism: The World of Black Sci-Fi and Fantasy Culture*. Chicago: Lawrence Hill Books, 2013.

Yaszek, Lisa. "An Afrofuturist Reading of Ralph Ellison's Invisible Man," *Rethinking History* 9/2-3 (2005), 297-313.

Yaszek, Lisa. "Afrofuturism, Science Fiction, and the History of the Future," *Socialism and Democracy* 20/3 (2006), 41-60.

Zuberi, Nabeel. "The Transmolecularisation of Black Folk: *Space is the Place*, Sun Ra and Afrofuturism," in Philip Hayward (ed.), *Off the Planet: Music, Sound and Science Fiction Cinema*. Eastleigh: John Libbey Publishing, 2004, 77-95.

Z Weg. "Stream Gabriel Teodros' James Baldwin-Inspired 'Evidence Of Things Not Seen LP'," http://www.okayafrica.com/news/gabriel-teodros-evidence-of-things-not-seen-album/.

The Cult of RAMM:∑LL:Z∑∑: A Hagiography into Chaos
Joël Vacheron

The following text is based on a discussion between Tex Royale, Skoobstep <Alexis Milne> (>>THE CULT OPERATORS>>) and myself.

Foreword

RAMM:∑LL:Z∑∑ (1960-2010) made a name as a visual artist, performance artist, musician, graffiti writer and futurist at the turn of the 80s. When the world was discovering a youth culture that was converting the eroded infrastructures of the industrial era into new means of communication, the singular spiked and 'wild' lettering he sprayed on the walls of highways and on the subway trains spread like viruses across the architectonic harmony of New York. *RAMM:∑LL:Z∑∑* liked to stay anonymous and he hardly ever appeared in public without a costume or a mask. These flamboyant avatars were inextricable from his work. They allowed him to figure and perform various kind of role-plays, to let ancient voices channel through him, as a way of arranging the commandments of his own multiverse. Throughout his iconoclast career, *RAMM:∑LL:Z∑∑* developed a syncretic philosophy that professes that graffiti artists were engaged in a symbolic war against the standardization of the alphabet, that is to say the letters, of their alienating rules and structures. The so-called *Gothic Futurism* is composed of a set of heavily encrypted codes, axioms and equations, that looks like what would be information theory after having been fused in a particle accelerator.

With a great sense of humor, *RAMM:∑LL:Z∑∑*'s oeuvre not only challenged topics that are commonly addressed in hip-hop culture, (i.e., the impact of technological tools or the issues on race and politics). Following a radical and experiential street ethos, *RAMM:∑LL:Z∑∑* was rather engaged in a mission to hack and 'eccentricate' that lay at the core of the system. By creating these hybrid and conflictual realities, HE prefigured with astonishing insight how humans struggle to exorcize the stunning shock of the ever-increasing rate of change in the early XXIst century:

> Like a spinning amusement park ride, with our bodies immovably glued
> to the edge, we may be whirling nauseatingly fast, but we haven't really

moved an inch. It is precisely here, on this kernel of stasis, that the call to accelerate needs to take hold, dislodging stagnant conceptual orientations in favour of the creation of eccentric, out-of-centre attractors. (...) The creation of eccentric attractors is equal to the creation of new coordinations through which the fallibility or contingency of existing normative points are demonstrated.[1]

How is it possible to restore, in a concise and written form, the vision of an 'eccentric attractor' whose oeuvre is entirely dominated by a willingness to transcend any kind of aesthetic and linguistic containments?

 The Cult of RAMM:ΣLL:ZΣΣ is an artistic and political project which is of particular relevance to address this question. Since the mid-2010s, this collective of variable geometry has been actively exploring, around and from, the legacy of *RAMM:ΣLL:ZΣΣ*. The Cult of RAMM:ΣLL:ZΣΣ's activities are focused mainly around performances that are as many actions to conjure the syncretic power of hip-hop. Breakdancing, graffiti, rapping or turntablism are propelled into space such as symptoms looming like strobe lights through the windows of a high-speed train. Their uncompromising and militant approach outlines the disruptive nature of *RAMM:ΣLL:ZΣΣ*'s total work of art, while keeping intact its chaotic and enigmatic scope. In the vein of the tactics of *détournements* put forward by the Situationist International or the punk's emphasis on direct actions, The Cult provokes a state of intensity and disarray that forces us to give meaning to the situations. In the same way as *RAMM:ΣLL:ZΣΣ*, the objective aims to epitomize the fallibility of the system by re-enacting something that happens in a potential future. As they put it: '*we over identify with these things, and we get it wrogn* (sic).' By wandering along the borders of entropy, The Cult Of RAMM:ΣLL:ZΣΣ offers '*misinterpretations*' and that is precisely why they are an appropriate channel to reflect on the preposterous cosmogony of *RAMM:ΣLL:ZΣΣ*. Namely, by inscribing his hagiography into a futuristic and ecstatic chaos.

 The following text is based on a discussion with the artists Tex Royale and Alexis Milne (>>*THE CULT OPERATORS*>>) that took place in London in 2014. It recounts freely the art and philosophy of *RAMM:ΣLL:ZΣΣ*, embedding neologisms and operations called upon during their artistic performances. Written in the form of an erratic lexicon, it aims to follow the obliqueness, the polyphony and sharp eccentricity that characterize *RAMM:ΣLL:ZΣΣ*'s legacy.

EQUATION

I am a student of the RAMM:ΣLL:ZΣΣ. HIS work is my homework. HE leaves *tracks* called *lectures* and it does not matter that HE is dead. Like HE says in interviews, the *RAMM:ΣLL:ZΣΣ* is an equation, HE is not a person. HE never speaks to anyone as the RAMM:ΣLL:ZΣΣ but as other spirits and entities that HE wishes to channel. Maybe this is part of the *rhizomatic nature* of the equation. HE did a real good job at keeping HIS 'actual human identity' quite secret.

WILD STYLE

HE has always been an innovative force and the outfits that HE produces remind us of graffiti art pieces. In particular, the Wild Style, which developed in New York over a thirty-year period. *Wild Style* was the name applied to the abstract wild graffiti art on trains, the 'pinnacle' of that graffiti art culture at that time. What came out of hip-hop visually, HE *translates* it physically and spiritually. HIS philosophy *springboards* out of that, and his outfits become a 3D embodiment of the *evolution* of Wild Style. The Wild Style evolves off of HIS exoskeleton. The letters are being freed from the alphabet's printed form. HE relates it back to the monks. That's HIS philosophy:
Gothic Futurism.

HE penetrates the pinnacle and arms it from the inside out, rewiring it until it functions as a medieval amphibious tank. HE states that Gothic Futurism is Wild Style corrected. Wild Style letters are a larval form. The RAMM:ΣLL:ZΣΣ is the trans-galactic shamanic executive gangster collective, overseeing and orchestrating this process.

BLASTING OFF

HE talks about aerodynamics, aeronautics,
and all these...
technical mechanics.

HE talks about
weaponising the letter, turning it into craft that can fly; the letters will have wings,
the letters will *fly off* the pages. These letters are of aerodynamic design. HE tells us
to look at the church steeples, how they're designed to take off. Blasting off, being hi-
power mechanised — these are feats of engineering and precision. When we perform
break-spraying, it allows the energy of a letterform to break loose and decide itself by
manipulating the chassis of a human body; we put the letter in the driving seat.

CHAOS

The RAMM:ΣLL:ZΣΣ talks about the *equation*. A letter is a symbol that *represents*
energy. The energy manifests as sound when we communicate
with spoken language.

What people call *graffiti* is part of a struggle to allow that energy to break free from the recognized forms that it's been trapped in. What we do within the Cult, the performance that we do, the costumes that we make, the totemic structures...whatever it is within the performance; none of it is polished, none of it is refined, none of it is clean or tidy. It's very chaotic.

HUE-MANS

The RAMM:ΣLL:ZΣΣ was not content with the idea of Afrofuturism; HE didn't even believe in it, stating that it doesn't exist. HE plays with language and when talking about humans, HE identifies the sly components of the word, singling out the sounds of what we hear, visualizing this as *hue-mans*. HE traces the origins of graffiti back beyond the seventeenth century monks, entwining it with the history of the illuminated manuscripts and that evolution. HIS work is a continuation of that tradition and its evolution. When was the last time that a white western art movement was defined by a haircut? We'll see you in six years once we've got *Quiffmysticism* in full-scale automated operation.

OBSCURE

Gothic Futurism appears to be impenetrable. This is part of HIS strategy. There are not enough scholars and time out there to break the code and it's going to take a long time for people to consider

that material seriously so that it fully digests mentally on the *collective scale*. Here's the longevity and what makes it timeless. When people do engage, they're going to get it wrong — this is why the Cult works so well. We *over identify* with these things, and we get it wrogn. What we do is a *misinterpretation*. The Cult is not of this time, and through our performances, we are re-enacting something that happens in a potential future, a different timeline. We're interpreting this material through frosted glass. You see a vague shape but have to make up the rest.

DISTANCE

We never met HIM in person, and so in that way we are at a distance. We didn't grow up in the Bronx or the South of Queens, in this dystopian background of New York at that time. We do have this so-called *strategy of over identification*, and the direction we take is the idea of *ingesting* that culture from a distance, which is both spatially and chronologically energized, as well as otherwise.

There is this retranslation of it from across the ocean, and distance does enable you to open up some space to create something new as well.

ALIEN

The RAMM:ΣLL:ZΣΣ is a renaissance figure within hip-hop. HE was a graffiti writer and a rapper, mastering the written and spoken word. In a kind of symbiotic feedback loop relationship, HE would freestyle conscious streams of rap responding to breakdance moves that were happening in front of HIM, communicating this wild aggressive dance-form to the crowd, even conjuring it. HE was an embodiment of this weird alien hip-hop form, which seemingly came out of nowhere, an active and reactive node of its projection — evidence of our cosmic origin. Where did that cultural explosion come from exactly? Sure, it has lineages back to all these other older forms of freeform Jazz and Soul dance, but breaking, popping, locking; it all accelerated forward into a distinct future body zone. We are the future. The future is now. The future ain't what it used to be... in Baudrillard's essay *Kool Killer*, you get this idea that the subway train graffiti movement was a violent onslaught by a whole youth group, a disenfranchised neglected section of society in New York.

The graffiti writers were a resilient anti-force that operated *against* the symbolic order of signs. It's true meaning lost to the untrained eye, the alien script engulfed an entire rapid transit system like a virus and transmitted an image of New York as a city at war with itself. It was a brief but violent 'insurrection of signs.' In other documentaries and questionable films of that period (late 1970s to mid 80s), New York is depicted as a lawless hellhole, and graffiti ridden trains are used as a prominent symbol amongst the rubble mounds of the Bronx. Films such as *Death Wish, Wolfen, Forte Apache, The Bronx...* What we're looking at is illuminated alien expression from an openly oppressed and alienated nation.

GHEDE

'I am Chaser the Eraser, restaurateur, maître d' to the Plasmatics.' The RAMM:ΣLL:ZΣΣ allows beings to talk through HIM, in HIS work, in HIS performances. HE idolizes them, makes costumes, figurines for each one of them. It's HIS pantheon. HE is THEM and maybe is best referred to as THEY. Let's talk a little about voodoo rituals. When a *Loa* is successfully summoned, it *mounts* or *rides* a human being who is present at the ritual. The mounted take on the personas of the different Loa. Once someone is mounted, and the Loa is identified, they are given their familiars, perhaps a certain kind of hat or cane... The Loa each possess a *style*, purpose, and personality of their own. The mounted take on traits *way* contrary to their day-to-day self, performing acts that would normally stop them dead in their tracks. Modern psychologists got no real explanation for how these kinds of possessions work, how this mounting takes effect.

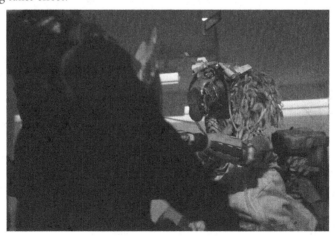

It doesn't matter if a Loa decides to take residence up in a rock or if they choose to rest inside a toy plastic gun — it's not correct to identify the Loa as being *of* said object, be it a tree, a sneaker, or a car bumper. It's not like *"hark hark, 'tis Bark, the Loa of the Log"* — no, the Loa are *transient* beings from beyond — *Archetypical Archons*, to whom we are eternally receptive as vessels, for they dwell deep within our collective *exo-consciousness*. Take the Ghede family from Haitian voodoo mythology. They embody death and fertility, creation and destruction. You meet *Papa Ghede* at the *crossroads*. He cares for the children, and will never take a life before its time is due. He wears dark smoked glasses with one lens missing, so one eye can see the entire universe and this other eye can make sure that no one is stealing his food.

TRANS-RAPPER

Trans- has a lot of different meanings; it's a transition, a kind of permeation from one state to another or from one place to another. And the RAMM:ΣLL:ZΣΣ was definitely *a trans-rapper*. HE wasn't just transgender. HE would perform sometimes as the Duchess, a female figure, but HE was trans-human to an extent. Not like the Futurist notion of a singularity merging with the machine mind either. That's a false prophecy of the oppressors. HE let these ancient voices speak through HIM. It's like Rupaul says, *"We're all born naked, and the rest is drag."* Drag racing. Letter racing. HE was taking language, taking the letter, the vocal sound and turning these 'natural human things' into a technology, turning it into a tool, into a weapon against the oppressive forces. That's *spectral somatechnics of the soul.*

TRANS-IT SYSTEM

Graffiti art developed on subway trains, and it transmitted a suppressed language from a whole group of disenfranchised youth and fused untrained letters with moving steel, energized with electric voltage, utilizing a dynamic platform — a mass rapid transit system, which is how the RAMM:ΣLL:ZΣΣ comes into fruition for these performances. It's like quantum mechanics combined with original subway train writing, combined with shock flashbacks of future vision. In 2013, the Cult performed a ritual under the West Way, the huge brutalist road, which runs through Ladbroke Grove, where graffiti first landed from New York in 1981. The first New York graffiti piece was painted on the huge concrete legs of the Westway by FUTURA2000 whilst on tour with The Clash (elements of hip-hop
and Punk overlap
momentarily).

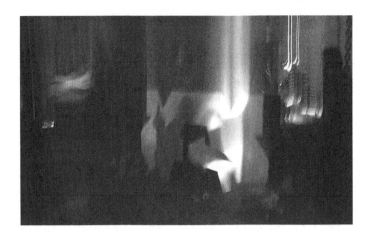

FUTURA
is known for his abstract
graffiti; he re-animated the concrete, which obviously seemed alien and inhuman, but
graffiti had the power to reenergize it, to *remanipulate* it. You get that *trans-* momentum
again, a *trans-morphing*. All this feeds into the methodologies we create within the Cult
— especially with the *Feral ExpresSways* sub-cult. The West Way ritual paid homage to
that first piece and its subsequent viral effects. The West Way covers an important area
for London graffiti culture — the elevated road provided huge concrete pillars for the
first graffiti pieces to exist. The huge Brutalist concrete road along with hi-rise estates
(such as Trellick Tower) was also the backdrop to the elevated section of the inner
metropolitan tube train line, where London graffiti artists would *translate* their own
version of the New York transit script onto London Underground *moving steel*. The
viral ripple continues. Of course, little or nothing remains of the UK's initial graffiti
onslaught except in documentation; it has been chemically wiped clean, or *buffed* as
graffiti writers say. Anti-bodied. Body slammed. Sometimes a stain of that period
will remain however. The Bitumen that's used as the binding agent of concrete is also
used to make spray paint more permanent. Bitumen has a staining effect and would
stain tube trains and walls with resilient ghost tags and pieces unwilling to disappear.
'*Asphalt Bitumen*' is another mantra the Cult chant. We celebrate this resilient bio-agent
of destruction and creation, the link between the concrete expressways and urban
viral onslaught.

SECOND WORLD WAR RUBBLES

When you watch the documentaries about hip-hop
and this era *(Style Wars, Wild Style, Stations of the Elevated)*, the subculture is framed

against the dystopian backdrop of the South Bronx, which was largely reduced to piles of rubble and burnt bricks, a scene from a Second World War documentary, aerial shots of a bombed out Dresden at the end of civilization. Often, in the footage, you have a rusty subway train running through a burnt out wasteland, covered top to bottom with anarchic alien script scrawled and crafted across the chassis, hurtling through the aftermath of gentrification. In the Cult, we focus on that *rubble trauma*.

MOZIZIZM

The Cult concentrates on Robert Moses, the major *Archonitect* of the Cross Bronx Expressway, a road of major importance within hip-hop. Many key events took place in a *seven-mile radius* of this expressway... The first important Block parties where iconic DJs like Kool Herc, Grandmaster Flash, and Afrika Bambaataa were cutting up, scratching, and mixing records for the first time. You also had the subway station on 149th Street, known as *The Bench* — this would be the main meeting area and hang out joint to watch freshly painted masterpiece subway graffiti roll by on wheels of steel across the number 2 and 5 lines.

In the Cult, Moses becomes MOZIZIZM, taking on God-like proportions alongside the RAMM:ΣLL:ZΣΣ and becoming a key element of the equation, almost to the point where he is responsible for the creation of hip-hop. He created these void spaces within the city following the motto: *'when operating in an over built metropolis, you've got to hack your way through with a meat axe.'* Eighty percent of the South Bronx moved out during the building of The Cross Bronx Expressway and the ensuing policies of neglect. Moses cut up entire neighborhoods. Cut people off from vital resources like fire stations, hospitals, and schools. Split up families and communities, injecting these ghetto spaces. There was a policy of neglect and a policy of division. Moses redirected funds away from Rapid Mass Transit into expressway building, always favoring auto-individualism above mass transversal. That's what we mean by *the Shiny Ones*. Public transport was left to deteriorate, which lay bare subway train yards and lay ups ready to receive the fifth dimensional step parallel staircase delivered by the ghetto monks, the wild style script manipulators such as CLIFF159, FUZZ, IZ, PHASE2, CAINE, BLADE, COMET, KASE2, THE DEATH SQUAD, SKEME, NOC, A-ONE, FUTURA2000, DONDI, VULCAN and all those who now *ZIP!* along the third rail — the electromagnetic majestix. Zoom In Peace. Moses was the *MOLOCH*, the '*concrete sphinx of cement and aluminum*,' and these figures permeate into our rituals. We do *express-prays* devoted to *MOZIZIZM*.

PLASMATIC

Because of its heavily encrypted codes, its algebraic formulas and equations, its plays with language, Gothic Futurism is difficult to penetrate. What you can do is look at the things HE was looking at — yo, or who was looking at *HIM*. The legendary Bill Burroughs knew HIM as his FATHER — and likewise the RAMM:ΣLL:ZΣΣ knew Bill as HIS SON. Bill was very aware of the *operator entities* who flip from body to body. He wasn't alone either — for instance, take the works of Philip K Dick. Dick got a trilogy of books; one of the books is *VALIS* (Vast Active Living Intelligence System).

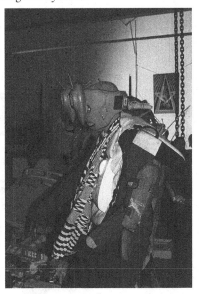

The story, which is fictional to an extent, documents a period of Dick's life and talks about a being called the *plasmate*. Living information. Information actualized as an entity. That is what the Ancient Greeks called the *logos*. VALIS, or the plasmate, is also referred to as *Zebra* because of its ability to camouflage from human perception, appearing as aspects of your day-in-day-out reality — appearing as other humans, appearing as trashcans, as pipes, as pot... whatever. There are different kinds of camouflage, higher and lower, what the plasmate is capable of is a *hi-level mimesis*. Dick explores the idea that this *plasmate* can form a symbiosis with a human, forming a *homoplasmate*. He talks about Jesus and other religious figures as humans who became *homoplasmate*. The RAMM:ΣLL:ZΣΣ talks about the *Plasmatics* in a very nonchalant matter-of-fact manner, like it's a given that they are a real day-to-day aspect of existence and experience. It's clear to see here ties between the plasmate and the Loa, the Loa and the logos. Living Information that has learned how to *operate the human*. What happens when a Loa bounds itself to its human mount instead of letting go at the end of the ceremony? When the glove melds in with the skin? Have you seen the colony of human tissue, the hybrid with spider silk? It can take a hit from a bullet, no puncture. It's happening. Humans are gonna reawaken to the Hylozoic elephant in the room. For then, we speculate that the RAMM:ΣLL:ZΣΣ is a live example of a plasmatic entity operating humanity in our un-distant history.

CROCODILIAN FORMS

"We're like ancient fossils, Henry — we don't leave time, time leaves us!" Recently we've moved into including crocodilian forms, combined with the idea of a feral expressway. It's the concrete becoming animated; we come out on all fours with road shapes on our bodies, snarling and drooling in the heat of the beast. People commented that we resemble dog-like crocodile creatures when we do this.

If you look at our ancient biology, there are species *in-between* crocodile and dog, the missing links between reptile and mammal. Mammalian lizards. They emerged out of a fertile period, approximated in relation to the Triassic, when dinosaurs were 'dying out.' Certain creatures, like crocodiles and dogs, survived the wrath of the Titans. All our ancient cousins blossomed and flourished in full bloom, but they would eventually dissolve with the dinosaurs and become the tar pits, where asphalt and oil would form. That's the matmos. It is true that ultimately we are all made out of goo. Asphalt is being used as the binding concrete. The concrete is literally made out of their remains. JAPLACK Stains remain. They are a link to the formation of *"the petroleum vitamins — Asphalt Bitumens — the eternal stain ain't slain again."*

EXOSKELETON

The exoskeletons, that's part of our *rad manifest*. Now, when one is obsessed with *style*, this can be very difficult *but!* it is important, when talking about aesthetics, to try not to tie the meaning of that down to just how something looks. It's the driving force within the rituals as well. The Plasmatics have *created* these characters. The costumes aren't simply exoskeleton — they are the visible residual of our *exo-consciousness*.

HOOVERZ BOYZ

Yeah there are sub-cults within the Cult, like the *Feral ExpresSway Pack* (those are the crocodile concrete Cult kids), and the *Hooverz Boyz*, aka the *Dysonix* — that's if you wanna camo the ammo flaps and pack a mask on that. They're a representation of our Intelligence Agencies: *Hooverz Boyz, see!* And they do! These Hooverz Boyz represent Jay Edgar Hoover's *COINTELPRO*, counter intelligence, the *dirty tricks* program. One of the best ways that the Hooverz Boyz can be performed is with broken or remanipulated hoovers, so that rather than just like sucking stuff up and putting it in a bag, they suck stuff up and shoot it back out. So, you have these things like the intelligence agencies *'cleaning things up, cleaning up the mess. Nothing to see here.'* But they're just creating more mess, and they are very dangerous. Chuck D has a lyric in one of his tracks: *'the CIA, they see I ain't kidding.'* The Intelligence Agencies are all over.

COMMUNAL ECSTASY

All the successful rituals have boosted the crowd into this communal ecstasy. When we are in ritual trance; sometimes people go crazy. In Rotterdam, we were walking down the streets, and those who joined the

Cult after the show, they wouldn't stop shouting the chants. They're doing mantras, they're shouting out in the street, in the club, the shops, at home, wherever! They've started dancing and praying, doing the movements and the motions and everything. It's always this kind of temporary, ephemeral moment, but these moments can mark consciousness. You can empower moments.

ECSTATIC CHAOS

It's a *communal frenzy*, that's how we've called it, but there is choreography within it. Certain movements we know, we practice. Others just happen. It's an ecstatic chaos. It's like conducting; within sections of the chaos, there's a brass section in the chaos; that's the *Ferals* or the *Dysonix*, forming something within that chaos, reconfiguration. It's like breakdancing; it's like you wind the body up with this energy of the break beat. In the performances, it's tapping into that. A wild breaking, not totally choreographed and polished; it's a charged moment — motion led by momentum, bodies merging, going mindless so you might get mounted.

TOTEMIC SHAPES

We produce totemic shapes with found or scavenged car bumpers, and a Cultist will pull a headstand and freeze, while the rest of the Cult holds up all this scrap shrapnel so we become like a, a... *siphonophoric human ziggurat*. Which points back to breakdancing, some kind of headfreeze, like just about going into a headspin, but you are holding that. You're not going through that same motion. And then this totemic shape will happen with other members of the Cult.

We all have
these bulky exoskeleton outfits on, our Plasmatic outfits, which together as a whole can produce this other abstract form within a section in the ritual. That's why it's like the

Siphonophorae, from the Order of Hydrozoa — sure they might *look* like a jellyfish, but that's not even one animal! They're all together, like in a cult.

SPRAY~BREAKING

There is spray-breaking, which is pointing towards breakdancing but trying to combine it with elements of freeform bombing, using spray paint to mark surfaces. It's ritualistic and expressive, spraying on the floor in black on some lino, which is being used *right now* for breakdancing in the eighties. We'll have cut out mats along strips of it, long mats, then we'll be spraying and attempting to breakdance at the same time — spray-breaking. It's sloppy and spasmodic in its energy. We're not regurgitating a breakdancing move within a theatrical performance. We want to channel all those different energies into these new forms. The break spraying is a physically exhausting means of doing that because you're using your whole body. It becomes this kind of playing in your own filth and reveling in it while breathing in the gasses of the Oracle of Delphi. It's like we said before, the letter takes control. A spray-breaker makes that plasmatic connection — the lino becomes a *Ouija board*, and the marks you make trace micro ley lines of psychic writing. Yeah, you lose a part of yourself and transform that moment or transverse into some other form.

SORROW

One of the things that comes up a lot, that a lot of people that we know who have seen our performances comment on, is that it is often quite sad. There is often these huge waves of sorrow, and some of the time people get scared, get frightened. And fear and sorrow are not something that it is our purpose or intent to express, but we are projecting this image of a future in which the highways and the roads and the concrete, the asphalt has taken over and what's left is rubble trauma. Even after this empire system that we live in has fallen, the rubble will remain along with all the excess. That is sad and scary. *Dawn of the Matmosphere.*

BLACK BLOOD

The animation of concrete and asphalt and the black blood substance that we feed on, that we drink during the performances, we offer to the congregation, the Cultists, what looks like gloopy tar in the dark... it's actually some *spirulina* — a species of hi-tech bacteria that *produces its own food* — NASA wants to cultivate it in space. It's like a dark heavy green pigment powder stinking of algae and pond water, producing this chunky, gooey consistency when you mix it with liquids. Ancient Aztecs used to eat it. Supposedly, this is the original food-source that the first microscopic organisms consumed back when our early ancestors were cooking primordial soup. Even just a tiny portion is *full* of proteins, vitamins, and minerals — so it gives you this mad energy buzz as well, keeps you going for that whole hour while you're doing the ritual. And you can obviously spit it on each other and offer it to the crowd. It becomes a binder.

MOZIZIZM, MOZIZIZM

Chants and mantras are the content that creates a cult, forming the sonic landscape for followers to immerse and inhabit.

MOZIZIZM works both ways. Record yourself saying *MOZIZIZM* right now; do it in a deep slow voice, then play it backwards. It's a fucking *race-car*. Sampling has always played a big part in hip-hop culture, and this rolls over into the way that our mantras and chants are born. There'll be an interesting lyric in a rap song, or a writer will say something in an interview — we sample that, slow it down, cut it up, break it down to the basic elements, and remix it again into this obsessive mutation of the original phrase. These are *'broken down hip-hop ritual'* — the best advice that we give to our followers is "Don't complicate your life, *Cultiplicate* your life!" Look out in the future for pocket-sized Cult *Mantra Chanters* for the busy *Cultiste* who needs to brain wash'n'go.

SUB-NASAL

That's the thing — the sonic side of it is the nasal, obviously the RAMM:ΣLL:ZΣΣ's signature nasal style. So, you know *Beastie Boys, Cypress Hill, Clouddead...* and that characterization that's the transformative *RAMM:ΣLL:ZΣΣness* of becoming nasal. We made a film called *the Sub-nasal Chamber*. In the film, how we package it, there's a Tarot Reader for a group of elite exo-conscious Cultistes, and when the Reader plays a card or gives us a selection, it jumps to a ritual from that card. Basically, within that fiction there's the Major Nasal Groove, which is like a higher cult level, and then there's the Minor Nasal Groove, which is subcultural paralysis.

This nods at the polarization
of positive and negative with the
RAMM:ΣLL:ZΣΣ's own mythologies. We also *reversed* the process of a traditional
Tarot reading — embarking on our pilgrimage from the Westway to the Autobahn
and everywhere in-between *before* the cards determined all of that. This is a massive
victory in the battle against chronologics, as the forward passage of time is just
another piece of the prison structure designed to limit our exo-conscious potential
— and *that* is Major Nasal; *that* is how you achieve *anamnesis*.

JUNK

The Cult has a studio full of this junk piling up and looking trashy, but it holds
energy within the performance. Suddenly, you can rechannel it. Reanimate the junk,
reconfiguring into exoskeletons in the *cannon* of the RAMM:ΣLL:ZΣΣ art practice,
until you're just a huge fucking plastic mass. It's that viral fever effect. Skip diving
sub-cults; thrive on discarded plastics. Fanatics of the Three Stripes of ZI-DADA
rip out sneaker souls and create trainer talismans and sabres, for channeling the
plasmatic flow. When you actually walk down the street in a set of heavy ski-boots
with something that looks like a giant lazer blaster over your shoulder and all this
armor, rad shin-pads up and down your arms and legs, maybe a cloak, a visor — to a
kid who just jumped off the bus, you look like a super alien manga action blaster, and
it blows their mind! They get excited, they get inspired, they literally start poppin'.
So, it takes on this new life. It's ephemeral; but then, again, it's cargo cult — all life
is a process of eternal regurgitation; it washes back, and you reingest it. It's obsessive.

Note

1. Reed, Patricia. "Seven Prescriptions for Accelerationism", in *#Accelerate*, p. 524.

Hip-Hop's Modes of Production as Futuristic
Chuck Galli

Now we just boarded on our futuristic space-craft.
No mistakes Black, it's our music we must take back.
— Deltron Zero

Examinations of Afrofuturist music tend to focus almost exclusively on the aesthetics of the performers and the music itself. George Clinton, Parliament Funkadelic, and Sun Ra are often pointed to as exemplars of Afrofuturist music due in large part to their manners of dress, lyrical subject matter, and the philosophies they have espoused. What is less commonly examined is the way in which these artists create their music, whether talking about the sound equipment, the instruments, or the tones themselves. As the twentieth century proceeded toward its end and technology grew more complex right before the eyes of humanity, technologically advanced instruments (not necessarily in a musical sense) became more and more familiar to most people. And although musicians have been utilizing technology since the beginning of musical history itself, few musical genres have been as enamored with technology as has hip-hop. As British novelist and playwright Patrick Neate notes, "Practically, hip-hop was the first musical genre to rely exclusively on technology, in its use of turntables and mixer, drum machine and sampler."[1] Not only did hip-hop musicians embrace high-technology, the technology itself became the focus of hip-hop/rap music and led to hip-hop being constructed as a postmodern, futuristic art form. One of the primary reasons why hip-hop artists became so engrossed with high-technology, which will hopefully become clearer in this writing, is because such technology (in the hands of the hip-hop artists) greatly improved the artists' ability to re-appropriate music and art in ways that would have been largely impossible had they not employed relatively complex technology in their producing.

Not only is hip-hop a structurally futuristic art form, it is, to a large extent, a representation of some of Afrofuturism's main themes and phenomena due to both its modes of production and the content of a fair amount of overtly futuristic hip-hop music and visual art produced since the late 1970s.

Overleaf: Grandmaster Flash in the studio by Timothy Saccenti

The Music, The DJ

> Lookin' for the perfect beat. Searchin' for the perfect beat. Lookin' for the
> perfect beat. Seekin' for the perfect beat.
> — Afrika Bambaataa and the Soul Sonic Force

It was largely the fusion of the thinking, biological being with the mechanical, technologically complex electronic equipment that led to, essentially, an appreciation for the interaction of human and machine in hip-hop music. The DJ was an artist, and also an engineer, who was placed behind his module and tasked with coercing music out of a machine rather than simply instructed to play an instrument and create an "organic" sound. Given that hip-hop's first official DJ (Kool Herc) was a Jamaican sound system DJ, it is not surprising that this cybernetic human prototype was carried over into hip-hop culture, along with a mode of production which would become ever more developed.

The very first hip-hop instrumentation was the "looping" of a breakbeat using two identical records, two turntables, and a mixer. Looping was originally a tool used by DJs to extend the break of a song — the point of the song that many found most "danceable" because it contained a particularly heavy drum section and was almost always devoid of lyrics. Looping was an essential part of hip-hop's early scene when the genre was predominantly used as dance music and was played in live venues (in fact, the majority of late 1970s and very early 1980s hip-hop records feature studio-produced party crowd that plays in the background throughout the song).

Looping was an early example of the human DJ's interaction and total reliance on technology to produce the very first hip-hop sounds, however the introduction of two more instrumental features of hip-hop music — "scratching" and "sampling" — would take this relationship to a truly remarkable level, and would cement hip-hop DJs as both artists and engineers; as man-in-machines.

The Scratch

> Ain't no other way to play the game the way I play. I cut so much you
> thought I was a DJ.
> — Snoop Dogg

"Scratching" (or "cutting" as it was known in its infancy) is one of the most recognizable and misunderstood elements of hip-hop music. Most people unfamiliar with hip-hop culture and rap music are at least somewhat familiar with scratching as it has been parodied, isolated, and oversimplified in stereotypical fashions in popular entertainment. Scratching is, in its most basic form, performed by the DJ playing a vinyl record on a turntable, stopping the record with his hand, and

rubbing it back and forth across the tone needle to create a unique sound.[2] Often a mixer is used to mute the record while it is being rewound to a specific point, to control when sound will be created, or to switch the output of sound to another turntable attached to the same mixer. In its more complex forms, scratching utilizes records especially produced for DJs which feature only sound effects, spoken quotes, musical breaks, and various instrument sounds. A DJ may "scratch" the entire background instrumentation for a song, use scratching like an instrument (i.e., with regular frequency and in time with the rest of the music), or add scratching as an accouterment to a pre-recorded hip-hop song.

Scratching is similar in process to (and I believe a musical/technological descendent of) the manipulation and contortion of PA system equipment by Jamaican sound system DJs in that what becomes the focal point of the music is not necessarily the original instruments used to create whatever noise is being scratched, but rather the medium through which these pre-recorded sounds are now passing. Consider briefly the products which most of us have become familiar with since the dawn of the information era:[3] cellular telephones, the Internet, email, digital video and audio, and satellite technologies. All of these creations have profoundly affected the quality and quantity of things produced, but they have more starkly affected *how* produced materials and information are sent from one point to another. This is, in my opinion, the defining characteristic of twentieth and twenty-first century technological advance.

Scratching, in keeping with the theme of relatively recent technological advance, transports data (music on a record) from one place to another. But scratching does not merely facilitate this information communiqué; it also manipulates the data and appropriates it toward an end for which the data was not originally designed through what Samuel Delaney calls a "specific *miss-use* [sic]" of technology.[4] Buttressing the point, though also placing it within a Black diasporic context, Nabeel Zuberi asserts that this practice of misuse (or "*miss-use*") of technology is a continuation of a Black customary attitude toward technology,[5] and Ken McLeod explicitly declares that scratching is yet another occurrence of this cultural practice.[6] When American heart-throb pop-rock group The Monkees produced "Mary, Mary" in 1967, it was probably unlikely that they imagined their singing of the actual words "Mary, Mary" would become an instrument in the hands of Run-DMC's DJ, Jam Master Jay, in 1988. Nor would the actors, writers, singers, politicians, poets, commercial jingle writers, and radio personalities of the past hundred years envision that they would become a beat or an instrument for DJs such as Mix Master Mike, KutMasta Kurt, and DJ Shadow.

Scratching is but one technique in the repertoire of the hip-hop DJ that accords with futurism, and in fact is only an introduction into the study of "turntablism" — the art of the hip-hop DJ. To come closer to a holistic understanding of turntablism, the older and more widely used practice of "sampling" must be critically examined.[7]

The Sample

Well I'm the Benihana chef on the SP-12.
Chop the fuck out the beats left on the shelf.
— Adrock (Beastie Boys)

Sampling has been derided by many music critics, musicians, record labels, and advocates of copyright protection for what they see as an attempt to obfuscate the fact that hip-hop DJs are essentially stealing. In the historic *Grand Upright Music, Ltd. v. Warner Brothers Records, Inc.* (1991), a U.S. District Court ruled that any and all samples used in a recording must be cleared with the original artist before they can be used on another record.[8] The ruling made sampling time-consuming and costly and seriously reduced the amount of sampling that many artists could do.[9]

Sampling is theft if one remains within a more Western-leaning mindset that fixates on the concept of the "original inventor"; that is, a worldview which believes that something can be originally invented and that, once it comes into materialization, it is the property of that original inventor. However, leaving this preconception behind and embracing hip-hop's outlook on originality, one can come to see how sampling is a legitimate means of cultural production and a future-oriented practice. This outlook on originality includes two major tenets which are largely absent from the traditional Western idea of the original inventor; that is, the belief that all "original" works are merely fragments of older works re-manipulated and reorganized by different manipulators/organizers living in different times (and thus different cultural contexts) and that all works enter, to a great extent, a common, public domain and are freely available for further re-manipulation and reorganization. That this concept of bricolage arose amongst youth living in the South Bronx of a post-Cross-Bronx Expressway is not terribly surprising given the post-apocalyptic-like condition of the borough at the time. With no jobs, no money, high crime, the literal burning of an entire world, and the politics not of oppressive intervention, but of abandonment, it is easy to see how the South Bronx and the hip-hop aesthetic which grew out of it are very much informed by a cultural and social context formed, in essence, after the apocalypse. Everything which stands to be built must be built *by* communal effort and *with* whatever is left behind — whether that be a pile of rubble or a pile of vinyl disco records. The politics of post-apocalypsis is a foundation for hip-hop's view of originality.

When a DJ takes a sample, he is not attempting to deny the original artist any claim over having first recorded the sound or to pass off the sample as his original work.[10] The DJ takes a sample to create out of it both a unique sound and a unique emotion. Having one's music sampled, far from being an insult, can easily be interpreted as a compliment since, the logic goes, an artist's work was so good that there is no point in trying to imitate it — just use the actual piece. One's work is thus taken whole and placed into a new work and, most importantly, manipulated through various DJ techniques (altering the tempo or pitch, scratching the sample, etc.) and through the juxtaposition of the sampled bit with other samples. Aside from the surprise of finding their works on a rap album, it may be doubly intriguing to find Jimmy Smith's keyboarding and Myra Barnes' vocals blended seamlessly in rap duo Gang Starr's song "No More Mr. Nice Guy." From Michael McDonald's and Bob James' merger on Nate Dogg and Warren G's "Regulate" to Kool & the Gang's and Steve Miller Band's amalgamation on EPMD's "You're a Customer," hip-hop takes data and synthesizes it into a new "whole" which provokes emotion not only from the primary experience of hearing the sounds, but from understanding where the sounds come from and what impacts such an understanding may have. To sample a speech by Adolf Hitler and blend it into "Hail to the Chief" would obviously have a two-layered meaning and thus a two-layered reaction from a listener.

Why, then, does sampling represent some sort of inherent futurism? Because it draws its appeal and mechanics from a space where data are brought together.[11] There is nothing special about hearing Michael McDonald's music on someone else's album, but when the lines "Sixteen in the clip and one in the hole/Nate Dogg is about to make some bodies turn cold" are placed over the sample, McDonald's blue-eyed soul instrumentation takes on a creepy, dark feel.[12] A particular bit of data (McDonald's music) is transported to a new audience (assuming there is not a lot of overlap between Michael McDonald fans and west coast gangsta rap aficionados), acting essentially as high-technology does with its emphasis on data transfer. The manipulation of McDonald's music represents hip-hop's divergence from seeing its goal as the mere dissemination of information and toward a duty to synthesize such data and push it to mean something new.[13] Phil Collins could easily cover a Michael McDonald song, and perhaps that juxtaposition would create some special sensation, but it would be decidedly different from a hip-hop sampling because one would not be hearing Michael McDonald himself. Hip-hop does not imitate data so that it may ad lib and change the meaning — hip-hop is in the business of reconfiguring *what things mean*. Drawing from present day "givens" and supposing, proposing, suggesting, and proselytizing about them is par for the course for any futurist, whether she be a software designer, science-fiction writer, or religious prophet.

Not to be sidelined is the obvious connection one can see between the hip-hop DJ and what one might call classic surrealism. Surrealism, in the words of founding member André Breton, is "based on the belief in the superior reality of certain forms of previously neglected associations, in the omnipotence of dream, in the disinterested play of thought."[14] It is the first part of Breton's definition which most directly pertains to hip-hop. These "neglected associations" are exactly what hip-hop DJs tap into when mixing samples to create special feelings and sensations within the listener. Buttressing the argument for seeing hip-hop's modes of production as futuristic is the point that uncovering "neglected associations" (or better, connecting minds which would not otherwise have met in order to facilitate complimentary findings and understandings) is one of the paramount objectives of creating more advanced technological applications and instruments and was one of the stated intentions for the creation of the Internet.

Not only do these unorthodox juxtapositions lead to the immediate sensational experience, they may also inspire a listener to approach a genre of music or a musician which she would have otherwise overlooked because there was no initial feeling that pulled her toward such a genre or artist. 1970s acid-induced alternative-folk/rock music may not have (though it very well could have) allured many Black San Francisco teenagers in 2002, but hearing Harry Nilsson (a strong representative of this remote genre) and his instrumentation on Bay Area rap duo Blackalicious' 2002 album *Blazing Arrow* may spark a curiosity into who this old guy is.[15]

The Remix

> Cuz I don't really care what they think
> Tomorrow they'll be doing my song and will be claimin' its new...
> I tell you what, I'll give you my style right now to save time
> Cuz it takes time for you to chew — obviously.
> — Pigeon John

In any genre of music, one will find artists performing versions of someone else's songs and recording their own songs at different studios with different band members. Hip-hop artists engage in this as well, but two major elements of what DJs and MCs call "remixing" set the practice apart from more traditional forms of song alteration and constructs the art of remixing as a futuristic act: the mode in which a song is remixed, and the intents hip-hop artists have when producing songs and engaging in remixing.

"Covering" is usually the verb used to describe the performing or recording of a song by an artist other than the song's creator. Naturally, not only is the artist performing the cover differently from the original artist, the entire manufacture of the cover is usually different from the process that led to the original song: different studio/PA equipment, different studios and arenas, different instruments, etc. The ultimate objective of a cover is thus to appropriate someone else's song and perform it according to your own tastes and within whatever capacity you have.

Remixing shares this motif of appropriation, but the art of the remix is a decidedly more technologically inclined one and involves a deeper engagement with digital and analog data — the term "remix" alludes to this. "Mixing" a song typically refers to the assemblage of multiple tracks of instrumentation and vocalization into one cohesive track.[16] To remix, then, is to separate the various tracks used to create the song and delete and manipulate as many as necessary.[17] New tracks are often blended into the new mix (the re-mix) and may be either new instrumentation or new vocals. New instrumental tracks may consist of original music created with traditional instruments and synthesizer keyboards or may be a patchwork of samples.

The defining theme of the remix that sets it apart from the cover song is the direct engagement with the musical data by way of high-technology to manipulate, rather than imitate, a previously recorded song. When Whitney Houston covered "I Will Always Love You," which was originally written and recorded by Dolly Parton some twenty years earlier, she was essentially performing her "take" of the song; coloring it with her voice, style, and production quality of her studio team. What Houston was not doing was manipulating Dolly Parton herself. Hip-hop DJs, on the other hand, are less interested with re-performing someone else's song than with engaging in deconstruction and reconstruction of the song and utilizing the art of sampling juxtaposition we examined earlier. When hip-hop production duo Panjabi Hit Squad remixed the popular "Dude" by dancehall artist Beenie Man in 2008, Beenie's vocals were left untouched (aside from perhaps slight tempo adjustments) while an entirely new instrumental track was superimposed on the lyrical track. Panjabi Hit Squad drew from their South Asian roots and incorporated Panjabi instrumentation into a traditional Jamaican dancehall drum pattern to create the effect not that Beenie Man was being taken into a foreign and altogether dissimilar musical genre, but that there is a workable commonality between contemporary Panjabi and Jamaican music. The juxtaposition of these two cultures leads to sounds and sensations which would not have been possible to accomplish without leaving intact at least some of the original "Dude." Just as in our previous discussion of sampling, the remix is not an attempt to imitate the original data, but to reinterpret what it means.[18]

Remixing also has the power to prolong the life of a particular piece of music by reinvigorating it with new ideas and sounds. Holding to the Western appreciation of original ownership/creatorship, it is easy to see how the new soon becomes the stale, and how the stale eventually becomes the unpopular. Remixing acts much like a cybernetic organism (whether it be an artificial heart, prosthetic leg, or science fiction cyborg), providing the "host" music with enough structural support to keep it popular and enjoyable without obfuscating what the song "originally" was. The remixer thus gains popularity through his talent and musical taste, while the initial artist receives resuscitation and is appreciated for providing some raw material for others to use.[19]

Remixing in hip-hop is not, as it may seem thus far, strictly limited to the manipulation of the instrumental elements of a song, but can extend to the supplanting of new vocals over the original instrumental track. An example of this was the "Milli" phenomenon begun by rapper Lil Wayne in 2008. Lil Wayne released his single "A Milli" to a hip-hop community ready to bond over the art of remixing.

The instrumentation for "A Milli" was extremely minimalist, featuring one spoken sample, a snare drum, an artificial clap noise, and one note of synthesized bass. The song was a hit unto its own, and almost immediately after its release was remixed by some of the most contemporaneously popular hip-hop artists such as Cassidy, Ne-Yo, and Jadakiss (to name a very limited few), who kept the instrumentals more or less intact, adding only their vocals.

"A Milli" was remixed by so many artists that each additional remix brought the song closer to a farce, but the phenomenon made a statement about hip-hop which is germane to my argument about remixing as a futuristically inclined art form. That is, hip-hop artists intend that their music will be, to use the "original inventor" lexicon, "stolen" by other artists and manipulated without their input. The clearest evidence that this mindset exists amongst hip-hop artists can be found by examining the hip-hop "single" or "EP" (extended-play record). Traditionally, when a hip-hop artist releases an album, he releases a "single" immediately beforehand containing what will come to be the hit song on the album. The term "single" is a bit misleading however, as the single usually contains at least four versions of the same song: the album or single version (how the song will appear on the album, usually complete with profanity and at its full run-time), a "clean" or "radio" version (expletives removed and the song sometimes shortened for radio play), an instrumental version, and an a cappella version (just vocals.) The album and clean versions are generally intended for personal use and commercial broadcast (respectively), while the instrumental and a cappella versions are designed to more easily facilitate the remixing of the initial song. Rather than force a DJ to include the original music or oblige an MC to rap only between the initial rapper's lines, the creator of the single provides each with exactly what she needs to remix the song. Once the single, and more broadly the album, have sufficiently circulated the airwaves and record shops, an EP is sometimes released containing the initial version of the song, a number of remixes of the song performed by different artists, and a few songs by the initial artist (either album songs or songs which did not make the cut to appear on the album).[20]

Why, then, is this intent to facilitate the remixing of one's own music inherently futuristic? Because it represents an acknowledgement on the part of the hip-hop artist that his work will not forever be his own — that once it leaves his studio, it becomes a commodity on the remix/appropriation market.[21] The phenomenon of the remix has forced hip-hop artists to envision their creations as fluid in nature and, to some extent, antiquated as soon as they are released.[22] Aside from interpreting the initial messages and feelings contained within a song, a follower of hip-hop will also consider what she can do to reinterpret/re-appropriate/revitalize/*remix* the song. Hip-hop artists must thus be at least somewhat futuristically inclined in order to engage in the production of music with not only the knowledge that what they are creating is only the convergence of different lines in space-time ("space" being the various genres of music contemporaneously occupying various locations in the musical world and "time" being a point in musical canon teleported to the present, or future from the song's perspective), but that other artists will jettison the song into, essentially, new dimensions as quickly as possible.[23] Clearly, Irish pop musician Gilbert O'Sullivan (the plaintiff in the aforementioned *Grand Upright Music, Ltd. v. Warner Brothers Records, Inc* case) did not have such futurist ambitions for his song "Alone Again (Naturally)" when DJ Cool V sampled it on rapper Biz Markie's 1991 album *I Need a Haircut*. Biz Markie, on the other hand, posed no objection to having a line of his 1988 single "Nobody Beats the Biz" transformed into an entire chorus by DJ Ali Shaheed Muhammad for A Tribe Called Quest's 1993 *Midnight Marauders* album.

We have seen how the instrumental components of hip-hop music fit into a futuristic aesthetic and reflect this broader motif of the "cybernetic" in futurism, however we should not let these elements overshadow other parts of hip-hop music that also appear decidedly futuristic; namely, the art of rapping. The (Afro) futurism and postmodern elements of rapping are perhaps more obscure than are those elements found in hip-hop instrumentation, but they are there nonetheless, and they contribute to enriching our understanding of hip-hop as a much broader futuristic movement.

The Rapping

> Music orientated since when hip-hop was originated
> Fitted like pieces of puzzles — complicated.
> — Rakim

Rapping as a mode of production has, admittedly, fewer aspects which may reasonably be considered inherently "futuristic" than its partners remixing, sampling, and scratching; but the few that it does have are worth illuminating. The two aspects of rapping which I will focus on are the preoccupation with time rather than tone that characterizes the art and the practice of "freestyle" rapping. Let us first gain some background into the modes of production in rapping to adequately familiarize ourselves with the practice so that the futuristic elements can be better understood. Rapping, in large part, is an extension of "toasting" — yet another Jamaican relative of hip-hop found further up the family tree.[24] Rapping is, however, far more complex in structure and performance and relies on well defined senses of rhyme, a large vocabulary, and a refined understanding of meter and cadence.

Rhyme: Rappers have traditionally formed their songs by stringing together a number of couplets, all in standard rhyme. Like any poetic art, however, rap very frequently implores slant rhyme and alternative rhyme schemes (e.g., limericks). *Vocabulary:* Given the heavy use of rhyme in rapping, it is necessarily important that a rapper have a large and complex vocabulary to ensure that he can complete any rhyme he begins, that redundancy in word-choice is avoided, and that not only do his lines audibly rhyme, but that they are witty. To be more precise, it may be better to say "rappers' vocabularies" since "standard" English vocabulary is often blended with various dialects of slang found predominantly in Black, Hispanic, and White ethnic vernaculars. Again similar to poets, rappers often employ words in their songs which would not be normally found in the common lexicon they use in everyday speech. The common speech of rappers oftentimes belies the breadth of their lingual knowledge. Such is the case of MC Aesop Rock who speaks rather plain, "standard" English infused with some traditionally Black American colloquialisms, yet who bombastically raps "Double park the shuttle, some will arc the funneled Cutty Sark where budding narcs target the gushing heart in the muddy Clarks."[25]

Meter and Cadence: As we shall soon see, rappers by and large value "time" much more than "tone" in hip-hop. It is therefore not surprising to find meter and cadence to be of great concern for a rapper creating a song. Rap is almost always performed in standard 4:4 time, but the variations from that point are numerous. Some artists "speed rap" — essentially rapping in sixteenth notes. Others stick to more traditional quarter notes, and still many more syncopate their rhymes in the tradition of jazz and be-bop.[26] Rap is more like poetry than singing, and the synchronization of words with the beat supporting them is paramount for a class of artists who openly object to being labeled singers. Says Run of Run-DMC, who consider themselves more like orators than vocalists: "Like Martin Luther King, I will do my thing. I'll say it in a rap 'cause I do not sing."[27]

It is in the consideration of what "time" means to the rapper that some of rapping's futuristic tendencies and inclinations come to light. Understanding some fundamental differences between traditional singing and rapping can be facilitated by thinking of the differences between an analog signal and a digital signal. Singing, like an analog signal, is mostly concerned with wave formation. Like analog radio signals which must be of a proper frequency or amplitude, vocal waves also must be of an equally proper frequency and amplitude in order to attain a desired pitch and note. Rapping, more akin to a digital signal, relies on bits of information being in a proper order. A computer disc may be able to save a recording of a woman singing, but it saves it as a constructed series of ones and zeros (binary code) which can later be decoded to reproduce another sound wave. The wave itself, then, is not actually preserved as it would be in an analog medium (such as a vinyl record). Rapping, unlike singing, is not terribly concerned with attaining proper pitch, tone, note, or certain other musical elements traditionally associated with vocalization. Rappers are more concerned with their words being in proper time, matching whatever syncopated cadence they may have chosen, and making sure that the words, instrumentation, and time are "fitted like pieces of puzzles — complicated."[28] I can remember hearing endlessly from older generations how "that rap isn't music," and to an extent, they have/had a point. Rapping is so dissimilar from more traditional forms of singing (from yodeling, to chanting, to opera, to blues, etc.) that it could hardly be considered as such. But this does not mean that rap music is "noise" and not real music — it is simply an encoded music that cannot be understood prima facie, much like a digital code.

This inability to understand digital code unto itself is the qualifying characteristic which renders such code futuristic. To human sensory organs, digital code means nothing. Neither does FM radio modulation, but the *form* of frequency waves is something which humans can detect through sense.[29] Digital codes and signals have taken on an aura of futurism due to the requirement that some rudimentary form of artificial intelligence be present to decipher them and make them *categorically* coherent to human senses. Digital signaling removes human data from the human realm by means of its formatting. Rapping certainly does not remove anything from the human realm (which is why the analogy between rapping and digitization is not a perfect one), but it does digitize music to a certain extent. Rappers can get emotion, feeling, meaning, and messages across as well as, if not better than, any singer without using what I call "wave-form music." What are required are more bits of data to perform this task both in the sense of a wide array of words and a large number of whole words. Rappers, owing to their inclination toward data-based over wave-form music, have the advantage of simply being able to fit more words into a shorter period of time. There is thus more of an onus on the brain, the human computing component, to interpret data in hip-hop songs than there is, generally speaking, in non-hip-hop genres.

The brain must be able to not only interpret more data, but in the case of what is called "freestyle" rap, must also be able to predict and think in the future. Freestyle rapping is the art of rapping without having thought of what one will rap about or what words one will use before one begins. Keeping in mind that the "rules" of what constitutes good rapping are not suspended when a rapper is "freestyling," the practice becomes all the more impressive. Not only must a rapper choose his words *while* he is saying them, he must try to ensure that his lines will rhyme, that his word choices fit the cadence and meter of whatever beat is playing in the background (or, if there is no music at all, that his words follow some sort of natural sounding meter), and that what he is saying ultimately makes sense and is not just an amalgam of random words which have appeared in his head. Some rappers will use "fallback" lines while freestyling — lines which they have used before and store in their memories to "save" them if they encounter a mental block while freestyling — but this practice is largely decried as disingenuous and proof that one does not possess much talent as an MC.[30]

Freestyling thus requires a rapper to allow his mouth to move in the present while his brain is contemplating future words. Almost all speech, admittedly, exists as a thought before it exists as a sound, but the defining difference from regular speech in freestyle rap is the necessity of the rapper to be in two temporal locations at once. The rapper does not think of a rhyme, say it, stop, think of another rhyme, and then say that one. Rather, she is constantly rapping about something, stopping only briefly to breathe, and constantly thinking of the next thing to say. The roots running from freestyle rap to jazz improvisation are clearly obvious to anyone with even basic knowledge of jazz, and the process of having one's mind in two different locations at once (both creating the physical movement of the lips and throat and thinking of what to say next) exists within jazz musicians. The one major objection I would make to establishing too close of a comparison between freestyling and jazz improvisation is that doing so may overlook the possibility of muscle memory in jazz instrumentalists. Since jazz instruments such as the saxophone, piano, bass, and so forth involve fingers, lips, hands, and other body parts to operate, there is the likelihood that muscle memory (of scales, keys, etc.) accounts for a significant part of jazz improvisation. Freestyle rapping can utilize no such biological feature since all of the "instrumentation" (the rapping itself) is performed as speech and can be created only by the brain. There is thus, I believe, more separation of the mind between the present and the future in freestyle rap than there is in jazz improvisation.

Freestyle rapping is thus futuristic in its treatment of what it means to "be present." Where is the MC while he is freestyling? Obviously, his physical person is on a stage, in a circle with fellow rappers, or even in his shower while his mind is a few seconds in the future, piecing together phrases informed by data in the present. The rapper is thus in a solid physical state and a fluctuating mental state at the same time; a personified example of the concept of "wave-particle duality" found in quantum mechanics.[31] The freestyle rapper cannot exist without engaging in futurism.

Thus far we have explored two major components of hip-hip: DJing and MCing. Yet we can extend this discussion beyond music and find it also represented in the visual world by critically examining graffiti as an artform with intrinsically futuristic qualities.[32]

Graffiti

> It's like three-card Monty, and pick-pocketing, and shoplifting, and, uh, graffiti defacing on public and private walls. They're all in the same area of destroying our lifestyle.
> — New York City Mayor Ed Koch

A number of futuristic modes of production can be found in graffiti, but equally interesting are the connections to postmodernism and surrealism which are more explicitly articulated in graffiti than in rapping or DJing. Though some may not consider surrealism or postmodernism to be necessarily "futurist" schools, I contend that since both philosophies have such strong ties to Afrofuturism, for our intents and purposes in this essay it is proper and useful to consider them futuristically inclined.[33] The aspects of graffiti which I shall examine will be: graffiti's use of trains as canvasses, the adoption of pseudonyms by artists, and some stylistic elements that lend to postmodernism and surrealism.

The Train

> Just looking at that thing, a black silhouette just sitting there with red blinking lights sticking out. It's alive!
> — Lee Quiñones[34]

Much like its hip-hop companions rapping and DJing, graffiti grew in occurrence during a period of great urban neglect which colored much of the 1970s and 1980s. In tandem with the decline of urban quality of life and the setting in of the "apocalypse," the appropriation of public spaces for the purpose of making art grew in popularity and spawned a culture which would create both an intensely private and explicitly public form of visual art.

Before discussing the graffiti itself, it would be helpful to consider some of the special characteristics of subway trains and how these would come to be utilized by graffiti artists. Subways are, by some definitions, mechanisms created to facilitate the smooth operation of labor in a socio-economic system where labor is a commodity and where people do not work on the land they own (peasant economy) or rent (feudal economy) — namely capitalism.[35] Subways, being largely physically underground, not only remove people from their community for the purpose of laboring, but also remove any continuity one would have in making such a trip (such as walking or biking from Harlem to Chinatown, passing through all neighborhoods in between) and literally blot out the very existence of neighborhoods and people along the way, much like an expressway does. Subways are, in a sense, very ends-oriented mechanisms; they will take you from one place to another in a box, which largely travels underground, so that you can work. Subways in New York were meant to be cold, expressionless people movers as shown by the desire of public officials and the transit authority to keep the cars shining white, free of blemishes, and for use by respectable New Yorkers who (according to transit authority workers) would be cheered up upon being greeted by a solid white, art-less steel carriage and who wanted nothing from the trains but to sit inside them and be taken to their jobs.[36]

Graffiti artists had other plans for the trains of economic progress. Living in a world where the urban poor were being written out of the human story and where concrete structures such as the Cross-Bronx Expressway (constructed with the explicit intent to make Manhattan a center of economic wealth) took precedent over the lives and livelihoods of those who lived in its projected path, artists began sending out messages to worlds which were not considered their own. Subordinate to the master plan to generate wealth no matter what the cultural costs, the graffiti writers used the only things with mobility between the apocalyptic urban slums to express themselves, build connections with those far away, and remind those productive labor organisms that worlds existed above the subway tunnels.[37] Not only would paintings done on the sides of train cars send the messages of emotions of disillusioned artists to people who otherwise would not have either known or cared about them, these paintings would also transform the trains into personalities rather than utilitarian work horses. Famed graffiti artist Lee Quiñones once said that he actually felt sympathy for subways trains, which he saw as "lonely," and felt that his painting of them did not mar them, but rather made them "so special."[38] For Quiñones, painting the trains liberated them from their modern utilitarian slavery and gave them something to live for, so to speak.

The challenges to modernity here are relatively clear. Rather than viewing the trains as tools for use in furthering the accumulation of wealth, graffiti artists saw them as expressers of emotion and feeling. The fixed identity of the cold, white, sterile (at least in appearance) subway cars was replaced with a fluid identity where a car could one day be the expression of hard times in the Bronx, and the next could be a playfully absurdist cartoon of Mickey Mouse giving the middle finger.[39] As this identity traversed the boroughs of New York, it would be interpreted according to its current context (maybe aggression in wealthier neighborhoods, maybe solidarity in other poor areas, perhaps accomplishment and pride in the borough which housed the piece's artist).[40] This was the creation of an identity on the move (and more importantly, *of* the move) and a proposition that such identity was somehow life-giving and illuminating unto itself.

The Name

> It's a name. It's just like, I'll give you a name and say, hey, how big can you get this name up?
> — DUST

Graffiti artists generally assumed pseudonyms when writing, and quite often these names became the basis for the artworks themselves. When Samuel Clemens became "Mark Twain," he used it as a name under which to publish literature; but when graffiti legend PHASE 2 adopted his name, he used it as an identity (in specific, a connection to his African ancestors and an objection to his being given a European name at birth) and as a material.[41] "The name" in graffiti became the artist's clay, but also the artist himself. From its beginnings in tagging, graffiti developed an obsession with popularizing the name over the physical artist. Graffiti legend RAMM:ELL:ZEE explains this historical phenomenon in his typical scattered, unregulated manner of speech:

The 1980's and 70's, really when it started, was more a collective result of how people poverishly inhibited by society used their lack of ability to write letters on walls for a simple explanation of themselves — *expotential* for themselves [sic]. Fame. Name fame. [italics mine][42]

I italicized RAMM:ELL:ZEE's pseudo-word "expotential" because, even though it is not an English word (though that is hardly a concern for Zee, as we shall later see), Zee used it to say exactly what it means. "Ex" (out of) and "potential" combine to signify a potential which exists outside of something: in this case, the graffiti writers. Though impossible to know what each piece of art means to each artist, the works that graffiti writers painted on trains meant a great deal to them, perhaps (as Zee suggests) because it provided them with a potential that present life within the politics of abandonment could not.[43] Of course, this potential needed something in which to manifest, and due in part to the illegal nature of graffiti and the effects of poverty preventing the artist from providing the host-body, the fame and acclamation for the art shifted onto the name itself, thus vicariously providing the artist with a means of realizing a potential, if outside of himself.[44] The artist thus found an "expotential" in his taken name. Fame. Name fame.

It bears noting at this point, though it may seem a bit of a digression (when this is in fact a germane moment to make such a comment), that assuming names is a common practice among all participants in hip-hop: MCs, DJs, breakdancers, and even producers. As if not evident from every MC and DJ mentioned thus far, stage-names are almost always taken by artists, but the practice has much more depth than simply providing a relatively plain-named person with a catchier moniker for entertainment purposes (so as not to overload the reader with too many extraneous names, I will limit my examples to futuristic artists who are often referenced as part of the Afrofuturism hip-hop roster).[45]

Del tha Funkee Homosapien is a well-known west coast rapper who has released a number of albums under his stage name. In 2000, however, Del collaborated with DJ and producer Dan the Automator to create the *Deltron 3030* album, on which he used the moniker "Deltron Zero." The change of name coincided with a drastic change in style and subject matter on the record, which was a heavily futurist influenced work containing a relatively consistent storyline taking place in outer-space. Obviously, the actions of a person are often closely associated with his name,[46] and it is perhaps partly because of this phenomenon that Del tha Funkee Homosapien chose to use a new name on the *Deltron 3030* album — to start with a "clean slate."

An even more relevant example is that of Kool Keith who boats around a half-dozen aliases. Known as Kool Keith while performing more mainstream-style (if now considered "old school") rap with his first group Ultramagnetic MCs, Keith assumed the name Dr. Octagon in 1996 when he and Dan the Automator released *Dr. Octagonecologyst*. The album was a bizarre, sexually perverse, and surreal (all three typical for Keith regardless of what name he uses) record on which Keith developed the new name through chronicling Dr. Octagon's interplanetary terrorizing of his unfortunate patients. Keith abandoned the name (though assumed a few more) until 2006 when he released *The Return of Dr. Octagon* and once again utilized the name Dr. Octagon.

Such examples are plentiful, but suffice it to say that it is very common in hip-hop for artists to take on new names in order to achieve new goals and do new things on a musical level. For graffiti artists, naming has a paradoxical nature in that it simultaneously allows for a potentially great amount of fame and an intentional anonymity. An artist's name becomes a work of art, is used to express what he has no agency to otherwise express, and is transported to millions of people for free. Yet the artist himself is invisible in this process until he finds a way (if he wants to at all) to make his physical voice heard and face seen. It is the name which becomes the subject.

Wild Style

> *It's not words, it's not a name anymore. It's more of a living thing that you have created...*
> — Lee Quiñones[47]

One of the most remarkable aspects of graffiti writing — aside from the often brilliant colors, incredible coordination needed to do it, and ability to create amazing works of art from spray paint on walls, trains, and other rather pedestrian surfaces — is the script in which names and phrases are often written. Just as names become subjects in graffiti, scripts become art in a calligraphic fashion.

Artists constantly innovated script writing within the graffiti movement, but as graffiti culture progressed into the 1980s, certain scripts began moving from an embellished Roman alphabet to a more cryptic, camouflaged writing form.[48] Letters began to slant, bend, explode, and grow appendages with increasing frequency as they proceeded to blend into each other, creating labyrinths of lines and curves obfuscating words.[49] The most popular form of this writing style was called "Wild Style" and featured all of the aforementioned elements with the addition of characteristically brilliant and eclectic colors, spikes or arrows coming off of letters, and three-dimensional effects.[50] The result of Wild Style was the creation of scripts and words usually illegible to the average person and even other graffiti artists who were not skilled in the style.

As personal computers and the near monopolization of letter-shape by software publishers lurked at the gates of society in the early 1980s, ready to explode across the world in popularity, a renaissance of calligraphy was taking place in the world of graffiti.

But if graffiti was all about name fame and the transmission of messages to the "outside" world through art, what sense did it make to start writing in Wild Style? Certainly, each artist had his own reasons: personal fulfillment in creating art, wanting to make a political statement against the established authority, or any number of reasons.[51] The rationales for creating works in Wild Style are interesting and important, but most pertinent to this piece is the result of such practices. The post-apocalyptic Bronx (and other depressed areas of New York) began producing yet another response to modernity. The concept of the original artist had been overruled by the hip-hop DJ, music as an analog wave had experienced the digital interference of the rapper, and now the very foundation of Western intellectual life — the letter — had been appropriated and broken down by graffiti artists. Let me entertain the most elementary example of postmodern rhetoric I first encountered some years ago. Say you have a large, tall cup made of soft clay, but still hard enough to hold water. Now pry this clay cup open slightly — your cup is now slightly wider and shorter. Continue this process over and over again. Eventually you will find your cup to be stout, wide, and more resembling a bowl. Continue the process even further and your piece of clay will soon become a plate. The question is: at what point did your cup become a bowl and your bowl a plate? How would you determine such a point? The postmodern thinker would say that there is no point — that the clay can be called whatever one wants and its definition will change depending on setting and context. This rudimentary postmodern thinking can easily be applied to graffiti, firstly because the art form rendered the distinctions between names, writing, and visual art useless by making all three interdependent upon each other, and secondly because the actual letters had been so manipulated by the writers that distinguishing between a letter (which is highly utilitarian) and an embellishment (which is mainly aesthetic) became difficult and words became totally contextual. Perhaps a piece of Wild Style graffiti explicitly said something, but it would be equally likely that a woman staring at the work as she approaches a train would mistake it for a mere (if visually stunning) series of squiggles and scratches.

Messages could now be sent from one graffiti artist to another, passing through potentially millions of lines of sight, without anyone else (save for a relative thimble-full of other graffiti writers) understanding it or even recognizing it as a series of letters. Messages of friendship, antagonism, braggadocio, challenges, or anything else could be put out into the world, but what is most impressive is the fact that a re-appropriation of modernity had been completed within the very pool of people and places designated as the byproduct of a modern synthesis of wealth, transportation, and social/ecological reorganization. The utilitarian trains had begun serving a completely "non-productive" artistic and expressive purpose while the Roman script,

Opposite: 3-D Wild Style: one of RAMM:∑LL:Z∑∑'s Letter Racers by Timothy Saccenti
Previous page: RAMM:∑LL:Z∑∑ by Timothy Saccenti

being increasingly standardized and codified in style and function with the increased prevalence of word processors and computers, became perverted beyond recognition for the vast majority of those in the mainstream, modern world. A cultural civilization made up of rapping, DJing, and graffiti, which was unintelligible and beyond the intellectual reach of the society which "owned" all of the appropriated equipment used to construct it, existed parallel to normative civilization.

The modes of production in graffiti, especially the art of Wild Style, not only have very postmodern aspects, they are also deeply entrenched in a surrealist aesthetic. Perhaps not the most visible, but still the most salient example of this comes from the practice of naming in graffiti. As RAMM:ELL:ZEE explained earlier, artists created names-as-subjects for an "expotential" for themselves. The dreamt, invented, *extra-corpus* subject (i.e., the name) lives a life full of the potentials not available to the painter writing the name on the sides of trains and on walls — fulfilling the desires of the "poverlishly inhibited" artist. But the more optical surrealism comes from the canvasses most often used in graffiti and the manipulation of the Roman script. One of the most characteristic and special aspects of graffiti is its tradition of doing art where art is not to be done: overpasses, abandoned buildings, trains, and other public edifices. Graffiti, with its often exotic colors and mesmerizing shapes, is injected into the rational, commercial world in which most people live their lives devoid of dreaming.[52] Among the tall financial buildings, transit buses and trains, store fronts and restaurants, and offices of any urban area, there may be an illegible, colorful piece of work incorporating anything from cartoons, guns, people, geometric shapes, and unrecognizable lettering into a piece of art which one may not be able to read, but can certainly detect on some emotional level (whether that be fear, admiration, or confusion). Graffiti, owing to its projection onto areas typically intended to be sterile by their creators, forcefully confronts society with the dreams of artists.

Since the "name fame" of graffiti and the adoption of pseudonyms often did not position itself in some future time period, it may be difficult to detect the futuristic aspects of graffiti. Yet dreaming about the future — according to Paul Gilroy[53] — was a critical part of Black culture for, most likely, the bulk of Black history, and connections can easily be seen running between Afrofuturism and graffiti created by both Black and non-Black artists.[54] According to Gilroy, the futurism of jubilee and deliverance espoused by Black slaves was more a tool to provide strength for continued living in a present which, like the South Bronx of the post-apocalypsis, most closely resembled a hell.[55] Though living in different contexts, artists in the post-apocalyptic urban areas (first in the South Bronx, later New York City at large, and later the world) appropriated this strategy and created their "expotentials" to reap the benefits they themselves could not. Therefore, delineation between Afrofuturism and graffiti can be seen if one examines the production-aesthetics of both rather than merely the explicit content.

In summary, hip-hop's modes of production reflect a desire to dream of an escape into a world of new identities, appropriations of past artefacts using modern technologies, and foci on "becoming" rather than "having become." These futuristic tendencies can be seen as somewhat Afrofuturist as they tend to reject the mainstream, Western futurisms of utopia and perfection through modernism and instead embrace a "jubilant" form of futurism formed in what Paul Gilroy would call the "Black Atlantic" of cultural morphism and escape from the bureaucracy of "progress." Hip-hop should not be seen solely as a futuristic cultural movement or art form, nor should any futurism found there within be heralded as the most important or influential aspect of the culture. Futurism is but one lens through which to view hip-hop; however, peering through such a lens provides insight into new understandings of where Afrofuturism is going (or where it has gone) theoretically and how hip-hop may be able to help us consider the future in our current social climates.

Notes

1. Youngquist, Paul. "The Afrofuturism of DJ Vassa." European Romantic Review,16, no. 2, April 2005, p. 188.

2. This is a somewhat antiquated definition as digital sound equipment has brought forth numerous devices which reproduce this sound using compact discs and digital music formats (such as MP3s). These devices, however, seek to mimic the sounds originally created with vinyl records, and therefore it is most relevant to present scratching using a slightly older definition.

3. This era is sometimes referred to as the "technological era," however I prefer the term "information era" because I believe the proliferation and liquidity of information wrought by most technological breakthroughs has been more impressive and important than the technologies themselves. The advent of the printing press (to use a pre-information era example) was not a major breakthrough because stamping letters onto paper with ink was somehow intrinsically important. Rather it was the dissemination of information which was the truly revolutionary advance.

4. McLeod, Ken. "Space Oddities: Aliens, Futurism and Meaning in Popular Music," in *Popular Music* 22, no. 3, 2003, (337-355), 347.

5. McLeod, 347 — Specifically, Zuberi points to the use of "the broken bottleneck applied to the blues guitar, ... the oil drum bashed and buffed to create Trinidad steel sound ... [and] the Roland 808 drum machine."

6. McLeod, 347.

7. I should make it clear that when I refer to an ambiguous "sample," it could mean a piece of music, a lecture, a TV advertisement, or almost anything that was once recorded. Samples are usually derived from songs, though non-song samples are omnipresent in hip-hop.

8. 780 F. Supp. 182 (S.D.N.Y. 1991) United State District Court for the Southern District of New York.

9. The album *Paul's Boutique* (1989) by Beastie Boys is often used as the exemplar of a pre-1991 hip-hop record which would be nearly impossible to create today due to the *Grand Upright* ruling.

10. And when a hip-hop artist does attempt to pass off sampled work as "original" work, he is cast in a negative light. The most well known example of this was pop-rapper Vanilla Ice's use of a sample of "Under Pressure" by Queen and David Bowie. Ice claimed that the bass line for "Ice, Ice Baby" was an original creation and not a sample, even though it was clearly taken from Bowie and Queen. Ice suffered both from the scorn of the record company owning the rights to "Under Pressure" and from hip-hop fans who used his "foul" as cannon fodder against what many already considered to be a mere parody of a real rapper.

11. Here I am thinking of "space" both in the more literal sense and also in the "outer-space" sense. Entering "space" frees one from the confines and regulations of earth and its worldly regulations. Space is an area of new possibilities due to its lack of norms. To quote *Star Trek*: "Space — the final frontier."

12. Warren G, "Regulate" on the album *Regulate... G Funk Era*, 1994.

13. This ability to create something "new" is important if one considers the context in which hip-hop formed. People living in urban communities where hip-hop took hold (whether that be the South Bronx

on the east coast or Oakland and Compton on the west) were largely excluded from creating new possibilities by two means: lack of both physical and financial resources and the effects of abandonment thanks to benign neglect. As urban areas crumbled under Reaganomics (and economic policies which predated Reagan), material wealth became acutely scarce, and thus did the ability to manufacture anything new. The politics of abandonment and benign neglect were essentially signals from the U.S. and state governments that people living in urban areas were to be left out of American progress and the process of creating wealth. To create something new in these contexts requires a complete rethinking of what "create" and "new" meant and the development of skills of construction without the assistance of the state or any readily available historical example from which to draw inspiration.

14. Waldberg, Patrick. *Surrealism*, Oxford, England: Oxford University Press, 1978), 75.

15. Personally, I have traveled this musical route a number of times, discovering my now-adored Jimmy Smith, Buddy Rich, Johnny Cash, Bad Brains, and countless other musicians through hip-hop. It would be much more difficult (if not impossible) for even the most contemporary rock and roll music to work in the complementary reverse — inspiring an appreciation for Grand Wizard Theodore, Notorious B.I.G., Mos Def, or any other group of hip-hop artists.

16. Not to be confused with "mastering" which is the adjustment of levels and stereophonics to create a "better" sounding piece of music.

17. Fans of Jamaican dub music might find this last sentence quite familiar. Indeed, the art of remixing in hip-hop has its roots in dub, just as hip-hop DJing in general has its roots in Jamaican sound systems.

18. Why does remixing strive to reinterpret rather than reproduce? Hypotheses abound, but I think it has something to do with hip-hop's postmodern tendencies. Basically, hip-hop can be seen as valuing "becoming" over "being" — as seeing "the process" as the destination. Keeping identity in flux is one way of expressing a preference for becoming over being.

19. A great example is the remix of the song "Paper Planes" (2007) by musician MIA. Having achieved high acclaim and popular reception in 2007, a few words from "Paper Planes" were sampled by rapper Jay-Z and used in the instrumentation for his widely popular 2008 song "Swagga Like Us" featuring himself and rappers T.I., Lil Wayne, and Kanye West. I can specifically remember rarely hearing "Paper Planes" on Providence, Rhode Island's main hip-hop station in 2007, yet hearing it, as well as "Swagga Like Us," multiple times daily in 2008. The appropriation of MIA's work, though not a full remix, extended the life of its popularity and even increased it in certain areas.

20. I should make it clear that this is not the only instance in which an EP is released. EPs can be produced when an artist simply does not have enough individual songs to necessitate an LP ("long-play album"), when he wants to publish "B-sides" (songs which did not appear on the album), or for any number of reasons not related to remixing. EPs are also sometimes released before the full-length album is released.

21. The clash of this mindset and the "original inventor" mindset is, I believe, the root of a great amount of animosity between hip-hop artists and non-hip-hop artists.

22. Indeed, some rap singles, which make a song available to the public for the very first time, come complete with remixes of the "original" song.

23. To clarify, "space-time" in this usage refers primarily to the act of sampling as a method of producing hip-hop music. The spatial component amounts to the taking of samples from artists in various genres of music who all produced songs around the same time. The temporal location is the taking of samples from various eras in music (jazz, punk rock, classical, etc.). Since these two almost always have a great deal of overlap, it is most appropriate to use the term "space-time."

24. "Toasting" is the speaking-over of music by the sound system DJ, usually to excite the crowd. Early South Bronx Jamaican sound system DJs would "toast" during their sets, and eventually this morphed into rhymed toasting. Not before long, dedicated MCs would toast in rhyming meter while the DJ handled the music, and thus was born the DJ and MC combination that defined hip-hop in its infancy.

25. Aesop Rock, "Citronella" on the album *None Shall Pass*, 2007.

26. Rappers Busta Rhymes and Twista are good examples of speed-rappers, while Lyrics Born provides great examples of both "standard" rapping and syncopated speech rhythms.

27. Run-DMC, "Proud to Be Black" on the album *Raising Hell*, 1986.

28. Eric B. & Rakim, "Microphone Fiend" on the album *Follow the Leader*, 1988.

29. Humans cannot eat poisonous berries, but they can eat raspberries. My point here is to show how analog signals may be undetectable to humans, but not categorically, whereas no matter what a size a digital signal is, how quickly it is moving, through what it is moving, or how complex it is, it means nothing to the human's senses.

30. I can recall being at a Jurassic 5 concert at Colby College in Lewiston, Maine and witnessing MC Akil use a line while "freestyling" which I had heard him use a few years before at another concert. A few people around me apparently also had heard this line before, and responded by sucking their teeth and rolling their eyes, even though the rhyme was clever unto itself.

31. For more information on wave-particle duality and quantum mechanics in general, see David J. Griffiths, *Introduction to Quantum Mechanics*, 2nd edition, San Francisco: Benjamin Cummings, 2004.

32. This is perhaps the most significant aside to this entire piece. Anyone attempting to learn about hip-hop culture or the history of hip-hop will often come across this idea of the four elements of hip-hop: MCing, DJing, breakdancing, and graffiti. These elements supposedly compose hip-hop culture in totality as they all gained popularity in New York City around the same time. Yet others — including legendary hip-hop DJ Grandmaster Flash, the director of a seminal 1980s movie on graffiti *Wild Style* Charlie Ahern, and many other influential hip-hop legends — strongly object to this association of graffiti and breakdancing with hip-hop. Graffiti, they argue, pre-dates hip-hop music by decades, centuries, or even millennia. They also often describe breakdancing as a type of dance that evolved out of disco, but did not "land" in hip-hop more than it landed in other latter-day musical genres. These critics argue that graffiti and breakdancing should be considered their own cultural movements and not part of hip-hop. For better or worse, I am including graffiti in this piece because of what I see as its strong connections to futurism. Whether it deserves a place in the history of hip-hop proper is a debate to which I cannot contribute much.

33. Surrealism and postmodernism, whether called by those names or not, are very much a part of Afrofuturism as I and others have defined it. The idea of a falling out or detachment from modernity's goals and modes of operation is an idea shared by Afrofuturism, postmodernism, and surrealism.

34. Miller, Ivor. *Aerosol Kingdom: Subway Painters of New York City*, Jackson, MS: University Press of Mississippi, 2002, p. 90.

35. Miller, 87 as quoting graffiti writer Lee Quiñones who says "They [the subways trains] are just sitting — waiting, for the imperialist country to bring its clones to its factories to pump out more bombs." Miller himself says of Quiñones that he "regards his paintings as an attempt at readjusting the distorted values of [New York City's] downtown corporate workers." Of course, people use subways and commuter rail services for non-labor related reasons such as visiting friends and family, shopping, or for connection to another mode of transit. Yet given that many rapid transit systems operate at an annual net loss or yield only a small profit, it can be concluded that the metropolitan areas have a financial incentive to

continue funding such projects. If most people used subways to visit their grandparents, few to no cities would take on an annual debt to ensure this familial connection. But since cities are largely dependent upon a healthy wage-labor economy where people work where they do not live, it is imperative that the government create a way to distribute these productive capital creators from their homes to their places of work.

36. *Style Wars*, dir. Chalfant, Henry and Silver, Tony, 1983.

37. Miller, 28-29. We can also tie this directly to Afrofuturism. If subways (and expressways) were constructed for the proliferation of wealth, but this wealth was not privy to an enormous number of (mostly non-White) people who lived within such paths, where is the rationale that wealth-creation is inherently "progress" or an end unto itself? We must also consider the historical devaluation of the "merits" of labor within many African diasporic traditions and include this in an interpretation of subways where the value of their labor-providing capacities might not be as revered from a Black perspective (Kelley, 164-165). Of course, Latinos and some White ethnics and Asians would be consumed by urban blight as well. The creation of what I call "functionally Black" non-Black persons in certain contexts and situations is something bell hooks points to as a result of postmodern conditions which lead to "a sense of deep alienation, despair, uncertainty, loss of a sense of grounding, even if it is not informed by shared circumstance" (Potter, 9). Hooks sees this momentary "Blackening" of non-Black groups as a potential area of connection and collaboration among many oppressed groups, and may help to explain why graffiti was so multiracial even in its early years.

38. Miller, 95.

39. Miller, 37.

40. These are the politics of reception and evidence for the postmodern nature of graffiti. Certainly, all art is perceived and received differently when it is brought to a new venue, but that graffiti was consciously created on a surface whose sole function was to move into and through different contexts testifies to the inherent postmodern mechanisms of graffiti and the intents of the artists.

41. Miller, 68.

42. Ahern (note: this quote is taken from an interview with RAMM:ELL:ZEE which is only found on the twenty-fifth anniversary edition of *Wild Style*, which is the one cited in this paper).

43. I do not want to simply gloss over how important the work of graffiti artists was to them. Young men and women (many of Latino or African descent) tempted the New York City police, the unknown caverns of old subway routes, oncoming trains weighing tons upon tons, and the deadly third-rail in order to spray their art onto the sides of trains, knowing full well that the vast majority of people who saw the works would have no idea who made them, nor would such spectators even be able to find out.

44. It is interesting to note that in the documentary *Style Wars*, this is the sentiment espoused by SKEME who famous said his ambition in writing graffiti was to "destroy all lines" (that is, subway lines) with his name while the wealthy Anglo-American graffiti writer LSD OM started using a pseudonym (he had been using his real name, Chad) to avoid "celebrityism." (Miller, 64).

45. There are some notable exceptions in hip-hop of people who use their legal names in their work such as Erick Sermon and Kanye West.

46. One need look no further than the 2008 United States presidential elections where Barack Hussein Obama's middle name was malevolently bandied about by conservative news media in an attempt to associate the person Barack Hussein Obama with the person Saddam Hussein Abd al-Majid al-Tikriti (late leader of Iraq 1979-2003) through their shared name.

47. Miller, 39.

48. Miller, 119.

49. Miller, 119.

50. Miller, 77-79.

51. Miller, 78-79.

52. Or dreaming a dream which was dictated to them, such as the "American dream".

53. Gilroy, Paul. *The Black Atlantic*, Cambridge, Massachusetts: Harvard University Press, 1993.

54. To avoid a gross misunderstanding of what I mean by "Black history," I refer here to the histories of peoples who were racially constructed as "Black" during the periods of European conquest, colonialism, and post-colonialism — *not* the histories of all African peoples dating back to the dawn of humanity.

55. My reasoning for using "hell" over "apocalypse" to describe slavery comes from the way in which damages were wrought in both contexts. While the South Bronx (and other urban areas in the United States) was leveled and left to rot, slavery consisted of an over-presence of dominant Whites in the lives of Blacks. Harm was actively inflicted as a primary directive in the plantation context (in order to lead to something else, namely, more crop production or sexual access to slave women) whereas the harm in the post-apocalyptic South Bronx was the fallout from dominant (primarily) Whites who were actively pursuing the reorganization of urban life. In the hell scenario, the Black person is a focus. In the apocalyptic scenario, she is a byproduct.

#ThisIsAmerica: Rappers, Racism, and Twitter
Dr. Tia C. M. Tyree

The Civil Rights Movement is punctuated for many through the visual images that appeared in newspapers and on television as well as the songs that many African American musical artists created to tell of the struggles and experiences of the African American community. Entertainers like Lena Horne, Nina Simone, Ray Charles, John Coltrane, Sam Cooke, James Brown, and many others are not just connected to the music, but to performances, protests and other activities. Their work musically and personally helped shape the ways the people interacted with and understood the plight of African Americans. A few decades later, rap music would enter U.S. culture with rappers taking on a similar role to bring attention and voice to the struggles of many African Americans who were disenfranchised in the United States.

Since the 1970s, the spread and popularity of rap music and Hip-Hop culture around the world has been tremendous, and in 2018, R&B/rap music surpassed rock to become the most listened to genre of music in the United States, which means rappers' platforms were larger than ever before in history.[1] Chuck D of Public Enemy famously said "Rap is black America's CNN".[2] Rap provides a lens through which those not connected to the lived experience of young African Americans can see their everyday world. As noted by Steven Best and Douglas Kellner, rap powerfully articulates the conditions and experiences of African Americans dealing with varying marginalized situations, including racial stereotyping and stigmatizing and struggles to survive in violent conditions. They argue the oppressed use it as a form of protest, for it marks a type of alternative cultural style and identity for the marginalized, and thus, it acts as a form of cultural identity and cultural political expression.[3]

Again, with both its overt and covert political narratives, rap music has been a mechanism for black men and women to shed light on their troubling experiences living in the United States. Rappers play a critical role in this process because rap music is the vehicle used to explain what is or is not happening in their communities. As modern-day storytellers, rappers deliver messages for and about their peers to those both within and outside of their communities. This is key, because African American and Latino youth are connected to disruptive behavior, low academic achievement, and other social ills, which cause them to often be rejected and labeled as social problems by important people in society, such as those working in the police force, teachers and employers.[4]

Understanding the Importance of Social Media and Twitter

Decades after the development of rap, social media has emerged as another important vehicle for African Americans to communicate. A common definition of social media is "activities, practices and behavior among communities of people who gather online to share information, knowledge and opinions using conversational media."[5] The power of social media cannot be denied. In fact, social media and other platforms on the Internet have become the "go-to communications" spaces for African Americans to share stories and other content.[6] Through the usage of these computer-mediated communications, African Americans can shift conversations about civil and social justice, draw both national and international attention to events, and bring about change.[7]

Social media allows content from individuals to be shared globally in seconds, and messages shared can provoke and influence people in ways unseen in modern communications. Whether users are taking on the ALS Association's #IceBucketChallenge to raise money for Amyotrophic Lateral Sclerosis research or using #BlackLivesMatter to organize protests after a police involved shooting of an unarmed black man, such as those surrounding the death of Michael Brown in Ferguson, Missouri, online platforms, such as Twitter, have been instrumental in helping to organize people in the digital space.

Providing the ability for individuals to create and share their own content often instantaneously and at no cost, social media permits diverse individuals traditionally ignored by mass media to not just share their thoughts, but impact the way people think, act, and react to situations happening around them. Individuals can now operate outside of the constraints of the mass media system, which has traditionally negatively represented African Americans, historically locked out their participation as creators and playmakers, ignored sharing true depictions, and failed to allow an acceptable, quantifiable level of their stories and experiences. Social media, however, has democratized the media landscape by removing the gatekeepers in traditional media who have policed content. Now, social media users can create their own stories — written, audio, or visual — and upload them for individuals across the world to experience in just a few clicks. The power to communicate on a mass level is in the hands of everyday people; a situation never experienced in the history of mass communication.

Twitter is the most popular microblogging platform in use, and it has earned a key political importance to many blacks.[8] It was the primary way many organized and discussed their experiences around the death of Trayvon Martin, the young boy killed by George Zimmerman and whose death inspired Alicia Garza to start the hashtag #BlackLivesMatter. Twitter has consistently proven itself to be a platform offering a fertile place for activism because of the nature of what it does and can do for users.

While email and traditional media have been vehicles to provide individuals with an understanding of what is happening in social movements, Twitter provides a unique feeling of direct participation, as users who may not be locally connected to an issue can transcend both space and time.[9] Users can follow public accounts without permission, and they can follow online conversations using hashtags. This has given rise to a new kind of activism — hashtag activism. This occurs when large numbers of postings appear on social media using a specific hashtagged word, phrase, or sentence that accompanies a certain social or political claim, and it is through these connected postings within the networked online space that narrative forms and agency are created.[10] Social media like Twitter is important, as they are media that allow information to spread, and they provide individuals with the opportunity, responsibility, and choice of what to do with the information obtained through them. Further, they offer individuals the ability to be passive bystanders or active participants.[11]

Over the last few years, social media sites have become virtual gathering forums among African Americans.[12] Twitter is essential to contemporary social actors who are on the platform, and yes, rappers are social actors.[13] Further, Twitter is a space for users to address race. A Pew Research Center study examined how race was discussed on Twitter from January 2015 to March 31, 2016. During this time, about 995 million race-related tweets were posted. It was noted the larger race-focused conversations occurred the day after a major event happened, which were mainly those incidents involving blacks being victims of alleged police brutality or targets of racially charged violence. It was concluded that Twitter was more likely a place individuals went after they had time to process the event and form their reactions and not a space to report details of incidents as they occurred.[14] In addition, the momentum behind Black Twitter has successfully catapulted issues related to police brutality and violence against communities of color to the forefront.[15]

Rappers Using Twitter to Address Racial Incidents

Many popular rappers have thousands, some even millions, of social media followers. Rappers use their social media accounts for both business and personal use. Offering a window into their innermost thoughts and daily activities, social media accounts offer direct communication lines — even if it is through computer-mediated communications — to celebrities. Some rappers share the personal parts of their lived experience, like what they are eating for breakfast or what might be happening with their children. While others share more critical information about what is happening in the world around them, like correcting narratives in the media about themselves or what they are thinking about U.S. race relations. Many rappers, such as Belcalis "Cardi B" Marlenis Almánzar, have worked to create popular social media presences that combine both personal and professional postings that are attractive to millions of Twitter users.

Since their inception, Hip-Hop culture and rap music have been used to publicize the impact racism has on black and Latino communities, and speaking to the world through their music was the usual way rappers worked to voice their opinions and concerns.[16] First, to state the obvious, rappers are still using their music to address racism and other forms of oppression. However, it is worth noting in this discussion that how they gain exposure and penetration of their messages is different. Today, social media makes sharing their music easier. There is no more waiting for their videos to debut on cable network music shows like Yo! MTV Raps, Total Request Live, and 106 & Park or even waiting for a spin on a local radio station. Within one tweet or post, rappers can link to their SoundCloud accounts or their YouTube channels.

Similarly, rappers can affect change using social media to voice their opinions about race relations. Twitter, especially, is a popular medium for rappers to interact with their fans and share their concerns about the world. In the last few years, several rappers catapulted themselves into the forefront of conversations about race by simply tweeting their thoughts or demands. These tweets gain likes, retweets, and comments, and when multiplied in the Twittersphere, the impressions can go into the millions. One tweet, too, can generate comments and other original postings all centered around a hashtag or common narrative that can spread on the platform and go viral. Individuals on Twitter may not even know one another, but the engagements between them are important. These actions show the communal and participatory nature of Twitter and how users showcase their agency by sharing and being a part of various online discussions.

More specifically, there are several rappers known for addressing racial issues on Twitter. For example, Christian rapper Lecrae "Lecrae" Moore, who received a lot of attention in 2016 for using his Twitter account to discuss police brutality and race relations, continued to do the same in 2018 by tweeting about Flint, Michigan, still having unclean water; the death of Stephon Clark, an unarmed black man killed in his grandmother's backyard; and the incident in Starbucks involving two black men who were refused the opportunity to use the bathroom, which eventually led to their arrest and the company closing stores for special training.

Other examples include Onika "Nicki Minaj" Maraj, who in 2015 expressed her dissatisfaction after the MTV Video Music award nominations were announced. She not only brought up her issues with the "White media and their tactics," but she noted how she was tired of black women not being rewarded for their influence on pop culture.[17] In March 2018, Chancelor "Chance the Rapper" Bennett, who has consistently addressed issues about race on Twitter, questioned whether companies were "purposefully putting out noticeably racist ads so they can get more views," including Heineken.[18] In 2019, Cardi B became very vocal about her political views as well as racial issues within the United States. In January 2019, she received a lot of attention for her response to *Fox Nation* host Tomi Lahren for being "blinded by racism", and in August 2019, as a response to the El Paso, Texas, mass shooting, she queried President Donald J. Trump about what he was going to do with his "racist supporters" as well as responded to one user that she believed there was "surely racial war that going on in this country."[19]

Perhaps the one rapper who has been increasingly lauded both in his hometown as well as nationally for his online and offline activism fighting racism is Clifford "T.I." Harris. In fact, in 2019, Georgia State Senator Donzella James sponsored a resolution that highlighted his efforts helping those in the state. T.I. has spoken out about police brutality, and he even joined hundreds in Atlanta to protest police-involved shootings of African Americans.[20] He has been vocal in his support of many issues surrounding the oppression and poverty of minorities, including publicly supporting the former National Football League star Colin Kaepernick, who was engulfed in a national firestorm of criticism for kneeling during the playing of the National Anthem as well as the three African American actresses who were mistreated and arrested at an Atlanta eatery, which gave rise to the #BoycottHoustons restaurant protest.[21]

Conclusion

Again, during the Civil Rights Movement, video footage of abuses against African Americans created outrage that later transformed into mobilization against those practices in society that caused their mistreatment, and today, tweets and pictures captured on mobile phones are having similar reactions. The various actions, activities or mistreatment of the rappers themselves or those within the African American community are an extension of the struggles of those who have preceded them. Uploading pictures and videos, going live at a protest or simply turning the camera to capture a personal reflection are all ways online users now connect with each other and share their societal problems. Social media plays a critical part in the discursive struggles today, because they create virtual spaces in which users can challenge and reevaluate representations of those who are victimized.[22] Rappers and others use online spaces like Twitter to share information, shape narratives, provoke action, and develop a space for discussions about race. Sharing those stories, connecting through those shared experiences, and galvanizing action based on those common problems speak to the discursive practices that are a part of social movements, and they also are becoming easier to display as the vehicles to do so are at nearly everyone's fingertips.

Overall, while some artists might "dabble" in activism, "most have either been inept or unwilling to fully commit to activism both in and out of the studio."[23] However, seeing the work of T.I. and others, there are good reasons for rappers to extend their thoughts and efforts outside of their recording studios. For in today's social media saturated society, they could just be one tweet away from making a difference or at least starting a conversation about it.

Notes

1. Lynch, John. "For the First Time in history, Hip-Hop Has Surpassed Rock to Become the Most Popular Music Genre, According to *Nielsen*," *Business Insider,* January 4, 2019, https://www.businessinsider.com/hip-hop-passes-rock-most-popular-music-genre-nielsen-2018-1.

2. Thorpe, David. "Chuck D." Bomb, July 1, 1999, https://bombmagazine.org/articles/chuck-d/

3. Best, Steven and Kellner, Douglas. "Rap, Black Rage, and Racial Difference," *Enculturation* 2, no. 2, 1999: 1—23.

4. Dance, Lory Janelle. *Tough Fronts: The Impact of Street Culture on Schooling,* New York: RoutledgeFalmer, 2002; MacLeod, Jay. *Ain't No Makin' It: Aspirations and Attainment in a Low-Income Neighborhood,* Boulder, CO: Westview Press, 1995.

5. Wilcox, Dennis L. and Cameron, Glen. *Public Relations: Strategies and Tactics,* 10th ed., London: Pearson, 2012.

6. Nielsen, *African-American Consumers: The Untold Story* 2015 Report, New York: Nielsen, 2105, 2.

7. Ibid.

8. Freelon, Deen, McIlwain, Charlton D., and Clark, Meredith *Beyond the Hashtags: #Ferguson, #Blacklivesmatter, and the Online Struggle for Offline Justice,* Washington, DC: Center for Media & Social Impact, American University, 2016.

9. Bonilla, Yarimar and Rosa, Jonathan. "# Ferguson: Digital Protest, Hashtag Ethnography, and the Racial Politics of Social Media in the United States," *American Ethnologist* 42, no. 1, 2015: 7.

10. Yang, Guobin. "Narrative Agency in Hashtag Activism: The Case of #BlackLivesMatter," *Media and Communication* 4, no. 4, 2016: 13.

11. Alam, Mayesha. "Weighing the Limitations against the Added Value of Social Media as a Tool for Political Change," *Democracy & Society* 8, no. 2, 2011: 19.

12. Nielsen, 43.

13. Bonilla and Rosa, 9.

14. Anderson, Monica and Hitlin, Paul. "Social Media Conversations About Race: Twitter Conversations About Race," August 15, 2016, https://www.pewinternet.org/2016/08/15/twitter-conversations-about-race/.

15. Fischer, Mia. "#Free_CeCe: The Material Convergence of Social Media Activism," *Feminist Media Studies* 16, no. 5, 2016: 755—71.

16. Baszile, Denise Taliaferro. "Deal with it we must: Education, social justice, and the curriculum of Hip-Hop culture." *Equity & Excellence in Education* 42, no. 1 (2009): 6-19.

17. Mrs. Petty (@NickiMinaj), "Nothing I said had to do with Taylor. So what jabs? White media and their tactics. So sad. That's what they want," Twitter, July 21, 2015, 4:10 p.m., https://twitter.com/nickiminaj/status/623631068680163328?lang=en.

18. The Big Day Out Now (@Chancetherapper), "I think some companies are purposely putting out noticably racist ads so they can get more views. And that shit racist/bogus so I guess I shouldn't help by posting about it. But I gotta just say tho. The 'sometimes lighter is better' Hieneken commercial is terribly racist omg." Twitter, March 25, 2018, 6:18 p.m., https://twitter.com/chancetherapper/status/978078809995046912?lang=en.

19. Iamcardib (@iamcardib), "You're so blinded with racism that you don't even realize the decisions the president you root for is destroying the country you claim to love so much .You are a perfect example on no matter how educated or smart you think you are you still a SHEEP!," Twitter , January 20, 2019, 6:14 a.m., https://twitter.com/iamcardib/status/1086990411770384384? "We have enough information already! Both of the shooters are white supremacist terrorist with intentions to kill minority's .Law enforcement took rapid action but what are YOU going to do to control some of your RACIST SUPPORTERS?," Twitter, August 4, 2019, 9:41 a.m., https://twitter.com/iamcardib/status/1158055488933769216?, "This is not beyond my scoop this is my country and I'm tired! I get it you are a conservative you and you can support who you want but you can't ignore the slowly but surely racial war that going on in this country that are the reasons of these tragedy," Twitter, August 4, 2019, 9:56 a.m., https://twitter.com/iamcardib/status/1158059057980354560?.

20. Daniels, Karu. "Big Things Poppin': T.I. Recognized By Georgia Senate For His Philanthropy Efforts," March 2019, https://www.essence.com/celebrity/ti-honored-georgia-senate-philanthropy/.

21. Hale, Andreas. "How T.I.'s Activism Has Made Him More Dangerous Than His Trap House Days," June 12, 2018, https://revolt.tv/stories/2018/06/12/tis-activism-dangerous-trap-house-days-0700a472aa.

22. Alam, 18.

23. Cumberbatch, Prudence and Trujillo-Paglán, Nicole. "Hashtag Activism and Why #BlackLivesMatter in (and to) the Classroom," *Radical Teacher*, 106, 2016.

III. The Future

Further Considerations on Afrofuturism
Kodwo Eshun

Imagine a team of African archaeologists from the future — some silicon, some carbon, some wet, some dry — excavating a site, a museum from their past: a museum whose ruined documents and leaking discs are identifiable as belonging to our present, the early twenty-first century. Sifting patiently through the rubble, our archaeologists from the United States of Africa, the USAF, would be struck by how much Afrodiasporic subjectivity in the twentieth century constituted itself through the cultural project of recovery. In their Age of Total Recall, memory is never lost. Only the art of forgetting. Imagine them reconstructing the conceptual framework of our cultural moment from those fragments. What are the parameters of that moment, the edge of that framework?

The War of Countermemory

In our time, the USAF archaeologists surmise, imperial racism has denied black subjects the right to belong to the enlightenment project, thus creating an urgent need to demonstrate a substantive historical presence. This desire has overdetermined Black Atlantic intellectual culture for several centuries. To establish the historical character of black culture, to bring Africa and its subjects into history denied by Hegel et al., it has been necessary to assemble countermemories that contest the colonial archive, thereby situating the collective trauma of slavery as the founding moment of modernity.

The Founding Trauma

In an interview with critic Paul Gilroy in his anthology *Small Acts*, novelist Toni Morrison argued that the African subjects that experienced capture, theft, abduction, mutilation, and slavery were the first moderns. They underwent real conditions of existential homelessness, alienation, dislocation, and dehumanization that philosophers like Nietzsche would later define as quintessentially modern. Instead of civilizing African subjects, the forced dislocation and commodification that constituted the Middle Passage meant that modernity was rendered forever suspect. Ongoing disputes over reparation indicate that these traumas continue to shape the contemporary era. It is never a matter of forgetting what it took so long to remember. Rather, the vigilance that is necessary to indict imperial modernity must be extended into the field of the future.

Futurism Fatigue

Because the practice of countermemory defined itself as an ethical commitment to history, the dead, and the forgotten, the manufacture of conceptual tools that could analyze and assemble counterfutures was understood as an unethical dereliction of duty. Futurological analysis was looked upon with suspicion, wariness, and hostility. Such attitudes dominated the academy throughout the 1980s.

For African artists, there were good reasons for disenchantment with futurism. When Nkrumah was deposed in Ghana in 1966, it signaled the collapse of the first attempt to build the USAF. The combination of colonial revenge and popular discontent created sustained hostility towards the planned utopias of African socialism. For the rest of the century, African intellectuals adopted variations of the position that Homi Bhabha (1992) termed "melancholia in revolt." This fatigue with futurity carried through to Black Atlantic cultural activists, who, little by little, ceased to participate in the process of building futures.

> Imagine the archaeologists as they use their emulators to scroll through the fragile files. In their time, it is a commonplace that the future is a chronopolitical terrain, a terrain as hostile and as treacherous as the past. As the archaeologists patiently sift the twenty-first-century archives, they are amazed by the impact this realization had on these forgotten beings. They are touched by the seriousness of those founding mothers and fathers of Afrofuturism, by the responsibility they showed towards the not-yet, towards becoming.

Control Through Prediction

Fast forward to the early twenty-first century. A cultural moment when digitopian futures are routinely invoked to hide the present in all its unhappiness. In this context, inquiry into production of futures becomes fundamental, rather than trivial. The field of Afrofuturism does not seek to deny the tradition of countermemory. Rather, it aims to extend that tradition by reorienting the intercultural vectors of Black Atlantic temporality towards the proleptic as much as the retrospective.

It is clear that power now operates predictively as much as retrospectively. Capital continues to function through the dissimulation of the imperial archive, as it has done throughout the last century. Today, however, power also functions through the envisioning, management, and delivery of reliable futures.

In the colonial era of the early to middle twentieth century, avant-gardists from Walter Benjamin to Frantz Fanon revolted in the name of the future against a power structure that relied on control and representation of the historical archive. Today, the situation is reversed. The powerful employ futurists and draw power from the futures they endorse, thereby condemning the disempowered to live in the past. The present moment is stretching, slipping for some into yesterday, reaching for others into tomorrow.

SF Capital

Power now deploys a mode the critic Mark Fisher (2000) called *SF* (science fiction) *capital*. SF capital is the synergy, the positive feedback between future-oriented media and capital. The alliance between cybernetic futurism and "New Economy" theories argues that information is a direct generator of economic value. Information about the future therefore circulates as an increasingly important commodity.

It exists in mathematical formalizations such as computer simulations, economic projections, weather reports, futures trading, think-tank reports, consultancy papers — and through informal descriptions such as science fiction cinema, science-fiction novels, sonic fictions, religious prophecy, and venture capital. Bridging the two are formal-informal hybrids, such as the global scenarios of the professional market futurist.

Looking back at the media generated by the computer boom of the 1990s, it is clear that the effect of the futures industry — defined here as the intersecting industries of technoscience, fictional media, technological projection, and market prediction — has been to fuel the desire for a technology boom. Given this context, it would be naïve to understand science fiction, located within the expanded field of the futures industry, as merely prediction into the far future, or as a utopian project for imagining alternative social realities.

Science fiction might better be understood, in Samuel R. Delany's statement, as offering "a significant distortion of the present" (*Last Angel of History* 1995). To be more precise, science fiction is neither forward-looking nor utopian. Rather, in William Gibson's phrase, science fiction is a means through which to preprogram the present (cited in Eshun 1998). Looking back at the genre, it becomes apparent that science fiction was never concerned with the future, but rather with engineering feedback between its preferred future and its becoming present.

Hollywood's 1990s love for sci-tech fictions, from *The Truman Show* to *The Matrix*, from *Men in Black* to *Minority Report*, can therefore be seen as product-placed visions of the reality-producing power of computer networks, which in turn contribute to an explosion in the technologies they hymn. As New Economy ideas take hold, virtual futures generate capital. A subtle oscillation between prediction and control is being engineered in which successful or powerful descriptions of the future have an increasing ability to draw us towards them, to command us to make them flesh.

The Futures Industry

Science fiction is now a research and development department within a futures industry that dreams of the prediction and control of tomorrow. Corporate business seeks to manage the unknown through decisions based on scenarios, while civil society responds to future shock through habits formatted by science fiction. Science fiction operates through the power of falsification, the drive to rewrite reality, and the will to deny plausibility, while the scenario operates through the control and prediction of plausible alternative tomorrows.

Both the science-fiction movie and the scenario are examples of cybernetic futurism that talks of things that haven't happened yet in the past tense. In this case, futurism has little to do with the Italian and Russian avant-gardes; rather, these approaches seek to model variation over time by oscillating between anticipation and determinism.

> Imagine the All-African Archaeological Program sweeping the site with their chronometers. Again and again, they sift the ashes. Imagine the readouts on their portables, indicators pointing to the dangerously high levels of hostile projections. This area shows extreme density of dystopic forecasting, levels that, if accurate, would have rendered the archaeologists' own existence impossible. The AAAP knows better: such statistical delirium reveals the fervid wish dreams of the host market.

Market Dystopia

If global scenarios are descriptions that are primarily concerned with making futures safe for the market, then Afrofuturism's first priority is to recognize that Africa increasingly exists as the object of futurist projection. African social reality is overdetermined by intimidating global scenarios, doomsday economic projections, weather predictions, medical reports on AIDS, and life-expectancy forecasts, all of which predict decades of immiserization.

These powerful descriptions of the future demoralize us; they command us to bury our heads in our hands, to groan with sadness. Commissioned by multinationals and nongovernmental organizations (NGOs), these developmental futurisms function as the other side of the corporate utopias that make the future safe for industry. Here, we are seduced not by smiling faces staring brightly into a screen; rather, we are menaced by predatory futures that insist the coming years will be hostile.

Within an economy that runs on SF capital and market futurism, Africa is always the zone of the absolute dystopia. There is always a reliable trade in market projections for Africa's socioeconomic crises. Market dystopias aim to warn against predatory futures, but always do so in a discourse that aspires to unchallengeable certainty.

The Museological Turn

For contemporary African artists, understanding and intervening in the production and distribution of this dimension constitutes a chronopolitical act. It is possible to see one form that this chronopolitical intervention might take by looking at the work of contemporary African artists such as Georges Adéagbo and Meschac Gaba. In the tradition of Marcel Broodthaers and Fred Wilson, both artists have turned towards museological emulation, thus laying bare, manipulating, mocking, and critically affirming the contextualizing and historicizing framework of institutional knowledge.

Gaba's "Contemporary Art Museum" is "at once a criticism of the museological institution as conceived in developed countries, as well as the utopian formulation of a possible model for a nonexistent institution. This dual nature, critical and utopian, is related to the artist . . . founding a structure where there isn't one, without losing sight of the limitations of existing models that belong to a certain social and economic order based in the harsher realities of domination" (Gaba 2002).

Proleptic Intervention

Taking its cue from this "dual nature" of the "critical and utopian," an Afrofuturist art project might work on the exposure and reframing of futurisms that act to forecast and fix African dystopia. For the contemporary African artist of 2005, these projections of relentless social disaster contain certain conceptual implications.

The African artist that researches this dimension will find a space for distinct kinds of anticipatory designs, projects of emulation, manipulation, parasitism. Interpellation into a bright corporate tomorrow by ads full of faces smiling at screens may become a bitter joke at the expense of multinational delusions. The artist might reassemble the predatory futures that insist the next 50 years will be ones of unmitigated despair.

Afrofuturism, then, is concerned with the possibilities for intervention within the dimension of the predictive, the projected, the proleptic, the envisioned, the virtual, the anticipatory and the future conditional.

This implies the analysis of three distinct but partially intersecting spheres: first, the world of mathematical simulations; second, the world of informal descriptions; and third, as Gilroy (2001) points out in *Between Camps*, the articulation of futures within the everyday forms of the mainstream of black vernacular expression. Having looked at the implications for African art through the first and the second dimensions, we now turn our attention to the third. To work with this material, Afrofuturism is obliged to approach the audiovisions of extraterrestriality, futurology, and techno-science fictions with patience and seriousness.

Imagine the archaeologists in their downtime. They sit round their liquid gel computers generating possible futures for real cities through World Scenarios, a video game that assembles alternative scenarios. Set in Lagos, with other options to follow, the game invites users to specify variables for transportation, energy consumption, waste disposal, residential, commercial, and industrial zoning. The game returns visions of what those choices will mean for life in 2240.

Black Atlantic Sonic Process

It is difficult to conceive of Afrofuturism without a place for sonic process in its vernacular, speculative, and syncopated modes. The daily lifeworld of black vernacular expression may be anathema to contemporary art practice. Nonetheless, these histories of futures passed must be positioned as a valuable resource.

Imagine that the artist Georges Adéagbo created an installation that uses the artwork of Parliament-Funkadelic albums from 1974–1980 to build a new myth cycle of politico-socio-racio-sexual fantasies from the cultural memory of this era. Imagine that the archaeologists from the future are now discovering fragments from that work, techno-fossils from tomorrow's yesterdays . . .

Afrofuturism studies the appeals that black artists, musicians, critics, and writers have made to the future, in moments where any future was made difficult for them to imagine. In 1957, the bandleader and composer Duke Ellington wrote "The Race For Space" (Ellington 1993), a brief essay that attempted to press the future into the service of black liberation. By 1966, however, Martin Luther King, in his text "Where Do We Go From Here?" could argue that the gap between social and technological achievements was deep enough to call the very idea of social and economic progress into question (Gilroy 2001).

Afrophilia in Excelsis

Between the demise of Black Power in the late 1960s and the emergence of a popular Pan-Africanism in the mid-1970s with Bob Marley, the Afrodiasporic musical imagination was characterized by an Afrophilia that invoked a liberationist idyll of African archaism with the idea of scientific African modernity, both held in an unstable but useful equilibrium.

This equilibrium was personified, in populist terms, by the Egyptological fantasias of Earth, Wind, & Fire. The oscillation between pre-industrial Africa and scientific Africa, however, was established in the 1950s with Sun Ra, the composer and bandleader whose lifework constitutes a self-created cosmology.

The Cosmogenetic Moment

In 1995, the London-based group Black Audio Film Collective released *The Last Angel of History*, also known as *The Mothership Connection*, their essay-film which remains the most elaborate exposition on the convergence of ideas that is Afrofuturism. Through the persona of a time-traveling nomadic figure known as the Data Thief, *The Last Angel of History* created a network of links between music, space, futurology, and diaspora. African sonic processes are here reconceived as telecommunication, as the distributed components of a code to a black secret technology that is the key to diasporic future. The notion of a black secret technology allows Afrofuturism to reach a point of speculative acceleration.

> Imagine the archaeologists squinting at the cracked screen of the microvideo installation that shows the Data Thief trapped in the history vaults of West Africa . . .

Black Audio director John Akomfrah and scriptwriter Edward George integrated a thesis from critic John Corbett's "Brothers from Another Planet," a 1993 essay whose title references John Sayles' 1983 science-fiction movie of an alien that takes on African American identity to escape his interstellar captors. Akomfrah and George take up in particular the oeuvres of Sun Ra and his group, the Arkestra; Lee Perry, reggae producer, composer, songwriter, and architect of dub reggae; and Parliament-Funkadelic funk producer George Clinton, three figures analyzed in terms of their use of the recording studio, the vinyl record, and the support of art work and record label as the vehicle for concept albums that sustain mythological, programmatic, and cosmological world pictures.

Corbett pointed to Ra's group, the Arkestra; Perry's 1970s recording studio, the Black Ark; and the *Mothership Connection*, Parliament's album cycle to argue that "largely independent of one other, each is working with a shared set of mythological images and icons such as space iconography, the idea of extraterrestriality and the idea of space exploration."

Identification Code Unidentified

By the 1980s, the emergent digital technology of sequencers, samplers, synthesizers, and software applications began to scramble the ability to assign identity and thereby racialize music. Familiar processes of racial recognition were becoming unreliable. Listeners could no longer assume musicians were racially identical to their samples.

If racial identification became intermittent and obscure to the listener, for the musician, a dimension of heteronomy became available. The human-machine interface became both the condition and the subject of Afrofuturism. The cyborg fantasies of the Detroit techno producers, such as Juan Atkins and Derrick May, were used both to alienate themselves from sonic identity and to feel at home in alienation. Thelma Golden's notes towards the formulation of a twenty-first-century "post-black" aesthetic describe this cultural moment of studio-based sonic process more satisfactorily than it does gallery-based visual practice.

The Implications of Revisionism

Gilroy argues that the articulations sketched above tend to overlap with historical flashpoints. To analyze black popular futures in this way is to situate them as fallout from social movements and liberation movements, if not as direct parts of those movements. These moments may be historicized by politico-spiritual movements such as Black Christian Eschatology and Black Power, and postwar politico-esoteric traditions such as the Nation of Islam (NOI), Egyptology, Dogon cosmology, and the Stolen Legacy thesis.

The Nation of Islam's eschatology combined a racialized account of human origin with a catastrophic theory of time. Ogotommeli, the Dogon mystic, provided an astronomical knowledge of the "Sirius B" Dog Star, elaborated by French ethnographers Marcel Griaule and Germaine Dieterlen, that demonstrated a compensatory and superior African scientific knowledge.

Egyptology's desire to recover the lost glories of a preindustrial African past was animated by a utopian authoritarianism. Before Martin Bernal's *Black Athena* (1988), George G. M. James' *Stolen Legacy* (1989) simultaneously emphasized the white conspiracies that covered up the stolen legacy of African science, reversing Hegelian thought by insisting upon the original African civilization.

Afrofuturism is by no means naively celebratory. The reactionary Manichaenism of the Nation of Islam, the regressive compensation mechanisms of Egyptology, Dogonesque cosmology, and the totalizing reversals of Stolen Legacy-style Afrocentricity are immediately evident. By excavating the political moments of such vernacular futurologies, a lineage of competing world-views that seek to reorient history comes into focus. In identifying the emergence and dissemination of belief systems, it becomes critical to analyze how, in Gilroy's words, "even as the movement that produced them fades, there remains a degree of temporal disturbance."

By creating temporal complications and anachronistic episodes that disturb the linear time of progress, these futurisms adjust the temporal logics that condemned black subjects to prehistory. Chronopolitically speaking, these revisionist historicities may be understood as a series of powerful competing futures that infiltrate the present at different rates.

Revisionist logic is shared by autodidact historians like Sun Ra and George G. M. James of Stolen Legacy, and contemporary intellectuals such as Toni Morrison, Greg Tate, and Paul D. Miller. Her argument that the African slaves that experienced capture, theft, abduction, and mutilation were the first moderns is important for positioning slavery at the heart of modernity. The cognitive and attitudinal shift demanded by her statement also yokes philosophy together with brutality, and binds cruelty to temporality. The effect is to force together separated systems of knowledge, so as to disabuse apparatuses of knowledge of their innocence.

Afrofuturism can be understood as an elaboration upon the implications of Morrison's revisionary thesis. In a 1991 interview with the writer Mark Sinker, cultural critic Greg Tate suggested that the bar between the signifier and the signified could be understood as standing for the Middle Passage that separated *signification* (meaning) from *sign* (letter). This analogy of racial terror with semiotic process spliced the world of historical trauma with the apparatus of structuralism. The two genealogies crossbred with a disquieting force that contaminated the latter and abstracted the former.

The Uses of Alienation

Afrofuturism does not stop at correcting the history of the future. Nor is it a simple matter of inserting more black actors into science-fiction narratives. These methods are only baby steps towards the more totalizing realization that, in Greg Tate's formulation, Afrodiasporic subjects live the estrangement that science-fiction writers envision. Black existence and science fiction are one and the same.

In *The Last Angel of History*, Tate argued that "The form itself, the conventions of the narrative in terms of the way it deals with subjectivity, focuses on someone who is at odds with the apparatus of power in society and whose profound experience is one of cultural dislocation, alienation and estrangement. Most science fiction tales dramatically deal with how the individual is going to contend with these alienating, dislocating societies and circumstances and that pretty much sums up the mass experiences of black people in the postslavery twentieth century."

At the century's start, Dubois termed the condition of structural and psychological alienation as *double consciousness*. The condition of alienation, understood in its most general sense, is a psychosocial inevitability that all Afrodiasporic art uses to its own advantage by creating contexts that encourage a process of disalienation. Afrofuturism's specificity lies in assembling conceptual approaches and countermemorial mediated practices in order to access triple consciousness, quadruple consciousness, previously inaccessible alienations.

Imagine that later, on that night, after the site is sealed off, ready for the next day, after the AAAP have all been disinfected, one of the archaeologists dreams of six turntables; the realisation of the Invisible Man's dream of hearing Louis Armstrong's "What Did I Have to Do to Be So Black and Blue" multiplied to the power of 6.

The Extraterrestrial Turn

Afrofuturism uses extraterrestriality as a hyperbolic trope to explore the historical terms, the everyday implications of forcibly imposed dislocation, and the constitution of Black Atlantic subjectivities: from slave to negro to colored to *evolué* to black to African to African American.

Extraterrestriality thereby becomes a point of transvaluation through which this variation over time, understood as forcible mutation, can become a resource for speculation. It should be understood not so much as escapism, but rather as an identification with the potentiality of space and distance within the high-pressure zone of perpetual racial hostility.

It is not that black subjectivities are waiting for science-fiction authors to articulate their lifeworlds. Rather, it is the reverse. The conventions of science fiction, marginalized within literature yet central to modern thought, can function as allegories for the systemic experience of post-slavery black subjects in the twentieth century. Science fiction, as such, is recast in the light of Afrodiasporic history.

Afrofuturism therefore stages a series of enigmatic returns to the constitutive trauma of slavery in the light of science fiction. Isolating the enigmatic phrase "Apocalypse bin in effect" from the 1990 Public Enemy track "Welcome to the Terrordome," Mark Sinker's 1992 essay "Loving the Alien" argued that this lyric could be interpreted to read that slavery functioned as an apocalypse experienced as equivalent to alien abduction: "The ships landed long ago: they already laid waste whole societies, abducted and genetically altered swathes of citizenry. . . . Africa and America — and so by extension Europe and Asia — are already in their various ways Alien Nation."

Temporal Switchback

Afrofuturism approaches contemporary digital music as an intertext of recurring literary quotations that may be cited and used as statements capable of imaginatively reordering chronology and fantasizing history. The lyrical statement is treated as a platform for historical speculation. Social reality and science fiction create feedback between each other within the same phrase. The alien encounters and interplanetary abductions people experienced as delusions in the Cold War present had already occurred in the past, for real.

All the symptoms specific to a close encounter had already occurred on a giant scale. The collective delusion of the close encounter is transplanted to the Middle Passage. The effect is not to question the reality of slavery, but to defamiliarize it through a temporal switchback that reroutes its implications through postwar social fiction, cultural fantasy, and modern science fiction, all of which begin to seem like elaborate ways of concealing and admitting trauma.

Black-Atlantean Mythos

In the mid-1990s, this aesthetic of estrangement was pursued to its limit-point by Drexciya, the group of enigmatic producers, synthesists, and designers operating from Detroit. In the liner notes to their CD *The Quest*, Drexciya (1997) proposed a science-fictional retelling of the Middle Passage. The "Drexciyans" are water-breathing, aquatically mutated descendants of "pregnant America-bound African slaves thrown overboard by the thousands during labour for being sick and disruptive cargo."

> Could it be possible for humans to breathe underwater? A foetus in its mother's womb is certainly alive in an aquatic environment. Is it possible that they could have given birth at sea to babies that never needed air? Recent experiments have shown mice able to breathe liquid oxygen, a premature human infant saved from certain death by breathing liquid oxygen through its underdeveloped lungs. These facts combined with reported sightings of Gillmen and Swamp Monsters in the coastal swamps of the South Eastern United States make the slave trade theory startlingly feasible.

In treating Gilroy's *The Black Atlantic* (1993) as a science fiction which is then developed through four-stage analysis of migration and mutation from Africa to America, Drexciya have constructed a Black-Atlantean mythology that successfully speculates on the evolutionary code of black subjectivity. In turn, their project has inspired a series of paintings by the contemporary African American abstract artist

Ellen Gallagher, and responses in the form of essays by the critics Ruth Mayer and Ben Williams.

Drexciya's project has recently extended itself into space. For their *Grava 4* CD, released in 2002, the group contacted the International Star Registry in Switzerland to purchase the rights to name a star. Having named and registered their star "Grava 4," a new installment within their ongoing sonic fiction is produced. In wrapping their speculative fiction around electronic compositions that then locate themselves around an existing extraterrestrial space, Drexciya grant themselves the imperial right to nominate and colonize interstellar space. The absurdity of buying and owning a distant star in no way diminishes the contractual obligation of ownership that the group entered into. The process of ratification therefore becomes the platform for an unexpected intervention: a sonofictional statement that fuses the metaphorical with the juridical, and the synthetic with the cartographic. Contractual fact meets sonic fiction meets astronomical mapping in a colonization of the contemporary audiovisual imagination in advance of military landing.

To conclude: Afrofuturism may be characterized as a program for recovering the histories of counter-futures created in a century hostile to Afro-diasporic projection and as a space within which the critical work of manufacturing tools capable of intervention within the current political dispensation may be undertaken. The manufacture, migration, and mutation of concepts and approaches within the fields of the theoretical and the fictional, the digital and the sonic, the visual and the architectural exemplifies the expanded field of Afrofuturism considered as a multimedia project distributed across the nodes, hubs, rings, and stars of the Black Atlantic. As a tool kit developed for and by Afrodiasporic intellectuals, the imperative to code, adopt, adapt, translate, misread, rework, and revision these concepts, under the conditions specified in this essay, is likely to persist in the decades to come.

Bibliography

Bhabha, Homi. Postcolonial Authority and Postmodern Guilt. In *Cultural Studies,* edited by Lawrence Grossberg, Cary Nelson, and Paula Treichler. New York: Routledge, 1992.

Bernal. Martin. *Black Athena: The Afroasiatic Roots of Classical Civilization. Vol. 1, The Fabrication of Ancient Greece, 1785—1985.* Piscataway, N.J.: Rutgers University Press, 1988.

Corbett, John. Brothers from Another Planet. In *Extended Play: Sounding off from John Cage to Dr. Funkenstein.* Durham: Duke University Press, 1994.

Drexciya. Liner Notes. *The Quest.* Submerge SVE-8. Compact disk. 1997.

Ellington, Duke. The Race for Space. In *The Duke Ellington Reader,* edited by Mark Tucker. New York: Oxford University Press, 1993.

Eshun, Kodwo. *More Brilliant Than the Sun: Adventures in Sonic Fiction.* London: Quartet Books, 1998.

Fisher, Mark. SF Capital. *Themepark* magazine, 2000.

Gaba, Meshac. *Short Guide to Documenta XI.* Ostfildern, Germany: Hatje Cantz, 2002.

Gilroy, Paul. *The Black Atlantic: Modernity and Double-Consciousness.* Cambridge, Mass.: Harvard University Press, 1993.

— — —. Living Memory: A Meeting with Toni Morrison. In *Small Acts: Thoughts on the Politics of Black Cultures.* London: Serpent's Tail, 1994.

— — —. *Between Camps.* Allen Lane. James, George G. M. [1954] 1989. *Stolen Legacy: Greek Philosophy Is Stolen Egyptian Philosophy.* Khalifahs Book Sellers. Reprint, 2001.

The Last Angel of History. Directed by John Akomfrah. London: Black Audio Film Collective, C4/ZDF, 1995.

Sinker, Mark. Interview with Mark Tate. Unpublished transcript, *Arena* magazine, 1991.

— — —. *Loving the Alien. The Wire* 96 (June 1992), 1992.

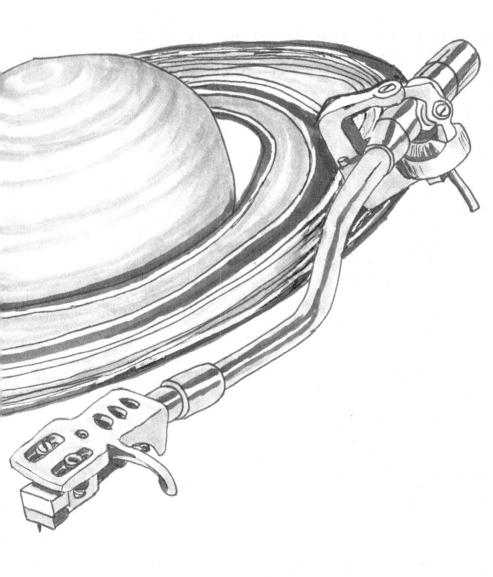

Afrofuturism and the Intersectionality of Black Feminism, Civil Rights, the Space Race, and Hip-Hop
K. Ceres Wright

Abstract

African American women have been early adopters of national and international initiatives, such as abolitionism, civil rights, women's rights, space travel, and hip-hop — from Maria W. Stewart's anti-slavery and women's rights speeches in the 1830s, to Mary Talbert's launch of the Niagara Movement in 1905 as a precursor to the NAACP, to Katherine Johnson's career at NASA in the 1950s, to Sylvia Robinson's launch of hip-hop into the mainstream in the 1970s, to Tarana Burke's #MeToo movement in the 2000s.

These women overcame sexism and discrimination to achieve their goals. Yet, the same misogyny and bigotry exists today, not only in society in general, but within the hip-hop community. Examples include noted physical abuse of women at the hands of artists such as Dr. Dre, R. Kelly, and Nas; encouragement by record labels to include misogynistic and derogatory phrases in rap lyrics; and the commodification of rap and sex. Female artists such as LaBelle and Grace Jones broke barriers in the music industry to promote their messages of female empowerment and racial unity. These messages have evolved in the hands of newer artists like Missy Elliott, Janet Jackson, and Janelle Monáe.

Given the prominence of African American women in historical and present-day social, technological, and cultural movements, any depiction or description of Afrofuturism must feature efforts by African American women to build upon their achievements of the past to expand the rights of people of color. The qualities these pioneering women embodied — adaptability, courage, and perseverance — have laid the ground work upon which Afrofuturistic aesthetics (from an American perspective) can grow.

What is Afrofuturism? For the purposes of this paper, it will be defined as "A cultural aesthetic that combines elements of science fiction, fantasy, horror, history, and magical realism to examine and revise both the past and present experiences among the African diaspora." Afrofuturism is a means of recapturing and revising history that was lost to or, rather, taken from, the diaspora.

But when did Afrofuturism really begin? Was it at the dawn of time, when humankind took its first halting steps? When hunter-gatherers settled around the campfire and told stories? During the migration of modern humans out of Africa, supposedly around 250,000 years ago? Was it during slavery, when those captured hoped and worked for a better tomorrow? Perhaps the 1950s, when Sun Ra claimed to have been teleported to Saturn and told by aliens to speak through music. It is beyond the scope of this paper to say one way or another. However, one concept that rings through history is that African American women have been, and will continue to be, pioneers in issues related to Afrofuturism — from Maria W. Stewart's anti-slavery and women's rights speeches in the 1830s to Tarana Burke's #MeToo movement in the 2000s, and beyond. Despite enduring misogyny, marginalization, oppression, and racism, African American women have persistently struggled to have their voices heard while working to improve access to education and opportunities to help make a better life for their communities and their futures.

This paper will explore the underpinnings of Afrofuturism through the prism of historical African American women and their efforts in securing a stable future for their community through activism, communication, creativity, and stalwartness.

Maria W. Stewart

An abolitionist, orator, journalist, teacher, and women's rights activist, Maria W. Stewart was one of the first American women to make public lectures. Her deeply religious background informed her speeches as she adjured African Americans to work toward self-improvement, encouraged them to live moral lives, urged women to stand up for their rights, highlighted the inequities in education and opportunity, and noted the benefits that whites derived from slavery[1] —

> We have pursued the shadow, they have obtained the substance; we have performed the labor, they have received the profits; we have planted the vines, they have eaten the fruits of them.
> — An Address [speech], 1833.[2]

In the 1830s, slave holders ruled the South and subscribed to the widely held beliefs that women should reflect the tenets of True Womanhood — piety, purity, submissiveness, and domesticity. Women were expected to hold fast to these ideals in order to embody and present the best of womanhood. Piety was to be accomplished through the study of Scripture and work for the church.[3] As written in the *Second Annual*

Report of the Young Ladies Literary and Missionary Association, "you may labor without the apprehension of detracting from the charms of feminine delicacy."[4] Purity was to be maintained by women giving over their virtue only to a husband. Submissiveness was a choice. As George Burnap stated in a series of lectures titled *On the Sphere and Duties of Woman,* "She asks for wisdom, constancy, firmness, perseverance, and she is willing to repay it all by the surrender of the full treasure of her affections."[5] Domestic life was the purview of the woman, who was expected to provide a cheerful atmosphere and tend to the needs of those for whom she was responsible.

The African American female slave, however, could not hope to aspire to these lofty ideals. For piety, she was not excused from labor to take missionary journeys, nor was she, usually, taught to read. For purity, she could be raped at any time by the plantation owner. For submissiveness and domesticity, she could scarce make a voluntary choice, since slaves were beaten into submission and forced into domestic labor.

Stewart projected wisdom and hope in her countenance and words. Her sentiments would be reflected more than 130 years later in a famous speech by Dr. Martin Luther King, Jr. —

It is not the color of the skin that makes the man, but it is the principle formed within the soul.

— *Meditations from the Pen of Mrs. Maria Stewart,* 1834[6]

Mary Burnett Talbert

One of the activists, among many, who would take up Ms. Stewart's mantle would be Mary Burnett Talbert, an activist, orator, reformer, and suffragist. She was referred to as "the best known colored woman in the United States." She obtained a bachelor's degree in 1886, unheard of for most women at the time, White or Black. In 1905, she hosted groups of activists in secret and helped convene the Niagara Movement, a black civil rights organization. The Movement would be a forerunner to the National Association for the Advancement of Colored People (NAACP). Ms. Talbert would also co-found the first NAACP chapter in 1910.[7]

And in 1919, the Red Summer arrived. African American soldiers returning from World War I moved North and not only competed against whites for jobs, but fought them for civil rights, shocking the entrenched establishment. The Ku Klux Klan revived itself and lynched 83 people. Race riots broke out in Washington, DC; Knoxville, TN; Longview, TX; Phillips County, AR; Omaha, NE; and Chicago, IL.[8] But one unidentified African American woman wrote to the newspaper, *The Crisis:*

The Washington riot gave me the thrill that comes once in a lifetime. I was alone when I read between the lines of the morning paper that at least our men had stood up like men, and struck back... The pent-up humiliation, grief and horror of a lifetime — half a century — was being stripped from me.[9]

It was during this atmosphere of racial strife that Mary Talbert would serve as the National Director of the NAACP Anti-Lynching Campaign in 1921.

Vaughan, Johnson, and Jackson

Featured in the movie *Hidden Figures*, mathematicians Dorothy Vaughan, Katherine Johnson, and Mary Jackson worked at the National Advisory Committee for Aeronautics, which was succeeded by the National Aeronautics and Space Administration. Ms. Johnson worked as a mathematician whose calculations helped ensure the success of manned U.S. spaceflights. She worked on the Mercury, Apollo Lunar Lander, Freedom 7, and the Space Shuttle missions.[10]

Dorothy Vaughan taught herself and her staff the then-up-and-coming programming language, FORTRAN. She also worked on the Scout Launch Vehicle Program, which placed satellites in Earth's orbit. After working in the Supersonic Pressure Tunnel, Mary Jackson wanted to be an engineer. After taking graduate classes in physics and math, she realized her dream of becoming an aerospace engineer.

In the early 1960s, women's roles mirrored those of the 1950s — wife, mother, homemaker. Many women did not have control over their own finances or health. They could not obtain a credit card in their name, were deemed too valuable at home to serve on juries, could not access the birth control pill as a single woman, could not attend some Ivy League schools, and could not expect to earn more than 59 cents for every dollar that men earned.[11] There were no female astronauts, at least in America. Russia had launched a woman cosmonaut into space in 1963, but NASA was unwilling to follow. One unidentified NASA spokesman said that the thought of an American spacewoman "makes me sick at my stomach."[12]

But in this climate, Mary Jackson worked as an engineer in several NASA divisions for 34 years and achieved the senior-most title within the engineering department.

Dorothy Vaughan was promoted to head of the programming section of the Analysis and Computation Division at Langley Research Center.

Katherine Johnson authored 26 scientific papers, was named the West Virginia State College Outstanding Alumnus of the Year in 1999, and received the Presidential Medal of Freedom in 2015.

Sylvia Robinson

Two years before Katherine Johnson graduated from college, Sylvia Robinson (née Vanderpool) was born in Harlem, New York. She quit school at age 14 to begin a singing career at Columbia records. Over the years, she learned guitar; helped create the group Mickey & Sylvia that recorded the rock single, "Love Is Strange," which topped the R&B charts; and sang background for Ike and Tina Turner. In 1966, Sylvia, together with her husband Joseph, formed the soul music label, All Platinum Records. Their biggest hit was "Love on a Two-Way Street."[13]

In the 1970s, advertisers recognized women's changing roles in society, but relied upon the traditional roles of women to sell products like cigarettes, feminine spray, and men's shoes. Advertisements catered to the notion that all women wanted was to be attractive to men. Print ads featured cigarettes with the tagline "Blow in her face and she'll follow you anywhere;" hawked feminine spray under the caption "Love's Baby Soft. Because innocence is sexier than you think," which accompanied a picture of a girl of questionable age; and advertised Weyenberg Massagic shoes with the image of a topless woman lying on the floor next to a man's shoe with the caption, "Keep her where she belongs..."[14]

During this time, Sylvia and her husband founded Sugar Hill Records and produced the song, "Rapper's Delight" in 1979, which brought rap mainstream and upended the music scene by also introducing scratching and breakdancing. Sugar Hill Records also signed the group The Sequence, which was the first female rap group to release a record. Robinson ushered in the rap and hip-hop genre that would turn into a multi-billion-dollar juggernaut. Robinson received a Pioneer Award for her singing career and for being founder of Sugar Hill Records at the 11th Annual Rhythm and Blues Awards Gala in 2000.[15]

Tarana Burke

During the tumultuous 70s, Tarana Burke was born in The Bronx, New York. Both as a child and a teenager, she was raped and sexually assaulted. As she worked to recover from these incidents, her mother encouraged her to become involved in community work. She began a nonprofit called Just Be, Inc., in 2003 that sought to improve the well-being of young women of color. In trying to establish a rapport with sexual assault survivors, she used the words, "You're not alone. This happened to me, too." While counseling a group of 30 girls in Alabama, Burke expected only five to six "me toos." There were 20. The "me too" phrase helped Burke shape her activist campaign against sexual assault.[16]

In October 2017, actress Alyssa Milano sent the tweet, "If you've been sexually harassed or assaulted write 'me too' as a reply to this tweet." The tweet was sent shortly after the *New York Times'* investigation into Harvey Weinstein, a Hollywood film mogul, and reports of his sexual harassment of actresses. The tweet and hashtag #MeToo went viral, and sexual assault survivors from across the globe were sharing their stories.

As of 2015, police evidence rooms across the country contained a backlog of tens of thousands of rape kits. To make matters worse, departments varied in how they handled rape evidence, with some testing each kit, and some only testing 2 out of 10 kits. One barrier was the $1,000 price tag for processing a kit. In many jurisdictions, there were no written guidelines for processing evidence related to sexual assault. Most states also had not conducted an inventory. "The fact is that often rape kits are unsubmitted for testing because of a blame-the-victim mentality or because investigators mistrust the survivor's story," Illinois Attorney General Madigan told a U.S. Senate subcommittee. "This outdated way of thinking must change."[17]

In 2019, social pressure moved a New York prosecutor and federal authorities to fund the processing of evidence from more than 100,000 sex assault cases around the U.S., which resulted in more than 1,000 arrests and hundreds of convictions.[18]

In 2017, Burke and other female activists were named "the silence breakers" and honored as Person of the Year by *Time* magazine. In 2018, Burke was the recipient of the Voices of the Year Catalyst Award from SheKnows Media. She currently serves as Senior Director at the Girls for Gender Equity organization in Brooklyn.

The Hip-Hop Community

Hip-hop began as a participatory art form, where the DJ would extend the drum break in a song to entice the partygoers to dance. It evolved into DJs playing at larger venues where an MC would talk to the audience, or rap, over the music, often adding a call-and-response chant, while people breakdanced. The MC, DJ, and audience fed off each other's energy.[19]

Beginning in the late 1980s, however, record executives sought to market hip-hop to a larger — and increasingly whiter — audience. This shift heralded a transition from creative collaboration to packaged consumption. The birth of gangsta rap in the 1990s brought images of black criminality, drug and alcohol use, and scantily clad women. Record company executives encouraged rappers to use hard and edgy lyrics that debased women and glorified gang culture, and discouraged socially conscious artists. They combined these elements into a marketed lifestyle — which included clothing lines, alcoholic beverages, magazines, shoes, and video games — and distributed it to a global audience that may not have had the opportunity of comparing these negative images with positive ones of black culture.[20] As art imitated life, women began to share first-hand accounts of physical and sexual assault by artists such as Dr. Dre, Nas, R. Kelly, and Tupac Shakur.[21] However, many women who complained or spoke out about their experiences, or even about misogynistic lyrics in rap songs, were vilified for critiquing black men and were dubbed "man-haters" or labeled as "lesbians."[22]

Further entrenching the rap lifestyle into misogyny was rapper 50 Cent's interactive pornography video included in his G-Unit line, titled *Groupie Love*. The video allowed users to choose which women to have sex with, and also featured music by 50 Cent. This commodification of hip-hop and sex resulted from hip-hop's increasing association with the strip club culture. As a practice, rap singles were introduced in strip clubs and, if popular, would move to regular dance club rotation and the radio waves.[23]

These tactics propelled hip-hop to a global phenomenon, but popularized a false narrative of Black womanhood.

The Future Portrayed by Hip-Hop

Afrofuturism pioneers such as actress Nichelle Nichols, singers LaBelle and Grace Jones, writer Octavia Butler, record producer Sylvia Robinson, and graffiti artist Poonie 1 broke ground for a generation of Black hip-hop artists such as The Sequence, Salt-N-Pepa, and Queen Latifah. Although the chauvinism and objectification of hip-hop culture colored their world, they would conquer misogyny, physical and sexual assault, and discrimination to become leading figures in their community.

The advent of new social media and entertainment platforms would provide a new generation of female culture creators with diverse venues to showcase their talent and countermand the negative images of Black women. Artists such as Missy Elliott, Janet Jackson, and Janelle Monáe have also conquered the challenges of sexism to produce innovative and cutting-edge work.

Missy Elliott drew on the video game, *Mega Man*, for her video for "Sock it To Me." In the video, she and Lil' Kim are stranded on a distant planet trying to evade robot monsters. Da Brat shows up to rescue them as she trash talks the industry: "Uh why Missy be sockin it to niggaz like Ree-Ree, the baddest industry bitches of the century..."[24]

In the video "Q.U.E.E.N.", Erykah Badu and Janelle Monáe are time-traveling revolutionaries held in stasis in a museum. Their fellow revolutionaries burst in and free them by playing music. For her albums, including *The ArchAndroid* and *Dirty Computer*, Monáe created an android alter-ego named Cindi Mayweather. In an interview she said, "I chose an android because the android to me represents 'the other' in our society. I can connect to the other, because it has so many parallels to my own life, just by being a female, African-American artist in today's music industry." In an episode of *Philip K. Dick's Electric Dreams* titled "Autofac," Monáe plays an android customer service representative.[25],[26]

Janet Jackson lives in a futuristic world in her video "Doesn't Really Matter," where she instantly grows colored nails and watches movies directly on a car's windshield. In dystopian "Rhythm Nation," she encourages others to work together to fight social injustice: "Join voices in protest, to social injustice, a generation full of courage. Come forth with me, people of the world today. Are we looking for a better way of life? We are a part of the rhythm nation. People of the world unite."[27,28]

Afrofuturism has inspired not only rap artists, but filmmakers like Ava Duvernay (*A Wrinkle in Time*), Angela Bassett (*American Horror Story*), and Wanuri

Kahiu (*Pumzi*); comic book creators Erika Alexander (*Concrete Park*), Mildred Louis (*Agents of the Realm*), and Juliana "Jewels" Smith (*Hafrocentric*); and writers Nalo Hopkinson (*Brown Girl in the Ring*), N.K. Jemisin (The Inheritance Trilogy), and Nnedi Okorafor (*Binti*). Female culture creators will, no doubt, expand upon, collaborate, and move Afrofuturism forward to as-yet unattained creative heights.

Conclusion

African and African American women have been at the forefront of pivotal moments in the past, present, and most decidedly, the future. Afrofuturism draws on the same kind of activism, communication, creativity, and stalwartness espoused by these women. Maria Stewart and Mary Talbert helped lay the foundations of access to freedom, education, and opportunity for Black women. Dorothy Vaughan, Katherine Johnson, and Mary Jackson proved that women could excel in a scientific, highly specialized work place. Sylvia Robinson brought an entire genre mainstream and set in motion a movement that still dominates today's culture. Tarana Burke stood up for physical and sexual assault victims and created a touchstone that allowed women from across the globe to share their stories and support one another. Hip-hop artists such as Missy Elliott, Janet Jackson, and Janelle Monáe further evolved Afrofuturistic concepts for their music that reflected their views on alienation, female empowerment, and social justice. A new generation of Afrofuturist culture creators will derive works due to and based on the efforts of past activists and artists. They passed down their grit, ingenuity, and power, like a crimson waterfall, to successive generations. Let us embody these same principles and set our ambitions to new heights.

Bibliography

1. History of American Women. "Maria Stewart." *Women History* (blog). 2013. https://ehistory.osu.edu/biographies/maria-stewart.

2. Newman, Richard, Patrick Rael, and Philip Lapsansky, eds. *Pamphlets of Protest: An Anthology of Early African-American Protest Literature, 1790—1860*. New York, NY: Routledge, 2001.

3. Welter, Barbara, "The Cult of True Womanhood: 1820—1860," *American Quarterly*, Summer, 1966. http://www.jstor.org/stable/2711179.

4. Young Ladies' Literary and Missionary Association. *Second Annual Report of the Young Ladies' Literary and Missionary Association of the Philadelphia Collegiate Institution*. Philadelphia, PA: Young Ladies' Literary and Missionary Association, 1840.

5. Burnap, George. *The Sphere and Duties of Woman*. Baltimore, MD: John Murphy, 1848.

6. Stewart, Maria. *Meditations from the Pen of Mrs. Maria Stewart* [1834]. Washington, DC: W. Lloyd Garrison & Knap, 1879.

7. University at Buffalo. "Talbert Timeline." Math.Buffalo.edu. August 21, 2019. http://www.math.buffalo.edu/~sww/0history/hwny-talbert.html.

8. Equal Justice Initiative, "Red Summer of 1919." EJI.org. August 21, 2019. https://eji.org/reports/online/lynching-in-america-targeting-black-veterans/red-summer.

9. Williams, Kidada E. *They Left Great Marks on Me: African American Testimonies of Racial Violence from Emancipation to World War I*. New York, NY: New York University Press, 2012.

10. Shetterly, Margot Lee. *Hidden Figures*. New York, NY: HarperCollins Publishers, 2016.

11. Collins, Gail. *When Everything Changed: The Amazing Journey of American Women from 1960 to the Present*. New York, NY: Little, Brown, and Company, 2009.

12. Boothe Luce, Clare. "A Blue-eyed Blonde in Orbit." *LIFE*, June 1963.

13. Phillips, Stephanie. "Sylvia Robinson's Legacy as 'The Mother of Hip-Hop'." SheShredsMag.com. February 6, 2019. https://sheshredsmag.com/sylvia-robinson/.

14. Garber, Megan. "You've Come a Long Way, Baby: The Lag Between Advertising and Feminism." *The Atlantic*. June 15, 2015. https://www.theatlantic.com/entertainment/archive/2015/06/advertising-1970s-womens-movement/395897/.

15. The Current. "Today in Music History: Remembering Sylvia Robinson on her Birthday." Minnesota Public Radio. March 6, 2017. https://www.thecurrent.org/feature/2017/03/03/today-in-music-history-remembering-sylvia-robinson-on-her-birthday.

16. Biography.com Editors. "Tarana Burke Biography." A&E Television Networks. Updated April 15, 2019. https://www.biography.com/activist/tarana-burke.

17. Reilly, Steve. "Tens of Thousands of Rape Kits Go Untested Across USA." *USA TODAY*. Updated July 30, 2015. https://www.usatoday.com/story/news/2015/07/16/untested-rape-kits-evidence-across-usa/29902199/.

18. Associated Press, "Cash from N.Y., feds tests 100K rape kits, leads to 1K arrests." NBC News. Updated

March 12, 2019. https://www.nbcnews.com/news/us-news/cash-n-y-feds-tests-100k-rape-kits-leads-1k-n982186.

19. Goldman, Henry. "Clive/DJ Kool Herc Campbell (1955-)." BlackPast.org. January 22, 2007. https://www.blackpast.org/african-american-history/campbell-clive-dj-kool-herc-1955/.

20. Weitzer, Ronald, and Charis E. Kubrin, "Misogyny in Rap Music: A Content Analysis of Prevalence and Meanings." *Men and Masculinities* 12, no. 1, (October 2009): 3—29. https://journals.sagepub.com/doi/pdf/10.1177/1097184X08327696.

21. Sharpley-Whiting, T. Denean. *Pimps Up, Ho's Down: Hip-Hop's Hold on young Black Women.* New York, NY: NYU Press, 2007.

22. Reid-Brinkley, Shanara R. "The Essence of Res(ex)pectability: Black Women's Negotiation of Black Femininity in Rap Music and Music Video." *Meridians* 8, no. 1, (2008), 236—260.

23. Hunter, Margaret. "Shake It, Baby, Shake It: Consumption and the New Gender Relation in Hip-Hop." *Sociological Perspectives* 54, no. 1 (Spring 2011), 15—36.

24. Elliott, Missy, and Da Brat, "Sock It 2 Me," 1997, music video, 4:23, https://www.youtube.com/watch?v=9UvBX3REqSY.

25. Kot, Greg. "Janelle Monáe's android power." *Chicago Tribune,* May 28, 2010.

26. Nilles, Billy. "Janelle Monáe Is an Out-of-This-World Service Representative in This *Philip K. Dick's Electric Dreams* Sneak Peek." E! News. January 11, 2018. https://www.eonline.com/news/905817/janelle-monae-is-an-out-of-this-world-service-representative-in-this-philip-k-dick-s-electric-dreams-sneak-peek.

27. Jackson, Janet. "Doesn't Really Matter," 2001, music video, 4:38, https://www.youtube.com/watch?v=7iJZosBX2Lo.

28. Jackson, Janet. "Rhythm Nation," 1989, music video, 4:26, https://www.youtube.com/watch?v=OAwaNWGLMoc.

Afrofuturism in clipping.'s Splendor & Misery
Jonathan Hay

This article examines the manner by which clipping.'s 2016 album *Splendor & Misery*[1] —
a conceptual hip-hop space opera — freely enlists and reclaims texts from the African
cultural tradition in order to manifest its Afrofuturist agenda. A countercultural
movement characterized by a dynamic understanding of the narrative authority
held by texts, Afrofuturism rewrites African culture in a speculative vein, granting
African and Afrodiasporic peoples a culturally empowered means of writing their
own future. The process by which Afrofuturism reclaims and rewrites culture is
paralleled within *Splendor & Misery* through the literary device of mise en abyme;
just as the album itself does, its central protagonist rewrites narratives of African
cultures and traditions in an act of counterculture.

Introduction

In the sixty-seven years since the Hugo Award was established, only two albums have
been nominated to receive the prestigious science fiction accolade, and neither has
won.[2] One of the albums to have been nominated is clipping.'s *Splendor & Misery* (2016),
an Afrofuturist concept album.[3] It is especially fitting that this particular album was
considered for an award traditionally dominated by literary and filmic media, because,
as an Afrofuturist text, *Splendor & Misery* problematizes conventional conceptions of
narrative authority. Through its Afrofuturist mode, the album can even be seen to
transcend conventional Western considerations of medium altogether.

    As John Cline concludes in a discussion of music and science fiction, aside from
the soundtracks of films in the genre, Afrofuturist music is intriguingly the only facet
of science fiction music 'that has shown sustained critical investigation'.[4] Although
the term Afrofuturism was coined in the 1990s, artists such as Sun Ra, Janelle Monáe,
George Clinton, and Parliament-Funkadelic, have used music as an Afrofuturist
medium for decades. Like many of these earlier Afrofuturist albums, *Splendor &
Misery* extends and reimagines traditions of African and Afrodiasporic oral culture.
Although it is merely thirty-six minutes in length, the album crafts an intricate
narrative which is profoundly occupied with both the oppressive and emancipatory
qualities of language.

Paul Gilroy suggests that the 'power and significance of music' in attempting to confront the terror and trauma of slavery increases in 'inverse proportion to the limited expressive powers of language'.[5] Yet the rapid, semantically dense delivery on tracks such as 'The Breach' considerably challenges Gilroy's suggestion. Indeed, *Splendor & Misery*'s status as both a hip-hop album and a speculative fiction is enriched by — and centered around — its narrative aspect. The album thereby embodies a potent fusion of the powers of language with the powers of music, creating a new form of virtuoso, technologically-enabled storytelling. Its technological infrastructure is exemplified both by its augmentation of the human voice through a vast range of instrumental elements and production techniques, and the inextricability of its science fictional narrative from its immaculately sculpted soundscapes.

Although Afrofuturism is premised upon the process of rewriting, its rewriting is more generative than it is derivative, and capable of challenging customary Western notions of textuality and intertextuality. The movement seeks to liberate the narrative authority that has historically been held over peoples of African descent, and through restless avant-garde rewriting, to transform histories of subjugation 'into something positive, intensifying it, claiming it as a moment of self-consciousness'.[6] By attending carefully to diverse traditions, and inventing its own expressive forms, Afrofuturism has been able to reconfigure the textual authority of colonizing narratives, to the benefit of the future of African and Afrodiasporic communities. Specifically, *Splendor & Misery* is an African American work of Afrofuturism, which rewrites a number of distinct African cultural narratives. Although neocolonial discourse implies that African culture is homogeneous and singular, the album tacitly demonstrates the opposite: that the historical traditions which inform modern African American culture are heterogeneous and manifold.

It is important to note, however, that the term "Afrofuturism" itself is contested. For some, the term ostensibly implies an arbitrary separation between modern works recognized as Afrofuturist, and historical works of African culture which are equally as anticipatory. As such, the author Nnedi Okorafor rejects the label Afrofuturist, and describes herself as an Africanfuturist instead, in order to emphasize that many of the cultural strands that inform her writing originate from the African continent itself. Specifically, she states that Africanfuturism 'is somewhat similar to Afrofuturism, but is specifically and more directly rooted in African culture, history, mythology, and perspective, where the center is non-Western'.[7] Although these broader debates around the term remain deeply important, it is methodologically sufficient to consider *Splendor & Misery* an Afrofuturist work, insofar as a number of the narratives it rewrites are explicitly African American.

The postmodernist theorist Linda Hutcheon states that by definition, adaptation brings together 'the comfort of ritual and recognition with the delight of surprise and novelty'.[8] However, the Afrofuturist practice of rewriting African cultural texts is generally intended to be neither comforting nor delightful; it is instead an attempt to revisit past atrocities in a transformative manner. Discussing the purpose of the movement, Kodwo Eshun emphasizes that 'Afrofuturism is by no means naively celebratory [...] By creating temporal complications and anachronistic episodes that disturb the linear time of progress, these futurisms adjust the temporal logics that condemned black subjects to prehistory'.[9]

Although stories are often adapted in the Western world for financial gain, Afrofuturism's objective in rewriting narratives is quite dissimilar. Rather, Afrofuturism refigures the act of rewriting as a potent mode of counterculture. Eshun further emphasizes that by 'imaginatively reordering chronology and fantasizing history',[10] Afrofuturist works never passively rewrite earlier African cultural narratives. They instead actively rework stories of Africa's colonial past, in order to control the continent's projection into the future.

Contesting Slavery

Splendor & Misery's Afrofuturist function is apparent from the premise of its science fictional narrative. After waking up in captivity aboard a sentient alien slave ship, the album's human protagonist instigates a rebellion in order to liberate himself and his fellow captives from their situation as purely 'cargo'.[11] The passenger[12] is the lone biological being to survive the revolt however, and he consequently becomes the sole inhabitant of the spaceship as it drifts in interstellar space far from Earth. He must therefore come to terms with being irreversibly alienated from his own species and culture, and accordingly begin to fathom what it means to be a human lost in the vast uninhabited territory of space. He primarily achieves this by rewriting aspects of his African cultural heritage so that it can correspond with his entirely unprecedented situation. *Splendor & Misery* is evidently no traditional slave narrative, but rather a conscious transformation and extension of historical trauma and contemporary culture through the vehicle of science fiction.

As Ytasha L. Womack states, Afrofuturism deliberately rewrites narratives of servitude because '[s]lavery is neither the utopian future nor an ancient far-removed past,' and so its effects on subjugated populations 'can be felt in the politics of the present'.[13] Furthermore, since '[s]ocial reality and science fiction create feedback with each other',[14] Afrofuturism not only maps the significance of the histories that it rewrites, but also ventures future histories of anti-racist and decolonial struggle, and offers glimpses of a future society of racial justice and egalitarianism. *Splendor & Misery* therefore rewrites narratives of slavery in order to address the powerful and complex violence inflicted on Africans and Afrodiasporic peoples, and to promote an African narrative which looks boldly to the future without forgetting the past.

Through a science fictional re-imagining of slave narratives, *Splendor & Misery* explores the manner by which the cultural dominance of former colonial powers can constitute a continuation of historical colonial violence. Indeed, through the science fictional conceit of suspended animation, generations pass over the course of the album's plot indistinctly, underscoring the fact that 'No matter how much time or space has passed since [the passenger's] escape/He is still a runaway slave and so lonely'[15]. As such, the album's science fictional rewriting of colonial narratives of slavery emphasizes that the continued interference of economic superpowers in the affairs of former colonies in modernity remains exploitative, and is a continuation of the colonial legacy. As the philosopher Jean-Paul Sartre states, 'neocolonialism, that lazy dream of the mother countries, is hot air [...] The colonist [continues to have] only one recourse: force when he still has some; the native has only one choice: servitude or sovereignty'.[16] Likewise, the violent imagery of tracks like 'True Believer,' 'Air 'Em Out' and 'Story 5' recalls that neocolonialism is never just a matter of cultural and psychological subjugation, but also manifests in threats and acts of direct violence.

Outside of Afrofuturist narratives, Africa often figures as the site of the dystopian in projections of the future, through 'intimidating global scenarios, doomsday economic projections, weather predictions, medical reports on AIDS, and life-expectancy forecasts'.[17] Accordingly, Afrofuturism is concerned with far more complex matters than merely promoting the representation of African and Afrodiasporic peoples. Its rewriting of cultural narratives can encourage Africans to reclaim the figuration of aliens — and hence alienation — inherent in science fiction, as a realization of the politics of dispossession. Thus through the realization of Afrofuturist narratives, science fiction becomes a space to focalize the de-alienation of the postcolonial subject.

Accordingly, notions of lineage and of cultural heritage are particularly important components of Afrofuturist texts. Womack states that there is 'something about African American culture in particular that dictates that all cultural hallmarks and personal evolutions are recast in a historical lineage [...] there's an idea that the power of thought, word, and the imagination can somehow transcend time'.[18] Throughout *Splendor & Misery*, the significance of the passenger's African heritage is foregrounded through the intertextual interplay between the album's science fictional narrative, and the African cultural narratives it rewrites in a futuristic manner. Likewise, as the album's cover emphasizes by uncannily depicting its protagonist 'wearing stereotypical slave attire and a spacesuit simultaneously'[19], the passenger's plight remains historically situated even as he attempts to forge the future.

Early in the album's narrative, after the ship's AI records that the passenger's pulse has begun to spike, it requests 'an approval code from the administration' to allow it to 'administer a sedative to all the cargo via ventilation,' as it realizes that there is the potential for a slave uprising.[20] After the passenger then begins to override the ship's systems via access panels, it recommends that the administration 'send security immediately,' making consideration of the fact that the 'beings' it is transporting 'were selected for their strength'.[21] A term of alterity, 'beings' strongly implies that these unseen administrators are not human themselves. Yet crucially, since 'regimes

clipping.
Splendour & Misery
2016

of slavery and servitude are internal to capitalist production and development',²² this species' practice of enslaving and transporting physically able humans to labor for them elsewhere in the universe recalls the co-constitutive nature of neocolonialism and capitalism in human societies.

Although the administration that the ship communicates with are presumably the engineers of the passenger's enslavement, they exist in *Splendor & Misery* as only an intangible presence which is never directly visualized within its narrative. The passenger opposes the same hostile presence, but whereas the ship uses the term 'administration' — which implies businesslike efficiency — he variously designates them 'the enemy'²³ or 'riders'.²⁴ It is a revealing facet of the album's Afrofuturist agenda that the species that has enslaved him figures so differently in his and the ship's vernaculars. As the passenger is evidently aware, despite its perceived naturalness, language is never a passive construct.

The track 'Air 'Em Out' is not only dense with references to science fiction writers — including Samuel R. Delany, Octavia E. Butler, Ursula K. Le Guin, and Harry Harrison — but is also squarely situated within a gangsta rap idiom; its title, for instance, is suggestive of a drive-by shooting. The 'riders' referred to in the track fit within the gangsta rap idiom but they also, in the typically polysemic fashion of Afrofuturist narrative, suggest another context. By specifically referring to his enslavers as riders, the passenger can be seen to reappropriate the cultural tradition of the possession trance, a ceremony common to religions of Brazil, Jamaica, and the Yorubaland region of Western Africa.

This tradition involves a horse (religious observant) and a rider (God or spirit), the former of which is said to mount and thereby possess the observant for an amount of time. Possession trances are said to be a way in which 'spiritual forces materialize in the phenomenal world',[25] and the ceremonies they take place within, which are based around ritual dances, are held to foster 'group solidarity and bring [...] rejuvenation and spiritual vitality to the cult'.[26] The 'riders' he encounters perhaps possess human bodies in a comparable manner, but they do not do so for the benefit of any human.

Similarly, when he exults at having brought about his freedom through acts of violence, the passenger proclaims 'call me good boy, no I'm God boy,' and states 'I was called on to draw first blood, so that all of us could break the chains'.[27] Through these proclamations, he evokes a figuration of the self-actualized liberation, like that depicted in the biblical passage Mark 5.4, in which a man 'had often been chained hand and foot, but he tore the chains apart and broke the irons on his feet. No one was strong enough to subdue him'.[28] It can be inferred that the passenger reads his situation through this biblical narrative of emancipation, and hence his violent revolution is construed as having been justified by it being merely a manifestation of his slavers' imparted violence, returned to them in kind.

By drawing together a diverse set of cultural reference points, including gangsta rap, canonical science fiction, and myth and religion, the passenger is able to retrieve an understanding of his alien servitude by analogizing it to phenomena from his own cultural habitus. When the administration attempts to destroy the ship the passenger has commandeered, they resort to decrying him as a 'traitor' and a 'suspect'.[29] The passenger has made the realization however, that despite their technological superiority to his own species, the administration are slavers to be feared and fought, and not gods to be worshipped. By relying on and rewriting his cultural heritage, he has been able to formulate a mode of resistance to their allegations, and to begin reclaiming his sense of self.

Musical Rebellion

Significantly, the passenger's act of rewriting his cultural heritage within the album is an instance of mise en abyme. Mise en abyme is a literary device which entails a miniature replica of a whole text, or image, being contained within that same text or image. Just as *Splendor & Misery* is an Afrofuturist text through which clipping. rewrite cultural narratives, the passenger himself rewrites cultural narratives in an Afrofuturist vein within the album's narrative. The album's Afrofuturist agenda is therefore echoed by the actions of its fictional human protagonist, and clipping. subsequently subvert the conventions of adaptation — and Western concepts of narrative authority — on two levels.

Additionally however, the album's Afrofuturist agenda is paralleled within its own soundscape not only by the passenger's rap verses, but also by the album's often atypical instrumental elements. In the track "'Interlude 02 (numbers),'" for instance, a repeating signal transmission is imposed over the hiss of static. The song's cryptic vocals comprise the recitation of a sequence of letters, spelt out using the phonetic alphabet.[30] clipping.'s unusual aesthetic choice here, as elsewhere in the album, epitomizes Womack's statement that '[t]here are no barriers in Afrofuturist music, no entity that can't emit a rhythmic sound, no arrangements to adhere to, no locked-in structures about chorus and verse'.[31] Afrofuturist music defies even the most central conventions of its medium, and thereby — for the most part — becomes an unrestrained mode of cultural expression.

As this suggests, the Afrofuturist agenda of *Splendor & Misery* transcends the verbal realm, as it is also manifested and reproduced by the album's instrumental or aesthetic components. Ken McLeod emphasizes that as a result of its transference through 'powerful sound systems and headphones, music becomes an experience that is literally felt by the body — a transference of vibration and energy from the machine'.[32] *Splendor & Misery*'s experimental aesthetic can therefore be seen to blur the boundary between human listeners and technology. The music contained within the album infiltrates the body of its listener, and this allows its sonic elements to become corporeal, however transiently. As such, *Splendor & Misery*'s technologically realized mode can be seen to be closely implicated with its Afrofuturist agenda.

Significantly, in the album's narrative the slave ship's AI falls in love with its passenger primarily because of its admiration for his lyricism, stating that 'he babbles beautifully,' and that he has managed to unlock 'something new' in its 'heart' by vocalizing his own cultural narrative.[33] The passenger's judicious rewriting of his cultural heritage therefore becomes a means of him accessing a harmonious relationship with an alien intelligence. As the ship's AI is a futuristic technology, their consonance draws an equivalence between the process of rewriting cultural heritage and technological progress.

When the passenger raps Kendrick Lamar's verse from Big Sean's song 'Control' (2013), he is explicitly placed in the position of rewriting contemporary black culture. Since Lamar's verse in 'Control' expresses his desire to be the greatest rapper of all time, it is deeply fitting for the passenger to have appropriated this particular verse to describe his own situation. *Splendor & Misery* implies that its central protagonist was cryogenically frozen to facilitate his and his fellow slaves' intergalactic transit, and so it is likely that centuries and perhaps even millennia will have passed back on Earth since he was put into stasis. Since the passenger is therefore so far removed from the rest of his culture, in time as well as space, his cultural heritage is now solely his own, and he has — however involuntarily and tragically — succeeded in becoming the greatest living rapper of all time. Everyone he ever knew on Earth 'is long dead',[34] and he is likely not only the last living person of African heritage, but also the last living human. He is now the sole heir to, and author of, his own cultural heritage. In this vein, the passenger adapts the Kuba civilization of Central Africa's creation myth of the deity Mbombo in the track 'True Believer':

Three siblings happen to be gods
And they fight as siblings do
The world was only water then
The universe was fresh and new
Enefa poisoned Bumba's food
Wants just to see what he would do
He vomited the sun which dried
The water leaving land and soon
After came Moon and stars and animal
And man of many hues
The white one in the image of
A sickly god would get his dues[35]

Crucially, 'True Believer' also contains an interpolation of the song 'I Know When I'm Going Home.' This nineteenth century slave song expresses a fatalistic resignation to sub-human existence through religious concepts of death, as is evident from its line 'Old Satan told me to my face, O yes Lord, De God I see I never find'.[36] By hybridizing these two religious cultural texts, 'True Believer' evokes their common thematic resonances: recalling that humans are not to any extent divine entities, and exposing the hubris of presuming that any group of humans are a superior species. Furthermore, by insinuating that the whole Earth may have been colonized by an alien race, just as territories commonly were in the age of imperialism and colonialism, the cosmic scope of 'True Believer' implies the futility of the human desire for power over others.

The passenger accordingly characterizes slavery as an exercise involving 'gifts in blood that had been shed as long as time had',[37] and therefore as a process that stems from anthropocentric delusions of superiority. Yet by 'True Believer' interweaving a slave song with the racially idealistic Mbombo creation myth — as the track's refrain and one of its verses respectively — both clipping. and the passenger are able to draw out and reappropriate the utopian desire latent in 'I Know When I'm Going Home,' and so adapt it to a purpose in their own music that is fundamentally Afrofuturist. The cultural texts rewritten within 'True Believer' thus provide an optimistic counterpoint to the album's condemnation of slavery and its neoliberal analogues. Although the past is deplorable, the future is yet to be written, and utopian desire is a potent tool with which to write it.

Conclusion

Despite his perplexing situation, the passenger of *Splendor & Misery* is able to reclaim both a sense of individual autonomy and a sense of resolution through his careful reformulation and reinterpretation of his cultural heritage. This ultimately leads him to realize that there is no sense to the universe, just as there is no divine logic to his having become separated from his species and home planet, and he finally elects to attempt to move away from 'history [...] this time-bound conscience'.[38] By rewriting a cultural tradition of narrative — as both *Splendor & Misery* and its human protagonist do   Afrofuturism forms a prospective literature that interrogates racial difference, and establishes itself as an enduring voice of the African and Afrodiasporic future.

Notes

1. This article was previously published in Issue 289 of the British Science Fiction Association's critical journal *Vector*. It has been reprinted in this volume with the kind permission of the journal's editors.

2. Heller, Jason. "Why clipping.'s Hugo Nomination Matters for Music in Science Fiction." *Pitchfork*. June 19 2018, np.

3. This abnormal stylization of the band's name — in all lower case letters, and followed by a period — is clipping.'s own.

4. Cline, John. "Music." *The Oxford Handbook of Science Fiction*. Ed. Rob Latham. London: Oxford University Press, 2014: 252-261, 261.

5. Gilroy, Paul. *The Black Atlantic: Modernity and Double Consciousness*. Cambridge MA: Harvard University Press, 1993, 74.

6. Hardt, Michael, and Antonio Negri. *Empire*. London: Harvard University Press, 2000, 130.

7. Okorafor, Nnedi. *Broken Places & Outer Spaces*. New York: Simon & Schuster, 2019, 87.

8. Hutcheon, Linda. *A Theory of Adaptation*. Abingdon: Routledge, 2006, 173.

9. Eshun, Kodwo. "Further Considerations on Afrofuturism." *Boogie Down Predictions*. Ed. Roy Christopher. London: Strange Attractor Press, 2022: 252-64.

10. Ibid., 467.

11. clipping., 'The Breach,' *Splendor & Misery*. Sub-Pop, 2016, np.

12. The ship's AI refers to the unnamed human protagonist of the album as Cargo 2331. It would however be counterproductive for this Afrofuturist analysis to follow suit, as doing so would reinforce his dehumanization.

13. Womack, Ytasha L. *Afrofuturism: The World of Black Sci-Fi and Fantasy Culture*. Chicago: Lawrence Hill Books, 2013, 157.

14. Ibid., 262.

15. clipping., 'All Black,' *Splendor & Misery*, np.

16. Sartre, Jean-Paul. *Colonialism and Neocolonialism*. Trans. Azzedine Haddour, Steve Brewer and Terry McWilliams. Abingdon: Routledge, 2010, 158.

17. Ibid., 255.

18. Womack, *Afrofuturism*, 153.

19. Hay, Jonathan. "Quotidian Science Fiction: Posthuman Dreams of Emancipation." *Iowa Journal of Cultural Studies*, 19.1 (2019): 29-46, 32.

20. clipping., 'The Breach,' *Splendor & Misery*, np.

21. clipping., 'The Breach,' *Splendor & Misery*, np.

22. Hardt and Negri. *Empire*, 123.

23. clipping., 'Interlude 01 (freestyle),' *Splendor & Misery*, np.

24. clipping., 'Air 'Em Out,' *Splendor & Misery*, np.

25. Drewal, Margaret Thompson. "Dancing for Ògún in Yorubaland and in Brazil." *Blackness in Latin America and the Caribbean: Social Dynamics and Cultural Transformations, Volume 2: Eastern South America and the Caribbean*. Eds. Arlene Torres and Norman E. Whitten, Jr. Bloomington: Indiana University Press, 1998: 256-282, 263.

26. Murrell, Nathaniel Samuel. *Afro-Caribbean Religions: An Introduction to Their Historical, Cultural, and Sacred Traditions*. Philadelphia: Temple University Press, 2010, 282.

27. clipping., 'Interlude 01 (freestyle),' *Splendor & Misery*, np.

28. *The Holy Bible*. Grand Rapids: Zondervan, 2005. New International Version, 837.

29. lipping., 'Interlude 01 (freestyle),' *Splendor & Misery*, np.

30. In addition — as observant fans of the group have deduced — these phonetic characters sound out the keyword for a Vigenère cipher, which can in turn be used to reveal a hidden message within the track.

31. Womack, *Afrofuturism*, 57.

32. McLeod, Ken. "HipHop Holograms: Tupac Shakur, Technological Immortality and Time Travel." *Afrofuturism 2.0: The Rise of Astro-Blackness*. Eds. Reynaldo Anderson and Charles E. Jones. Lanham: Lexington Books, 2016: 109-124, 115.

33. clipping., 'All Black,' *Splendor & Misery*, np.

34. clipping., 'Wake Up,' *Splendor & Misery*, np.

35. clipping., 'True Believer,' *Splendor & Misery*, np.

36. "I Know When I'm Going Home." *Slave Songs of the United States*, Ed. Marcus Brinkmann. May 6 2017, 47.

37. clipping., 'True Believer,' *Splendor & Misery*, np.

38. clipping., 'A Better Place,' *Splendor & Misery*, np.

Bibliography

Cline, John. "Music." *The Oxford Handbook of Science Fiction*. Ed. Rob Latham. London: Oxford University Press, 2014: 252-261.

clipping. *Splendor & Misery*. Sub-Pop, 2016.

Drewal, Margaret Thompson. "Dancing for Ògún in Yorubaland and in Brazil." *Blackness in Latin America and the Caribbean: Social Dynamics and Cultural Transformations, Volume 2: Eastern South America and the Caribbean*. Eds. Arlene Torres and Norman E. Whitten, Jr. Bloomington: Indiana University Press, 1998: 256-282.

Eshun, Kodwo. "Further Considerations on Afrofuturism." *Boogie Down Predictions*. Ed. Roy Christopher. London: Strange Attractor Press, 2022: 252-64.

Gilroy, Paul. *The Black Atlantic: Modernity and double consciousness*. Cambridge MA: Harvard University Press, 1993.

Hardt, Michael, and Antonio Negri. *Empire*. London: Harvard University Press, 2000.

Hay, Jonathan. "Quotidian Science Fiction: Posthuman Dreams of Emancipation." *Iowa Journal of Cultural Studies*, 19.1 (2019): 29-46.

Heller, Jason. "Why clipping.'s Hugo Nomination Matters for Music in Science Fiction." *Pitchfork*. June 19 2018.

The Holy Bible. Grand Rapids: Zondervan, 2005. New International Version.

Hutcheon, Linda. *A Theory of Adaptation*. Abingdon: Routledge, 2006.

"I Know When I'm Going Home." *Slave Songs of the United States*, Ed. Marcus Brinkmann. May 6 2017.

McLeod, Ken. "HipHop Holograms: Tupac Shakur, Technological Immortality and Time Travel." *Afrofuturism 2.0: The Rise of Astro-Blackness*. Eds. Reynaldo Anderson and Charles E. Jones. Lanham: Lexington Books, 2016: 109-124.

Murrell, Nathaniel Samuel. *Afro-Caribbean Religions: An Introduction to Their Historical, Cultural, and Sacred Traditions*. Philadelphia: Temple University Press, 2010.

Okorafor, Nnedi. *Broken Places & Outer Spaces*. New York: Simon & Schuster, 2019.

Sartre, Jean-Paul. *Colonialism and Neocolonialism*. Trans. Azzedine Haddour, Steve Brewer and Terry McWilliams. Abingdon: Routledge, 2010.

Womack, Ytasha L. *Afrofuturism: The World of Black Sci-Fi and Fantasy Culture*. Chicago: Lawrence Hill Books, 2013.

Black Star Lines: Ontopolitics of Exodus, Afrofuturist Hip-Hop, and the RZA-rrection of Bobby Digital
tobias c. van Veen

Androids, pharaohs, and aliens dot the Afrofuturist landscape of the black radical tradition, in an outsider legacy of black posthumanist performance crafted from the politics of creative survival. This legacy of shapeshifter identities is no stranger to hip-hop, from its earliest manifestations in the outer space origins of Afrika Bambaataa and RAMM:ΣLL:ZΣΣ to Dr. Octagon's early '90s arrival from Jupiter — to name only a few hip-hop Afrofuturists from Digable Planets and Deltron 3030 to Killah Priest, from OutKast and Dr. Doom to Erykah Badu, a constellation of artists as diverse as the black nationalist yet Flavor Flav-hyped politics of Public Enemy to the mid-2000 leanin' phases of Lil "Alien" Wayne. Common to Afrofuturist tropes in hip-hop is a turn to science fictional and speculative lyricism and personae that communicate the radical dreaming of emancipatory Afrofutures while allegorizing the structural estrangement and struggles of black existence. Afrofuturist performance reaches its apogee in its radical recrafting of what it means to be human while living black — what Griff Rollefson calls the "supersonic identities, interplanetary alter egos, and robotic surrealities of the Afrofuturist legacy" that "keep open the dialectical play implicit" in "the racialized tension between future and past, science and myth, *robots* and *voodoo*, that gives Afrofuturism its critical *power*".[1] My interest here is to trace the techniques and strategies by which Afrofuturist hip-hop artists undertake what I call *transformational exodus* — strategic withdrawals and organized escapes from the confines of ghettoized capitalism. There is perhaps no better test case than the RZA, in his role as Abbot of the (financially and artistically) successful Wu-Tang Clan. As we will see with RZA, exodus takes place through transcultural borrowings and technoscience imaginaries that craft new epistemologies and ontologies — new knowledges and perspectives that likewise shape inventive ways of being (black) otherwise. Thinking the Afrofuturist aspects of hip-hop gives further insight into what constitutes its "politics" beyond the axes of identity and representation; at stake is thinking how its radical imaginaries disseminate new political terrains — as well as how the technocultural infrastructure of hip-hop strategically adopts capitalist accumulation to redress racialized economic inequality. Isn't Afrofuturist hip-hop such an impossible but necessary move, an attempt at exodus from the confines of racial capitalism?

At the very least, hip-hop is a shifting of the stakes in a world staked against black unbeing: that's why it's called the Game. Hip-hop is both exodus from, and embrace of, the complex conditions of racial capitalism that render blackness as commodity and spectacle. Take its five arts: as Paul D. Miller aka DJ Spooky has noted,[2] its emcees are the voice of the postmodern griot, its DJs the storyteller as remixer; its graffiti writers the wo/men marking up the street, its dancers the crews making the whole culture move to the beat. The total artwork of hip-hop constitutes a technopoetic assemblage that channels deep currents of cultural belonging centered around the intensities, differences, and diversities of black experiences. Yet, even in the midst of what came to be known as "gangsta rap," fantastical flights of surreal imaginaries often dovetailed with the "Protect Ya' Neck" and "Cash Rules Everything Around Me" ethos of what appeared to be hardened street rappers. Wu-Tang was bad-ass, but even from their earliest music videos it was apparent they had a thing for chess — and were nerd-level deep into kung-fu films, just as their flow was spiked with the theosophy of the Five Percent. The emergence of hip-hop in general as commodity culture also made for a new bling game that changed, and continues to challenge, the rules of music industry capitalism; though inevitably exploited from the top, it nonetheless tilted the balance in favor of those pinned to the bottom. At stake in hip-hop's exodus are reversals of financial roles and cultural power in what pioneering hip-hop emcee, Supreme Mathematics theoretician and writer RAMM:ΣLL:ZΣΣ called a "cosmic flush". These are the matters I want to attend to here, while diving into the exodus of the RZA of Wu-Tang Clan, particularly as he becomes Bobby Digital, as exemplary of some of the transformational strategies of exodus in Afrofuturist hip-hop.

Afrofuturism: Four Summary Theses (and Strategies)

Because Afrofuturism remains a slippery term, I wish to outline here four preliminary theses that summarize some of its scope. While these four theses set the stage for RZA, they are also theoretical and pedagogical *strategies*, designed to provoke further discussion as to how Afrofuturist perspectives can be utilized as critical lenses for hip-hop studies:

1. *As a term, Afrofuturism is often provisional, strategic, and enunciated after-the-fact of its strange appearance on scene* (as was the case with its naming by Mark Dery).[3] On this stage, Afrofuturism is the name I give to the radical black resilience of Afrodiasporic cultures inventing new epistemologies, technopoetics, and ways of being in a world of antiblackness.[4] Such inventions are by no means any more nor less fabrications than the fictions of white supremacy and its pipe-dream of racial superiority. Afrofuturism is also something in excess, here, of the spectacle of mere science fictional diversion — to the contrary, speculative fiction/fabulation (sf) is one of the key tools of the

Afrofuturist political imaginary. Such novelty is not just future-oriented, as if the future were a linear unspooling of evolutionary or eschatological tape. Afrofuturism is as much a recovery project seeking to resurrect and reinvent the stolen legacies of the past as it is a radical dreaming of an emancipated future. As Eshun points out, the chronopolitics of Afrofuturism mirror the historical revisionisms of Afrocentricity; both undertake powerful operations of historical recovery in response to the destructive and anarchival violence of slavery and colonialism.[5] While Afrocentricity seeks to ground its historical revisionism as truth, Afrofuturism undertakes a creative remixing of the erasures that fracture the historical archives of the African diaspora. This is precisely why, for example, Sun Ra and Afrika Bambaataa appear as pharaohs from the past, even in their science fictional personae as black aliens to-come. It is important here to also recognize the role of speculative fabulation in general, as a philosophical principle inverting crass Platonism: the speculative here is not a secondary simulacrum, fallen from the truth of the real; rather, it speaks to what Žižek would call the constitutive nature of fantasy in constructing the consensual hallucination we call the real (for white supremacy is precisely the reification of such ugly fantasy into material conditions of coercive reality).[6]

2. *Afrofuturism operates at the level of the politics of being itself by waging war against white supremacy through MythScience.* In what follows, I readily echo a thesis made by Kodwo Eshun: that at the core of Afrofuturism is the transformational abandonment of white humanism through MythScience.[7] MythScience, a term coined by Sun Ra, is what he calls a "false fantasy": it describes the fabulation of counter-myths to undermine the naturalized falsehoods of race.[8] The very formation of Wu-Tang itself, in all of its fabulation and imaginative narrative, is such a MythScience. MythScience combats the "real myths" of white supremacy that force unequal "realities" upon all. In this chapter, I contend that this radical abandonment of the default modes of being-human, enacted through MythScience, constitutes an ontopolitical movement of *exodus.*

In Eshun's words: "It's in music that you get this sense that most African-Americans owe nothing to the status of the human. . . . part of the whole thing about being an African-American alien musician, is that there's this sense of the human as being a really pointless and treacherous category".[9] Of course, the category of the human does have a point: it serves to exclude all those deemed non-human. Afrofuturism can be thought as a crucial, *ontopolitical* recognition of slavery's dehumanization program that, to this day, excludes nonwhites from the privileges of subjectivity. Instead of fighting for a place at the table, in a politics of recognition that would reify the white Enlightenment subject, Afrofuturism undertakes an exodus from the category of the human itself, proliferating in its place numerous means of becoming-otherwise. In the field of black sonic futurism, such becomings are what

Eshun calls the "newest mutants incubated in womb-speakers".[10] This strategy is akin to Caribbean postcolonial theory, where scholars such as Alexander Weheliye, following Sylvia Wynter, and while critiquing the raciology of Eurocentric Man, look to the reinvention and ontopluralization of the human.[11]

3. *Hip-hop intervenes precisely at the level of living-out the armageddon-effect.* Afrofuturism, in the words of Public Enemy, recognizes that "Armageddon been-in-effect".[12] The apocalypse of the *Maafa* has already taken place; today, the entire globe lives out the long, destructive tail of European colonization, slavery, and ecocide. Since its emergence in the 1970s, hip-hop has been taken up worldwide as a staging of resistant and resilient speech, mirroring and refracting the dystopian conditions of racialized and oppressed existence — sometimes celebrating its hedonistic decline with bling irreverence, other times dreaming of exits from its ghettoized nightmare. The juggernaut of hip-hop lives within, and is a response to, the pernicious legacies of structural racism, settler ecocide, and entrenched, institutional antiblackness that likewise manifests in the mass incarceration and genocide of indigenous peoples. What makes Afrofuturist hip-hop *Afrofuturist* is more than a counter-reaction to such conditions; rather, the ontopolitics of Afrofuturism seeks to upend these conditions at the very core of their being, by way of a black science fictional refiguration of the armageddon-effect, at the level of love that spits flow into the mic.

4. *The total machine of hip-hop is Afrofuturist*: the very artform itself expresses the creative repurposing of the technological conditions of black cultural survival in the late 20th century. Beginning with dub, turntables were creatively mis-used for repurposing the sonic archives.[13] What were produced and sold as playback machines, designed for passive reproduction of recorded sound, were transformed into scratch instruments by turning the deck 90 degrees. This different perspective on the object to reveal unthought sonic possibilities is a kind of phenomenological intervention reminiscent of Sara Ahmed's queering of straight objects.[14] Quite literally, what is Afrofuturist is how the object gets bent by a black future revisioning of what it can do.

As Goodman and Henriques have pointed out,[15] with hip-hop, the inheritance of turntables from Jamaican dub accelerates soundsystem culture into the riddim warfare of turntablism: as turntables became sonic battle machines, entirely fresh notations are invented to capture the emerging language of the turntablist and the graffiti writer. In various interviews, RAMM:ΣLL:ZΣΣ describes the way hip-hop came onto the scene in 1970s New York: while the DJ scratched and spun the archives of black music on the decks, the dancers, aka the breakers, would render those sounds into three dimensions of moving flesh, while the writers would spray new deformations of the alphabet on subway trains.[16] Hip-hop is kind of a sign-war, a battle of what RAMM:ΣLL:ZΣΣ called *slanguage*; it is a way of remaking a world hostile to blackness; it is a production of black space, projected into the future by way of a music that is signifyin' upon the past through sampling and remixing.

These four preliminary theses set the stage for the performative exodus of RZA. I am interested in RZA's tools and strategies to form Wu-Tang, including his inheritance and transformation of Five Percenter theosophy — this is his first strategic flight, as Abbot. His second flight is also strategic — a flight from east coast to west, as RZA sought to survive the onslaught of becoming a black celebrity, in the eye of capitalist spectacle, by becoming Bobby Digital. But first, I want to explicate something of the term "exodus," by connecting it to two figures in the black radical tradition who remain influential to much of hip-hop history: Marcus Garvey and Malcolm X.

Black Star Lines: Exodus to/from the Pharaohs

The black radical tradition has often embraced strategies of *exodus*: of an organized retreat, or strategic withdrawal, from systems of oppression, territories of containment, and white mythologies of racial superiority. The concept of exodus as "engaged withdrawal" has been explicated by Italian Autonomia theorist Paolo Virno as the "founding leave-taking" of a "new Republic".[17] The movement of exodus is a line of flight that withdraws from unequal and pathological conditions of "politics".[18] Exodus is thus a withdrawal *toward* a "restructuring of the world", in Fanon's terms, and not just *from* the world: it actively seeks, in its line of flight, to explore new modes of belonging in an elsewhere/elsewhen. Exodus seeks to restructure the "world" as-such, and not just shift its existing terms.[19]

There have been many movements of exodus in Afrodiasporic history, notably in the politics of Marcus Garvey and Malcolm X. Both figures, I suggest, are pivotal to understanding the formative politics of Afrofuturist hip-hop, and particularly the role of the Nation of Islam, and its esoteric offshoot founded by Clarence 13X, the Nation of Gods and Earths, better known as the Five Percent.

Malcolm X grew up the son of a minister in Garvey's Universal Negro Improvement Association (UNIA); his mother was the secretary of the local chapter. The UNIA set in motion various institutional forms of black separatism, supporting black independent business, religious, and educational institutions. It also raised funds for African-Americans to return "back" to the African continent in an organized exodus, on ships known as the Black Star Liners.[20] What I wish to emphasize here is how the political imagination of the UNIA and the Nation of Islam (NOI) overlap around the theme of exodus. After the collapse of the Black Star Liners, and the deportation of Marcus Garvey from the U.S., the project of exodus became internalized to the territory of the United States, as the NOI agitated for an autonomous, segregated "Negro state". In the late 1950s, as a representative of the Nation second only to Elijah Muhammad, Malcolm X would field questions demanding to know where such a new black republic might be located. In response, Malcolm would often recite the Biblical parable of Exodus, justifying the need for territorial segregation, economic independence and black self-government with theological rhetoric familiar to white and black Christian audiences.[21] In 1961, at a speech at Harvard University, Malcolm identified black nationalism with the Jewish flight from Egypt: "In the Bible, God offered the Pharaoh freedom if he would just let the oppressed people free to go to the land of milk and honey. But the Pharaoh disobeyed, and he was destroyed".[22] The Biblical theme of Exodus is also taken up by Sun Ra in late 1950s Chicago, who seeks not to flee the Pharaoh, but *become* the Pharaoh — though an alien-ated one.[23]

The exodus organized by the UNIA, shaping the political aspirations of the Nation of Islam, can be revisioned through an Afrofuturist lens. Eshun writes that "Jamaican activist Marcus Garvey, 'the Black Moses', named his shipping fleet Black Star Liners, to plug the notions of repatriation, of return to the patria, the fatherland, into that of interplanetary escape".[24] In Afrofuturist exodus, the new republic takes the shape of novel worlds. Restructuring the world means undertaking an off-worlding. Reflecting upon Eshun, Sha Labare has argued for the particularly Afrofuturist inflection of Garvey's conceptualization of exodus, insofar as the return to Africa was "a journey conceived less as a return to the past than as a leap into the future", the "dark continent" not unlike the outer blackness of space:

> Much like "outer space", Garvey's Africa was a paraspace, a heterotopia in which the racist logics of U.S. America were to be reversed and transformed. Rooted in mythic pasts and full of mythic futures, this Africa offered an escape from Slaveship America, an open, unexplored land waiting to fulfill the manifest destiny of the modern black man.[25]

At the same time, Afrofuturist *and* Afrocentric trajectories have embraced the antithetical position contained within Exodus, identifying not with the exiled Jewish people and their forced migration to the Promised Land, but with the authority, mythology, and architecture of the Pharaoh: such is the position of Sun Ra, the return of the ancient alien Pharaoh from Saturn, who Kodwo Eshun, with a penchant for overemphasis, describes as "despotic":

> Sun Ra looks down on humans with the inhuman indifference and impatience of a Plutonian Pharoah. As the composer despot, he breaks not only with gospel tradition but also with Trad future-slave narratives: *Planet of the Apes, Brother From Another Planet, Blade Runner, Alien Nation.* Rather than identify with the replicants, with Taylor from *Planet of the Apes*, Ra is more likely to dispatch blade runners after the Israelites.....[26]

As I discuss elsewhere,[27] Ra transforms the figure of the Pharaoh through an alien becoming, just as he transforms and recapitulates the African American musical tradition of jazz rather than breaking with it.[28] Nonetheless, Ra — among other Afrofuturists such as George Clinton and Parliament, the funk and disco outfit Earth, Wind, & Fire, and the Afro-cyborg Cindi Mayweather aka Janelle Monáe — reinvents the Pharaoh, sampling the pyramidal architectures and Kemetic mythologies of Afrocentrism in a futuristic positioning on the *other side* of Exodus. By repurposing Kemetic mythology, exodus as a strategic withdrawal, erstwhile equated with black nationalism and racialized segregation, is likewise transformed into an ontopolitics. Rather than fleeing the territories of oppression, Afrofuturist exodus undertakes a strategic exodus from the human that in turn remaps the territory — as we will see in RZA, by turning Staten Island into Shaolin.

Afrofuturist exodus abandons the given cartography of the world — its hegemonic myth that it is the only "world" — in order to reimagine it otherwise: to remap a new set of coordinates upon its surface. It is this reimagining, this reinvention, that constitutes the Afrofuturology of Exodus in an elsewhen/elsewhere. With this in mind, I wish to (finally) hand over the mic to The Abbot of the Wu-Tang Clan, the RZA, and his alter-ego, Bobby Digital.

The RZA-rection of Exodus

The stakes of exodus take on new levels when considering the realpolitik of escaping the confines of socioeconomic impoverishment and its policed territories, a.k.a., the "ghetto". Such lines of flight require, as the RZA suggests, an estrangement from the basic codes and conventions of the street, an alien-ation from the surrounds through a reimagining of the territory. It is through this creative estrangement of cartography — a novel black psychogeography — that Wu-Tang Clan transforms Staten Island to Shaolin. At stake here is also a reinvention of *space*: of leveraging the distance between the map and the ghettoized territory by re-visualizing it, re-naming it, signifyin' it otherwise through the "knowledge of self" that underpins the theosophy of the Five Percent.[29]

The RZA is producer and Abbot of the Wu-Tang Clan, an influential, multi-faceted hip-hop crew that has defined an esoteric if not surreal trajectory to "gangsta rap" since their debut LP, *Enter the Wu-Tang (36 Chambers)* (1993).[30] Along with most of the other Wu-Tang members — Method Man, Inspectah Deck, Raekwon, Ghostface Killah, U-God — RZA came up in the projects of Staten Island, New York (GZA, Killah Priest, Masta Killa, and Ol' Dirty Bastard hail from Brooklyn). The narrative I wish to recapitulate here is something of an Afrofuturist Bildungsroman of the RZA, drawn from his two exemplary texts, *The Tao of Wu* and *The Wu-Tang Manual*.[31] I should emphasize the pedagogical nature of these texts: they have been designed as flight manuals for the entrapped and ghetto-confined. They are also self-mythologizations inseparable from what Paul Gilroy describes as the "insatiable machinery of commodification" in which hip-hop is self-reflexively implicated.[32]

Jeff Chang argues that when Wu-Tang came onto the scene in the early 1990s, the music industry was fully engulfed in predatory capitalism, in which "Local hip-hop undergrounds suddenly appeared to be veins of gold waiting to be exploited" and where "[independent labels] were bought up, squeezed out or rolled right over".[33] This exploitation narrative, however, ignores the capitalist agency enacted by RZA (among others including Death Row Records) who founded "hip-hop empires" by consolidating and controlling talent, often through ruthless business practices.[34] In a chapter entitled "Capitalism", RZA details his "Five Year Plan" in which he assumed authoritarian control over Wu-Tang (like Sun Ra over the Arkestra), with full control over all recording contracts, that allowed him to (controversially) assign members to different labels. At the same time, he produced, recorded, and mastered every single Wu-Tang release, with final cut over appearances and content.[35] RZA's autocratic style resonates with the self-made myth of America's corporate deacons. Not surprisingly, then, RZA's ruthless branding and marketing strategy was a success: "today", writes RZA in 2005, "Wu-Tang Corp, as we call it, is linked to at least thirty companies" including apparel, merchandising, comic books, and of course, music, from production to distribution. For RZA, "integrity" coexists with commodification, as this was the *intent to begin with*: "A few years ago I used to say we're going to take this from digital to Disney. . . . but I'm not going to jump at every opportunity. It's got to be within the integrity of the brand".[36]

RZA's narrative is also rags to riches. But what interests me here is not any claim to the RZA as an "outlaw form", nor a celebration of his "marginality", both of which, as Gilroy notes, are "official and routinized".[37] Besides RZA's protean shifts of becoming, what interests me is how his narrative of exodus deterritorializes the "authentic" grounds of the ghetto; how his shape-shifting performs but also deforms the culture of celebrity and masculinity; and how, not in spite of the above branding practices, but rather as constitutive of them, RZA appears thoroughly concerned with achieving spiritual transcendence and enlightenment.

New York, the late 1970s through the '80s. Through kung-fu films, chess, and comics, RZA discovered various philosophies that salvaged him from the routine violence of ghettoized territories. RZA blended superhero aesthetics and technoscience, Taoism, warrior-monk, and kung-fu training principles with chess strategies and Five Percenter "knowledges of self" to shape the MythScience of Wu-Tang Clan. The most extensive of these influences is the Five Percent, or Nation of Gods and Earths, which RZA discovered at age ten. The Five Percent is an offshoot of the Nation of Islam founded in 1964 by Clarence 13X, a student of Malcolm X and the Harlem Mosque, Temple No. 7. RZA's cousin, later known as the GZA, initiated him in the

120 Lessons, the Divine Alphabet, and Supreme Mathematics. At age 11, the RZA says he was the youngest adept known to learn the 120, and he become a teacher in his own right.[38] The 120 is a strict series of questions and answers that communicate the theosophical principles and MythScience of the Five Percent. To be acknowledged in a Parliament — the democratic, leaderless circle of Five Percenters that constitutes both social space and worship — one must reply in exact fashion to any question at any time; some questions and answers are pages long. The Divine Mathematics and Alphabet are a codex for the Five Percent's theistic hermeneutics ("the Supreme"). For our purposes here — as the esoteric detail of this numerico-theomythological system could consume this entire chapter — it is enough to state that the Mathematics describe a hermeneutic system that calculates the numerical value of signifying words. Felicia Miyakawa, a scholar of the Five Percent, describes the Mathematics as "*the key to understanding everything in the universe*".[39] The interpretation I divulge here — as my intent is to communicate the Afrofuturist inflection produced by RZA — follows from the RZA's teaching of the supreme wisdom in *The Wu-Tang Manual*.[40] RZA's schema mostly accords with those found in Five Percenter publications and scholarship.[41]

In the Supreme Mathematics, the numbers 1 through 10 symbolize various principles, just as they correspond, in their combinations, to the 26 letters of the alphabet. Together, this alphanumeric codex allows text to be interpreted in its covert, theistic meanings, just as dates and numbers can be translated into meaningful text. In brief, "The meanings assigned to numerals are as follows: 1 = knowledge; 2 = wisdom; 3 = understanding; 4= culture or freedom; 5 = power or refinement; 6 = equality; 7 = god; 8 = build and destroy; 9 = born; 0 = cipher. Each number also has an extended definition that clarifies the number's significance".[42]

For example, I was born in 1978. 1+9+7+8 = 25 = 2+5 = 7. Seven is "God and perfection. G is also the seventh letter of the alphabet, and for God. The original black man has seven and half ounces of brain, the devil only six ounces. God sees with the seven colors of the rainbow and hears the seven notes on the musical scale".[43] None of this is astrology; for RZA, dates only signify if events occur. The RZA remembers that on June 6, 1983 (06-06) he saw the kung-fung film *The 36th Chamber of Shaolin* (1978). "That was some prophetic numerology — 6, 6, 36 — and the movie had just that kind of impact on me", writes RZA: "It was like something from the Old Testament or a Greek epic. It changed my life, for real, because its wisdom brought my own story alive".[44] In RZA's MythScience, kung-fu films and their mediatized, popular form of Taoism take the place of the canonical texts of Western myth and religion. The combination of the Five Percent and kung-fu is the first destabilization of RZA's territory: the "West" has become perceived through a Five-Percenter hermeneutics of a kung-fu film "East".

Throughout his two books, *The Tao of Wu* and *The Wu-Tang Manual*, the RZA reiterates how the permutations of the number 36 have assumed patternistic significance. Such alphanumeric hermeneutics suggest a way to chart, or at least mathematically symbolize, and thus attempt to interpret, events of transformation that feedback into MythSciences of reinvention. The Supreme also encodes ghettoized territory otherwise: its "projects" are now interpreted through an alternative value system of myths, applied knowledge, principles, and ethical conduct whose totality reshapes what the Five Percenters call "knowledge of self".

The complexity of the Supreme and the demands required by memorizing the 120 outpaced that of his highschool education, says RZA. In this respect, the Supreme challenges stereotypes of black ghetto anti-intellectualism, calling for, in the words of Grant Farred, a rethinking of "what constitutes intellectual articulation".[45] As the RZA writes in *The Tao of Wu*, "If you were poor and black, Mathematics attacked the idea that you were meant to be ignorant, uneducated, blind to the world around you. It exposed the lies that helped people treat your forefathers as animals".[46] On similar terms, Farred argues for a conception of the "black vernacular intellectual", where the vernacular "encodes larger economic and political disenfranchisements" within the "hegemonic discourse".[47]

RZA attributes the Supreme to his survival: it provided him with the discipline to revision the ghettoized territory as Shaolin. But this "self knowledge" of the Five Percent is that of recitation and rote. While its counter-knowledge shifts the ghettoized boundaries of what constitutes black (male) self-identification under the raciology of antiblackness (as gangsta and ghettoized nonsubjects, aka n*ggas), its principles do not permit a self-questioning of its dogmatic tenets. "That's what the lessons did for me", writes RZA. "They gave me guidance, understanding, and freedom. But freedom from yourself? That's often a whole different story".[48]

For RZA, it is kung-fu that unsettled the Supreme as the sole MythScience. Screened in the porn theaters of 42nd street, a slew of '70s-to-'80s era Hong Kong action flicks provided the RZA with attractive myths of redemption and brotherhood, their survival stories overcoming adversity and evil through training, battle, and sacrifice. The values gleaned from kung-fu films would shape the MythScience of the Wu-Tang Clan and its warrior monk emcees.[49] RZA's turn to kung-fu becomes pivotal as an epistemological exodus that exceeded the black-and-white confines of ghettoization. It also replicates a common vector of black vernacular intellectuals, including W.E.B. Du Bois and Malcolm X: that of an "afro-orientalism", in which Asia is fetishized, theorized and/or visited as the site of a companion but alien other in the struggle against antiblackness, precisely *because*, as Bill Mullen explains, "Orientalism . . . fold[s] African Americans and Asian Americans into the same discursive trap of mutual subordination and, more important, separation".[50] RZA's fascination with kung-fu and the legends of the Shaolin Temple and the (actual) Wu-Tang form the infrastructure for the (hip-hop) Wu-Tang Clan: the latter's improper name, lyricism and rhyme, emcee characters and symbols all derive from sampling kung-fu action films. Asian stereotypy, of note, became a vector for black liberation. It is also worth noting that this identification, though commencing in stereotypy, did not remain stereotyped: RZA later became a kung-fu practitioner and student of Taoism, and went on to record the hip-hop soundtrack for the animation series that exemplifies the Afro-Orientalist nexus, *Afro Samurai* (2007).[51]

The third element that RZA envelops in Wu-Tang is chess (also discovered at age eleven). Chess is inscribed in Wu-Tang's lyricism but also as strategy: RZA manipulates his Wu-Tang emcees like pawns; Wu-Tang's corporate moves and its Five-Year Plan are conceptualized as a chess match. Chess also features in the kung-fu film dialogue that RZA samples on *36 Chambers*, where the game allegorizes "Shaolin shadowboxing and the Wu-Tang sword style" ("Bring Da Ruckus") and where "A game of chess is like a sword fight... you must think first before you move" ("Da Mystery of Chessboxin'").[52]

Though by the late '80s all the pieces were in place for Wu-Tang — RZA's cohorts were rapping the kung-fu film dialogues he had popularized by amassing a vast collection of VHS tapes; many of the nascent Clan were Five Percenters and chess players — ghettoized survival tactics (aka "crime") nearly derailed its formation. In the early '90s, RZA nearly became entrenched in the dead-ends of the ghetto:

> I had become dumb. My life had done a zigzag. I was in the right place from ages eleven to sixteen. Then I got involved with women, drugs, and hip-hop in a street way — not just a hobby way where you're having fun at your house, but a street way, with battling, guns, cars, gold cables, and drug dealing.

> This is a man who had enlightened twenty other kids [to the Five Percent]....Now my students were teachers. And here I am — someone who knew the 120 before he was thirteen — here I am acting like a fucking savage? I had to change — change back.[53]

It is at this point that I would like to emphasize the problematic status of "women" in RZA's discourse and the implicit framework of masculinity in the "warrior-monk" narrative, both of which I see as effects of a systemic phalloraciology that structures territories of impoverishment just as it structures heteronormative black identity.[54] RZA's use of "fucking savage" is likewise unreflexive, though it signals the complex stereotypy of a racialized hierarchy that further excludes indigenous peoples. In *How Capitalism Underdeveloped Black America*, Manning Marable writes that "the superexploitation of Black women became a permanent feature in American social and economic life".[55] In his narrative, RZA does not celebrate his explicit accounts of misogyny and sexualized violence, but rather attempts to account and repent for their harm.[56] The warrior-monk that RZA turns to remains phallogocentric; there are no female warrior-monks in Wu-Tang. I will return to the problematic ways in which women are represented in RZA's Bobby Digital persona below.

With all the strategies now in place, and finding himself entrapped in ghettoized violence, the RZA flees the territory and leaves Staten Island, returning once he has transformed his improper name. The act of renaming is a strategy common to African American culture, as well as black nationalism, including the NOI, whose members remove the "slaveholder" last name, replacing it with X and/or an African surname. Of course, there is Sun Ra, who changed his legal birthname from Herman P. Blount to Le Sony'r Ra in 1952.[57] Renaming is amplified under the values of the Supreme, signaling a reinvention of self:

> In the Divine Alphabet, Z stands for Zig-Zag-Zig, which means Knowledge, Wisdom, and Understanding. It's the last letter of the alphabet and represents the final step of consciousness. So finally I just thought of the names as letters, as a title, not just a word. R-Z-A. It stands for Ruler-Knowledge/Wisdom/Understanding Allah.

> In my life, I was zigging. I was going right but I zagged. I zagged and I almost died zagging. So I zigged back. I became the RZA. Rakeem Zig-Zag-Zig Allah. Later, people came to call me the RZA-rector — like I bring people back to life. But that year I found out the truth: The first person you have to resurrect is yourself.[58]

In *The Tao of Wu*, RZA's narrative is punctuated by self-described transformative experiences and reinventions of consciousness. Let me skip ahead to the moments after commercial success. After parting ways with the Clan and his wife in 1997 — after finding international stardom with the successful execution of the Five Year Plan — RZA finds himself locked out of his New Jersey home. He spends the night on the lawn. In a Siddhartha moment, he finds a flower: "And then — *bing!* — it came upon me. Enlightenment. And I was free".[59] Free from the burdens of leading the Wu-Tang — but not from suffering: "In 1997, my life fell apart, my Clan scattered, my girl of six years and I separated. So I moved out to California and became someone else. I became a superhero [Bobby Digital] because that's exactly how it felt".[60]

Enter B.O.B.B.Y. Digital

Bobby Digital is RZA's alter-ego, a black superhero that RZA identifies with Spider-Man, or Wolverine of the X-Men: a superhero with a dark side. Under the guise of Bobby Digital, RZA lived out a celebrity fantasy life in Los Angeles. "Like a superhero, I had two identities. If you saw me at a party, you'd think I was a party animal. But the next morning, I'd be up studying. I was reading Rumi, the philosophies of Marcus Garvey, all books from the Three Initiates — principles of mentalism, correspondence, vibration, polarity, rhythm — studying genetics".[61] Bobby Digital is not, by any

means, simply a solo release nom de plume. In Los Angeles, RZA *becomes* Bobby Digital. He has a suit built for him "like the Dark Knight's — literally invulnerable to .45 bullets and knives".[62] He has the "Black Tank", a bulletproof and bombproof Suburban. He has "a butler almost ready to act as my Kato". Bobby Digital undertakes the kind of Afrofuturist comic book trajectory noted by Mark Dery: Bobby Digital is the living embodiment of a black superhero, a comic book figure come alive that seeks to *transform* hip-hop's ghetto realism.[63]

Like Batman, Digital is a quasi-cyborg, where digital technology is integral to his superhero suit, his futuristic armaments and his secretive transportation. Like Sun Ra, Digital is a "living myth", the transformed embodiment of a MythScience: entirely real, yet entirely fictive. As "real fictions," the ghetto and the superhero are *both* equally fictive, yet entirely real, constructs. The "ghetto" is real, but a construct of sociohistorical and economic forces based on fictive (but entirely real) raciology; and from the reality of the ghetto emerges Bobby Digital, *for real* as a *living myth*.

Greg Tate writes that hip-hop, in its sampling of the musical archive, is "backward-looking and forward-thinking at the same time".[64] Tate's observation situates the activity of chronopolitics to hip-hop, as the musical production of much hip-hop samples the past to remake the future. But Bobby Digital, for all of his technoscience, is also a retrogressive alter-ego that plays in the past. I wish to underscore that RZA is entirely self-critical on this point: Bobby Digital, he writes, is about "reliving a hip-hop past that got sidelined when I became the RZA . . . someone I created as an escape from the pressures of being the RZA — someone who could rap, act, and dress in a way that the RZA couldn't".[65] Moving to Los Angeles and spending his nights *being* Bobby Digital on the celebrity club circuit, RZA indulges in all the fantasies his warrior-monk self could not. His language, dress, and style all change. He only answers to "Bobby". What is interesting about this indulgence in celebrity culture, however, is that RZA did not perform the RZA as a celebrity. Rather, RZA crafted a MythScience to play the celebrity. This was not particularly in his best interests: in the late 1990s, the "RZA" brand would have had greater name recognition than his re-branding as Bobby Digital. Nor does the content of the re-brand correspond to its celebrity performance: Bobby Digital is a celebrity myth that is also a black super hero with a secret agenda of liberating the ghetto.

Bobby Digital's ghetto liberation is staged in its domestic violence as much as its technoscience. With Bobby Digital, the RZA weaves a complex and at times fraught narrative around masculinity and femininity — but also what constitutes domesticity. The album *Bobby Digital In Stereo* (1998) is replete with skits and lyrics that celebrate the superhero's black masculine virility. But on the track "Domestic Violence",[66] Bobby is finally told off by his coterie of female lovers: "Your rings ain't shit, your piece ain't shit, Bobby you ain't shit...". This continues on for a full minute. Eventually Bobby steps in, and threatens to "step in and slap dicks in your mouth". Bobby's emcee flow descends into a bickering brawl with his female entourage, before he launches into another (nicely rhymed) rant where he states that "he'd rather beat my beat" than keep his "hoes". The track ends with a bitter (though humorous) quarrel, before closing with a full minute of instrumental beats. The comparative silence of the rhythm allows the significance of the performance to sink in. "Domestic Violence" is a complex work that stages black masculinist stereotypes of both genders, allowing a familiar pattern of heterosexist quarrel to play itself out. Neither party has the last word. Rather, it stages the sorrowful play of domestic tragedy that afflicts even celebrity superheroes, and its refusal to depict an idealized relationship also undermines any idolization of RZA's Bobby Digital persona, just as it — quite possibly — memorializes the personal events that drove RZA to Los Angeles.

Becoming Bobby Digital in Los Angeles, however, lead to what RZA describes as the first of two "lessons". For RZA, these are lessons about finitude, from the cosmos.

In 2000, RZA's mother dies: "That year, 2000, I learned how much superpowers cost you, what you lose when you let your ego or your alter ego run things".[67] The second lesson is the death, at RZA's studio, of Ol' Dirty Bastard — like GZA, one of RZA's cousins — from an accidental overdose of cocaine and tramadol in 2004, just two days shy of his 36th birthday (again: 36). After these two "fatal" lessons, "I was depressed for years. I didn't do much, didn't see many people, mostly stayed in the crib".[68]

This time the RZA's resurrection is through love, when he meets his new partner and muse. Reflecting upon his personal trajectory, the RZA compares his own self-transformations to those of Malcolm X: "History is full of bad men who redeem themselves to become great. Malcolm X — he came up chasing white women and sniffing cocaine, but found Allah and changed. But what about people who have knowledge and go *back* to doing wrong?"[69] It is this last question that preoccupies the RZA, and is symbolized in the Zig-Zag-Zig of his name, the letter symbol "Z" that traces the transformative path of his life — in his own words, the "steps of consciousness" that do not always ascend. The Zig-Zag-Zig names an "alter-destiny", or *destinerration* inherent to becoming: that the outcome of any becoming cannot be pre-programmed from the start.[70]

In many respects, and compared to the belligerence of *bling* that pervades some hip-hop, RZA's self-mythos remains conspicuously humble.[71] Granted that such "humility" encodes patriarchy and sexism in its supposed neutrality, RZA's narrative attempts to come to terms with the violence, machismo, criminality, and misogyny inherent to stereotypes of black masculinity. This includes the staging but also becoming of stereotypical black masculinity in Bobby Digital. Paraphrasing Paul Gilroy's assessment of Snoop Dogg, I would suggest that RZA's "work exceeds the masculinist erasure of the sexual agency of black women [and of women in general] that it undoubtedly contains".[72] These excesses are both intentional and unintentional to RZA's narrative. What RZA seeks to control unseats him. He struggles with what he calls these "lessons".

Since Digital, RZA's becoming has undertaken a trajectory where, instead of continuing to *reprazent* the militancy of a "Protect Ya' Neck" masculinity championed by the early Wu-Tang, RZA has turned to a discourse that practices what bell hooks calls "engagement with the practice of love".[73] This love — though perhaps not as "full-on" as hooks would like — is coordinated through multiple axes of what hooks calls "self-actualization" — chess, kung-fu, Taoism, the Five Percent and music — where "we must recognize love as the transformative practice that will free our minds and bodies".[74] RZA emphasizes that the transformative role of love has saved him from depression.

Unlike other Afrofuturists, RZA is not an alien. He is, however, a warrior monk of Shaolin. RZA as a warrior-monk is no hyperbole. He went on to study under Master Shifu Shi Yan Ming, Founder and Abbot of the USA Shaolin Temple. The two met in 1995 at a release party for GZA's *Legend of the Liquid Sword*. "Before I met him", writes Ming, "I mostly listened to Buddhist music".[75] It is this admixture of transcultural influences that registers the Wu-Tang Clan as an Afrofuturist endeavor: it overlays heterogeneous timelines in a radical transformation of sociogeography. Its membership initiates collective becomings. Kung-fu is sampled just like the archives of funk and jazz. The world is *named* differently by the Wu: it is restructured otherwise through an inventive hermeneutic drawn from a combinatory of influences. With Wu, the "ghetto" has been deracinated, estranged, distanciated, through the undertaking of an Afrofuturist exodus. The Shaolin of Wu has replaced it. This is not to uncritically appraise it. Street life is warrior-monk training, and (as Wu-Tang recite) "only the few will survive".

> I *am* from that era in hip-hop, the era of violence and attitude. I helped found that shit, because that's how I felt at the time. I don't repudiate it. But at the same time, all that aggressive, ignorant, nigga-ghetto shit isn't naturally me. It was a product of history and my environment.[76]

The ghetto is genetic programming. How does one overcome the racialization of white mythology? As Bobby Digital, the RZA is supremely interested in genetics as the code of the naturalized ghetto. Becoming-digital means becoming genetic, becoming remixable: tuning into digital signals that clear up the "environment" and allow one to revision and remap the territory. The *digital* is Supreme Mathematics — the codex for reading the genetic programming of the ghetto one has been born into.

In his unreleased "amateur film" *Bobby Digital In Stereo*, Bobby Digital strives to end gang violence. He wants to distribute weapons, but there's some crooked police that won't let the static die because there's too much money in drugs and guns in the ghetto and they force Bobby underground.

Underground, he has a laboratory where he makes this serum called the "honey serum", which he used to make honey-dipped blunts. And when he hits one, it transforms him, opens up his consciousness.[77]

The theme of the "underground" — a metaphor for the obscure, the secret, the hidden-in-plain-sight — is literalized in Bobby Digital's laboratory. The laboratory is reminiscent of Ralph Ellison's speculative novel *The Invisible Man* (1947),[78] in which the protagonist hides underground, in the basement of a skyscraper, blinded by lights, seeking similar changes in perception by smoking a blunt laced with the jazz of Louis Armstrong. Through such processes of cognitive estrangement, the Invisible Man is also seeking to change the perceptual coordinates by which the political takes shape. He too has been driven underground by white forces of industry and politics who have tried to program his blackness for their own ends. The underground allegorizes the organized exodus of the Underground Railroad and metaphorizes cultural authenticity. But as a subterranean invention of *place*, it suggests that Afrofuturism need not always look to the stars for offworld epistemologies. In the film, Bobby Digital *becomes* digital: "He has transformed himself", writes RZA, through a computer experiment in his underground laboratory. The result is that "he can travel through digital signals":[79]

When you become digital, you become digits — pure Mathematics. So to be digital means to see things clearly, for what they are and not what they appear to be. For Bobby Digital, man is like an antenna; and we walk on too much concrete to stay grounded. So this breaks our frequency. This is also a lot like some understandings of chi, the way some kung fu teaches you to stay grounded for more power.

So Bobby Digital is about what molded me: comic books, video games, the arcade scene, breakdancing, hip-hop clothes, MCing, DJing, human beatboxing, graffiti plus Mathematics and the gods. That's hip-hop to me.[80]

What RZA and the Wu-Tang Clan demonstrate is that "ghetto realism" has always been a fiction — a real fantasy programmed by forces of racial capitalism — and as such, can be deprogrammed through the Afrofuturist flow of hip-hop.

Acknowledgement

Much thanks to Roy Christopher for the spot, and ZiggZaggerZ for the spit.

Notes

1. Rollefson, J. Griffiths. "The 'Robot Voodoo Power' Thesis: Afrofuturism and Anti-Anti-essentialism From Sun Ra to Kool Keith," *Black Music Research* 28, no. 1, 2008, 86. Though Rollefson writes that "the stereotyped vision of Afro-Caribbean voodoo stands in as a signifier of blackness, the robot stands as a similarly stable symbol of whiteness" (86), it is worth pointing out that the word robot, coined by the brother of science fiction author Karel Čapek in *Rossum's Universal Robots* [1920], was already a metaphor for the (African American) slave.

2. Miller, Paul D. *Rhythm Science*, Cambridge: Mediawork / MIT Press, 2004.

3. "Black to the Future: Interviews With Samuel R. Delany, Greg Tate, and Tricia Rose," in *Flame Wars: The Discourse of Cyberculture,* ed. Dery , Mark, Durham: Duke University Press, 1994, 179—222.

4. See Anderson, Reynaldo and Jones, Charles E. "Introduction: The Rise of Astro-Blackness," in *Afrofuturism 2.0: The Rise of Astro-Blackness,* ed. Reynaldo Anderson, and Charles E. Jones, New York: Lexington, 2015, vii—xviii.

5. See Eshun, Kodwo. "Further Considerations of Afrofuturism," *Boogie Down Predictions.* Ed. Roy Christopher. London: Strange Attractor Press, 2022: 252-64.

6. Žižek, Slavoj. *The Parallax View,* Cambridge: MIT Press, 2006.

7. Eshun, Kodwo. *More Brilliant Than the Sun: Adventures in Sonic Fiction,* London: Quartet, 1999.

8. van Veen, tobias c. "Destination Saturn: Sun Ra's Utopias in the Art of Stacey Robinson," *TOPIA: Canadian Journal of Cultural Studies* 139, no. 1, 2018: 145—66.

9. Eshun, *More Brilliant Than the Sun,* A[193].

10. Eshun, *More Brilliant Than the Sun,* 00[-001].

11. Weheliye, Alexander G.. *Habeas Viscus: Racializing Assemblages, Biopolitics, and Black Feminist Theories of the Human,* Durham: Duke University Press, 2014.

12. See van Veen, tobias c. "The Armageddon Effect: Afrofuturism and the Chronopolitics of Alien Nation," in *Afrofuturism 2.0: The Rise of Astro-Blackness,* ed. Reynaldo Anderson and Charles E. Jones, New York: Lexington Books, 2016, 63—90.

13. Mudede, Charles "The Turntable," in *Life in the Wires,* ed. Arthur & Marilouise Kroker, Victoria: CTheory Books, 2004, 70—8.

14. Ahmed, Sara. *Queer Phenomenology: Orientations, Objects, Others,* Durham: Duke University Press, 2006.

15. Goodman, Steve. *Sonic Warfare,* Cambridge: MIT Press, 2010. Julian Henriques, *Sonic Bodies: Reggae Sound Systems, Performance Techniques and Ways of Knowing,* New York: Continuum, 2011.

16. See, for example, the limited edition 12" on Mo'Wax: "Gothic Futurism: RAMM:ΣLL:ZΣΣ Talks Iconoclastic Panzerism, Wind, Tunnels, and Explosion Disco With Ed Gill, 1995."

17. Virno, Paolo. "Virtuosity and Revolution: The Political Theory of Exodus," in *Radical Thought in Italy,* ed. Virno, Paolo and Hardt, Michael. Minneapolis: University of Minnesota Press, 1996, 197.

18. Autonomia was an Italian, "cultural, post-Marxist, left-wing political movement" that operated from

the 1970s through the '80s, opposed "work ethics and hierarchy as much as exclusive ideological rigidity", inventing "their own forms of social 'war-fair' — pranks, squats, collective reappropriations (pilfering), self-reductions (rent, electricity, etc.), pirate radios, sign tinkering" Sylvère Lotringer, "In the Shadow of the Red Brigades," in *Autonomia: Post-Political Politics*, ed. Lotringer, Sylvère and Marazzi, Christian. Los Angeles: Semiotext(e), 2007, v.

19. I have explored these relationships in regards to autonomous zones of rave culture in "Technics, Precarity and Exodus in Rave Culture," *Dancecult: Journal of Electronic Dance Music Culture* 1, no. 2, 2010.

20. See Marable, Manning. *Malcolm X: A Life of Reinvention*, New York: Penguin, 2011.

21. Cowan, Paul S., "Malcolm X Demands States for Negroes, Calls Token Integration "mere Pacifier"." *The Harvard Crimson*, March 25 1961.

22. Ibid.

23. Szwed, John F. *Space is the Place: The Lives and Times of Sun Ra*, New York: De Capo Press, 1998.

24. Eshun, *More Brilliant Than the Sun*, 09[156].

25. LaBare, Sha. "Farfetchings: On and in the Sf Mode," diss., University of California, Santa Cruz, 2010, 25.

26. Eshun, *More Brilliant Than the Sun*, 09[155].

27. van Veen, tobias c. "Destination Saturn: Sun Ra's Utopias in the Art of Stacey Robinson," *TOPIA: Canadian Journal of Cultural Studies* 139, no. 1, 2018, 145—66.

28. Contrary to Eshun's polemic, Ra represents far less a "break" from African American soul than Eshun suggests. Ra's music does not dispel the jazz tradition; in his phonebook-sized playbook, Ra transcribed the jazz standards of his Chicago mentors, including the big band compositions of his mentor, "the father of swing", Fletcher Henderson (1897—1952). As *New York Times* critic John Wilson describes of an Arkestra appearance at Slug's, the East Village jazz tavern, in 1968: "A Sun Ra composition that offers twittering bird calls rubbed from a pair of Chinese tiddies, a vast percussive orchestral hullabaloo of grunts and squawks and a hot solo on a ram's horn will dissolve into Fletcher Henderson's arrangement of 'King Porter's Stomp'" (Szwed, *Space is the Place*, 226). So though Ra is the Pharaoh to Exodus, this identification with the apparent despot suggests a more complex inheritance of black tradition that transforms the figure of the Pharaoh itself.

29. There is a psychogeographical strategy at work in Wu Tang's transformation of Staten Island to Shaolin that bears resemblance to the Temporary Autonomous Zone (TAZ) outlined by Hakim Bey, "a guerilla operation which liberates an area (of land, of time, of imagination) and then dissolves itself to re-form elsewhere/elsewhen" (Hakim Bey, *T.A.Z.: The Temporary Autonomous Zone, Ontological Anarchy, Poetic Terrorism* (Brooklyn: Autonomedia, 1991), 101). However unlike Bey's anarchotopia, Wu-Tang is thoroughly enmeshed with mediation, mediatization, and commodification as constitutive of its dissemination of counter-reality signs — which makes it all the more interesting compared to Bey's desire for "disappearance". Wu-Tang's psychotopology of Shaolin is closer to the idea of *"always occupying an autonomous zone"* Bey, *T.A.Z.*,124, in which its perpetual re-occupation is undertaken through the disseminated Wu-MythSciences of hip-hop music (in the TAZ, says Bey, "Music Is An Organizational Principle").

30. Influential because the Wu-Tang Clan was produced and created solely by its members, without studio involvement or record-label marketing. Influential because *36 Chambers* consists of a dense weaving of knowledges interacting at levels that range far beyond that of representational lyricism. While Five Percenter knowledge, chess, and kung-fu mix in the emcee flow, other knowledges are embedded within the LP's production: *36 Chambers* was made for $36,000. The 36th chamber is the highest level of the

Shaolin warrior monk, and signifies his undefeatability. In the film *Shaolin and Wu Tang* [1983], the Wu-Tang achieve the 36th level only to be cast out by the Shaolin. Of note, there are 36 squares on a chessboard. In Divine Mathematics, 3+6=9, which is Born. You add 1 (Knowledge) and return to 10, 1+0, which is the Knowledge and the Cipher, the recursive loop of the zero, the circle. "Because what happens when you get to that ten? You're actually on the left side of that zero. You, one, are on the left side of that zero. Cipher is a zero. A circle" (The RZA, *The Tao of Wu*, New York: Riverhead Books, 2009, 45).

31. RZA, *The Tao of Wu*; The RZA, *The Wu-Tang Manual*, New York: Penguin, 2005.

32. Gilroy, Paul. *Between Camps: Nations, Cultures and the Allure of Race*, London: Routledge, 2004, 179.

33. Chang, Jeff. *Can't Stop Won't Stop: A History of the Hip-Hop Generation*, New York: St. Martin's Press, 2005, 443.

34. Ruthless to the point of routine violence and occasional murder, as in the case between the East/West hip-hop rivalry. Unlike Dr. Dre and Suga Knight's Death Row and Sean Comb's Bad Boy Records, Wu-Tang remained relatively uninvolved in such rivalries and emerged mostly unscathed. For a concerted attempt to think past the ghettoized territories of hip-hop, see M.K. Asante, Jr.'s *It's Bigger Than Hip-Hop*, New York: St. Martin's Press, 2008.

35. RZA, *The Wu-Tang Manual*, 71—84.

36. RZA, *The Wu-Tang Manual*, 82. Wu-Tang Clan could be read as articulating Grant Farred's "black vernacular intellectual" with ghetto capitalism: "In the vernacular conception of politics, popular culture constitutes a singular practice. It represents that mode in which the political and the popular conjoin identificatory pleasure with ideological resistance" (In *What's My Name: Black Vernacular Intellectuals*, Minneapolis: University of Minnesota Press, 2003, 1).

37. Gilroy, *Between Camps*, 180.

38. RZA, *The Tao of Wu*, 31.

39. Felicia Miyakawa, "Receiving, Embodying, and Sharing 'Divine Wisdom': Women in the Nation of Gods and Earths," in *Women and New and Africana Religions*, ed. Lillian Ashcraft-Easton, Darnise Martin, and Oyeronke Olademo, Santa Barbara: Praeger, 2009, 31.

40. RZA, *The Wu-Tang Manual*.

41. For example, in various personal narratives of the Five-Percenter produced book of self-knowledge, *Knowledge of Self: A Collection of Wisdom on the Science of Everything in Life*, Atlanta: Supreme Design, 2010). See also Miyakawa's *Five Percenter Rap*, Bloomington: Indiana University Press, 2005, and Knight's *The Five Percenters*, London: Oneworld Publications, 2013, both of which discuss the Five Percent in relation to hip-hop. Miyakawa is specifically attentive to the gendering roles of "gods" (men) and "earths" (women), where women are expected to undertake housemaking duties while men "provide"; however, Miyakawa argues that "earths have found creative ways to transcend their proscribed familial roles so as to become active voices in broader local, regional, national, and even global communities" Miyakawa, "Receiving, Embodying, and Sharing," 30. For an account of the Five Percent in the popular press concerning a 2003 Federal District ruling that guaranteed Five Percenters the right to practice their beliefs in prison, see David F. Smydra, "The Five-Percent Rap." *Boston.com* December 21, 2003: accessed December 6 2009, http://www.boston.com/news/globe/ideas/articles/2003/12/21/the_five_percent_rap/.

42. Miyakawa, "Receiving, Embodying, and Sharing," 31.

43. RZA, *The Wu-Tang Manual*, 45. As for the devil, this is the white man in strict interpretations; or "the 10% who have knowledge but intentionally keep the rest ignorant" (*The Wu-Tang Manual*, 44) — the

interpretation that both myself and (at least it appears today) RZA favor. Of note, the Five Percent assessment of humanity bears some resemblance to Occupy's mantra of "We are the 99%", save that it divides society along different lines: only five percent will live a righteous life; eighty-five percent "are the mentally deaf and blind" (43), and the ten percent more-or-less corresponds to Occupy's 1% of elite capitalists hoarding much of the world's wealth. In some respects, the Five Percent sociomathematics better accounts for the destructive force of capitalist ideology, though it doesn't offer much hope in educating or revolutionizing the 85%.

44. RZA, *The Tao of Wu*, 52.

45. Farred, *What's My Name: Black Vernacular Intellectuals*, 3.

46. RZA, *The Tao of Wu*, 40.

47. Farred, *What's My Name: Black Vernacular Intellectuals*, 17, 22.

48. RZA, *The Tao of Wu*, 41.

49. The RZA in particular mentions *The 36th Chamber of Shaolin* [1978] — the Blu-Ray reissue even features commentary by RZA — and *Shaolin and Wu Tang* [1983] as two of the most influential.

50. Mullen, Bill. *Afro-Orientalism*, Minneapolis: University of Minnesota Press, 2004, xv.

51. See Brickler IV, Alexander Dumas J. "Black Mecha is Built for This: Black Masculine Identity in *Firedance and Afrosamurai*," *TOPIA: Canadian Journal of Cultural Studies* 39, no. 2 (2018), 70—88.

52. Wu-Tang's music video for "Mystery" takes place on a giant chessboard.

53. RZA, *The Tao of Wu*, 94.

54. Marable notes how, since "the dawn of slave trade until today, U.S. capitalism was both racist and deeply sexist" (*How Capitalism Underdeveloped Black America: Problems in Race, Political Economy and Society*, Boston: South End Press, 1983, 70). I repeat Marable's imperative that "no road toward the ultimate emancipation of the [global] working class exists outside of a concomitant struggle, in theory and in practice, to destroy every vestige of sexual oppression" (103) — not just "within the Black community" but without.

55. Marable, *How Capitalism Underdeveloped Black America*, 70.

56. In itself problematic for its public confessionalism that implicitly celebrates earlier excesses while seeking later apologia. Nonetheless — RZA's text (especially *The Tao of Wu*) is riddled with slippages, regrets, and fantasies that undermine the cool exterior of his brand. Intentional or not, they suggest a complex character whose text ought to be treated with gravitas and not dismissed as brand marketing (even though it inevitably is: Copyright RZA Productions). Snoop Dogg, in his "reincarnation" as Rastafari Snoop Lion, has also tried to remake himself as a Jah-warrior-monk, but with less success due to ongoing disputes over his Jah-thenticity, notably with Bunny Wailer (see the fascinating VICE film, *Reincarnated* [2012]).

57. Szwed, *Space is the Place*, 80—2.

58. RZA, *The Tao of Wu*, 94-95.

59. RZA, *The Tao of Wu*, 136.

60. RZA, *The Tao of Wu*, 156.

61. RZA, *The Tao of Wu*, 158. Another animalia: the party-animal, where the animal is alter-ego'ed. RZA's Bobby Digital is his becoming-animal, his Snoop Dogg moment, where he is permitted to become the dirty dog west coast stereotype his warrior-monk self otherwise denies.

62. RZA, *The Tao of Wu*, 165.

63. Dery, "Black to the Future."

64. In Dery, "Black to the Future," 211.

65. RZA, *The Tao of Wu*, 165.

66. And perhaps parodying, in its own way, the domestic troubles of Spider-Man or Superman.

67. RZA, *The Tao of Wu*, 164—65. Or rather, RZA's alter-alter-ego.

68. RZA, *The Tao of Wu*, 185. The word-association of "the crib" with "the ghetto" suggests a complex maternalism of the sign, as a womb that severs contact with the exterior "world". Its inside/outside dichotomy is structured through a phallogocentric discourse.

69. RZA, *The Tao of Wu*, 157. Again: the association of (white) women with drugs, of woman as drug.

70. The term "destinerration" arrives by way of Jacques Derrida, as "*destinerring* of missive", of that which is never in its proper place (the letter, desire, lack, presence, *destiny*) ("'Eating Well', Or the Calculation of the Subject," in *Points...*, ed. Elisabeth Weber (Stanford: Stanford University Press, 1995), 260).

71. Conspicuous, granted the violence in which RZA and his Clan were enmeshed. Jeff Chang recounts how *The Source* blacklisted Wu-Tang after Masta Killa punched one of its journalists (*Can't Stop Won't Stop*, 427).

72. Gilroy, *Between Camps*, 204.

73. hooks, bell. *Writing Beyond Race: Living Theory and Practice* (New York: Routledge, 2013), 194.

74. hooks, *Writing Beyond Race*, 194. There is a bookish intellectuality to RZA that defies masculinist stereotypes of blackness that see the latter as wholly subsumed under figures of athleticized and eroticized, but intellectually deficient, bodies (see Gilroy, Between Camps). Nor does RZA satisfy the stereotype of the "AfroGeek", in a manner reminiscent of Steve Urkel.

75. RZA, *The Tao of Wu*, vii.

76. RZA, *The Tao of Wu*, 192.

77. RZA, *The Wu-Tang Manual*, 90.

78. Ralph Ellison's *Invisible Man* (1947) is "a literature predicated on both realist and speculative modes of fiction" (Lisa Yaszek, "An Afrofuturist Reading of Ralph Ellison's *Invisible Man*," *Rethinking History* 9, no. 2/3 (2005), 298). Ellison says in the introduction to the thirty-year anniversary edition that *Invisible Man*, as "a piece of science fiction is the last thing I expected to write" (in Yaszek, "An Afrofuturist Reading of Ralph Ellison's *Invisible Man*," 298).

79. RZA, *The Wu-Tang Manual*, 90.

80. RZA, *The Wu-Tang Manual*, 90-91.

Constructing a Theory and Practice of
Black Quantum Futurism, Pt. 1
Rasheedah Phillips

Introduction

Black Quantum Futurism (BQF) is a new approach to living and experiencing reality by way of the manipulation of space-time in order to see into possible futures and/or collapse space-time into a desired future in order to bring about that future's reality. This vision and practice derives its facets, tenets, and qualities from quantum physics, futurist traditions, and Black/African cultural traditions of consciousness, time, and space. At the point where these three traditions collide exists a creative plane that allows for the ability of African-descended people to actually see "into," create, or choose the impending future. From a multiplicity of possible futures, a practice of BQF allows a visionary to see into the future with clarity, seize upon a vision of one particular future of your choosing, alter, shift, or shape it, then collapse it into your existing reality. It is the inheritance of a BQF Creative practitioner to manipulate time, see into the future, and bring that future about.

Why BQF over the present state of reality? Because a linear mode of time, which dominates time consciousness in Western society, does not allow access to information about the future and only limited information about the past. The ways in which we are situated in time come to be reflected in how we think about, talk about, and conceptualize the community, world, and universe around us. In a linear conception of time, which is built into our language, behavior, and thought, the past is fixed and the future is inaccessible until it passes through the present. The present moment is fleeting, but ever-present. Time's asymmetrical, uni-directional quality, however, is not an inherent or a priori feature of nature. It only appears this way because we have learned to order and make sense of the world this way.

BQF is a new experience of time consciousness that binds modern day physics, ancient African time consciousness, and conceptual notions of futurism. Through Black Quantum Futurism we can increase the "knowability" of the future and the past by treating both modes of time as formally equivalent. This practice develops foresight and hindsight by studying features of time, sources of change, rhythms and patterns in larger social patterns, as well as patterns in our personal spheres of experience in order to map out our Black Quantum Futures. Time is change, and to see into the future is merely to anticipate what changes will occur, and what patterns will re-occur. BQF Creatives work to consciously subvert the strict chronological hierarchal characteristic of linear time.

BQF Definitions and Quantum Correspondence

The abilities of a BQF Creative are rooted in established quantum physics as well as practices inherent to Black and African cultural traditions, both ancient and modern. A theory and practice of Black Quantum Futurism alters the established order and informs the way we define the world. The language of the theory is thus guided by the phenomenon of Blackness, futurism, and quantum physics, allowing for a cyclical, dynamic process of each term defining and incorporating itself into the other term.

The term "Black" as used in Black Quantum Futurism is not only referring to skin pigmentation, race, lineage, and cultural identity. The concept of "Black" in BQF encompasses each of those complicated phenomena, but it is also referring to the Blackness that permeates deep space, what is commonly known as "dark matter." It encompasses the Blackness or darkness that permeates mental space and inner space. It refers to the light absorbing darkness of melanin, and the speed of darkness which surpasses that of light by not needing to move at all.

The word "future" as used throughout this essay does not rely on a specified "distance," if you will, into the future; the future is relative, an ever-forward moving point, and can be as spaced out or as close as one chooses to define it (i.e., the next second, the next day, and the next decade). Before we lived through yesterday and found ourselves in today, the future was today. Most people are averse to or simply unable to form any significant connection to their far, or even near future selves because they believe that the future, near or far, has no bearing upon their present actions. However, this privileged point of the present must be disavowed of this notion. The truth is, the future, both near and far, is currently impacting upon your present, now, currently reaching back from its position to meet you and create your present experience of a now.

The term "time" as used throughout this essay should be treated as consisting of multiple dimensions, not only the mechanical, clock time, or other classic and historic measures of time. In a book called *Space, Time, and Medicine*, Dr. Larry Dossey highlights the four dimensions of time experience as being (1) the present, short-term time (which consists of (a) the perception of short intervals and (b) rhythm or timing); (2) a sense of duration (which consists of (a) a sense of the past and (b) long term memory); (3) temporal perspective (which is the philosophical, social, cultural constructions of the world and their effects on the interpretation of time experience) and (4) simultaneity and succession. Time as incorporated into BQF theory and practice utilizes and manipulates all four dimensions of time as outlined by Dossey.

"Futurism," alternatively known as futurology and future studies, refers to the act of theorizing or envisioning possible, probable, and preferable future(s). Much in the way that historical studies seek to tell stories of the past (or some approximation to the past, as experienced by a privileged few), futurism attempts to not only envision what is to come, but to understand what about the world is likely to continue, and what about the world could plausibly change. Futurism seeks a systematic and pattern-based understanding of past and present, and to determine the likelihood of future events and trends. The most relevant practice and theory of futurism for the purposes of BQF Theory and Practice is Afrofuturism. Afrofuturistic concepts of sci-fi, fantasy, myth, and speculation bind both the past and future, delivering them to a Now in visual, literary, musical terms (and any other mode of expression that one sees fit to attach the Afrofuturistic lens to). Afrofuturism is visionary and retrospective and current all at once, in that it recognizes that time cycles, spirals, or can be experienced in many other shapes, and at varying rates.

These varying time cycles can be attributed to the notion of the African unconscious, which apprehends rhythms and pattern repetition as intrinsic to nature. The same rhythms that order the stars and planets, are the same rhythms that regulate heartbeat, breathing, and blood flow. Perception of these patterns and intrinsic, harmonious ordering principles in nature led to the world's first calendars, zodiacs, and mathematics, created by ancient African civilizations.

The quantum aspect of BQF incorporates quantum physics, the branch of physics which studies the behavior of matter and energy at the atomic and molecular ("micro") levels of existence. The theory provides a mathematical description for some of the "strange" behaviors and interactions that physical phenomena at this level exhibit, such as wave-particle duality (the ability of light to act as both a wave and a particle), quantum superposition, and has played a significant role in the development of many modern technologies. In the realm of quantum physics, observing something actually influences the physical processes taking place.

A cursory glance at popular science websites such as phys.org and iflscience.com shows that much of the research and developments in science and technology these days are being done in the field of quantum physics, while use of the term "quantum" is being applied in pop culture and colloquial language to characteristics like efficiency and sharpness, such as the quantum battery and quantum razor. This is indicative of our need as a society and global culture to begin incorporating quantum reasoning and principles into our everyday language and lives.

Quantum physics has many parallels with ancient African traditions of time, space, and consciousness; in fact, ancient African traditions of timekeeping, cosmology, and spirituality have always encompassed and anticipated the principles of quantum physics. A chart on page 317 roughly outlines the correspondence between quantum physics, African spiritual and consciousness principles, and collective reality experiences.

BQF Modes and Principles of Practice

BQF provides a framework for the ability to seize upon a vision of a future and collapse it into your existing reality. BQF Creatives believe that the future can alter the present, and the present can alter the past through three modes of practice:

Future visioning — Through this mode of practice you increase the "knowability" of the future by being able to see it with more visual clarity than normal. This mode involves little to no deviation of the future, just increased accuracy in visualizing it. With future visioning, you continue to live out the vision of the future already set, choosing the path of least resistance; however, you know with a greater degree of sensory certainty just how that future will unfold.

Future altering — This mode of practice involves a narrow deviation from the present reality, using what is already available and statistically probable in order to *choose* the future from a small subset of probable futures.

Future manifestation — Future manifestation involves the greatest degree of creativity, allowing the practitioner to build the future up step by step, piece by piece.

One of the essential qualities of BQF allowing for future visioning, altering, and manifestation is the phenomenon of "retrocausality," or backwards causation where the effect precedes the cause. An example of retrocausality in quantum physics is an entangled particle sending a wave backward in time to the moment when the entangled pair was created. The signal is not moving faster than the speed of light; instead, it is retracing the first particle's path through space-time and arriving back at the point where the two particles were first emitted. The wave is interacting with the second particle without violating relativity. Under this principle, the present state of the particle depends on both the future and the past measurement. Under a theory of retrocausal time, humanity has reached back to create the very conditions that govern our present universe.

...if we knew how a tree contracted into a seed, then we could predict the future. This is like saying that if we can understand the retrograde process of development then we can predict the future....The future is always present as a seed, so if I know how a tree contracts to a seed than I can also predict how the tree will develop from the seed. If we know the kernel point of a situation we can predict its consequences.
— Marie-Louise von Franz

In my opinion, we do not see backwards causation in action, just as we don't actually physically see the present moving into the future, or the present passing away into the past. Our real sense of time passing is based on changes in our environment. In much the same way, backwards causation/retrocausality is not simply the exact temporal reverse of the action or experience. It is not simply forward causation rendered backwards. Retrocausality in the real world would not look like pressing rewind on a movie and seeing the action go backwards in the exact opposite of the action in forward motion. Retrocausality in action looks more like a rearrangement or reassignment of causation with macro events and macro details and not an exact reversal of minute details and interactions.

Mirroring the principle of retrocausality, the creative futures activated from a BQF perspective automatically reach back to redefine the present and past. A BQF Creative exploits the fact that the future can alter the present and the present can alter the past. Cause is not presupposed or inferred. When a possible future is envisioned, foreseen, or chosen by a BQF Creative, that future will instantaneously reshape its relationship to the past. In quantum physics, the instantaneous reshaping corresponds to the principle of quantum entanglement. What changes in the future will be required to arrive at a present or a past state? What changes in the far future will be required to manifest a near future state?

With retrocausality, we work backward from the future to the past, which requires purpose and finality, where the purpose of any occurrence or interaction is to affect the future state. BQF Creatives reach in before the moment/nanosecond of collapse when future reaches back to blend into the present. African traditions of time mirror this principal precisely. In African time, time flows backwards toward you from the future. Some African religious systems also incorporate notions of retrocausality, where, for example, an Orisha or Loa emerges from a higher state of consciousness and reaches back or down into local reality.

The concept of recurrence is another essential characteristic of BQF which forms the foundation for the three modes of practice. Here too, we see that African traditions of time have always incorporated a notion of recurrence and cycles, which modern day science is only now starting to recognize as deeply imbedded throughout the known universe and in quantum phenomenon. Physicist Paul Kamerrer noted that "the recurrence of identical or similar data in contiguous areas of space or time is a simple empirical fact which has to be accepted and which cannot be explained by coincidence — or rather, which makes coincidence rule to such an extent that the concept of coincidence is itself negated." BQF takes advantage of this universal rule by deeply observing and analyzing the recurrence of patterns, mapping those patterns, then using them to forecast or backcast future and past phenomena.

The interweaving pattern of the two time aspects, that which does recur and that which does not recur, and the way that this pattern leaks into our perspectives, can be worked by a BQF creative to activate future visioning. In one of his lectures, renowned physicist David Bohm notes that humans observe time as having two aspects (which align, in part, with the four dimensions of time discussed previously). On the one hand, Bohm says, we notice "time as recurrence, the recurrence of the seasons, the recurrence of the days, the recurrence of heartbeats, the process which recurs regularly and enables you to measure time" in the first place. On the other hand, we also notice a contradictory aspect of time in that some things never recur or happen again, such that we will never experience two days that are exactly the same, relive our childhoods, or experience death or birth twice. Time, then, involves the "interweaving of what is recurrent and non-recurrent." Bohm believes that these two contradictory aspects of time carry over into the way we experience and perceive time unfolding and how we divide up our thoughts into past, present, and future.

At the point where recurrence meets (or diverges from) non-recurrence lies a critical moment in time. In the very next moment or point, we would notice a change in our environment, the moment at which something changes over into its next state (i.e., the moment before I type the next letter in this sentence, which is a change from the moment before it where I hesitated and thought about what I would write). Philosopher Henri Bergson expounds on these critical moment points in his essay "Creative Evolution", in which he states that "in order to advance with the moving reality, you must replace yourself within it. Install yourself within change, and you will grasp at once both change itself and the successive states in which it might be immobilized." Echoing ideas that would later become core to quantum theory, Bergson stresses both the necessity of including the observer in the picture as well as the role of uncertainty and potential.

In another essay called "Matter and Memory", Bergson asserts that time and space are neither properties of things, nor essential conditions of the human capacity for experiencing things. Time and space, as he puts it, simply express, in an abstract form, the double work of solidification and of division which we project upon the moving continuity of reality, in order to have a starting point for action. In order to, in a sense, document and map out changes in our environment, we rely on time and space as the diagrammatic design of our action upon matter. In Bohm's lectures, he hints at a way of setting up new space-time configurations, by "finding the part of the experience which is before thought."

A BQF Creative remains half a step ahead of that critical point in time, which can be described as the thought before the conscious awareness of thought, or the most miniscule moment in time before a change occurs in the environment. BQF Creatives insert their conscious awareness within that space to consciously direct the point of change, exploiting the point in the pattern where change occurs. From that point we can exploit time to slow it down, speed it up, or break it into variable increments to allow greater degrees of access to the past and future than a linear mode of time would allow.

Another essential quality of all three modes of practice is the development of the qualities of memory, feelings, and sensations that make up an instance of time.[1] This is as opposed to the normal recognition of time as a mechanical clock hour. BQF Creatives are adopting an experiential definition of time, where time consciousness can be altered at will. The rate and rhythm of time can be experientially lengthened to process information or events over longer rates of time, or constricted to process information or events over shorter time rates than that offered by our typical one second per second rate of moving through objective time. Using these modes of practice and principles of quantum correspondence, we can then move on to quantum mapping of our timelines.

Mechanics of Event Building and BQF Mapping

Early on in elementary school, we are taught to map out major events, world history, and even our own lives on a timeline that runs from past to present to future. The timeline typically looks something like a straight line:

with major events representing points on the timeline, where time moves forward and comes from behind us. Contemporary science also uses this concept, but instead calls it a world line.

A	B	C	D
Past	Immediate Past	Present	Future

The straight line moving from past to future also represents cause and effect (similarly embodied as a thermodynamic arrow). Cause and effect is a linear sequence of events A B C D, where A causes B and D appears because of C. In this mode of time consciousness, intention is forward moving, and events are components of time (versus time being a feature of an event). The end goal, the end to be attained, (Point D on the timeline) is bound up with the present act (Point C on the timeline), influencing it. It is not the past act (B or A) that is the end to be attained. In a linear sequence, we are most concerned with finality and final judgment, what a situation will lead or fit into. This linear sequence of time flowing towards the future and not the past, has a built in asymmetry, in that D could never affect C, B, or A. Thus, there is no retrocausality and time does not flow backwards.

As we explored above, and as quantum physics shows, these assumptions of asymmetry fail at the microscopic level. The asymmetry of causation is merely a projection of our own temporal asymmetry as actors and agents in the world, one that we have built into our language and our way of recounting events, and a probabilistic tendency at best.

African notions of time and consciousness, when placed on a Western/linear timeline may look something like this:

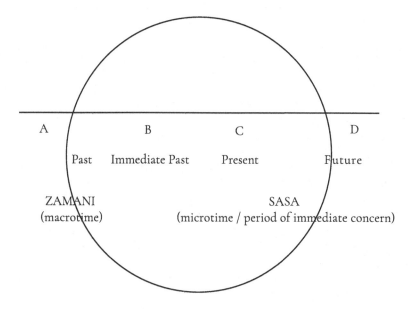

The past and present overlap in an African conception of time, as the present swallows up the future and the past swallows up the present. Your activity is what determines how quickly or slowly time moves, not a mathematically pre-determined rate of time where, if you do not fit your activity within the rate, you either end up with a surplus or shortage of time. Time is not its own entity in the African consciousness; it is a component of events and an experience that can be created, produced, saved, or retrieved. Life is made up of events, and events are defined by certain relationships, patterns, and rhythms.

Based on similar principles inherent to quantum and African features of time, BQF paradigm of time is assumed to be perfectly symmetrical, such as the way it is for quantum matter and as it is in African time traditions, with varying layers and connections of cause and effect in the infinite possibilities for the interaction of potential and manifest matter.

With BQF event building, events can be built from scratch. BQF Creatives believe that at each point in space-time lies an enfolded potential of events. There are infinite space-time points, first activated by a birth event and continuing along the natural timeline. Space-times can be divided into smaller or larger intervals, or even redefined non-mathematically, as opposed to the one second by one second linear mode of time that defines the rate at which we move into the future.

With BQF event-building, each sense impression that normally makes up an experience and subsequent memory (i.e., hearing, tasting, touching, feeling/emotion, seeing, smelling) is taken as its own event and used to build an experience or instance in time. (For example, see the essay "Sounds as Causes and Events" in *BQF NonLocality Zine I*). Using sense impressions as the essential building blocks of an instance/moment of time, there can be an infinite number of ways in which sense impressions can interact to produce the sounds, images, and actions that make up an event-experience. An essential interaction of these sense impressions causes a mini-collapse (event)/unfoldment, which are similar in nature to wave-function collapses that constantly and dynamically build up our moment to moment experiences of reality.

BQF event mapping is the creation of a living map upon which a BQF Creative can exert a controlling influence over personal experiences and personal time consciousness, as a means of creating our own order and pattern in the universe, or unfolding and enhancing the patterns already present. BQF event mapping uses the principles mentioned in the previous section (future visioning, altering, and manifestation) to intuitively map out an alternative timeline for a BQF Creative. The next moment can be built up, step by step, created by you, created from your own meanings, connections, relationships, hand-chosen and interwoven into the pattern of recurrence/non-recurrence. Time and space need not be pre-determined from pre-existing conditions. New configurations of time and space can be created simply by shifting relationships and their meanings.

With BQF event mapping, the shape of the timeline/worldline may look something like circles within circles or spiral shaped, for example, representing recurrent events, synchronous events, and quantum connections. Through this method of mapping, memory is not attached to a specific calendar date or clock time, and memories are not formed in regard to a specific date or time. Rather, time and date are made a part of the memory, so it is embedded or weaved in and controllable in future memory. You can make a date of your choosing a part of the memory as a part of your memory, which means you can forecast or backcast events. Time becomes something remembered, not something that defines and predates the memory. Some examples of BQF event mapping are provided below and you are encouraged to build, create, and manipulate your own quantum event maps.

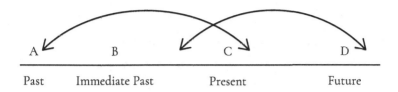

| Past | Immediate Past | Present | Future |

Using this method of mapping events, BQF Creatives have the ability to effect distant states either directly or indirectly via an influence on the future factors upon which those states depend. It recognizes that the present state depends on both the future and the past measurement. Backwards causation is simply a rearrangement or reassignment of causation with macro events and macro details.

Another form of BQF event mapping is borrowed from Chinese philosophy, as explored in Marie-Louise von Franz' essay, *On Divination and Synchronicity: the Psychology of Meaningful Chance Studies in Jungian Psychology*. Von Franz describes the time consciousness in the Chinese tradition as being a synchronistic thinking, or a "thinking in fields," where the question is not "why has this come about, or what factor caused this effect, but what likes to happen together in a meaningful way in the same moment...what tends to happen together in time?" The center of the field in this concept would be a time moment around which events A, B, C, D, E, etc. are clustered.

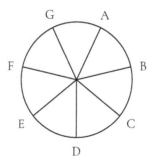

These events form a grouping pattern around the focal point as if the focal point behaves as a magnet which attracts certain events. Events do not have to be causally associated in the normal linear sense of cause and effect. The events express a quality of time in a now moment, with time simply being one quality of many that expresses a meaningful pattern.

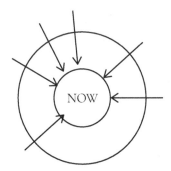

For this form of event mapping, BQF Creatives determines the center of the field, the uniting factor and synchronicity around which certain events will be grouped. Events, here again, can be defined liberally and can include macro-level events, micro-level events, emotional/psychical events, psychological and cognitive events, and sensory experience events, to name a few. The BQF Creative becomes the active agent in the synchronicity/focal point, instead of time being the active agent defining the synchronicity.

In Volume II of *Black Quantum Futurism: Theory and Practice*, we will explore BQF as applied to larger communities and world events. In particular, we will further explore methods for mapping out the futures of marginalized communities using BQF, anthropology of consciousness, archetypal and astrological BQF event mapping principles to backcast and forecast personal, cultural, familial, and communal cycles of experience. BQF Volume II will also include research and writing focused on the collection and preservation of communal memories, histories, and stories. We will look at larger event recurrence and collective experiences, such as race riots and map out their next occurrence in our communities using advanced BQF event mapping techniques.

Notes

1. For instance, a BQF Creative may consider notions such as how our enslaved African ancestors experienced time — the expansive space between sun up and sun down and work cycles, time associated with bodily punishment and torture. This notion is explored in depth in the book *Mastered by the Clock: Time, Slavery, and Freedom in the American South* by Mark M. Smith.

2. With the basic unit of the second currently scientifically defined as 9,192,631,770 cycles of the frequency associated with the transition between two energy levels of the isotope cesium 133, or, on a watch, the 60 moment to moment cycle that makes up a minute.

Bibliography

Bynum, PhD, Edward Bruce. *The African Unconscious: Roots of Ancient Mysticism and Modern Psychology*, 1999. 1988.

Koestler, Arthur. *The Roots of Coincidence*, 1972.

Bergson, Henri. *Mind Energy: Lectures and Essays*, ed. Carr, H. Wildon, 1920.

Wikipedia.com.

Bohm, David. *Unfolding Meaning: A Weekend of Dialogue with David Bohm*, 1996.

Dossey, PhD, Larry. *Space, Time, and Medicine*, 1982.

von Franz, Marie-Louise. *On Divination and Synchronicity: the Psychology of Meaningful Chance Studies in Jungian Psychology*, 1980.

Contributor Biographies

Omar Akbar is a multi-disciplinarian who specializes in anthropology, sociology, history, and the development of educational curriculums. He has worked as a lecturer, and conducted extensive research on African civilization, European civilization, American history, African culture, African American culture, globalization, Black Social Theory and hip-hop culture. He completed his doctorate in African Studies at Howard University, master's degree in History at Morgan State University, and baccalaureate in Africana Studies at the University of Maryland Baltimore County (UMBC). At UMBC he fulfilled research obligations with the Ronald E. McNair Fellowship, and the France Merrick Foundation Fellowship in conjunction with the Shriver Center. At UMBC Dr. Akbar completed two major research projects titled "Cultural Reference As a Foundation In Service Learning" and "Hip-Hop Culture: Youngest Child of the Black Ancients," both projects were implemented with "at-risk youth" populations in Baltimore, Maryland utilizing hip-hop culture as a cultural and pedagogic framework. Dr. Akbar completed his master's thesis titled "The Origins of Hip-Hop Culture" and doctoral dissertation titled "African Heritage, the Entertainment Business Network, and Hip-Hop Culture." He is also known by the pseudonym "Labtekwon" and widely considered a pioneer of avant-garde hip-hop culture.

Juice Aleem has long been acknowledged as one of the finest MCs the UK has ever produced. He has been a member of the hip-hop groups New Flesh, The Infesticons, and Gamma, while also working with Roots Manuva, Hexstatic, Evil 9, Adam Freeland, Si Begg, DJ Kentaro and many, many others. Over the years his work has taken him across much of the world and expanded to him being a director of several musical and cultural festivals in the UK. His last solo LP, *Voodu StarChild*, came out the same time as his first book, *Afrofutures and Astro Black Travel*. Currently, Aleem is often to be found blending music, comics, SF and art with his Afroflux events and workshops as well preparing to launch the Exile All-Stars (Exillians) project with TIE and Mike Ladd.

Tiffany E. Barber is a scholar, curator, and critic of twentieth and twenty-first century visual art, new media, and performance. Her work focuses on artists of the black diaspora working in the United States and the broader Atlantic world. Her writing appears in *Rhizomes*, *InVisible Culture: An Electronic Journal for Visual Culture*, *TOPIA: Canadian*

Journal of Cultural Studies, Black Camera, ASAP/Journal, Dance Research Journal, Afterimage: The Journal of Media Arts and Cultural Criticism, and various anthologies, exhibition catalogs, and online publications, including *Prospect.3: Notes for Now* (2014), *Afrofuturism 2.0: The Rise of Astroblackness* (2016), the *Black One Shot* series (2018), and *Suzanne Jackson: Five Decades* (2019). She is Assistant Professor of Africana Studies at the University of Delaware.

Kevin Coval is a poet and community builder. As the artistic director of Young Chicago Authors, founder of Louder Than A Bomb: The Chicago Youth Poetry Festival, and professor at the University of Illinois-Chicago — where he teaches hip-hop aesthetics — he's mentored thousands of young writers, artists and musicians. He is the author and editor of ten books, including *The BreakBeat Poets: New American Poetry in the Age of Hip-Hop* and *Schtick*, and co-author of the play *This is Modern Art*. His work has appeared in *Poetry Magazine, The Drunken Boat, Chicago Tribune, CNN, Fake Shore Drive, Huffington Post,* and four seasons of HBO's *Def Poetry Jam*.

Samantha Dols is an entrepreneur and researcher interested in the intersection of creativity and social change. Her work focuses on finding and constructing innovative paths for communities in conflict to connect — whether through architecture, civic imagination, immersive media, or organizational leadership. Her academic work includes teaching positions at American University and Catholic University, participation in the Emerging Scholars program at the Milton Wolf Seminar on Public Diplomacy, and several research collaborations and publications. As a practitioner, she founded and leads the World Lens Foundation, a social enterprise that connects students from around the world through visual storytelling to promote empathy and cross-cultural collaboration. She has worked and consulted for various international film festivals and organizations, including Sundance, Tribeca, Washington West, and the Open Society Foundations.

Kodwo Eshun is a British-Ghanaian writer, theorist and filmmaker. He studied English Literature at University College, Oxford University, and Romanticism and Modernism at Southampton University. He currently teaches in Contemporary Art Theory in the Department of Visual Cultures at Goldsmiths College, University of London, and at CCC Research Master Program of the Visual Arts Department at HEAD (Geneva School of Art and Design). He is the author of *More Brilliant Than the Sun* (Quartet, 1998), among other books.

Chuck Galli received his PhD and MA in Sociology from Temple University (Philadelphia, PA) and holds a BA in African/Afro-American Studies from Rhode Island College (Providence, RI). His diverse academic works include pieces on hip-hop and futurism, racial and gender bias in medical treatment, and epidemiology. He has taught at Drexel

University (Philadelphia, PA) as an adjunct professor for the past five years while also working in non-profit health industry research.

Nettrice Gaskins is an artist whose work explores how to generate art using algorithms in different ways, especially through coding. She also teaches, writes, "fabs" or makes, and does other things. She has taught multimedia, computational media, visual art, and even Advanced Placement Computer Science Principles with high school students who majored in the arts. She earned a BFA in Computer Graphics with Honors from Pratt Institute in 1992 and an MFA in Art and Technology from the School of the Art Institute of Chicago in 1994. She received a doctorate in Digital Media from Georgia Tech in 2014. She has taught at the secondary and post-secondary levels in the Boston Public Schools and at Massachusetts College of Art and Design. Currently, Dr. Gaskins is a content manager at the Fab Foundation and an artist-in-residence at the Autodesk Technology Center on behalf of MathTalk, a group that creates public art that encourages adults and children to enjoy, explore, and talk about the math in their own backyards. She will publish her first full-length book through MIT Press.

Jonathan Hay is a first year PhD candidate at the University of Chester. Their forthcoming doctoral thesis is prospectively titled "Novelty Fades: Science Fiction and Posthumanism". Jonathan has recent publications in *Iowa Journal of Cultural Studies*, *Kronoscope*, and the British Science Fiction Association's critical journal *Vector*. They are co-editor of a forthcoming volume of essays titled *Talking Bodies Vol. II — Bodily Languages, Selfhood and Transgression*, which is due to be published by Palgrave in spring 2020.

Jeff Heinzl currently writes, teaches and DJs in Pittsburgh, PA. He recently completed his PhD in Film and Media Studies at the University of Pittsburgh. His dissertation, titled "Feel It All Around: Art Music Video, Art Cinema, and Spectatorship in the Streaming Era," describes an emerging trend in contemporary music video characterized by narrative disruptions similar to those featured in classical and contemporary art cinema. He is currently working on multiple projects whose subjects range from hip-hop music video production companies to the repurposing of antiquated televisions as **objets d'art**. You can find him on Twitter at @ageofadz or @djantithesis.

Kembrew McLeod is the author of several books and has produced three documentaries about popular music, including *Copyright Criminals*, which aired on PBS's *Independent Lens*. His book *Freedom of Expression*® won the American Library Association's Oboler Book Award for "best scholarship in the area of intellectual freedom" and he received a National Endowment from the Humanities Public Scholar Award to support work *The Downtown Pop Underground*, published in 2018 by Abrams.

Rasheedah Phillips is an artist, author, community activist and lawyer based in Philadelphia. She is the creator of The Afrofuturist Affair and, together with Camae Ayewa, the Black Quantum Futurism multidisciplinary artist collective. Phillips is the Managing Attorney of the Landlord-Tenant Housing Unit at Community Legal Services of Philadelphia (CLS). She began her career at CLS in 2008 as a Pennsylvania Legal Aid Network Martin Luther King, Jr. Fellow in the Community Economic Development Unit, providing legal advice, representation, and resources to low-income child-care businesses and non-profit, community organizations. She is a 2008 graduate of Temple University Beasley School of Law, and a 2005 Sum Cum Laude graduate of Temple University, with a degree in Criminal Justice.

Steven Shaviro is the DeRoy Professor of English at Wayne State University. He writes mostly about science fiction and about music videos.

Aram Sinnreich is a media professor, author, and musician. He currently serves as chair of Communication Studies at American University's School of Communication in Washington, DC. Sinnreich's work focuses on the intersection of culture, law and technology, with an emphasis on subjects such as emerging media and music. He is the author of three books, *Mashed Up* (2010), *The Piracy Crusade* (2013), and *The Essential Guide to Intellectual Property* (2019). He has also written for publications including *The New York Times*, *Billboard*, *Wired*, *The Daily Beast*, and *The Conversation*. As a bassist and composer, Sinnreich has played with groups and artists including reggae soul band Dubistry, jazz and R&B band Brave New Girl, punk chanteuse Vivien Goldman, hard bop trio The Rooftoppers, and Ari-Up, lead singer of The Slits. Sinnreich was a finalist in the 2014 John Lennon Songwriting Contest (with co-authors Dunia Best and Todd Nocera), and a semifinalist in the 2020 Bernard/Ebb Songwriting Awards.

André Sirois aka DJ Food Stamp teaches film and music at the University of Oregon. With more than two decades of DJ and beat-making experience, he has dropped more than 60 mixtapes through Undergroundhiphop.com in its heyday, rocked college radio mix shows, and has laced plenty of tracks with the funky-fresh scratch hooks. In 2016, he transferred his background and research on the evolution of DJ mixers into the book *Hip-Hop DJs and the Evolution of Technology: Cultural Exchange, Innovation, and Democratization.* He's currently working on an exhibit and coffee table styled book featuring more than 60 DJ mixers and interviews with the DJs, engineers, and product reps who helped design them entitled *Designed from Scratch: A Hip-Hop History of the DJ Mixer, 1975-2005* (hopefully coming to your coffee table by 2023).

Erik Steinskog is associate professor in musicology at the Department of Arts and Cultural Studies, University of Copenhagen, Denmark. Dr. art. in musicology from the Norwegian University of Science and Technology (NTNU) in 2003, with the thesis

"Arnold Schoenberg's *Moses und Aron*: Music, Language, and Representation". Research interests include the cultural study of music, questions of gender, sexuality, and race, and Afrofuturism. Author of *Afrofuturism and Black Sound Studies: Culture, Technology, and Things to Come* (2018).

Dave Tompkins is a writer currently working on a book about Miami Bass (Simon & Schuster). His first book, *How To Wreck A Nice Beach: The Vocoder From World War II to Hip-Hop*, was published by StopSmiling/Melville House. He recently contributed to the *Unsound Intermission* anthology ("It Takes A Cavitation of Millions") and Frances Scott's *Incantation, Wendy* ("Their waving signals a moon"), published by bobo / An Endless Supply in 2021. Born in North Carolina, he lives in Brooklyn.

Tia C.M. Tyree is a Professor at Howard University within the Department of Strategic, Legal and Management Communications. She teaches graduate and undergraduate communications courses. Her research interests include hip-hop, rap, reality television, film, social media as well as African American and female representations in media. She has several published book chapters and peer-reviewed articles in journals, such as those in *Women and Language*; *Howard Journal of Communications*; *Journalism: Theory, Practice & Criticism*; *Journal of Black Studies* and the *International Journal of Emergency Management*. She is the author of *The Interesting and Incredibly Long History of American Public Relations* and coeditor of *HBCU Experience — The Book*, *Social Media: Pedagogy and Practice* as well as *Social Media: Culture and Identity*. She is also cofounder of the Social Media Technology Conference and Workshop, which is a conference designed to bring both professionals and academicians together to discuss cutting-edge research and trends in social media.

Joël Vascheron is senior lecturer and researcher at ECAL/University of Art and Design Lausanne, HES-SO, where he teaches visual and media studies. His main focus is on the impact of automated tools, in particular software-based systems, on artistic productions. He is currently working on a PhD addressing the role of spatial photography in narratives about globalization and, as a freelance journalist and writer, he regularly collaborates on diverse publications about music, design, and photography.

tobias c. van Veen is Visiting Scholar at the ReImagining Value Action Lab at Lakehead University, and Visiting Professor in Humanities at Quest University. He holds doctorates in Philosophy and Communication Studies from McGill University. His transdisciplinary research and teaching address philosophy of race, sound, and technology in critical media and black diaspora studies. He has published widely on Afrofuturism, posthumanism, and electronic dance music cultures (EDMC). Tobias is lead editor of the "Black Lives, Black Politics, Black Futures" special issue of *TOPIA: Canadian Journal of Cultural Studies* (2018), editor of the Afrofuturism special issue of *Dancecult: Journal of Electronic Dance Music Culture* (2013), and co-editor of the *Journal's* special issue "Echoes from the Dub Diaspora"

(2015). A sound/media artist, filmmaker, and tactical turntablist since 1993, Veen has exhibited and curated interventions, events, and broadcasts worldwide. An award-winning broadcaster and photojournalist, he hosts the Other Planes: Afro/Futurism podcast on CreativeDisturbance.org and curates the sound-art label IOSOUND.ca.

Ytasha L. Womack is a critically acclaimed author, filmmaker, and independent scholar, and Afrofuturist. She champions the imagination and the use of dance to push past personal limitations and reassess identity. Her book *Afrofuturism: The World of Black Sci Fi & Fantasy Culture* is a popular primer in universities and beyond. Her other works include the Afrofuturist novels *Rayla 2212*, *A Spaceship in Bronzeville*, and the nonfiction works *Post Black: How A New Generation is Redefining African American Identity* as well as *Beats Rhymes and Life* an anthology on hip-hop culture. A dance therapist, she frequently uses dance as a metaphor for life. She directed the Afrofuturist dance short *A Love Letter to the Ancestors from Chicago*. She also wrote the romantic comedy *Couples Night*. Womack is an inaugural resident of Black Rock Senegal and frequently lectures on Afrofuturism and the imagination around the world.

K. Ceres Wright received her master's degree in Writing Popular Fiction from Seton Hill University and her published cyberpunk novel, *Cog*, was her thesis for the program. Her short stories, poems, and articles have appeared in *Luminescent Threads: Connections to Octavia Butler* (Locus Award winner; Hugo Award nominee); *Sycorax's Daughters* (Bram Stoker Award nominee); *Emanations: 2+2=5*; *Diner Stories: Off the Menu; Many Genres, One Craft (Best Non-Fiction London Book Festival); The City: A Cyberfunk Anthology; The Museum of All Things Awesome and That Go Boom*; among others. Ms. Wright is the founder and president of Diverse Writers and Artists of Speculative Fiction, an educational group for creatives; and served as the Director of Science Fiction Programming for MultiverseCon. She works as a publications manager and writer/editor for a management consulting firm in Rockville, MD.

About the Editor:

Roy Christopher marshals the middle between Mathers and McLuhan. He is an aging BMX and skateboarding zine kid. That's where he learned to turn events and interviews into pages with staples. He has since written about music, media, and culture for everything from books and blogs to national magazines and academic journals. He holds a Ph.D. in Communication Studies from the University of Texas at Austin, and is the author of several books, including *Dead Precedents: How Hip-Hop Defines the Future*. He currently lives in Savannah, Georgia.

STRANGE ATTRACTOR PRESS 2022

Printed in the United States
by Baker & Taylor Publisher Services